THE PROHIBITION C
EXCEPTIONAL CIR(

Can torture be justified in exceptional circumstances? In this timely work, Michelle Farrell asks how and why this question has become such a central debate. She argues that the ticking bomb scenario is a fiction that blinds us to the reality of torture, and investigates what it is that this scenario fails to represent. Farrell aims to reframe how we think about torture, and critically reflects on the historical and contemporary approaches to its use in exceptional situations. She demonstrates how torture, from its use in Algeria to the 'War on Terror', has been misrepresented, and appraises the legalist, extra-legalist and absolutist assessments of exception to the torture prohibition. Employing Giorgio Agamben's theory of the state of exception as a foil, Farrell deconstructs these approaches and goes on to propose her own theory of exceptional torture.

MICHELLE FARRELL is a Lecturer in law at the School of Law and Social Justice, University of Liverpool.

THE PROHIBITION OF TORTURE IN EXCEPTIONAL CIRCUMSTANCES

MICHELLE FARRELL

CAMBRIDGE
UNIVERSITY PRESS

CAMBRIDGE
UNIVERSITY PRESS

University Printing House, Cambridge CB2 8BS, United Kingdom

Cambridge University Press is part of the University of Cambridge.

It furthers the University's mission by disseminating knowledge in the pursuit of education, learning and research at the highest international levels of excellence.

www.cambridge.org
Information on this title: www.cambridge.org/9781316603413

© Michelle Farrell 2013

First published 2013
First paperback edition 2015

A catalogue record for this publication is available from the British Library

Library of Congress Cataloguing in Publication data
Farrell, Michelle, 1981–
The prohibition of torture in exceptional circumstances / Michelle Farrell.
pages   cm
Based on the author's thesis (doctoral) – National University of Ireland
Galway, 2011, under title: On torture.
Includes bibliographical references and index.
ISBN 978-1-107-03079-4 (hardback)
1. Torture (International law)   I. Title.
KZ7170.F37 2013
341.6'5–dc23   2013008188
ISBN 978-1-107-03079-4 Hardback
ISBN 978-1-316-60341-3 Paperback

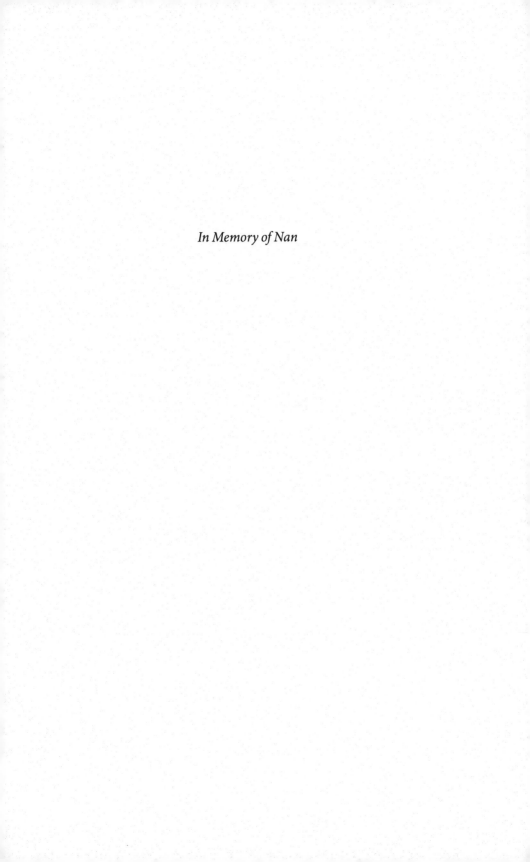

In Memory of Nan

CONTENTS

FOREWORD
LOUIS E. WOLCHER

Within the circle of academic discourse about human rights, the customary way of thinking about torture in the post September 11 world has for
a long time been obsessed with – one might even say has fetishised – the
so-called 'ticking time bomb scenario' (TTBS). After paying lip service to
the nearly universal modern chorus of moral and legal condemnation of
the use of torture by the state as a general matter, mainstream academics
in thrall to the TTBS have tended to focus their formidable intellectual
energy on what they believe to be the one case where the argument for
torture is strongest. As the TTBS is usually imagined, a terrorist bomb or
other mechanism of mass destruction is set to go off in the near future,
thereby precipitating hundreds (or thousands or millions) of casualties
amongst the civilian population. The authorities believe they know that a
particular person in their custody knows where the engine of destruction
is located and/or how to disable it, but he or she will not disclose this information in response to 'normal' investigative techniques. Thus constructed
in the form of an abstract thought experiment, the TTBS poses the question whether it is moral, or legal, or both, for agents of the state to subject
such a person to various forms of torture (including what the Bush administration euphemistically called 'enhanced interrogation techniques' such
as waterboarding) in order to obtain putatively life-saving information that
the suspect refuses to reveal under the influence of less drastic measures.

The TTBS seems to pose the sort of 'either/or', 'yes or no' question –
'Is torture justified in this scenario or not?' – that Jacques Derrida called
'violent, polemical and inquisitorial ... We may fear that it contains some
instrument of torture – that is, a manner of interrogation that is not the
most just.'[1] In other words, it takes the paradoxical form of something

Louis E. Wolcher is Charles I. Stone Professor of Law, University of Washington School of
Law.

[1] Jacques Derrida (tr. Mary Quaintance), 'Force of Law: The "Mystical Foundation of
Authority"', (1990) 11 *Cardozo Law Review* 919, 923.

akin to an academic torture device on the very subject of torture's legitimacy. Fortunately, every now and then a book comes along that does not arrogantly presume to instruct the reader what to think about a conventionally defined problem such as the TTBS. Instead, such a book attempts to uncover the problematic nature of convention itself – that is, of *what* we choose to think about and *how* we choose to think about it. The present volume is such a book. Its author's insights into the violence that is concealed and enabled by excessive use of the TTBS in academic and political discourse is a refreshing reminder that it is possible to think critically (and compassionately) about the theory and practice of human rights without immediately taking sides on a pressing 'problem' whose very taken-for-granted *frame of reference* is what actually poses the greatest problem.

Dr Farrell identifies three types of conventional positions or opinions that together characterise the logical space marked out for us in advance by the way the TTBS is usually constructed. They are: (1) the *absolute torture prohibition*, which, in line with international law, resolutely refuses to sanction torture in this or any other circumstance; (2) the *qualified torture prohibition*, which seeks to formalise a narrow legal exception to the general rule against torture through procedural devices such as 'torture warrants'; and (3) the *pragmatic absolute torture prohibition*, which officially denounces all torture as illegal but still manages to give a wink of approval at the extra-legal use of torture by agents of the state in certain extraordinary circumstances.

What unites all three of these approaches, Farrell maintains, is what might be called their pernicious moral and political *performativity*. Not only do they fail theoretically to resolve or even address the use of torture in exceptional situations, but more importantly they constitute speech acts whose intellectual cacophony drowns out the screams of those on whom torture is, as Farrell puts it, 'actually practiced in the liberal democratic state'. In other words, the book shows that the TTBS is a beguiling fiction that renders the realities of everyday state practices amounting to torture morally and legally invisible. Appropriating some powerful theoretical tools from the philosopher Georgio Agamben,[2] the book's principal insight is that the discourse of the TTBS transforms the figure of the alleged terrorist-who-knows-about-the-ticking-time-bomb into a 'bare life' that is utterly excluded from the legal sphere by means of a Schmittian

---

[2] See Giorgio Agamben (tr. Daniel Heller-Roazen), *Homo Sacer: Sovereign Power and Bare Life* (Stanford University Press, 1995).

state of exception.[3] This implies, in turn, that in so-called 'normal' situations outside the context of the TTBS everyone has human rights that the state protects and no one is being tortured. One of the book's most powerful contributions to the theory of human rights is to demonstrate the fundamental falsity of this implication by shining a bright light on the ubiquity of torture as it is actually practised by liberal and constitutional states.

In the end, this remarkable book gives proof of a simple but fundamental truth: that taking a moral and political stand against real instances of torture is not the same as simply being for a principle that forbids torture or against a principle that allows it. In essence, thinkers such as Farrell criticise conventional approaches to law and morality by criticising the universal extension of the stringent logic of consistency to the real conduct of men and women. Such logic does not allow us the space to notice that, in the words of Theodor Adorno, 'perennial suffering has as much right to expression as a tortured man has to scream'.[4] To paraphrase Adorno, lines such as 'No man should be tortured; there should be no concentration camps' are undoubtedly true as an impulse, as a reaction to news that torture is going on somewhere. But at the same time '[t]hey must not be rationalized; as an abstract principle they would fall promptly into the bad infinities of derivation and validity.'[5]

The present book does human rights scholars and practitioners the inestimable favour of showing that the widespread academic and political obsession with developing a rationalised abstract formula for dealing with the scenario of the ticking time bomb threatens to lead us into a sort of bad infinity where we keep on overlooking instances of actual torture in order to take notice of the sort of 'torture' that only occurs inside works of fiction. The book thus belongs alongside other important theoretical contributions on the relationship between law and violence, including especially Walter Benjamin's 'Critique of Violence',[6] which Farrell herself discusses in Chapter 3.

In one way or another, these contributions to critical thought can trace their lineage back to the very first text in the Western canon that dares to comment on the intimate relationship between law and violence. I am

---

[3] See Carl Schmitt (tr. George Schwab), *Political Theology: Four Chapters on the Concept of Sovereignty* (Cambridge, MA: MIT Press, 1985).

[4] Theodor Adorno (tr. E. B. Ashton), *Negative Dialectics* (London: Routledge, 1973), p. 362.

[5] *Ibid.* p. 285.

[6] See Walter Benjamin, 'Critique of Violence', in *Reflections: Essays, Aphorisms, Autobiographical Writings*, tr. Edmund Jephcott (New York: Schocken Books, 1978), p. 277.

referring of course to the Greek poet Pindar's famous fragment 169, the first four lines of which can be rendered in English as follows:

> *Nomos* [signifying both law *and* custom] is lord of everything,
> Of mortals and immortals king.
> High violence it justifies,
> With hand uplifted plundering.[7]

Readers would do well to approach the present volume with an attitude, like Pindar's, that remains simultaneously critical *and* compassionate. I believe the book will amply reward those who are able to remain open to the essential task of subjecting customary ways of thinking and being to the kind of relentless ethical scrutiny that Dr Farrell brings to them here.

---

[7] Pindar (tr. C. M. Bowra), 'The Power of Custom', in T. F. Higham and C. M. Bowra (eds.), *The Oxford Book of Greek Verse in Translation* (Oxford: Clarendon Press, 1938), p. 330.

ACKNOWLEDGEMENTS

When I picked up J. M. Coetzee's *Waiting for the Barbarians* for some light reading during the writing stage of my Ph.D. thesis, I had no idea how deeply it would influence my understanding of torture and of human rights more generally. I also did not realise that the Magistrate's struggle would become central to my own conclusions. *Waiting for the Barbarians* ends on a beautifully ambiguous note. Reflecting on a year of turmoil in the history of Empire, the Magistrate thinks to himself: 'There has been something staring me in the face, and still I do not see it.'[8] His inability to see, capture and conclude on the unfolding history and meaning of Empire, as well as his complicity to Empire, resonates with me as I try to see and make sense of what stares at me. In this unending effort, I have been guided and inspired by a number of individuals.

Above all, I would like to thank my Ph.D. supervisor, Dr Kathleen Cavanaugh, for her years of enthusiasm, expertise and provocation, her seemingly endless patience but mainly for trusting that I would eventually see something. I would also like to particularly thank my external examiner, Professor Louis Wolcher, who, through his scholarship and comments, has opened my eyes to new ways of seeing. Professor William A. Schabas has been an inspiration to me (not to mention infectious in his enthusiasm) since I first undertook my LLM at the Irish Centre for Human Rights. Finally, I would like also to give special thanks to Professor Edward Peters. My copy of his seminal text *Torture* is well thumbed for a good reason. Moreover, Professor Peters has kindly engaged with me on matters of substance and provided me with important comments, particularly as I moved this work from Ph.D. to book.

I would like to give special thanks to the team at Cambridge University Press for their hard work, guidance and patience with me in finalising this manuscript.

---

[8] J. M. Coetzee, *Waiting for the Barbarians* (London: Vintage Books, 2004), p. 170.

xiii

I spent a number of years at the Irish Centre for Human Rights as an LLM and Ph.D. student, as a postdoctoral research fellow and as a contract lecturer. Those years were foundational in so many ways for my academic career but, more importantly, they have set me up with friends for life. During my time there, I was lucky to meet, to learn from and to receive advice from a number of former and current staff. I would like, therefore, to thank Ray Murphy, Vinodh Jaichand, Shane Darcy, Joshua Castellino, Elvira Dominguez Redondo, Peter Fitzmaurice, Noam Lubell, Nadia Bernaz and Annysa Bellal. I have benefited from discussions with, and the friendship of, many 'Centre' folk including Andrea Breslin, Anthony Cullen, Josh Curtis, Aoife Daly, Fidelma Donlon, Annabel Egan, Roja Fazaeli, Niamh Hayes, Edel Hughes, Michael Kearney, Yvonne McDermott, Nicholas McGeehan, Eadaoin O'Brien, Joseph Powderly and John Reynolds.

A number of people have read and commented on drafts of this work. I would particularly like to thank Niamh Hayes, Andrea Breslin and John Reynolds for great comments and proofreads, always at the right time. I would also like to thank Fiona de Londras for her wonderfully critical reading of the introduction, not to mention her encouragement along the way. All errors are, of course, my own.

I would like to thank the National University of Ireland, Galway for initially providing me with a doctoral fellowship and for later providing me with a Write-Up Bursary. I would also like to thank the National University of Ireland for the award in 2010 of NUI E. J. Phelan Postgraduate Fellow in International Law. With this Fellowship I was in a position to devote my time to updating the Ph.D. for publication. I undertook the Fellowship at the Irish Centre for Human Rights and benefited so much from the experience of being a member of staff there.

Finally and notably, I would like generally to thank my family – immediate and extended – and my close friends. My parents, Brigid and Michael, are amazing people. They have never doubted my chosen career path, difficult and unrewarding as it may have looked to them at times. They are also endlessly selfless. To them and my brother Neil I must also give special thanks for remaining patient with me during the write-up period. I must thank my brother Stuart for being such a reliable source of cheer. Clare and Enagh, I must thank for the moral support; it's good to know you two are always there.

TABLE OF CASES

African Commission on Human and People's Rights

International Court of Justice

International Criminal Tribunal for the Former Yugoslavia

International Criminal Court

National Decisions

~

Introduction

This book is prompted by the disquieting discourse on the legal and moral justifiability of torture in extraordinary or so-called 'ticking bomb' situations. From the literature on this discourse, there are three representative academic positions concerned with the question of providing for an exception to the prohibition on torture in such ticking bomb situations that merit review. First, the qualified torture prohibition proposes that there should be a legally accommodated exception to the torture prohibition in ticking bomb situations. Second, the pragmatic absolute torture prohibition proposes that the absolute torture prohibition must be maintained whilst allowing for the extra-legal use of torture in ticking bomb situations.[1] Third, the absolute torture prohibition, in line with international law, proposes that there can be no exception to the torture prohibition in any situation because the torture prohibition is an archetype of the rule of law.[2] Significantly, each of these proposals has in common a concern for the preservation of the rule of law in a crisis situation. The first and second proposals diverge from the third in attempting to regulate or accommodate exceptional torture. These proposals to regulate or accommodate torture are motivated not by torture advocacy, but by the view that torture would, or should, be used in such an exceptional situation.[3]

I argue that the ticking bomb scenario, which frames this debate on torture, signals the innate tension between the rule of law and the state of

---

[1] This language is adopted from Oren Gross' extra-legal model, which will be used to exemplify the pragmatic absolute position. See Oren Gross, 'Chaos and Rules: Should Responses to Violence Crises Always Be Constitutional?' (2003) 112 *Yale Law Journal* 1011, 1099.

[2] Jeremy Waldron, 'Torture and Positive Law: Jurisprudence for the White House' (2005) 105 *Columbia Law Review* 1681, 1742.

[3] Alan M. Dershowitz, 'Tortured Reasoning' in Sanford Levinson (ed.), *Torture: A Collection* (Oxford University Press, 2004), p. 266; Oren Gross, 'Are Torture Warrants Warranted? Pragmatic Absolutism and Official Disobedience' (2004) 88 *Minnesota Law Review* 1481, 1520.

exception in the liberal democratic[4] or constitutional state and, in addition, that this scenario and the torture debate bear little or no relation to real situations in which torture occurs. Giorgio Agamben's theory of the state of exception is, therefore, placed within this discourse in order, first, to tease out why the proposals to regulate or accommodate torture in ticking bomb situations fail, normatively and theoretically, to resolve or adequately address the question of the use of torture in exceptional situations and, second, to theorise the space in which torture is actually practised in the liberal democratic state. By theorising this space, it is possible to broaden the frame for thinking about torture and for thinking about what it means to debate the justifiability of torture. In order to achieve this objective of reframing how we think about torture, it is necessary to understand what it is about torture that the ticking bomb scenario fails to represent; in other words, it is necessary to reveal the 'fiction' of the ticking bomb scenario. Borrowing the question from Darius Rejali, the book, consequently, asks: 'if it is a fiction, how does it exercise the power of a black hole in modern memory? How does it bend all argument to its narrative, preventing light breaking beyond the edges to the realities of torture?'[5]

A.   What is torture?

The United Nations Convention against Torture and Other Cruel, Inhuman and Degrading Treatment or Punishment defines torture in Article 1(1) as:

> any act by which severe pain or suffering, whether physical or mental, is intentionally inflicted on a person for such purposes as obtaining for him or a third person information or a confession, punishing him for an act he or a third person has committed or is suspected of having committed, or intimidating or coercing him or a third person, or for any reason based on discrimination of any kind, when such pain or suffering is inflicted by or

---

[4] By 'liberal democratic' state, I am referring broadly to pluralistic states in which the governing party is elected (at regular intervals) with the consent of the people and in which there is a check on executive power, a free and independent judiciary and a constitution or statute protecting core human rights and/or civil liberties. On the meaning of liberal democracy, see Peter Leyland, *The Constitution of the United Kingdom: A Contextual Analysis* 2nd edn (Oxford: Hart Publishing, 2012), p. 3; On the development of the liberal and of the democratic state and on human rights in the liberal-democracy, see C. B. Macpherson, *The Real World of Democracy* (Oxford University Press, 1966), pp. 4–11 and p. 57.

[5] Darius Rejali, *Torture and Democracy* (Princeton University Press, 2007), p. 547.

at the acquiescence of a public official or other person acting in an official capacity. It does not include pain or suffering arising only from, inherent in or incidental to lawful sanctions.[6]

Torture, according to this definition, contains four elements: first, the element of severity; second, the element of intent; third, the element of purpose; and fourth, the involvement of, or acquiescence by, a state official.[7]

The Convention against Torture also contains a state obligation 'to prevent ... other acts of cruel, inhuman and degrading treatment or punishment *which do not amount to torture*'.[8] This suggests that torture is, to use the words of the former European Commission on Human Rights, 'an aggravated form' of cruel, inhuman and degrading treatment or punishment.[9] In the *Greek Case*[10] the European Commission elaborated on the formula contained in Article 3 of the European Convention on Human Rights. Article 3 states: 'no one shall be subjected to torture or to inhuman or degrading treatment or punishment'.[11] The Commission reasoned that the term torture 'is often used to describe inhuman treatment, which has a purpose such as the obtaining of information or confessions, or the infliction of punishment, and it is often an aggravated form of inhuman treatment'.[12] The Commission did not specify in the *Greek Case* that the term 'aggravated' was intended to mean a more severe level of suffering than the level of severity required for the treatment to be considered as 'inhuman'.[13]

---

[6] United Nations Convention against Torture and Other Cruel, Inhuman and Degrading Treatment or Punishment (adopted 10 December 1984, entered into force 26 June 1987) 1465 UNTS 85, 113 Article 1(1).

[7] Manfred Nowak and Elizabeth McArthur, *The United Nations Convention Against Torture: A Commentary* (Oxford University Press, 2008), p. 28.

[8] Convention against Torture, Article 16(1), (emphasis added). As Nowak and McArthur have pointed out, the Convention against Torture does not contain a specific human right not to be subjected to torture or to other forms of ill-treatment. It is clear from the language of Article 16(1) that the Convention 'only creates a State obligation to prevent cruel, inhuman or degrading treatment or punishment'. See Nowak and McArthur, *The United Nations Convention against Torture*, p. 540.

[9] *Denmark et al. v. Greece (The Greek Case)* (1969) 12 Yearbook of the European Convention on Human Rights, p. 186.

[10] *Ibid.*

[11] Convention for the Protection of Human Rights and Fundamental Freedoms (European Convention on Human Rights, as amended) (ECHR) Article 3.

[12] The *Greek Case*, p. 186.

[13] *Ibid.* According to the Commission, 'inhuman treatment covers at least such treatment as deliberately causes severe suffering, mental or physical.'

The European Court of Human Rights has, since the *Greek Case*, developed a rich jurisprudence on Article 3 of the Convention.[14] In deciding whether acts fall within the scope of prohibited treatment or punishment under Article 3, the Court requires ill-treatment to attain 'a minimum level of severity', the assessment of which is 'relative'; 'it depends on all the circumstances of the case, such as the duration of the treatment, its physical or mental effects and, in some cases, the sex, age and state of health of the victim, etc'.[15] The three categories of prohibited ill-treatment – 'torture', 'inhuman' and 'degrading' – have been interpreted by the Court as overlapping but distinct.[16] The Court tends to distinguish torture from inhuman treatment in two ways. The Court attaches 'a special stigma to deliberate inhuman treatment causing very serious and cruel suffering'.[17] In addition, it follows the reasoning of the *Greek Case* and endorses the Convention against Torture's definition of torture by emphasising the purposive element of torture.[18] However, although it is not uniformly the case, the Court does tend to rely on the severity of suffering as the decisive criterion.[19]

Reliance on the element of severity to differentiate torture from inhuman treatment obfuscates their distinction. Following Nigel Rodley's approach,[20] it will be argued that purpose ought to be the distinguishing element.[21] Manfred Nowak, who also adopted this approach, further

---

[14] Fionnuala Ní Aoláin, 'The European Convention on Human Rights and Its Prohibition on Torture' in Sanford Levinson (ed.), *Torture: A Collection* (Oxford University Press, 2004), p. 213.

[15] *Ireland* v. *United Kingdom* (App. No. 5310/71) ECHR 18 January 1978, para. 162. See also Ní Aoláin, 'The European Convention', p. 217.

[16] Michael K. Addo and Nicholas Grief, 'Does Article 3 of the European Convention on Human Rights Enshrine Absolute Rights' (1998) 9 *European Journal of International Law* 510, 511.

[17] See *Ireland* v. *United Kingdom* (1978), para. 167.

[18] See, for example, *Selmouni* v. *France* (App. No. 25803/94) ECHR 28 July 1999, para. 98; *İhlan* v. *Turkey* (App. No. 22277/93) ECHR 27 June 2000, para. 85; *Kişmir* v. *Turkey* (App. No. 27306/95) ECHR 31 May 2005, para. 129.

[19] See, for example, *Gäfgen* v. *Germany* (App. No. 22978/05) ECHR 1 June 2010, para. 108. See also, Nigel S. Rodley and Matt Pollard, *The Treatment of Prisoners Under International Law* 3rd edn (Oxford University Press, 2010), p. 87; Steven Dewulf, *The Signature of Evil: (Re)Defining Torture in International Law* (Antwerp: Intersentia, 2011), p. 199.

[20] Nigel Rodley served as United Nations Special Rapporteur on Torture and other Cruel, Inhuman and Degrading Treatment or Punishment from 1993 to 2001.

[21] Nigel S. Rodley, 'The Definition(s) of Torture in International Law' (2002) 55 *Current Legal Problems* 467, 489. See also, Rodley and Pollard, *The Treatment of Prisoners*, p. 123. Rodley and Pollard take the position that 'the purposive element is the sole or dominant element distinguishing torture from cruel or inhuman treatment'.

maintained that the powerlessness of the victim, in addition to the purposive element, is essential to understanding the distinction between torture and other ill-treatment.[22] Nowak has, consequently, asserted:

> the decisive criteria for distinguishing torture from [cruel, inhuman and degrading treatment or punishment] may best be understood to be the purpose of the conduct and the powerlessness of the victim rather than the intensity of the pain or suffering inflicted, as argued by the European Court of Human Rights and many scholars.[23]

By introducing the notion of powerlessness,[24] Nowak aimed to convey the point that subjection to torture presupposes a situation in which the victim 'is under the total control of another person'.[25] The purposive element approach to defining torture does not dispense with the element of 'severe pain or suffering, whether physical or mental'. It does dispense with the notion that torture constitutes a calibrated level of suffering, degrees beyond that of inhuman treatment.[26] Moreover, it emphasises that it is not the defined level of 'pain or suffering' that determines the paradigm of torture, rather that the paradigm of torture is different from inhuman or degrading treatment or punishment because of the context in which such pain or suffering is endured.[27] As such, the purposive element approach

---

[22] Nowak, who served as United Nations Special Rapporteur on Torture from 2004 to 2010, endorsed this position in his capacity as Special Rapporteur. See UNCHR, 'Report of the Special Rapporteur on the Question of Torture, Manfred Nowak' (2005) UN Doc. E/CN.4/2006/6, para. 39. See also Manfred Nowak, 'What Practices Constitute Torture? US and UN Standards' (2006) 28 *Human Rights Quarterly* 809, 833; Manfred Nowak and Elizabeth McArthur, 'The Distinction between Torture and Other Cruel, Inhuman or Degrading Treatment or Punishment' (2006) 16 *Torture* 147.

[23] UNCHR, 'Report of the Special Rapporteur: Manfred Nowak', para. 39.

[24] As Rodley and Pollard have observed, the concept of 'powerlessness' introduced by Nowak is not an element of the definition of torture and should not be understood as such. It is best understood rather as a 'factual description of the situation in which torture typically occurs', that is, when the victim is deprived of personal liberty or is under the effective physical control of the authorities. See Rodley and Pollard, *The Treatment of Prisoners*, p. 119, n. 192.

[25] UNCHR, 'Report of the Special Rapporteur: Manfred Nowak', para. 39. Similar to Nowak, David Sussman has argued that torture is distinguishable by its situational impact upon the victim. He described this not as powerlessness but as 'the experience of a kind of forced passivity in a context of urgent need, a context in which such passivity is experienced as a kind of open-ended exposure, vulnerability and impotence'. See David Sussman, 'Defining Torture' (2006) 37 *Case Western Reserve Journal of International Law* 225, 227.

[26] Rodley and Pollard, *The Treatment of Prisoners*, p. 124.

[27] In this regard, Marnia Lazreg has argued: '[i]t is the totality of the torture *situation* that needs to be grasped in order to understand that torture is not definable in terms of bodily

to the definition of torture provides a more accurate account of the phenomenon of torture.

B.   Torture and counterterrorism

The prohibition of torture is a fixture of international law that cannot easily be unravelled. The prohibition is one of only a few human rights provisions that permit of no limitation or restriction and no derogation even in times of war or other public emergency.[28] In addition, the prohibition on torture is widely recognised as a peremptory norm of international law or *jus cogens*.[29] The prohibition on torture is, by and large, uncontested; that is to say, no state argues that the use of torture ought to be generally permissible. The near-universal consensus in favour of the prohibition, reflected in its status as a peremptory norm of international law, a norm of customary international law and in numerous international and regional human rights treaties, shows a commitment to the normative rejection of torture. In spite of this commitment, however, the practice of torture persists; its prevalence is a conspicuous reminder of the gap between the norm and its realisation. In a report on the phenomena of torture, cruel, inhuman and degrading treatment or punishment as assessed in the five years of his mandate as Special Rapporteur, Nowak described the reality as 'alarming'.[30] According to Nowak, the practice of torture and ill-treatment is widespread 'in the majority of the countries on our

---

harm or psychological torment alone'. See Marnia Lazreg, *Torture and the Twilight of Empire: From Algiers to Baghdad* (Princeton University Press, 2008), p. 6.

[28] Nowak and McArthur, *The United Nations Convention against Torture*, p. v.

[29] *Questions Relating to the Obligation to Prosecute or Extradite (Belgium v. Senegal)* Judgment [2012] ICJ Reports 2012, para. 99; *Prosecutor v. Anto Furundzija* (Trial Judgment), IT-95–17/1-T, International Criminal Tribunal for the former Yugoslavia (ICTY), 10 December 1998, para. 144. See also Lauri Hannaiken, *Peremptory Norms (Jus Cogens) in International Law: Historical Development, Criteria, Present Status* (Helsinki: Lakimiesliiton Kustannus Finnish Lawyer's Publishing Company, 1988), p. 508; Theodor Meron, *Human Rights and Humanitarian Norms as Customary Law* (Oxford: Clarendon Press, 1989), p. 31; Erika de Wet, 'The Prohibition of Torture as an International Norm of *Jus Cogens* and its Implications for National and Customary Law' (2004) 15 *European Journal of International Law* 97; Alexander Orakhelashvili, *Peremptory Norms in International Law* (Oxford University Press, 2006), p. 43.

[30] UNHRC, 'Report of the Special Rapporteur on Torture and Other Cruel, Inhuman and Degrading Treatment or Punishment, Manfred Nowak: Study on the Phenomena of Torture, Cruel, Inhuman and Degrading Treatment or Punishment in the World, Including an Assessment of Conditions of Detention' (2010) UN Doc. A/HRC/13/39/Add. 5, para. 9.

planet'.[31] Regarding the practice of torture specifically, Nowak concluded that, for the most part, torture victims are 'ordinary persons suspected of having committed ordinary crimes' and that 'the major structural reason for the widespread practice of torture in many countries is the malfunctioning of the administration of justice and, consequently the lack of respect for safeguards'.[32] The pervasiveness of the practice is, according to Nowak, also due to it being used in 'combating terrorism, extremism or similar politically motivated offences'.[33] This widespread practice of torture does not call into question the rationale of the universal norm; rather it emphasises the precise need for a blanket ban on torture, for widespread implementation and enforcement of the prohibition on torture and the Convention against Torture and for effective oversight and accountability mechanisms.

The contemporary discourse on torture is less concerned with the ordinary and everyday perpetration of torture and the struggle for its elimination. The torture discourse is fixated on the *exception* to the prohibition in *exceptional* circumstances. Frank Ledwidge and Lucas Oppenheim have pointed out that 'much ink has been spilled on the question of whether torture is ever justified' and, as a result, inadequate attention is currently paid to the practice of torture in many of the world's criminal justice systems.[34] The question of whether torture is ever justified, to which Ledwidge and Oppenheim refer, is generally posed in the form of the ticking bomb scenario, the contemporary framework for thinking about torture.[35] There are countless variations on this ticking bomb scenario.[36] The construct posits a hypothetical situation in which an individual (or suspected 'terrorist') is in custody, and the authorities are certain this individual has the necessary information to prevent an impending attack that will claim the lives of many people. This individual

---

[31] *Ibid.*

[32] UNHRC 'Report of the Special Rapporteur on Torture and Other Cruel, Inhuman and Degrading Treatment or Punishment, Manfred Nowak' (2010) A/HRC/13/39, paras. 69 and 71.

[33] UNHRC 'Report of the Special Rapporteur: Manfred Nowak' A/HRC/13/39/Add. 5, para. 9.

[34] Frank Ledwidge and Lucas Oppenheim, 'Preventing Torture: Realities and Perceptions' (2006) 30 *The Fletcher Forum for World Affairs* 165.

[35] UNHRC 'Report of the Special Rapporteur: Manfred Nowak' A/HRC/13/39/Add. 5, para. 43.

[36] For a collection of the various ticking bomb scenarios that have been proffered in the literature, see Yuval Ginbar, *Why Not Torture Terrorists? Moral, Practical, and Legal Aspects of the 'Ticking Bomb' Justification for Torture* (Oxford University Press, 2008), pp. 379–86.

is unwilling to talk, but the authorities believe – or are certain – that the information can be extracted under torture. The question that the hypothetical situation poses, therefore, is whether or not it is justifiable, excusable or otherwise legitimate to torture the individual. Within this ticking bomb framework, the appropriateness of the *absolute, non-derogable* torture prohibition in *all circumstances* is a matter of debate. This ticking bomb scenario is, on the one hand, a thought experiment presented in order to elicit an intuitive response to the question of whether or not torture ought to be applied. It may also be conceived as a rhetorical device presented in order to persuade the listener of the necessity for torture. On the other hand, the ticking bomb scenario is the touchstone used by states, in practice, for describing a set of circumstances in which the prohibition on torture is presented as unreasonably impeding the possibility of saving lives.[37] In essence, however, the ticking bomb scenario is a signal of the fundamental 'tension' between the rule of law and the exception.[38]

Since the events of 11 September 2001, in the context of counterterrorism, the torture prohibition has been called into question at a rhetorical level and defied in practice by a number of governments through their counterterrorism policies. The absolute and non-derogable character of the prohibition on torture, the definition of torture, the principle of non-refoulement and the non-admissibility of evidence extracted by torture are amongst the elements of the prohibition that have been undermined by the practices and policies of a number of states. Nowak has summarised the ways in which states have, since the events of 11 September, abrogated the prohibition on torture:

> Even democratic governments contributed to the erosion of this fundamental principle of the international rule of law by adopting an extremely limited definition of torture, by openly advocating torture and/or ill-treatment as a legitimate measure of saving the lives of innocent people in the 'ticking bomb' scenario, by outsourcing torture to private companies and detention centres outside their own territory, such as Guantánamo Bay, by creating secret places of detention for suspected terrorists, by sending these individuals for interrogation purposes to countries known for their systematic practice of torture, sometimes on the basis of diplomatic

---

[37] Matthew Hannah, 'Torture and the Ticking Bomb: The War on Terrorism as a Geographical Imagination of Power/Knowledge' (2006) 96 *Annals of the Association of American Geographers* 622, 623.

[38] Nasser Hussain, *The Jurisprudence of Emergency: Colonialism and the Rule of Law* (Ann Arbor: University of Michigan, 2003), p. 2. Hussain describes his study as engaging with the 'tension between … the requirements of the sovereign emergency and the constraints of the rule of law'.

assurances provided by such governments, by closely cooperating with intelligence agencies in other countries which apply torture to extract information from suspected terrorists and by various other means.[39]

Whilst Nowak acknowledged that *even* democratic governments have contributed to the erosion of the norm prohibiting torture, it is, in fact, from within liberal democratic states that arguments that contest the logic of the prohibition on torture have emerged. In particular, by advocating for a restrictive definition of torture, by approving the legality of lists of coercive interrogation techniques and by invoking the logic of the ticking bomb, attorneys for the United States government under the Bush administration attempted to carve out a space wherein practices that contravene the prohibition on torture could be considered acceptable.[40] The actual practice of torture and other ill-treatment, which, it is suggested, stemmed from this official discourse of arguing 'away the rules of torture', was brought into sharp focus by the conditions in the Guantánamo Bay detention facility and, in particular, following the publication of the Abu Ghraib photographs documenting apparent detainee abuse.[41] It is now well known that the United States, under the Bush administration, also made use of a system of secret detention and so-called extraordinary rendition; a system that Dick Marty has described as a global 'spider's web'.[42] Extraordinary rendition is contemporaneously commonly understood to refer to the extra- or non-judicial transfer of an individual from one state to another for the purpose of interrogation, where such interrogation is likely to be conducted through the use of unlawfully coercive methods, including torture, whilst the individual is in *incommunicado* detention.[43] The fact that this form of extraordinary rendition features

---

[39] Nowak and McArthur, *The United Nations Convention against Torture*, p. v.

[40] John T. Parry, 'The Shape of Modern Torture: Extraordinary Rendition and Ghost Detainees' (2005) 6 *Melbourne Journal of International Law* 516, 522. See also, Paul W. Kahn, *Sacred Violence: Torture, Terror, and Sovereignty* (Ann Arbor: University of Michigan Press, 2008), p. 5. The Bush administration's policy with respect to the use of treatment that concerns the prohibition on torture, inhuman and degrading treatment or punishment can be traced in the declassified memoranda that have come to light since 2004. For a collection of the memos released up to 2005, see Karen J. Greenberg and Joshua L. Dratel (eds.), *The Torture Papers: The Road to Abu Ghraib* (Cambridge University Press, 2005).

[41] Greenberg and Dratel, *The Torture Papers*, p. xiii.

[42] Dick Marty, 'Alleged Secret Detentions and Unlawful Inter-State Transfers of Detainees Involving Council of Europe Member States', Council of Europe Doc. 10957 (12 June 2006), p. 9.

[43] See UNHRC, 'Joint Study on Global Practices in Relation to Secret Detention in the Context of Countering Terrorism of the Special Rapporteur on the Promotion and

the use of unlawful interrogation techniques for the ostensible purpose of intelligence-gathering distinguishes it from the preceding understanding of the term.[44] These practices of secret detention and extraordinary rendition were tolerated, and thus legitimised, by numerous other states. In June 2007, in a report submitted to the Council of Europe, Rapporteur Dick Marty found that the practice of secret detention and unlawful transfer was made possible because of the collaboration of a number of states, including several members of the Council of Europe.[45] Marty also confirmed that he had enough 'evidence to state that secret detention facilities run by the CIA did exist in Europe from 2003 to 2005, in particular in Poland and in Romania'.[46] According to Marty, his sources confirmed that Abu Zubaydah and Khalid Sheikh Mohamed were amongst the high value detainees held in secret detention and subjected to 'enhanced interrogation techniques' in Poland.[47] The United Kingdom continues to be

Protection of Human Rights and Fundamental Freedoms while Countering Terrorism, Martin Scheinin; the Special Rapporteur on Torture and Other Cruel, Inhuman and Degrading Treatment or Punishment, Manfred Nowak; the Working Group on Arbitrary Detention represented by its Vice Chair, Shadeen Sardar Ali; and the Working Group on Enforced or Involuntary Disappearances represented by its Chair, Jeremy Sarkin (19 February 2010) A/HRC/14/42, p. 3; David Weissbrodt and Amy Bergquist, 'Extraordinary Rendition and the Torture Convention' (2006) 46 *Virginia Journal of International Law* 585, 588 (describing extraordinary rendition as a euphemism for 'abduction of terror suspects not in order to bring them to justice in the United States but rather to transfer them to a third country'); The Committee on International Human Rights of the Bar of the City of New York and The Center for Human Rights and Global Justice, 'Torture by Proxy: International and Domestic Law Applicable to "Extraordinary Renditions"' (New York: NYU School of Law, 2004), p. 4 (defining extraordinary rendition as the 'transfer of an individual, with the involvement of the United States or its agents, to a foreign state in circumstances that make it more likely than not that the individual will be subjected to torture or cruel, inhuman or degrading treatment').

[44] Extraordinary rendition originally referred to the covert practice of 'obtaining' individuals from other countries in order to stand trial in the United States. Parry, 'The Shape of Modern Torture' 529; Weissbrodt and Bergquist, 'Extraordinary Rendition' 586.

[45] Dick Marty, 'Secret Detentions and Illegal Transfers of Detainees involving Council of Europe Member States: Second Report', Council of Europe Doc. 11302 (7 June 2007), p. 3. In his original report Marty had found that Sweden, Bosnia–Herzegovina, the United Kingdom, Italy, the former Yugoslav Republic of Macedonia, Germany and Turkey 'could be held responsible to varying degrees' for violations of the rights of specific individuals who were victims of the extraordinary rendition programme. He also found that these and a number of other countries 'could be held responsible for collusion – active or passive – involving secret detention and unlawful inter-state transfers of a non-specified number of persons whose identity so far remains unknown'. See, Marty, 'Alleged Secret Detentions', pp. 59–60.

[46] Marty, 'Alleged Secret Detentions', p. 4.

[47] *Ibid.*, p. 24.

scrutinised for its own policies and practices vis-à-vis the prohibition on torture. There are a number of cases in which it is alleged that British officials cooperated in the torture and ill-treatment of individuals detained abroad.[48] Judicial proceedings in the United Kingdom with respect to Binyam Mohamed, who was subjected to torture during his two year period of *incommunicado* detention in a number of prisons abroad, whilst being held 'at the behest of the United States',[49] have confirmed that 'the relationship of the United Kingdom government to the United States authorities ... was far beyond that of a bystander or witness to the alleged wrongdoing'.[50] In addition to its involvement in secret detention and extraordinary rendition, there have been a number of inquiries into the alleged torture and ill-treatment of detainees by British troops in Iraq.[51]

These practices have not altered the international legal landscape. The legal response remains intact: 'no exceptional circumstances whatsoever ... may be invoked as a justification of torture.'[52] The policies and practices implemented in the aftermath of 11 September by governments such as the United States and the United Kingdom have also been widely criticised and condemned. At the same time, however, the prohibition on torture continues to be clouded by the appeal to exception. Emergency or ticking bomb rationale is used to represent ordinary circumstances as extraordinary; the rare situation, which the phrase purports to describe, repeats itself everywhere so that the extraordinary becomes the ordinary. In conducting fact-finding missions in his capacity as Special Rapporteur, Nowak witnessed this phenomenon in practice. He described the number of 'alleged "exceptional circumstances", "unique situations" etc.' that were

[48] See Joint Committee on Human Rights, 'Allegations of UK complicity in Torture' (2008–09 HL 152, HC 230) 7–12; Human Rights Watch, 'Cruel Britannia: British Complicity in the Torture and Ill-Treatment of Terror Suspects in Pakistan' (New York: Human Rights Watch, 2009).

[49] These facts related to the treatment in detention of Binyam Mohamed were presented during the habeas corpus case of Guantánamo detainee Fahri Saeed Mohammed in the United States in 2009. See *Fahri Saeed Bin Mohammed et al. v. Barack H. Obama et al.*, United States District Court for the District of Columbia 1347 (17 November 2009), pp. 64–8. See also Amnesty International, 'USA: See No Evil: Government Turns the Other Way as Judges Make Findings about Torture and Other Abuse' (London: AMR 51/005/2011), p. 13.

[50] *R (B Mohamed) v. Secretary of State for Foreign and Commonwealth Affairs* [2008] EWHC 2048 Admin (21 August 2008), para. 88.

[51] Lord Robert Aitken, 'The Aitken Report: An Investigation into Cases of Deliberate Abuse and Unlawful Killing in Iraq in 2003 and 2004' (London: Ministry of Defence, January 2008); Sir William Gage, 'The Report of the Baha Mousa Inquiry' (2011 HC 1452).

[52] Convention against Torture, Article 2(2).

presented to him during his five-year mandate as 'somewhat astounding and instructive'.[53] According to Nowak:

> In many of my fact-finding missions, Government officials indicated that their country was currently confronted with an unrivalled and critical security challenge ranging from 'global war on terror', internal armed conflict and secessionist movements to high rates of violent crime and drug offences. Against this background, officials of all ranks at least implicitly put the absoluteness and non-derogability of the torture prohibition into question and on some occasions portrayed it as an academic or theoretical, if not naïve ideal which lacks applicability and a sense of realism.[54]

This might suggest that due to the prioritisation of security concerns in the aftermath of 11 September and the concomitant defence of torture for the prevention of acts of terrorism, the strength of the prohibition has waned, leading to a generalised defence of the practice of torture. Yet the question remains as to how and why torture is so extensively perpetrated. Indeed, there may be a 'change in the Zeitgeist' with respect to minimal standards,[55] and this change may, at least in part, explain why, in the current landscape, the use of torture has been more openly defended. Torture, however, has a long history of employment in order to deal with supposedly 'extraordinary situations'.[56] The ticking bomb scenario merely provides a contemporary, or 'liberal', rubber stamp.[57] Although torture continues to be publically eschewed, its practice, both historically and contemporaneously, suggests, as Shue argued in 1978, that Pandora's Box has long been open.[58]

C.   Reading the debate on torture

The prohibition of torture remains absolute under international law. That said, both the rhetoric of the ticking bomb and state practices and policies

---

[53] UNHRC 'Report of the Special Rapporteur: Manfred Nowak' A/HRC/13/39/Add. 5, para. 44.

[54] *Ibid.*

[55] *Jalloh* v. *Germany* (App. No. 54810/00) ECHR 11 July 2006 (Concurring Opinion of Judge Zupančič).

[56] Edward Peters, *Torture* (Philadelphia: University of Pennsylvania Press, 1996), p. 7. See also Parry, 'The Shape of Modern Torture' 522 (arguing that torture is exceptional conduct because, first, states tend to invoke the necessity defence to justify torture and, second, torture is linked with states of emergency and not with ordinary practices).

[57] David Luban, 'Liberalism, Torture, and the Ticking Bomb' (2005) 91 *Virginia Law Review* 1425, 1427.

[58] Henry Shue, 'Torture' (1978) 7 *Philosophy and Public Affairs* 124.

have tested the limits of the 'legalist approach' to the prohibition.[59] The debate on torture is concerned with the question of whether limitation or exception ought to be applied to the prohibition on torture in the exceptional situation captured in the ticking bomb scenario. This debate has generated arguments and proposals that contest, either explicitly or implicitly, the absolute and non-derogable prohibition on torture in all circumstances. The qualified torture prohibition proposal and the pragmatic absolute prohibition proposal are two accounts of how such an exception ought to be accommodated to meet the exigencies of the exceptional situation whilst remaining faithful to the rule of law. This situates the prohibition on torture within a more general debate on the appropriate balance to strike between liberty and security in crisis situations. However, proposals to accommodate exceptions to the torture prohibition, such as the torture warrant system advocated by Alan Dershowitz or the extra-legal measures model put forward by Oren Gross, run into the broader jurisprudential problem of the state of exception as presented by Agamben. These proposals are premised on the idea that torture is being practised – or would be practised in a ticking bomb situation – in flagrant violation of the rule of law and without legal accountability. Yet neither the torture warrant system nor the extra-legal measures model can offer a solution as to how torture might be practised in conformity with the rule of law. In deconstructing these proposals – in discovering why they would fail to operate as mechanisms to achieve the goal of preventing acts of terrorism whilst remaining faithful to the rule of law in exceptional circumstances – the jurisprudential problem of the state of exception materialises. This jurisprudential problem exists in the complex relationship that the exception establishes between law and political fact.[60] The attempt to ascribe the exception to the legal order, through the torture warrant procedure, or to distance the exception from the legal order, through the extra-legal measures model, is mirrored in debates about whether emergency powers can be regulated within law or whether they exist outside of law.[61] Just as this binary conception of emergency powers (as either inside or outside of law) fails to account for the phenomenon of states of emergency, the proposals to accommodate torture fail to account for the phenomenon of exceptional torture.

[59] Joan Fitzpatrick, 'Speaking Law to Power: The War against Terrorism and Human Rights' (2003) 14 *European Journal of International Law* 241, 242.

[60] Giorgio Agamben (tr. Kevin Attell), *State of Exception* (University of Chicago Press, 2005), p. 2.

[61] On this, see Leonard C. Feldman, 'Terminal Exceptions: Law and Sovereignty at the Airport Threshold' (2007) 3 *Law, Culture and Humanities* 320, 325. Feldman has posited

The exception to the prohibition on torture is discernible. The practice of torture by liberal democratic states during actual or perceived states of emergency or in countering terrorism occurs to an extent that can hardly be described as aberrational. As Paul Kahn has asserted:

> Ordinarily, we may tolerate some slippage between the generality of a legal prohibition and its application to exceptional circumstances. Law is always applied with a certain amount of discretion. But in a war on terror – past and present – torture seems to be a regular feature, not an occasional point of slippage.[62]

Reports of torture are generally met with denial or with the claim that the conduct was the doing of 'a few bad apples'.[63] When the use of torture is acknowledged, it is condemned. Prosecutions, however, tend to be minimal.[64] In a context where torture is practised extensively, reiterating that this behaviour violates international law and that the prohibition on torture is a peremptory, absolute and non-derogable norm is the obvious response. Such a response tells us that torture is illegal and ought not to be practised; however, it does not address the reality that torture *is* practised by liberal democratic states despite an absolute ban. It does not, therefore, bring us any further in understanding the narratives constructed by states, or the political and juridical procedures implemented by states, that allow torture to be practised inside of the law and outside of the law simultaneously.

Other commentators on the phenomenon of exceptional torture have varying but distinct points of departure for considering the practical, legal and moral issues presented by the ticking bomb scenario. The efficacy of torture is one such point of departure. Those who advocate or defend the use of torture in ticking bomb situations claim that such torture is necessary in order to elicit the information required to prevent the impending attack. There is an inherent assumption of the efficacy of torture. If torture could be proven to be generally ineffective in the elicitation of information in exigent circumstances, as some commentators and experts argue, this would decouple torture from the ticking bomb scenario: why torture if it is not going to work? There are, however, methodological and ethical

that the 'debate over "torture warrants" is an instance of a broader debate – over the relationship between law and the exception'.

[62] Kahn, *Sacred Violence*, p. 83.

[63] John T. Parry, *Understanding Torture: Law, Violence and Political Identity* (Ann Arbor: University of Michigan Press, 2010), p. 1.

[64] Kahn, *Sacred Violence*, p. 83.

issues with this approach. It is difficult to envisage an empirically sound method of proving that torture is always and everywhere ineffective. For example, the most valuable data required to carry out such a study is likely to be inaccessible for national security or state secrecy reasons. In any event, even if an irrefutable empirical study could prove the inefficiency of torture generally, it is foreseeable that such a study would, nevertheless, be confronted with the practical issue of whether torture *might* just work in this one exceptional case. The efficacy of torture approach is also ethically challenging. Whilst it might be practically significant to convince states that torture is an inefficacious method of acquiring reliable information, too much weight is thereby placed on the side of practicality. The integrity of this approach is undermined because it suggests, however unintentionally, that torture ought not to be practised because torture does not work, rather than because of its illegality or because of the ethical questions that its practice raises. In other words, the 'torture does not work' argument points only to a practical flaw in the debate.[65]

Another approach to tackling the question of exceptional torture is to challenge the plausibility of the ticking bomb scenario itself; the ticking bomb scenario has frequently been described as a fantastical construction and, thus, unlikely to manifest in reality. This approach encounters the same methodological and ethical obstacles as the efficacy approach. It would prove problematic to produce a reliable and conclusive study that shows that something like a ticking bomb scenario is always illusory. Accessing the required data and demonstrating that such a scenario *could* never unfold are just two of the striking impediments. In addition, as with the question of torture's efficacy, this line of reasoning, on its own, is circumstantial and, therefore, it really only circumvents the moral and legal conundrum. This is not to suggest that there is not merit in analysing the discourse and arguments that accompany each. However, such analyses remain trapped in the torture/ticking bomb nexus, a nexus that this book seeks to overcome.

A third approach to confronting the question of exceptional torture would be to enter the debate by adopting a legal and moral position on the justifiability of using torture in ticking bomb situations. The dominant

---

[65] Amnesty International, *Report on Torture* 2nd edn (London: Duckworth, 1975), p. 24. Bagaric and Clarke also raise this point as a response to their critics who proffer the 'torture does not work' argument. They maintain that '[p]resumably, if this obstacle was overcome the critics would then agree with the proposal'. See, Mirko Bagaric and Julie Clarke, *Torture: When the Unthinkable is Morally Permissible* (Albany: State University of New York Press, 2007), p. 53.

approach in the literature on torture and the ticking bomb has been to debate the question of whether torture can be justified or excused in such situations and to put forward a legal and/or moral position.[66] In his study on the reciprocal relationship between torture and terror, Paul Kahn demonstrated the inefficacy of this approach:

> As it is framed, this debate will get nowhere. Scholars will proclaim the prohibition on torture to be a necessary principle ... while our political practices will regularly employ torture. We will express surprise at the 'excesses' of our security forces, yet we intuitively know that torture is virtually inevitable. So we will be sidetracked into debates about the point at which 'rough treatment' becomes torture, about the necessity defense, or about the jurisdiction of courts. These are strategies of avoidance by definition, exception, and exclusion. The few scholars who defend torture will appeal to the logic of material calculation – torture's contribution to the greater good – but they will be met with countercalculations ... This debate will not change anyone's mind, for it never reaches the deepest issue.[67]

Kahn avoids becoming entangled in what he dubs the 'sideshow' of debating torture by undertaking a theoretical investigation into torture as a 'political phenomenon'.[68] He inquires into the political–theological meaning of torture as a product of the 'sacrificial space of sovereignty' beyond law.[69] Torture, according to Kahn, is an act of degradation that negates the terrorist's self-sacrifice for their sovereign.[70] For Kahn, the 'deepest issue' is, thus, the culture of sacrificial violence in which we remain embedded, where torture and terror form a reciprocal relationship.[71] Terror, Kahn asserts, 'is met with torture, and torture with terror'.[72] He contends that the events of 11 September opened this space of sovereignty beyond law in which torture is practised.[73] Kahn characterises torture as a failure of the law,[74] and, moreover, he concludes that torture is inevitable in the face of terrorism: 'The terrorist with weapons of mass destruction may well put an end to our dream of a global community of human rights'.[75] This conclusion calls to mind Carl Schmitt's distinction between friend and

---

[66] Of course, there are exceptions to this. Kahn's study is one. See also Feldman, 'Terminal Exceptions' 325.

[67] Kahn, *Sacred Violence*, p. 172.   [68] *Ibid.*, pp. 4, 173.

[69] *Ibid.*, pp. 15, 169, 179, n. 2.   [70] *Ibid.*, p. 76.

[71] *Ibid.*, p. 173.   [72] *Ibid.*, p 11.

[73] *Ibid.*, p 14. See also Fiona de Londras, 'Book Review: Paul W. Kahn, Sacred Violence' (2009) 19 *Law and Politics Book Review* 371, 374.

[74] Kahn, *Sacred Violence*, p. 175.   [75] *Ibid.*, p. 178.

enemy as the definition of the political: 'A world in which the possibility of war is utterly eliminated, a completely pacified globe, would be a world without the distinction of friend and enemy and hence a world without politics.'[76] Kahn describes torture as an inherently political practice and an inexorable response to terrorism. In focusing on the 'character of the political imagination that makes possible the exception' and 'on sacrifice as the archetype of political behaviour that is beyond law',[77] we are, however, no closer to answering the question of *how* torture is accommodated in the liberal democratic state; nor are we any closer to understanding why the ticking bomb scenario has such a pervasive grip on the discussion of torture.

Therefore, whilst the 'deeper issue' to which Kahn refers preoccupies this study, distinct from Kahn's approach, torture is not considered a sacrificial practice in the space of sovereignty *beyond* law; rather, torture is understood as a political practice in which law is deeply implicated. Edward Peters' assertion that judicial torture is the '*only* kind of torture' illuminates this understanding.[78] Peters insists upon the 'judicial character' of torture in an attempt to preserve the core meaning of a concept that has been both sentimentalised and politicised.[79] He argues that, although judicial torture was virtually abolished from Western European criminal legal procedure by the early nineteenth century, in the course of the twentieth century law increasingly became 'an engine of the state, and torture, therefore, an engine of the law'.[80] Peters is not exclusively referring to the totalitarian regimes of Stalinism and National Socialism, the obvious cases in which law became an 'engine of the state' and torture, thus an 'engine of the law' – the state itself having been subordinated to ideology.[81] In this context he also discusses the extensive use of torture by the French army and police in Algeria, as one example amongst others, where legal safeguards, 'entrenched in the homeland', were not applied in the colony.[82] Peters employs the term judicial torture to convey the point that torture,

---

[76] Carl Schmitt (tr. George Schwab), *The Concept of the Political* (University of Chicago Press, 2007), p. 35.

[77] Kahn, *Sacred Violence*, p. 179, n. 2.

[78] Peters, *Torture*, p. 7.

[79] Edward Peters, 'Memorandum on Torture: 12/2010' (Unpublished, Personal email correspondence 8 December 2010). Peters, *Torture*, p. 7.

[80] As Peters notes, this was the phrase used by William Blackstone around 1769 in his brief consideration of torture where he described the 'rack' as 'an engine of the state, not of law'. See Peters, *Torture*, pp. 102, 108.

[81] *Ibid.*, pp. 131–2.   [82] *Ibid.*, p. 135.

whilst not sanctioned by the judiciary as in medieval Europe,[83] remains a practice 'essential to the state's notion of order'.[84] According to Peters, his own endorsement of the term 'judicial torture' shows its logic when one takes into account the extent to which the United States administration sought legal approval for its interrogation practices in the aftermath of 11 September: 'That the US administration first turned to their attorneys for legal advice indicates that they perceived the problem of adverse interrogation to be a legal one.'[85] M. Cherif Bassiouni has pointed out that the government lawyers constructed the torture memos 'to allow their clients to rely on their advice, and thus eventually avoid responsibility'.[86] At this point it is not necessary to contemplate whether legal approval was sought in order to provide legal cover. What is explicit, particularly taking into account President Barack Obama's stated position against the prosecution of government agents who acted on the legal advice of the Office of Legal Counsel,[87] is the judicial character of the torture practised during the Bush administration.

[83] John H. Langbein, 'The Legal History of Torture' in Sanford Levinson, *Torture: A Collection* (Oxford University Press, 2004), pp. 93–4.

[84] Peters, *Torture*, p. 7.

[85] Peters, 'Memorandum on Torture'.

[86] M. Cherif Bassiouni, 'The Institutionalisation of Torture under the Bush Administration' (2006) 37 *Case Western Reserve Journal of International Law* 389, 403.

[87] On 22 January 2009, his second day in office, President Barack Obama reacted to the policies implemented by the Bush administration by ordering the revocation of the Bush administration's 'enhanced interrogation policy'. See Exec. Order No. 13491, 74 Fed. Reg. 4893 (Jan. 27, 2009), which revokes Exec. Order No. 13440, 72 Fed. Reg. 40707 (July 24, 2007). However, despite continued pressure to open a truth commission, public inquiry or criminal investigation into the policies and practices of the Bush administration, the Obama administration has remained committed to a policy of 'looking forward'. On 16 April 2009, following the release and publication (as a result of litigation filed by the American Civil Liberties Union under the Freedom of Information Act) of four memos detailing the authorised interrogation techniques that were issued by the Department of Justice's Office of Legal Counsel under the Bush administration, Obama stated: 'We have been through a dark and painful chapter in our history. But at a time of great challenges and disturbing disunity, nothing will be gained by spending our time and energy laying blame for the past.' He also stated that government agents who had used the techniques authorised by the memos would not be prosecuted: 'In releasing these memos, it is our intention to assure those who carried out their duties relying on good faith upon legal advice from the Department of Justice that they will not be subject to prosecution.' See The White House, Office of the Press Secretary, 'Statement of Barack Obama on Release of OLC Memos' 16 April 2009. In a statement made on 21 April 2009, Obama reiterated that it would be inappropriate to prosecute those 'who carried out some of these operations within the four corners of legal opinion or guidance that had been provided from the White House'. Questioned about the possibility of prosecuting those who formulated the legal decisions, he remarked that this would be a decision for the Attorney General. See

The practice of torture is therefore both exceptional – insofar as it is not normative or prescribed by law – and judicial – insofar as it entails the suspension of the prohibition of torture. Giorgio Agamben's theory of the state of exception endeavours to address this apparent paradox and for our purposes serves as a useful conceptual prism.[88] The application of his theory serves as a foil for the proposals to legally or extra-legally capture the ticking bomb scenario, and, further, it provides a means to theorise the space of exceptional torture. Agamben becomes the interlocutor as he challenges the idea that the exception can be located either inside or outside of the law.[89] His characterisation of the state of exception thus provides a control for checking various models and proposals for the accommodation or regulation of exceptional torture.[90] Agamben's theory of the state of exception is also used to investigate the space that is opened when the liberal democratic state practises torture. In confronting the rationale of the torture warrant system and the extra-legal measures model, and in discovering what is structurally unsound within these proposals, the question arises as to whether torture already constitutes an act of exception. It follows, therefore, that the state of exception also challenges the possibility of an *absolute* prohibition on torture.

To Agamben, the state of exception – that is the temporary suspension of the rule of law – reveals itself as the 'fundamental structure of the

The White House, Office of the Press Secretary, 'Remarks by President Obama and King Abdullah of Jordan' 21 April 2009. The report of the Office of Professional Responsibility, which investigated the Office of Legal Counsel's memos on 'enhanced interrogation techniques', concluded that attorneys John Yoo and Jay Bybee had 'committed professional misconduct' by failing to exercise 'independent legal judgement and render thorough, objective, and candid legal advice'. See US Department of Justice, Office of Professional Responsibility, 'Investigation into the Office of Legal Counsel's Memoranda Concerning Issues Relating to the Central Intelligence Agency's Use of "Enhanced Interrogation Techniques" on Suspected Terrorists' (29 July 2009), p. 11. The Office of the Attorney General, however, rejected the findings of the Office of Professional Responsibility on the basis that, in its view, whilst the memos were flawed, the standard of 'professional misconduct' had not been reached. See US Department of Justice, Office of the Deputy Attorney General, 'Memorandum for the Attorney General' (5 January 2010), p. 2.

[88] The term 'state of exception' is not used in this study to connote emergency powers, public emergency or state of emergency. It does not refer to 'a special kind of law' governing a factual situation, nor does it describe factual circumstances or a provision or decree instituted to deal with a situation of crisis. It has a theoretical nuance insofar as it describes the interface of law and politics: 'it defines law's threshold'. See Agamben, *State of Exception*, p. 4. Thus, the terms state of emergency and public emergency will be used interchangeably in this study when referring to international human rights law; the term state of exception will be used in a theoretical sense.

[89] Agamben, *State of Exception*, p. 23; Feldman, 'Terminal Exceptions' 329.

[90] Feldman, 'Terminal Exceptions' 322.

legal system'.[91] For Agamben, the main concern is not only, or even, that the exception has become permanent or the rule.[92] Rather, he determines the state of exception, which demands the sovereign decision, to be the ontological structure or foundation 'of the political space in which we … live' wherein that which is excluded – the exception – transcends positive law and is included within the (suspended) legal order.[93] Agamben characterises the figure of the state of exception as bare life or *homo sacer*, 'a human victim who may be killed but not sacrificed'.[94] Bare life is lived by an individual who is stripped, in Hannah Arendt's words,[95] of the 'right to have rights'.[96] Agamben views the concentration camps established under National Socialism both as the extreme materialisation or manifestation of the state of exception and as the continued potentiality of the state of exception.[97] Agamben's point is not to deny the unprecedented and unique horror of what happened in the camps.[98] His concern is with the 'juridico-political structure' that made the camps possible:[99]

> The correct question to pose concerning the horrors committed in the camps is, therefore, not the hypocritical one of how crimes of such atrocity could be committed against human beings. It would be more honest, and, above all, more useful, to investigate the juridical procedures and

[91] Giorgio Agamben (trs. Vincenzo Binetti and Cesare Casarino), *Means Without Ends: Notes on Politics* (Minneapolis: University of Minnesota Press, 2000), Preface. See also Giorgio Agamben (tr. Daniel Heller-Roazen), *Homo Sacer: Sovereign Power and Bare Life* (Stanford University Press, 1998), p. 9 (describing the state of exception as the 'hidden foundation' of the political system).

[92] Walter Benjamin (tr. Harry Zohn), 'On the Concept of History' in Howard Eiland and Michael W. Jennings (eds.), *Walter Benjamin: Selected Writings, Vol. IV, 1938–1940* (Cambridge, MA: The Belknap Press, 2003), p. 392. See also, Agamben, *Homo Sacer*, p. 12.

[93] Agamben, *Means Without Ends*, p. 36 and Agamben, *Homo Sacer*, p. 17.

[94] Agamben, *Homo Sacer*, p. 83.

[95] Agamben's writings in general, and his elaboration of the notion of 'bare life' in particular, are heavily influenced by Arendt. However, whilst Agamben, in his concern with biopolitics, draws inspiration from Arendt's discussion of rights in *The Origins of Totalitarianism*, his focus is on the question of sovereign power, whereas Arendt is concerned with the relationship between rights and the nation-state. See Judith Butler, 'I Merely Belong to Them' (2007) 29 *London Review of Books* 26, 28. See also Agamben, *Homo Sacer*, pp. 126–35; Hannah Arendt, *The Origins of Totalitarianism* (New York: Harcourt Books, 1968), pp. 290–302.

[96] Arendt, *The Origins of Totalitarianism*, p. 296.

[97] Agamben, *Homo Sacer*, pp. 166, 174; Agamben, *Means Without Ends*, pp. 36–44.

[98] Giorgio Agamben (tr. Daniel Heller-Roazen), *Remnants of Auschwitz: The Witness and the Archive* (New York: Zone Books, 2002), p. 31; Agamben, *Homo Sacer*, p. 166.

[99] Agamben, *Homo Sacer*, p. 166.

deployments of power by which human beings could be so completely deprived of their rights and prerogatives that no act committed against them could appear any longer as a crime.[100]

In his concern with the 'juridico-political structure', Agamben again echoes Arendt. Arendt, in her report on the trial of Adolf Eichmann, drew attention to the inadequacy of 'juristic concepts' in representing the criminal facts that were the subject of that trial.[101] She was pointing to the entire reversal of the notion of exception in the Third Reich where the crimes committed constituted not an exception to the rule, but the rule itself.[102] Like Arendt, Agamben claims that the juridico-political structure that enabled the exception to become the rule was not fully grasped in the context of National Socialism. His further claim is that this juridico-political structure – that is, the state of exception – is, in fact, determinative of modernity.[103] Such an assertion allows him to make what might seem to be an irreverent assertion:

> [I]f the essence of the camp consists in the materialisation of the state of exception ... then we must admit that we find ourselves virtually in the presence of a camp every time such a structure is created, independent of the kinds of crime that are committed there and whatever its denomination and specific topography.[104]

By imagining the paradigm of torture as a representation of the state of exception, Agamben's theory is applied as the analytical framework for theorising the practice of torture.

Agamben has been described as the 'contemporary disciple' of the German legal theorist and jurist Carl Schmitt;[105] his theory has been considered as a 'less radical' version of Schmitt's.[106] There are, however, important differences between Agamben's theory of the state of exception and Schmitt's writings on the sovereign exception. Indeed Schmitt has been described as the 'outstanding legal theorist of the *notion of*

---

[100] *Ibid.*, p. 171.
[101] In fact, since Arendt refers to 'all these trials', she appears to be referring, more generally, to the Nuremburg trials. Hannah Arendt, *Eichmann in Jerusalem: A Report on the Banality of Evil* (New York: Penguin Books, 1994), p. 292.
[102] *Ibid.*, p. 291.
[103] Agamben, *Homo Sacer*, p. 166.   [104] *Ibid.*, p. 174.
[105] Costas Douzinas, *Human Rights and the End of Empire: The Political Philosophy of Cosmopolitanism* (Abingdon: Routledge-Cavendish, 2007), p. 6.
[106] David Dyzenhaus, *The Constitution of Law: Legality in a Time of Emergency* (Cambridge University Press, 2006), p. 39.

exception',[107] and there has been a substantial resurgence of interest in his writings, particularly since the events of 11 September. Schmitt's writings have, in this regard, been applied to explain exceptionalism from international standards by the United States administration in its 'war on terror'.[108] Agamben does draw heavily upon Schmitt's account of the sovereign as 'he who decides on the exception'.[109] In addition, Agamben has recourse to the essential critique that Schmitt makes of liberal constitutionalism faced with an emergency. Schmitt argued that liberal constitutionalism, by attempting to devolve decision-making on the exception through a series of checks and balances, denies the sovereign decision on the exception.[110] This denial, according to Schmitt, is a fiction because the exception that the liberal constitution attempts to regulate with precision cannot regulate itself.[111] That is to say, the exception requires a decision. Whilst the constitution can regulate who makes this decision, the nature of the decision cannot be regulated. Schmitt identified the juristic nature of this decision, thus dismantling the idea that the exception is purely legal or normative or purely extra-legal.[112] For Schmitt, resolving the problem of the exception necessitated recognition of the unlimited authority to decide.[113] He maintained that the authority to decide exists prior to positive or constitutional law but that the decision is a juristic one because the sovereign who makes this decision straddles the threshold of law.[114]

Agamben departs from Schmitt at the point at which Schmitt attempts to resolve the contradiction of the exception in the liberal constitution. Schmitt honed in on the decision as the locus of the liberal constitution's failure to come to terms with the exception. In order to correct this, Schmitt espoused an authoritarian position: he viewed the decision on the exception as the legally constituted, legitimate purview of the sovereign. In contrast, Agamben accepts the fact of the political nature of the decision on the exception but his analysis is diagnostic and, unlike Schmitt,

---

[107] Dan Diner and Michael Stolleis (eds.), *Hans Kelsen and Carl Schmitt: A Juxtaposition* (1999), cited in Oren Gross, 'The Normless and Exceptionless Exception: Carl Schmitt's Theory of Emergency Powers and the "Norm/Exception" Dichotomy' (2000) 21 *Cardozo Law Review* 1825, 1826 (original emphasis).

[108] See, for example, Adrian Vermeule, 'Our Schmittian Administrative Law' (2009) 122 *Harvard Law Review* 1095, 1149; Christopher Kutz, 'Torture, Necessity and Existential Politics' (2007) 95 *California Law Review* 235, 238; William E. Scheuerman, 'Carl Schmitt and the Road to Abu Ghraib' (2006) 13 *Constellations* 108, 118–20.

[109] Carl Schmitt (tr. Georg Schwab), *Political Theology: Four Chapters on the Concept of Sovereignty* (University of Chicago Press, 2005), p. 1.

[110] *Ibid.*, p. 7.   [111] *Ibid.*, p. 14.   [112] *Ibid.*, p. 13.

[113] *Ibid.*, p. 12.   [114] *Ibid.*, p. 7.

his objective is not to give the exception a normative content;[115] rather it is to explain the dialectic between law and authority in real terms. This is necessary, for Agamben, because he recognises that the state of exception has itself become prosaic in the liberal democratic state. Agamben, therefore, does not focus on the state of exception as a problem caused by a separation of powers to be resolved by recognising, as the sovereign, 'he' who truly decides.[116] Moreover, Agamben does not espouse authoritarianism. He demonstrates, rather, how the state of exception is absorbed within the liberal democracy such that the state of exception has become an indistinguishable point of confluence between public law and political fact. For Agamben, therefore, the problem of the state of exception in the liberal democracy is not Schmitt's diagnosis of paralysis in the face of emergency; the problem for Agamben, rather, is that the state of exception does function in the liberal democratic state.[117]

Bas Scholten regards Agamben as having erected 'a straw man' with his theory of the state of exception. He deems Agamben's state of exception to misrepresent what is, in reality, governments 'abusing the law and acting in bad faith'. According to Scholten, Agamben's work deprives 'the law of all its complexities, diversity, openness and constraints (and thus normativity)'.[118] Because he denies the law its 'normativity', Agamben's theory therefore prevents him from being able to identify 'violations, abuses and misuses of the law'.[119] As such, 'Agamben's methodology can tell us ... little about the law'.[120] Scholten, however, misunderstands Agamben's concern with the state of exception. Agamben's argument is not that norms are unidentifiable or that norms do not exist. Nor is he preoccupied by the accountability aspects of 'impunity of violations of international law by governments that nevertheless still claim to be applying law'.[121] Rather, Agamben observes that the application of the norm is increasingly replaced by the state of exception, that is, in short, the suspension

---

[115] Austin Sarat, 'Introduction: Toward New Conceptions of the Relationship of Law and Sovereignty under Conditions of Emergency' in Austin Sarat (ed.), *Sovereignty, Emergency, Legality* (Cambridge University Press, 2010), pp. 1, 3.

[116] Agamben, *Homo Sacer*, p. 173. See also Bruno Gullì, 'The Ontology and Politics of Exception: Reflections on the Work of Giorgio Agamben' in Matthew Calarco and Stephen DeCaroli (eds.), *Giorgio Agamben: Sovereignty and Life* (Stanford University Press, 2007), pp. 219, 235 (pointing out that the state of exception exceeds the already fading 'distinction among legislative power, executive power, and juridical power').

[117] Agamben, *State of Exception*, p. 86.

[118] Bas Scholten, 'Defending Our Legal Practices: A Legal Critique of Giorgio Agamben's State of Exception' (2009) 1, 2 *Amsterdam Law Forum* 113, 124.

[119] *Ibid.*, 121.   [120] *Ibid.*, 123.   [121] *Ibid.*, 120.

of the norm. Agamben recognises a futility in reiterating that 'violations of law are taking place'.[122] He attempts to inquire into the structure of the state of exception that allows such violations to take place. Therefore, in the same way that he does not, for example, focus on the role of international criminal law in ending impunity or in promoting accountability for international crimes, the omission of reflection on judicial review in Agamben's work ought not to be understood as his dismissal of the practice; it is simply not the concern of his inquiry.

In attempting to demonstrate what is irrelevant in Agamben's work, Scholten rhetorically asks: 'Imagine you are detained in Guantánamo. What should your lawyer be doing? Should she be arguing in court that according to precedents and legal doctrine current practices are simply illegal? Alternatively, should she be wandering around in an open space of human praxis'?[123] Yet, ironically, Scholten's question actually highlights the relevance of Agamben's concern with the state of exception. As Judith Butler has pointed out, for those indefinitely detained in Guantánamo, 'the law is effectively suspended in both its national and international forms.'[124] Whilst from the perspective of international law, and from Scholten's perspective, such indefinite detention might be easily recognisable as illegal detention, the situation of the detainees in Guantánamo resulted from 'the production of a paralegal universe that goes by the name of law'.[125] Agamben's effort is not to deny the law the possibility of

---

[122] *Ibid.*, 121.   [123] *Ibid.*, 124.

[124] Judith Butler, *Precarious Life: The Powers of Mourning and Violence* (London: Verso, 2004), p. 51. Butler argues that the exception produced by the withdrawal of the norm, as articulated by Agamben, is supplemented by a matrix of rules enforced by delegated sovereigns, that is by a Foucauldian structure of 'governmentality'. See, Butler, *Precarious Life*, pp. 61–2; see also Feldman, 'Terminal Exceptions' 331. Nasser Hussain also applies a governmentality analysis to Guantánamo. Hussain argues, moreover, that the state of exception cannot account for the form of governance enacted in Guantánamo. See Nasser Hussain, 'Beyond Norm and Exception: Guantánamo' (2007) 33 *Critical Inquiry* 734, 735 and 749. Also critical of a state of exception explanation for Guantánamo, as applied by Agamben and others, Fleur Johns argues that the detention facility is constituted by 'elaborate regulatory efforts by a range of legal authorities', and that this regime is not one demonstrating the state of exception but the retreat or the 'annihilation' of the exception. See Fleur Johns, 'Guantánamo Bay and the Annihilation of the Exception' (2005) 16 *European Journal of International Law* 613, 614. For an analysis critical of Agamben's account of the history of the state of exception, in the United States in particular, see Charles R. Venator Santiago, 'From the Insular Cases to Camp X-Ray: Agamben's State of Exception and United States Territorial Law' (2006) 39 *Studies in Law, Politics and Society* 15. A detailed engagement with these critiques of the state of exception as applied to Guantánamo is beyond the scope of the current work.

[125] Butler, *Precarious Life*, p. 61.

re-establishing the applicability of the norm in the individual case; rather he attempts to unmask *how* such 'paralegal universes' are produced. In other words, his concern would likely be with the a priori question of how – that is, by what juridical and political procedures – 'you' came to be detained in Guantánamo at all.

This ontological approach allows accepted or established frames for thinking about events to be called into question.[126] As regards the state of exception, Agamben asks us to rethink the exception and its association with the norm. The attempt to placate an exception to the torture prohibition with a concern for the rule of law in ticking bomb situations relies on a circumscribed understanding of the exception, and of the norm – the prohibition of torture. Moreover, the debate about torture in such situations rests on a production of the ticking bomb event and its causal relationship with torture, which edits out 'other possibilities for apprehension'.[127] Before attempting to reframe how we think about torture, it is first necessary, therefore, to shed light on what is missing from the ticking bomb scenario's 'rendition of reality'.[128]

Chapter 1 examines the prohibition of torture under international law, specifically as it relates to the question of the use of torture in exceptional circumstances as captured in the notion of the ticking bomb scenario. This chapter is explanatory insofar as it provides an account of the status and definition of the right to be free from torture under international law. It is not my contention that the prohibition on torture is in need of substantial reform. I do argue, however, that the integrity of the legal prohibition of torture is dependent on a dogmatic interpretation both of the absolute nature of the prohibition and of the definition of torture. Thus, the motivation of the perpetrator must not be considered where violations of the prohibition are at issue. In addition, the definition of torture should not rely on the severity of pain and suffering as the decisive criterion for distinguishing torture from other forms of ill-treatment.

By examining the origins, usages and critiques of the ticking bomb scenario, Chapter 2 attempts to understand how this scenario emerged as the apogee of justifications for the practice of torture. The objective is, on the one hand, to illustrate how the ticking bomb scenario exerts an amnesic effect on our understanding of torture and, on the other hand, to illuminate this memory of torture by showing that the ticking bomb scenario frames the debate on torture so as to obscure the 'realities of

[126] Judith Butler, *Frames of War: When is Life Grieveable?* (London: Verso, 2010), p. 9.
[127] *Ibid.*, p. 12.   [128] *Ibid.*

torture'.[129] The chapter reviews a number of contexts in which the ticking bomb scenario has been presented as part of the narrative, or as the justification or rationale, for the state practice of torture. It then analyses the contours of the debate on the justifiability of torture in ticking bomb situations.

Chapter 3 examines, from a theoretical perspective, the structure of the state of exception. The chapter sets out from the premise that states of emergency 'challenge the state's commitment to govern through law'.[130] It is shown that responses to states of emergency tend to be considered from either of two perspectives. On the one hand, the state of emergency is posited as a juridical problem; the response to the emergency is considered to be constituted by law. On the other hand, the state of emergency is posited as a problem of fact or a political problem; the response to the emergency is thus considered extra-legal, albeit with legal consequences. The chapter then shows how Agamben cuts through this binary conception of states of emergency to present his theory that the state of exception is constitutive of the juridical order. Employing Agamben's theory facilitates analysis of how torture is practised in the liberal democratic state from a perspective that breaks through the torpid recognition of torture simply as a violation of international law. In this regard, the chapter seeks to understand the juridical and political structure of torture as a paradigm of the state of exception.

Chapter 4 identifies and critically evaluates the three representative academic positions concerned with the question of accommodating an exception to the torture prohibition in exceptional situations: the qualified torture prohibition, the pragmatic absolute torture prohibition and the absolute torture prohibition. As this chapter will reveal, in the case of the torture warrant proposal and the extra-legal measures model, the narratives that are woven around the ticking bomb scenario implode when viewed in a critical light. By contrast, because Waldron approaches the torture question from outside of the frame of the ticking bomb scenario, he provides an alternative way of thinking about torture. All three approaches, however, raise feasibility questions in the light of the state of exception.

Chapter 5 examines the relevance of morality to the prohibition on torture, on the one hand, and to the debate on the justifiability of torture,

---

[129] Rejali, *Torture and Democracy*.

[130] Victor V. Ramraj, 'No Doctrine more Pernicious? Emergencies and the Limits of Legality' in Victor V. Ramraj (ed.), *Emergencies and the Limits of Legality* (Cambridge University Press, 2008), pp. 3–4.

on the other hand. First, it outlines a number of accounts that call into the question the assumption that the abolition of torture across Europe towards the end of the eighteenth century was attributable to the progress of Enlightenment thought. Attention then turns to the contemporary torture debate and the deontological and consequentialist reasoning that divides opinion on the question of justifiability. Torture is then considered within the broader contexts of rights' protection in the liberal democratic state and of the state of exception. In this final analysis, the chapter attempts to theorise the space of exceptional torture.

1

State of law

It is hardly radical to remark that the definition of torture is unclear and somewhat intangible. The chapter that follows does not claim to rectify this by, for example, redefining torture. Rather this chapter pries open both the absolute character of the prohibition and the definition of torture for analysis and offers positive legal conclusions in favour of a rigid application of the absolute prohibition and of a purposive element approach to the definition. These conclusions are reached in full knowledge that they juxtapose somewhat awkwardly with the underpinning thread of analysis in this work: the notion of absolute as a fiction and of law as incapable of adequately capturing the act of torture.

A. The international legal framework for the prohibition of torture: from the Universal Declaration to the Convention against Torture

(1) Universal Declaration of Human Rights

Article 5 of the Universal Declaration of Human Rights states: 'No one shall be subjected to torture or to cruel, inhuman or degrading treatment or punishment.'[1] Nigel Rodley remarks that this provision 'appeared naturally and uncontroversially' in the Declaration.[2] The natural appearance of this provision is unsurprising. By the end of the eighteenth century, torture had become viewed as 'a direct attack on the core of human dignity'.[3] The atrocities committed during the Second World War, however, fresh in the minds of the drafters of the International

---

[1] Universal Declaration of Human Rights (adopted 10 December 1948) UNGA Res. 217 A (III), Article 5.

[2] Nigel S. Rodley, *The Treatment of Prisoners Under International Law* 2nd edn (Oxford University Press, 1999), p. 18.

[3] Manfred Nowak, *UN Covenant on Civil and Political Rights: CCPR Commentary* 2nd edn (Kehl: N. P. Engel Verlag 2005), p. 158.

Bill of Rights,[4] undoubtedly contributed to the rationale of Article 5.[5] The extensive and 'extremely cruel' practice of torture by the totalitarian regimes of Stalinism and National Socialism brought to the fore the reality that torture was, by no means, a historical phenomenon.[6] The inclusion of the provision was prompted by the agreement amongst the drafters of the Declaration that effective measures would need to be implemented in order to prevent the recurrence of such atrocities.[7]

The torture provision provided surprisingly little debate at the drafting stages.[8] It was recognised early in the process, however, that the precise meaning of the term torture was unclear and might require further elaboration. In addition, the propriety of medical experimentation and the potential justification for the infliction of suffering were issues raised by René Cassin, the French representative on the Drafting Committee. Cassin was commenting on Article 4 of the draft outline of an International Bill of Rights prepared by the Secretariat, which stated: 'No one shall be subjected to torture, or to any unusual punishment or indignity.'[9] He pointed to the need for a clearer definition of torture and suggested, in that regard, that the Commission ought to take into consideration such questions as: 'Do some humans have the right to expose others to medical experiments and do any have the right to inflict suffering upon other human beings without their consent, even for ends that may appear good?'[10] Charles Malik, the Lebanese representative, also 'found ambiguity' in the word

---

[4] At its second session, the Commission on Human Rights applied the term 'International Bill of Rights' to the series of documents, namely a declaration on human rights, a convention or covenant on human rights and measures of implementation, with which the Economic and Social Council had charged the Commission with drafting. For the debates on the alternative forms that the International Bill of Rights might have taken, see UNCHR (1947) UN Doc. E.CN.4/SR.7; UNCHR (1947) UN Doc. E.CN.4/SR.9; UNCHR (1947) UN Doc. E.CN.4/SR.10; UNCHR (1947) E.CN.4/21 p. 3.

[5] UNCHR (1948) UN Doc. E/Cn.4/AC.1/SR.23, p. 3. See also Barry M. Klayman, 'The Definition of Torture in International Law' (1978) 51 *Temple Law Quarterly* 449, 461; Rodley, *The Treatment of Prisoners*, p. 18.

[6] Manfred Nowak and Elizabeth McArthur, *The United Nations Convention Against Torture: A Commentary* (Oxford University Press, 2008), p. 2.

[7] Ann-Marie Bolin Pennegård, 'Article 5' in Gudmundur Alfredsson and Asbjørn Eide (eds.), *The Universal Declaration of Human Rights: A Common Standard of Achievement* (The Hague: Martinus Nijhoff Publishers, 1999), p. 123.

[8] William A. Schabas, *The Death Penalty as Cruel Treatment and Torture: Capital Punishment Challenged in the World's Courts* (Boston, MA: Northeastern University Press, 1996), p. 27.

[9] UNCHR (1947) UN Doc. E/CN.4/21, p. 9.

[10] UNCHR (1947) UN Doc. E/CN.4/AC.1/SR.3, p. 13. See also, Klayman, 'The Definition of Torture' 449 (for an account of the drafting of Article 5 of the Universal Declaration).

torture and expressed his opinion that it should be defined more carefully. Specifically, he asked whether 'forced labor, unemployment or dental pain might be considered torture'.[11] During the second session of the Drafting Committee, however, Malik explicitly delinked the need for definitional clarity from the proposed provision with reference to the Nazi atrocities:

> The basic idea was to explain in an international instrument that the conscience of mankind had been shocked by the inhuman acts in Nazi Germany, and therefore a positive and condemnatory article was needed. Considering what had happened in Germany he felt that it was better to err on the side of vagueness than on the side of legal accuracy.[12]

The issue of the potential justification for the infliction of suffering, raised by Cassin, did not arise again in the drafting of Article 5 of the Universal Declaration. At any rate, attention turned away from the perceived ambiguity of the term torture. The Drafting Committee, working on the Secretariat draft, focused instead, on the one hand, on elaborating upon the accompanying phrases of the draft secretariat provision and, on the other hand, on the subject of medical and scientific experimentation.[13] The discussion was limited. This was partly due to the fact that an amended version of the Secretariat draft, which read '[n]o one shall be subjected to torture or to cruel, inhuman or degrading treatment or punishment', was approved by the Commission as part of an article that also dealt with the prohibition of slavery.[14] Consequently, the discussion of the slavery provision overshadowed discussion of the torture provision contained in the same article.[15] When the final version was adopted by the General Assembly on 10 December 1948, the torture provision had been separated into a distinct article.[16] With respect to the approved draft of Article 5 of the Universal Declaration, Barry Klayman remarks:

> During the course of the debates … many of the delegates had expressed their misgivings about the substantive content of the ban against torture

[11] See UNHCR (1947) E/CN.4/AC.1/SR.3, p. 13.
[12] UNCHR (1948) E.CN.4/AC.1/SR.23, p. 3. At this point the discussion was geared towards the drafting of a covenant and not a declaration. See Johannes Morsink, *The Universal Declaration of Human Rights: Origins, Drafting and Intent* (Philadelphia: University of Pennsylvania Press, 1999), p. 10.
[13] Klayman, 'The Definition of Torture' 459.
[14] *Ibid.*, 460; Schabas, *The Death Penalty*, p. 28.
[15] Klayman, 'The Definition of Torture' 460.
[16] *Ibid*; Schabas, *The Death Penalty*, p. 28.

and solemnly spoke of the need for greater specificity and definiteness. Whilst not articulated, much of the pressure to clarify the torture prohibition was eased as a result of the decision to follow the Declaration, which was to be a nonbinding statement of ideals and objectives, with another set of international instruments which would be more definite and legally binding upon states.[17]

In spite of such misgivings, since the adoption of the Universal Declaration on 10 December 1948, Article 5 has provided the language for the provisions prohibiting torture in a number of other international human rights instruments.

(2)   International Covenant on Civil and Political Rights

Article 7 of the International Covenant on Civil and Political Rights states: 'No one shall be subjected to torture or to cruel, inhuman or degrading treatment or punishment. In particular, no one shall be subjected without his free consent to medical or scientific experimentation.'[18] This clause was adopted by the Commission on Human Rights as early as 1949 following a proposal by Lebanon that the wording remain the same as Article 5 of the Universal Declaration.[19] During the discussion on what became Article 7 of the Civil and Political Rights Covenant, the character of the prohibition of torture as an individual right, expressed in the wording 'no one shall be', was emphasised.[20] In addition, the discussion stressed the meaning of the word torture as encompassing both mental and physical torture.[21] It was also agreed that the word 'treatment' was to be understood as broader in scope than the word 'punishment'; however, it was not to be understood as encompassing 'degrading situations arising from socio-economic conditions'.[22] The second clause of Article 7 developed out of a proposal submitted to the Drafting Committee in

---

[17] Klayman, 'The Definition of Torture' 460.
[18] International Covenant on Civil and Political Rights (adopted 16 December 1966, entered into force 23 March 1976) 999 UNTS 171, Article 7.
[19] UNCHR (1949) E/CN.4/193. See also M. J. Bossuyt, *Guide to the 'Travaux Préparatoires' of the International Covenant on Civil and Political Rights* (Dordrecht: Martinus Nijhoff Publishers, 1987), p. 150; Schabas, *The Death Penalty*, p. 28; Nowak, *UN Covenant on Civil and Political Rights*, p. 159.
[20] Bossuyt, *Guide to the 'Travaux Préparatoires'*, p. 150; Nowak, *UN Covenant on Civil and Political Rights*, p. 159.
[21] *Ibid.*
[22] Nowak, *UN Covenant on Civil and Political Rights*, p.159.

1947 by the United Kingdom delegate.[23] The *Travaux Préparatoires* show that its inclusion was intended as a response to the Nazi atrocities committed in the concentration camps.[24] The discussion on this clause was 'all-consuming' and dominated the Drafting Committee's efforts.[25] This was so because, whilst consensus was reached on the necessity of including this provision, the delegates were faced with the problem of finding a formulation that 'prohibits criminal experiments while not ruling out at the same time legitimate scientific and medical practices'.[26] As a result of the lengthy consideration of this second clause, the clause prohibiting torture received little consideration.[27] The final text of Article 7 was adopted by the General Assembly on 16 December 1966. Klayman concludes that the original clause contained in the Universal Declaration was maintained, despite some dissatisfaction, because delegates feared that a more specific formulation would unduly restrict the application of the prohibition.[28] Article 7 of the Covenant on Civil and Political Rights was, thus, formulated in such a way as to assure its widest possible application.[29]

(3)   European Convention on Human Rights

Article 3 of the European Convention on Human Rights states: 'No one shall be subjected to torture or to inhuman or degrading treatment or punishment.'[30] This provision differs from Article 5 of the Universal Declaration of Human Rights only insofar as it omits the word cruel. The drafting of Article 3 of the European Convention 'provoked little controversy'.[31] In 1949 the Consultative Assembly of the Council of

---

[23] UNCHR (1947) E/CN.4/AC.1/4/Add.4. This proposal stated: 1. No Person shall be subjected to: (a) Torture in any form; (b) any form of physical mutilation or medical or scientific experimentation against his will; (c) cruel or inhuman punishments.

[24] Bossuyt, *Guide to the 'Travaux Préparatoires'*, p. 151; Nowak, *UN Covenant on Civil and Political Rights*, p. 188.

[25] Klayman, 'The Definition of Torture' 465.

[26] Nowak, *UN Covenant on Civil and Political Rights*, p. 188. For an analysis of the preparatory work on the prohibition of medical or scientific experimentation, see also Bossuyt, *Guide to the 'Travaux Préparatoires'*, p. 151.

[27] Klayman, 'The Definition of Torture' 466.

[28] *Ibid.*, 466.   [29] *Ibid.*

[30] Convention for the Protection of Human Rights and Fundamental Freedoms, 4 November 1950, 213 UNTS 221 (entered into force 3 September 1953), Article 3.

[31] Malcolm D. Evans and Rodney Morgan, *Preventing Torture: A Study of the European Convention for the Prevention of Torture and Inhuman or Degrading Treatment or Punishment* (Oxford University Press, 1998), p. 70.

Europe began its deliberations on a draft of the European Convention on Human Rights and Fundamental Freedoms.[32] The Consultative Assembly discussions were based on a draft Convention prepared by the Legal Committee of the European Movement.[33] Discussion on this document culminated in the Teitgen Report of 5 September 1949.[34] Article 2 of the draft appended to the Teitgen Report read: 'In this Convention, the Member States shall undertake to ensure to all persons residing within their territories: (1) Security of person, in accordance with Articles 3, 5 and 8 of the United Nations Declaration.'[35] During the debates the representative of the United Kingdom, Seymour Cocks, suggested two amendments to the draft texts and, in doing so, he sparked a detailed debate on the substance of the prohibition of torture.[36] Cocks suggested that paragraph 1 of Article 2 be supplemented to include the following:

> In particular no person shall be subjected to any form of mutilation or sterilisation, or to any form of torture or beating. Nor shall he be forced to take drugs nor shall they be administered to him without his knowledge and consent. Nor shall he be subjected to imprisonment with such an excess of light, darkness, noise or silence as to cause mental suffering.[37]

Cocks also proposed that Article 1 of the draft include the following:

> The Consultative Assembly takes this opportunity of declaring that all forms of physical torture ... are inconsistent with civilised society, are offences against Heaven and Humanity and must be prohibited. They declare that this prohibition must be absolute and that torture cannot be permitted for any purpose whatsoever, either for extracting evidence, for saving life or even for the safety of the State. They believe that it would be better even for Society to perish than for it to permit this relic of barbarism to remain.[38]

Cocks maintained that his objective in proposing this amendment was 'to give greater emphasis ... to the condemnation of torture', which he felt was mentioned 'almost too casually' in the report.[39] In defending his plea for the elaboration of the torture prohibition, he referred to the history of

---

[32] Council of Europe, European Commission on Human Rights, 'Preparatory Work on Article 3 of the European Convention on Human Rights' (1956) D.H (56) 5, 1.
[33] Evans and Morgan, *Preventing Torture*, p. 69.   [34] *Ibid.*
[35] Council of Europe, 'Preparatory Work' 1.
[36] Klayman, 'The Definition of Torture' 471.
[37] Council of Europe, 'Preparatory Work' 2.
[38] *Ibid.*, 3.   [39] *Ibid.*

the abolition of torture and to its resurgence and use in Nazi Germany.[40]
He concluded his statement with the following words:

> I feel that this is the occasion when this Assembly should condemn in the
> most forthright and absolute fashion this retrogression into barbarism. I say
> that to take the straight beautiful bodies of men and women and to maim
> and mutilate them by torture is a crime against high heaven and the holy
> spirit of man. I say that it is a sin against the Holy Ghost for which there is
> no forgiveness. I declare that it is incompatible with civilisation. Therefore,
> I ask this Assembly to announce to the whole world that torture is wholly
> evil and absolutely to be condemned and that no cause whatever – not even
> the life of a wife, a mother or a child, the safety of an army or the security of
> a State – can justify its use or existence. I say that if a State, in order to sur-
> vive, must be built upon a torture chamber, then that State should perish. I
> do not believe in that necessity. It is the States which are built upon torture
> chambers which will perish, as Nazi Germany perished.[41]

Cocks' proposals confronted the 'basic ethical dilemma' posed by the question of whether torture could ever be justified.[42] Clearly, he rejected the idea
that it could. In response to Cocks' proposals, Sir David Maxwell Fife, also
representing the United Kingdom, lauded the sentiment of the proposals
but pointed out that this sentiment was already expressed in Article 5 of the
Universal Declaration. He also remarked that placing such an emphasis on
this particular provision would throw the whole draft Convention out of
balance and, in doing so, potentially weaken other provisions that were
not specifically mentioned.[43] The French representative, Mr André Philip,
suggested as a compromise that the Assembly consider adopting a separate resolution that would not be included in the draft Convention.[44] The
French Rapporteur, Pierre-Henri Teitgen, responded to Cocks' proposals
with a warning that an overly specific provision might lead to unintended
consequences: 'if ... he enumerates a certain number of means of torture
which he wishes to have prohibited, he risks giving a wholly different interpretation from that which he hopes to make, namely that the other processes of torture are not forbidden. And this is certainly the opposite of
what he intends.'[45] Teitgen reiterated the point that the best way to express
the fundamental principle was by way of a general prohibition on torture.[46]
Cocks accepted Philip's proposal and withdrew his amendment.[47]

---

[40] *Ibid.*, 3–4.   [41] *Ibid.*, 4–5.
[42] Klayman, 'The Definition of Torture' 471.
[43] Council of Europe, 'Preparatory Work' 5.
[44] *Ibid.*, 7. See also Evans and Morgan, *Preventing Torture*, p. 71.
[45] Council of Europe, 'Preparatory Work' 8.   [46] *Ibid.*
[47] The subject of Cocks' proposals was then placed in a draft resolution, which read:

(4)   Other regional human rights instruments

The American Declaration of the Rights and Duties of Man,[48] adopted as a non-binding resolution of the Ninth International Conference of American States in 1948, contains no specific reference to the prohibition of torture and other ill-treatment. Scott Davidson observes, however, that the Inter-American Commission on Human Rights 'has always assumed that they are subsumed under Article I of the declaration'.[49] Article I provides that '[e]very human being has the right to life, liberty and the security of his person'.[50] In addition, Article XXV of the Declaration protects 'the right to humane treatment' of the detained and Article XXVI prohibits the 'cruel, infamous or unusual punishment' of 'every person accused of an offense'.[51] The American Convention on Human Rights, adopted in 1969, includes the prohibition on torture in Article 5, which concerns the 'right to humane treatment'.[52] The provision prohibiting torture is phrased in the same terms as Article 5 of the Universal Declaration, although the terms 'treatment' and 'punishment' are, as William Schabas points out, reversed 'for no apparent reason'.[53] In addition, the torture provision

> The Consultative Assembly solemnly declares that any use of torture by public authorities or individuals is a crime against humanity and can never be justified on the grounds that it is being used for extracting information, to save life or to protect the interests of the State or on any grounds whatsoever.
>
> The Assembly records its abhorrence at the subjection of any person to any form or mutilation or sterilisation or beating.

Whilst the first paragraph was accepted, the second paragraph proved controversial due to objections from Denmark, Sweden and Norway with regard to the domestic permissibility of sterilisation and an objection from the United Kingdom because of the domestic permissibility of corporal punishment for certain offences. Unable to resolve the question, the Assembly referred the entire text to the Legal Committee and decided to reconsider the matter in the next Assembly. This resolution was not pursued by the Assembly. See Evans and Morgan, *Preventing Torture*, p. 73.

[48] American Declaration of the Rights and Duties of Man, OAS Res. XXX, adopted by the Ninth International Conference of American States (1950) reprinted in Basic Documents Pertaining to Human Rights in the Inter-American System, OEA/Ser.L.V/II.82 doc.6 rev. 1, 17 (1992).

[49] Scott Davidson, 'The Civil and Political Rights Protected in the Inter-American Human Rights System' in David J. Harris and Stephen Livingstone (eds.), *The Inter-American System of Human Rights* (Oxford University Press, 2004), p. 226.

[50] American Declaration of the Rights and Duties of Man, Article I.

[51] *Ibid.*

[52] American Convention on Human Rights (Pact of San José), signed 22 November 1969, entered into force 18 July 1978, OASTS 36, O.A.S. Off. Rec. OEA/Ser.L/V/11.23, doc. 21, rev. 6 (1979), reprinted in 9 ILM 673 (1970), Article 5.

[53] Schabas, *The Death Penalty*, p. 41.

includes a clause on the respect of the inherent dignity of detained persons: 'No one shall be subjected to torture or to cruel, inhuman, or degrading punishment or treatment. All persons deprived of their liberty shall be treated with respect for the inherent dignity of the human person.'[54] In addition to these general treaties, on 9 December 1985 the Organization of American States adopted the Inter-American Convention to Prevent and Punish Torture.[55]

The African Charter on Human and Peoples' Rights,[56] adopted in 1981, states in Article 5: 'Every individual shall have the right to the respect of the dignity inherent in a human being and to the recognition of his legal status. All forms of exploitation and degradation of man, particularly slavery, slave trade, torture, cruel, inhuman or degrading punishment and treatment shall be prohibited.'[57] Fatsah Ouguergouz observes that the positive guarantee of respect for human dignity contained in the first clause of Article 5 'expresses the fundamental idea on which the concept of human rights is based' and that its 'recapitulation is all the more significant in that it is linked, more or less directly, with the formal expression of the individual's right to recognition of his legal status and to the prohibition of all forms of exploitation and degradation of man'.[58] He connects the restatement of the inherent dignity of the human being to the continent's history of colonisation and slavery.[59]

(5)   Declaration and Convention against Torture

According to Nigel Rodley, two principal factors contributed to the adoption of the Declaration on the Protection of All Persons from Being

---

[54] American Convention on Human Rights, Article 5(2).

[55] Inter-American Convention to Prevent and Punish Torture, adopted 9 December 1985, entered into force 28 February 1987, OASTS 67, O.A.S. Off. Rec. OAS/Ser.L/V/1.4 rev. 9 (2003). See Fredy H. Kaplan, 'Combating Political Torture in Latin America: An Analysis of the Organization of American States Inter-American Convention to Prevent and Punish Torture' (1989) 15 Brooklyn Journal of International Law 399.

[56] African Charter on Human and Peoples' Rights, adopted 27 June 1981, entered into force 21 October 1986, O.A.U. Doc. CAB/LEG/67/3 Rev. 5, reprinted in 21 ILM 58 (1982), 7 HRLJ 403 (1986), Article 5. For documents pertaining to the drafting history of the African Charter, see Christof Heyns (ed.), Human Rights Law in Africa (The Hague: Kluwer Law International, 2002), pp. 65–106.

[57] African Charter on Human and Peoples' Rights, Article 5.

[58] Fatsah Ouguergouz, The African Charter on Human and Peoples' Rights: A Comprehensive Agenda for Human Dignity and Sustainable Democracy in Africa (The Hague: Kluwer Law International, 2003), p. 110.

[59] Ibid.

Subjected to Torture and Other Cruel, Inhuman or Degrading Treatment or Punishment in 1975.[60] Rodley argues that the 'Situation in Chile' provided the political impetus to act.[61] Following the overthrow of the democratically elected government of Salvador Allende in Chile on 11 September 1973 by the military junta under General Augusto Pinochet, reports of the practice of torture became widespread and, as Rodley points out, circulated amongst the delegations to the General Assembly.[62] Amnesty International's one year Campaign for the Abolition of Torture, established in December 1972, 'contributed the political context for an initiative at the UN'.[63] The aim of the Amnesty International campaign was to raise public awareness about the practice of torture worldwide, but it also lobbied for the adoption of stronger international norms.[64] This combination of factors created the context for the adoption of Resolution 3059 on 2 November 1973, the draft of which was originally introduced by Sweden.[65] Resolution 3059 reaffirmed existing norms prohibiting torture and placed the question of torture and other ill-treatment on the agenda for discussion 'at a future session' of the General Assembly.[66] The following year, Draft Resolution 3218 was introduced by the Netherlands.[67] According to Resolution 3218, adopted during the 29th session of the General Assembly on 6 November 1974, due to 'the increase in the number of alarming reports on torture, further and sustained efforts' were necessary to protect the prohibition on torture and other ill-treatment, in all circumstances.[68] Operative paragraph 4 of the Resolution directed the Fifth United Nations Congress on the Prevention on Crime and the Treatment

---

[60] Declaration on the Protection of All Persons from Being Subjected to Torture and Other Cruel, Inhuman or Degrading Treatment or Punishment UNGA Res. 3452 (XXX) 9 December 1975.

[61] Rodley, *The Treatment of Prisoners*, p. 21. See also J. Herman Burgers and Hans Danelius (eds.), *The United Nations Convention against Torture: A Handbook on the Convention against Torture and Other Cruel, Inhuman and Degrading Treatment or Punishment* (Dordrecht: Martinus Nijhoff Publishers, 1988), p. 14.

[62] Rodley, *The Treatment of Prisoners*, p. 21.

[63] *Ibid.*, p. 20. See also Winston P. Nagan and Lucie Atkins, 'The International Law of Torture: From Universal Proscription to Effective Application and Enforcement' (2001) 14 *Harvard Human Rights Law Journal* 87, 96; Burgers and Danelius, *The United Nations Convention against Torture*, p. 13.

[64] Ann Marie Clark, *Diplomacy of Conscience: Amnesty International and Changing Human Rights Norms* (Princeton University Press, 2001), p. 44.

[65] Rodley, *The Treatment of Prisoners*, p. 21.

[66] UNGA Res. 3059 (XXVIII) 2 November 1973.

[67] UNGA Res. 3218 (XXIX) 6 November 1974; Rodley, *The Treatment of Prisoners*, p. 21.

[68] UNGA Res. 3218 (XXIX) 6 November 1974.

of Offenders to consider 'rules for the protection of all persons subjected to any form or detention or imprisonment against torture and other cruel, inhuman or degrading treatment or punishment'.[69] This laid the basis for the drafting of the Declaration against Torture.[70] The Declaration against Torture evolved out of the text of a draft declaration submitted to the Fifth United Nations Congress by Sweden and the Netherlands. The text of the draft declaration was broadly supported at the Congress and it found its way to the United Nations General Assembly.[71] On 9 December 1975 the General Assembly adopted the Declaration against Torture.[72]

On the same day a second resolution was passed by the General Assembly, in which it was noted that 'further international efforts' were required 'to ensure adequate protection for all' against torture and other ill-treatment.[73] Operative paragraph 2 of that Resolution requested the Commission on Human Rights 'to study the question of torture and any necessary steps for: (a) Ensuring the effective observance of' the Declaration against Torture.[74] On 8 December 1977 Resolution 32/62 was passed, in which the Commission on Human Rights was requested to draw up a draft convention against torture and other ill-treatment 'in the light of the principles embodied in' the Declaration against Torture.[75] A second resolution was passed that requested the Secretary-General 'to draw up and circulate among member states a questionnaire soliciting information concerning steps ... taken, including legislative and administrative measures, to put into practice the principles' of the Declaration against Torture. The 'grave concern' expressed in this Resolution 'over continued reports from which it appears that some countries are systematically resorting to' torture and other ill-treatment provides the contextual rationale for the focus of initiative upon the question of torture.[76]

When the Commission on Human Rights began its discussions in February 1978, it had two draft conventions, one from the International Association of Penal Law and the other from the Swedish Government, available for discussion.[77] The Working Group established to draw up the draft convention selected the Swedish draft as the basis for deliberations.[78] That draft was substantively based on the Declaration against Torture;

---

[69] Ibid.
[70] Rodley, The Treatment of Prisoners, p. 26.   [71] Ibid.
[72] Declaration on the Protection of All Persons from Being Subjected to Torture.
[73] UNGA Res. 3453 (XXX) 9 December 1975.   [74] Ibid.
[75] UNGA Res. 32/62 8 December 1977.   [76] Ibid.
[77] Burgers and Danelius, The United Nations Convention against Torture, p. 34.
[78] Ibid., p. 38; Nowak and McArthur, The United Nations Convention against Torture, p. 4.

however, it did include an additional provision specifying the principle of *non-refoulement*.[79] In addition, it elaborated upon the draft declaration's criminalisation of torture by proposing the principle of universal jurisdiction and it suggested mechanisms for the prevention of torture, including an international monitoring mechanism to be entrusted to the Human Rights Committee, the supervisory body established under the Civil and Political Rights Covenant.[80] Between 1978 and 1984 the Working Group ironed out 'most of the controversial issues' in the Swedish draft of the Convention.[81] Amongst the amendments, it was decided that a specific Committee against Torture would be established to monitor compliance with the Convention.[82] On 10 December 1984 the United Nations Convention against Torture and Other Cruel, Inhuman and Degrading Treatment or Punishment was unanimously adopted by the General Assembly.[83]

B.   The international prohibition of torture: scope of application

(1)   *The torture prohibition as a norm of* jus cogens

The prohibition on torture is widely recognised as a peremptory norm of general international law or *jus cogens*. The Vienna Convention on the Law of Treaties provides, in Article 53:

> A treaty is void if, at the time of its conclusion, it conflicts with a peremptory norm of general international law. For the purposes of the present Convention, a peremptory norm of general international law is a norm

---

[79] Burgers and Danelius, *The United Nations Convention against Torture*, p. 35. Burgers and Danelius note that the inclusion of this provision was inspired by the jurisprudence of the European Commission on Human Rights.

[80] Nowak and McArthur, *The United Nations Convention against Torture*, p. 4.

[81] *Ibid.*, p. 5. For the drafting history of the Convention against Torture, see Burgers and Danelius, *The United Nations Convention against Torture*, pp. 31–107. See also Ahcene Boulesbaa, 'An Analysis of the 1984 Draft Convention Against Torture and Other Cruel, Inhuman or Degrading Treatment or Punishment' (1986) 4 *Dickinson Journal of International Law* 185; Matthew Lippman, 'The Development and Drafting of the United Nations Convention against Torture and Other Cruel, Inhuman and Degrading Treatment or Punishment' (1994) 17 *Boston College International and Comparative Law Review* 275.

[82] Nowak and McArthur, *The United Nations Convention against Torture*, p. 5.

[83] United Nations Convention Against Torture and Other Cruel, Inhuman or Degrading Treatment or Punishment (adopted 10 December 1984, entry into force 26 June 1987) GA Res. 39/46, 39 UN GAOR, Supp. (No. 51), UN Doc. A/39/51, 197 (1984), reprinted in 23 ILM 1027 (1984), minor changes reprinted in 24 ILM 535 (1985), 5 HRLJ 350 (1984).

accepted and recognized by the international community of States as a
whole as a norm from which no derogation is permitted and which can be
modified only by a subsequent norm of general international law having
the same character.[84]

Strictly speaking, this provision refers only to the invalidity of treaties
that conflict with a peremptory norm. Lauri Hannaiken considers, however, that as a consequence of this provision, acts provided for by treaty,
but which conflict with a peremptory norm, are unlawful. He reasons
that this leads to a 'comprehensive prohibition of all acts contrary to peremptory norms ... Otherwise peremptory norms would be made nearly
meaningless; the State concerned need only take care not to conclude a
formal treaty referring to the violation'.[85] Theodor Meron similarly reasons that certain norms and values are of such importance to the international community that they 'merit absolute protection and may not be
derogated from by States, whether jointly by treaty or severally by uni-
lateral or executive action'.[86] The substance and application as well as the
utility and practical effect of *jus cogens* is, nevertheless, questioned and
contested.[87] In that regard, the concept of *jus cogens* has been metaphorically described as an 'empty box'.[88] The mystery surrounding the substance of *jus cogens* might be uncovered to some degree if such norms are
accepted as 'a form of customary international law'.[89] The juridical utility
of this form of 'super-custom'[90] is, as yet, unclear.

[84] Vienna Convention on the Law of Treaties (adopted 22 May 1969, entered into force 27
January 1980) 1155 UNTS 331, Article 53.
[85] Lauri Hannaiken, *Peremptory Norms (Jus Cogens) in International Law: Historical
Development, Criteria, Present Status* (Helsinki: Lakimiesliiton Kustannus Finnish
Lawyer's Publishing Company, 1988), p. 6.
[86] Theodor Meron, *The Humanization of International Law* (Leiden: Martinus Nijhoff,
2006), p. 397.
[87] See, for example, Anthony D'Amato, 'It's a Bird, It's a Plane, It's *Jus Cogens!*' (1990) 6
Connecticut Journal of International Law 1, 6.
[88] Andrea Bianchi, 'Human Rights and the Magic of *Jus Cogens*' (2008) 19 *European Journal
of International Law* 491.
[89] Jordan Paust, 'The Reality of *Jus Cogens*' (1991) 7 *Connecticut Journal of International
Law* 81, 82. The International Court of Justice, in the case of *Belgium v. Senegal*, also suggests this association. See *Questions Relating to the Obligation to Prosecute or Extradite
(Belgium v. Senegal)* Judgment [2012] ICJ Reports 2012, para. 99.
[90] William A. Schabas uses this phrase in his discussion of *jus cogens* in the *Belgium
v. Senegal* decision. See William A. Schabas, 'Antigone, jus cogens and the international court of justice', 22 July 2012, available at: http://humanrightsdoctorate.
blogspot.co.uk/2012/07/antigone-jus-cogens-and-international.html (last accessed
29 July 2012).

In the case of *Prosecutor* v. *Furundzija*[91] the International Criminal Tribunal for the Former Yugoslavia held that the peremptory norm prohibiting torture comprises a deterrent effect:

> Clearly, the jus cogens nature of the prohibition against torture articulates the notion that the prohibition has now become one of the most fundamental standards of the international community. Furthermore, this prohibition is designed to produce a deterrent effect, in that it signals to all members of the international community and the individuals over whom they wield authority that the prohibition of torture is an absolute value from which nobody must deviate.[92]

The Tribunal also held that peremptory norms have further effects at the domestic level insofar as they 'de-legitimise any legislative, administrative or judicial act authorising torture'.[93] According to the Tribunal:

> It would be senseless to argue, on the one hand, that on account of the *jus cogens* value of the prohibition against torture, treaties or customary rules providing for torture would be null and void *ab initio*, and then be unmindful of a State say, taking national measures authorising or condoning torture or absolving its perpetrators through an amnesty law.[94]

Accordingly, national measures that authorise or condone torture, including amnesty laws, may not be afforded international legal recognition. In addition, the Tribunal emphasised that perpetrators of torture remain bound to comply with the prohibition on torture despite authorisation at the domestic level.[95]

In the *Democratic Republic of the Congo* v. *Rwanda*[96] the DRC argued that the Rwandan reservation to Article IX of the Genocide Convention ought to be considered invalid because it sought to prevent the Court from safeguarding norms of a peremptory character. The Court held that the peremptory character of an international rule may not provide a basis for the jurisdiction of the Court, which is always grounded in the consent of the parties.[97] In his separate opinion, Judge *ad hoc* Dugard took the opportunity to elucidate his thoughts on the concept of peremptory

---

[91] *Prosecutor* v. *Anto Furundzija* (Trial Judgement), IT-95–17/1-T, International Criminal Tribunal for the former Yugoslavia (ICTY), 10 December 1998.

[92] *Ibid.*, paras. 153–154.   [93] *Ibid.*, para. 155.

[94] *Ibid.*   [95] *Ibid.*

[96] *Case Concerning Armed Activities on the Territory of the Congo* (New Application: 2002) (*Democratic Republic of the Congo* v. *Rwanda*), Jurisdiction of the Court and Admissibility [2006] ICJ Reports 1, paras. 64 and 125.

[97] Bianchi, 'Human Rights and the Magic of *Jus Cogens*' 502.

norms. Dugard agreed with the decision of the Court and accepted the premise of the judgment that 'the scope of jus cogens is not unlimited and that the concept is not to be used as an instrument to overthrow accepted doctrines of international law'.[98] He argued, however, that *jus cogens* should play a pivotal role in the judicial process in guiding judicial interpretation. According to Dugard, judicial decision-making requires a weighing of competing principles and competing interpretations and a judge is guided by principles and polices 'in order to arrive at a coherent conclusion that most effectively furthers the integrity of the international legal order'.[99] Norms of *jus cogens*, he suggests, provide guidance in establishing what constitutes the most important rights and goals of the international legal order:

> Norms of *jus cogens* are a blend of principle and policy. On the one hand, they affirm the high principles of international law, which recognize the most important rights of the international order ... while, on the other hand, they give legal form to the most fundamental policies or goals of the international community ... This explains why they enjoy a hierarchical superiority to other norms in the international legal order. The fact that norms of *jus cogens* advance both principle and policy means that that they must inevitably play a dominant role in the process of judicial choice.[100]

As such, Dugard holds that norms of *jus cogens* provide guidance, rather than a blanket trump card, in establishing the values required to sustain the integrity of judicial decision-making and the international legal order more broadly.[101]

Judge Cançado Trindade, in his separate opinion in *Belgium* v. *Senegal*, describes *jus cogens* as ascribing 'an ethical content to the new *jus gentium*'.[102] The idea that emerges from his discussion is the unshakeable existence of the prohibition even in the face of manoeuvres designed to escape it: 'Torture is absolutely prohibited in all its forms, whichever misleading and deleterious neologisms are invented and resorted to, to attempt to circumvent this prohibition.'[103] Judge Cançado Trindade's

---

[98] *Case Concerning Armed Activities on the Territory of the Congo*, Separate Opinion of Judge *Ad Hoc* Dugard, para. 6.

[99] *Ibid.*, Separate Opinion of Judge *Ad Hoc* Dugard, paras. 9–10.

[100] *Ibid.*

[101] Bianchi, 'Human Rights and the Magic of *Jus Cogens*' 504.

[102] *Questions Relating to the Obligation to Prosecute or Extradite (Belgium v. Senegal)* Judgment [2012] ICJ Reports 2012, Separate Opinion of Judge Cançado Trindade, para. 182.

[103] *Ibid.*

analysis suggests *jus cogens* to represent a kind of permanent antidote to legal positivism. What the practical consequences are remains vague; there is a sense that the pre-eminent value of *jus cogens* lies in its rhetoric.

(2) *The offence of torture*

Article 4 of the Convention against Torture is central to the Convention's objective of fighting impunity.[104] Article 4 requires States Parties to the Convention to make torture an offence under their domestic criminal law, and it requires the punishment of perpetrators of, or participants in, torture through appropriate penalties that take into account the grave nature of the offence:[105]

1. Each State Party shall ensure that all acts of torture are offences under its criminal law. The same shall apply to an attempt to commit torture and to an act by any person which constitutes complicity or participation in torture.
2. Each State Party shall make these offences punishable by appropriate penalties which take into account their grave nature.

Whilst the Committee against Torture does not 'explicitly provide for a specific punishment or type, extent and level of sentence', the Committee has considered short sentences, ranging from several days to two years, as an inappropriate penalty.[106] In the case of *Guridi* v. *Spain* in 2005, the Committee against Torture found a violation of Article 4 for the first time.[107] The applicant in that case had been subjected to torture. Three civil guards were found guilty in a Spanish provincial court of torture and each was sentenced to imprisonment of four years, two months and one day and ordered to pay the complainant compensation. In a judgment of 30 September 1998 the Supreme Court reduced their sentences to one year. In July 1999 the Ministry of Justice granted them pardons.[108] The Committee ruled that 'the imposition of lighter penalties and the granting of pardons to the civil guards are incompatible with the duty

---

[104] Nowak and McArthur, *The United Nations Convention against Torture*, p. 229.
[105] Convention against Torture, Article 4.
[106] Nowak and McArthur, *The United Nations Convention against Torture*, pp. 239–41.
[107] *Kepa Urra Guridi* v. *Spain*, Communication No. 212/2002, UN Doc. CAT/C/34/D/212/2002 (2005). See also Nowak and McArthur, *The United Nations Convention against Torture*, p. 251.
[108] *Guridi* v. *Spain*, paras. 2.3, 2.5, 2.6.

to impose appropriate punishment'.[109] With respect to the granting of amnesties, in General Comment 2 to Article 2 of the Convention against Torture, the Committee states that 'amnesties or other impediments which preclude or indicate unwillingness to provide prompt and fair prosecution and punishment of perpetrators of torture or ill-treatment violate the principle of non-derogability'.[110] The Committee appears to reason that the 'no exceptional circumstances' dictum of the Convention imposes an obligation to prosecute and punish the perpetrators and that failure to satisfy this obligation violates the principle of non-derogation. The Human Rights Committee has also found amnesties to be incompatible with Article 7 of the Civil and Political Rights Covenant. According to General Comment 20:

> The Committee has noted that some States have granted amnesty in respect of acts of torture. Amnesties are generally incompatible with the duty of States to investigate such acts; to guarantee freedom from such acts within their jurisdiction; and to ensure that they do not occur in the future. States may not deprive individuals of the right to an effective remedy, including compensation and such full rehabilitation as may be possible.[111]

In 1994, in the case of *Rodríguez* v. *Uruguay* before the Human Rights Committee,[112] the applicant, who had been subjected to torture by the police during the military regime, complained that the amnesty law enacted in 1986 denied him redress because of the failure to investigate the abuses allegedly committed by the military authorities, to punish those responsible and to compensate the victims'.[113] Noting that the law precluded 'the possibility of investigation into past human rights abuses' in a number of cases, thus, preventing the 'State party from discharging its responsibility to provide effective remedies to the victims of those abuses',[114] the Human Rights Committee found a violation of

---

[109] *Ibid.*, para. 6.7.
[110] UNCAT, 'General Comment 2' (2007) CAT/C/GC/2/CRP.1/Rev.4, para. 5.
[111] UNHCR, 'General Comment 20' (1992) in 'Note by the Secretariat, Compilation of General Comments and General Recommendations adopted by the Human Rights Committee (2008) HRI/GEN/1/Rev.9 (Vol. 1) 200, para. 15.
[112] *Rodríguez* v. *Uruguay*, Communication No. 322/1988, UN Doc. CCPR/C/51/D/322/1988 (1994).
[113] *Ibid.*, para. 3.
[114] *Ibid.*, para. 12.4.

Article 7 in connection with Article 2(3)[115] of the Civil and Political Rights Covenant.[116]

Article 5 of the Convention against Torture requires States Parties to establish their jurisdiction over the offence of torture 'in a comprehensive manner in order to avoid safe havens for perpetrators of torture'.[117] Article 5(1) specifies that states shall provide territorial jurisdiction over the offence of torture as well as jurisdiction '[w]hen the alleged offender is a national of that State' and '[w]hen the victim is a national of that State if that State considers it appropriate'.[118] States Parties are thus obligated 'to take the necessary legislative measures to establish jurisdiction in their respective domestic criminal codes'.[119] Article 5(2) also provides for universal jurisdiction over torture.[120] A State Party is required 'to take such measures as may be necessary to establish its jurisdiction over such offences in cases where the alleged offender is present in any territory under its jurisdiction and it does not extradite him pursuant to article 8'.[121] In *Belgium* v. *Senegal* the International Court of Justice confirmed the obligation under Article 7(1),[122] in connection with Article 5(2), to prosecute persons alleged to have committed acts of torture or to extradite them to a country with jurisdiction to instigate criminal

---

[115] Article 2(3) states:

Each State Party to the present Covenant undertakes:

(a) To ensure that any person whose rights or freedoms as herein recognized are violated shall have an effective remedy, notwithstanding that the violation has been committed by persons acting in an official capacity;

(b) To ensure that any person claiming such a remedy shall have his right thereto determined by competent judicial, administrative or legislative authorities, or by any other competent authority provided for by the legal system of the State, and to develop the possibilities of judicial remedy;

(c) To ensure that the competent authorities shall enforce such remedies when granted.

[116] *Rodríguez* v. *Uruguay*, para.13.

[117] Nowak and McArthur, *The United Nations Convention against Torture*, p. 254.

[118] Convention against Torture, Article 5(1).

[119] Nowak and McArthur, *The United Nations Convention against Torture*, p. 254.

[120] Lippman, 'The Development and Drafting of the United Nations Convention Against Torture' 316.

[121] Convention against Torture, Article 5(2).

[122] Article 7(1) states: 'The State Party in the territory under whose jurisdiction a person alleged to have committed any offence referred to in article 4 is found shall in the cases contemplated in article 5, if it does not extradite him, submit the case to its competent authorities for the purpose of prosecution.'

proceedings. The Court held that Senegal must immediately take the necessary measures to submit the case of Mr Hissene Habré, accused of acts of torture and other crimes committed in Chad, 'to its competent authorities for the purpose of prosecution, if it does not extradite him'.[123] In regard to the obligation to prosecute or extradite, the Court held: 'Extradition is an option offered to the State by the Convention, whereas prosecution is an international obligation under the Convention, the violation of which is a wrongful act engaging the responsibility of the State.'[124]

(3)   Torture under international humanitarian law

The prohibition of torture in international humanitarian law finds its roots in various sources including the Lieber Code of 1863.[125] The Lieber Code, drafted by Francis Lieber, a professor at Columbia University, during the American Civil War and proclaimed by President Abraham Lincoln,[126] represents the first attempt to codify the law of war. With respect to the prohibition of torture, Article 16 states: 'Military necessity does not admit of cruelty – that is, the infliction of suffering for the sake of suffering or for revenge, nor of maiming or wounding except in fight, nor of torture to extort confessions.'[127]

Jean Pictet describes the principle of humane treatment as the 'leit-motiv' of the Four Geneva Conventions of 1949:[128] 'No war, no impera-tive reason of national security, no military necessity can justify inhumane treatment.'[129] The significance of the prohibition of torture as an intrinsic aspect of the principle of humane treatment is evidenced by the fact that, during the drafting of the Geneva Conventions, a French proposal for a preamble to the Conventions included the prohibition

---

[123] *Questions Relating to the Obligation to Prosecute or Extradite (Belgium v. Senegal)* Judgment [2012] ICJ Reports 2012, paras. 118–119.

[124] *Ibid.*, para. 95.

[125] William A. Schabas, *The UN International Tribunals: The Former Yugoslavia, Rwanda and Sierra Leone* (Cambridge University Press, 2006), p. 206.

[126] William A. Schabas, 'The Crime of Torture and the International Criminal Tribunals' (2006) 37 *Case Western Reserve Journal of International Law* 349.

[127] F. Lieber, 'Instructions for the Government of the United States in the Field by Order of the Secretary of War', United States War Department, Adjutant General's Office, General Orders No. 100, 24 April 1863.

[128] Cited in Cordula Droege, '"In Truth the Leitmotiv": the Prohibition of Torture and Other Forms of Ill-Treatment in International Humanitarian Law' (2007) 89 *International Review of the Red Cross* 515, 516.

[129] Droege, '"In Truth the Leitmotiv"' 516.

on torture.[130] No preamble was included in the Conventions, however, as agreement could not be reached on its content.[131] Each of the four Geneva Conventions provides that the relevant category of protected persons shall not be subjected to torture.[132] Article 17 of the Third Geneva Convention Relative to the Treatment of Prisoners of War specifies that '[n]o physical or mental torture, nor any form of coercion, may be inflicted on prisoners of war to secure from them information of any kind whatever'.[133] Torture is also defined as a grave breach of each of the Geneva Conventions.[134] Additional Protocol I, devoted to international armed conflicts, supplements the four Geneva Conventions.[135] Article 75 of Additional Protocol I, which refers to fundamental guarantees, prohibits 'torture of all kinds, whether physical or mental'.[136] Common Article 3 of the four Geneva Conventions, which applies to armed conflict not of an international character, provides a minimum guarantee of protection against subjection to inhumane treatment.[137] Article 3(1) specifies: 'Persons taking no part in the hostilities, including members of the armed forces who have laid down their arms and

---

[130] Theodor Meron, 'The Humanization of Humanitarian Law' (2000) 94 *American Journal of International Law* 239, 246.

[131] *Ibid.* The proposed preamble stated:

> The High Contracting Parties, conscious of their obligation to come to an agreement in order to protect civilian populations from the horrors of War, undertake to respect the principles of human rights which constitute the safeguard of civilization and, in particular, to apply, at any time and in all places, the rules given hereunder:
> ... (4) Torture of any kind is strictly prohibited.
>
> These rules which constitute the basis of universal human law, shall be respected without prejudice to the special stipulations provided for in the present Convention in favour of protected persons.

[132] Geneva Convention for the Amelioration of the Conditions of the Wounded and Sick in Armed Forces in the Field, 12 August 1949, 6 UST 3114, 75 UNTS 31, Article 12; Geneva Convention for the Amelioration of the Conditions of the Wounded and Sick and Shipwrecked Members of Armed Forces at Sea, 12 August 1949, 6 UST 3217, 75 UNTS 85, Article 12; Geneva Convention Relative to the Treatment of Prisoners of War, 12 August 1949, 6 UST 3316, 75 UNTS 135, Articles 17 and 87; Geneva Convention Relative to the Protection of Civilian Persons in Time of War, 12 August 1949, 6 UST 3516, 75 UNTS 287, Article 32.

[133] Third Geneva Convention, Article 17.

[134] First Geneva Convention, Article 50; Second Geneva Convention, Article 51; Third Geneva Convention, Article 130; Fourth Geneva Convention, Article 147.

[135] Protocol Additional to the Geneva Conventions of 12 August 1949, and Relating to the Protection of Victims of International Armed Conflicts (Additional Protocol I), 1125 UNTS 3, 1977, Article 1(3).

[136] *Ibid.*, Article 75(2)(ii).

[137] Article 3 common to the Four Geneva Conventions.

those placed hors de combat by sickness, wounds, detention, or any other cause, shall in all circumstances be treated humanely.'[138] It further states, without ambiguity: 'To this end, the following acts are and shall remain prohibited: (a) Violence to life and person, in particular murder of all kinds, mutilation, cruel treatment and torture; ... (c) Outrages upon personal dignity, in particular humiliating and degrading treatment.'[139] In regard to the wording of this provision, Pictet comments, '[n]o possible loophole is left, there can be no excuse, no attenuating circumstances'.[140] Of items (a) and (c), he remarks that these are 'acts which world public opinion finds particularly revolting'.[141] Additional Protocol II, which develops and enhances Common Article 3, echoes its language with respect to the provision for humane treatment. Article 4 provides that 'all persons who do not take a direct part or who have ceased to take part in hostilities, whether or not their liberty has been restricted ... shall in all circumstances be treated humanely, without any adverse distinction', and it specifies that 'violence to the life, health and physical or mental well-being of persons, in particular, murder as well as cruel treatment such as torture, mutilation or any form of corporal punishment ... are and shall remain prohibited at any time and in any place whatsoever'.[142]

(4)   The crime of torture

Both the Statute of the International Criminal Tribunal for Former Yugoslavia (ICTY)[143] and the Statute of the International Criminal Tribunal for Rwanda (ICTR)[144] include acts of torture in the crimes

---

[138] Article 3(1) common to the Four Geneva Conventions.

[139] Ibid.

[140] Jean S. Pictet (ed.), Commentary IV Convention Relative to the Protection of Civilian Persons in Time of War (Geneva: ICRC, 1958), p. 38.

[141] Ibid., p. 38.

[142] Protocol Additional to the Geneva Conventions of 12 August 1949 and Relating to the Protection of Victims of Non-International Armed Conflicts (Additional Protocol II), 1125 UNTS 609, 1977, Article 4.

[143] Statute of the International Criminal Tribunal for the Former Yugoslavia, UN Doc. S/Res/827 (1993). Torture is similarly listed as a crime against humanity and as a war crime in the Statute of the Special Court for Sierra Leone. See Agreement between the United Nations and the Government of Sierra Leone on the Establishment of a Special Court for Sierra Leone, Freetown, 16 January 2002, Statute of the Special Court, Articles 2(f) and 3(a).

[144] Statue of the International Criminal for Rwanda, UN Doc. S/Res/955 (1994).

enumerated.[145] Under Article 3 of the ICTY statute, torture constitutes a grave breach of the Geneva Conventions, and under Article 5 the act of torture is included as a crime against humanity.[146] Under Article 2 of the ICTR statute, torture is listed as a crime against humanity.[147] In addition, it is listed as a war crime under Article 4 referring to violations of Common Article 3 and Additional Protocol II.[148] The Rome Statute of the International Criminal Court includes torture amongst the enumerated acts that constitute crimes against humanity.[149] Torture as a crime against humanity is defined as 'the intentional infliction of severe pain or suffering, whether physical or mental, upon a person in the custody or under the control of the accused; except that torture shall not include pain or suffering arising only from, inherent in or incidental to, lawful sanctions'.[150] Torture is also listed as a war crime when committed both in international armed conflict and in armed conflict not of an international character.[151]

(5)   No exceptional circumstances

Across the spectrum of international human rights treaties, both general and specific, the prohibition of torture is framed as an absolute right that permits of no derogation, even in states of emergency. Article 7 of the Civil and Political Rights Covenant is assured without any restriction or limitation whatsoever.[152] In addition, under Article 4 of the Civil and Political Rights Covenant, Article 7 is specified as a non-derogable right:[153]

1. In time of public emergency which threatens the life of the nation and the existence of which is officially proclaimed, the States Parties to the present Convention may take measures derogating from their obligations under the present Convention to the extent strictly required by

---

[145] Torture was not referred to in the Charter of the International Military Tribunal, adopted in August 1945, but was included in the list of crimes against humanity in Control Council Law No. 10, adopted in December 1945. See Schabas, 'The Crime of Torture' 351.

[146] ICTY Statute, Articles 2(b) and 5(f).

[147] ICTR Statute, Article 3(f).

[148] ICTR Statute, Article 4(a).

[149] Rome Statute of the International Criminal Court of 1998 (37 ILM 999, 1998), Article 7(1)(f).

[150] *Ibid.*, Article 7(2)(e)

[151] *Ibid.*, Articles 8(2)(a)(ii) and 8(2)(c)(i).

[152] Nowak, *UN Covenant on Civil and Political Rights*, p. 157.

[153] International Covenant on Civil and Political Rights, Article 4(2).

the exigencies of the situation, provided that such measures are not inconsistent with their other obligations under international law and do not involve discrimination solely on the ground of race, colour, sex, language, religion or social origin.

2. No derogation from articles 6, 7, 8 (paragraphs 1 and 2), 11, 15, 16 and 18 may be made under this provision.[154]

In its General Comment on Article 7 of the Civil and Political Rights Covenant, the Human Rights Committee has explained that the aim of Article 7 is 'to protect both the dignity and the physical and mental integrity of the individual'.[155] In addition, the Human Rights Committee establishes that Article 7 applies irrespective of whether the acts are 'inflicted by people acting in their official capacity, outside their official capacity or in a private capacity'.[156] Article 7 thus creates both a negative duty on states party to the Covenant not to engage in torture or other prohibited ill-treatment and a positive duty to protect individuals under its jurisdiction from acts committed by private individuals.[157] The Human Rights Committee also reiterates the absolute and non-derogable status of the prohibition:

> The text of article 7 allows of no limitation: The Committee also reaffirms that, even in situations of public emergency such as those referred to in article 4 of the Covenant, no derogation from the provision of article 7 is allowed and its provisions must remain in force. The Committee likewise observes that no justification or extenuating circumstances may be invoked to excuse a violation of article 7 for any reasons, including those based on an order from a superior officer or public authority.[158]

The Human Rights Committee makes it clear that Article 7 not only prohibits the use of torture and other ill-treatment in states of emergency, it also rules out the possibility for a justification defence, such as the defence of necessity, to be invoked to justify the use of torture. In this respect, in its consideration of Israel's second periodic report in 2003, the Human Rights Committee explicitly declared the defence of necessity to be incompatible with the Civil and Political Rights Covenant:

---

[154] *Ibid.*, Article 4(1)(2).

[155] UNHCR, 'General Comment 20' (1992).

[156] *Ibid.*

[157] Association for the Prevention of Torture and Center for Justice and International Law, 'Torture in International Law: A Guide to Jurisprudence' (Geneva: Association for the Prevention of Torture and Center for Justice and International Law, 2008), p. 13.

[158] UNHCR, 'General Comment 20', 200.

The Committee is concerned that interrogation techniques incompatible with article 7 of the Covenant are still reported frequently to be resorted to and the 'necessity defence' argument, *which is not recognized under the Covenant*, is often invoked and retained as a justification for [Israeli Security Agency] actions in the course of investigation.[159]

Like Article 7 of the Civil and Political Rights Covenant, Article 3 of the European Convention on Human Rights does not limit the exercise of the right. Under Article 15 of the European Convention, the prohibition on torture is also enumerated as a non-derogable right even '[i]n time of war or other public emergency threatening the life of the nation'.[160] Similarly, under Article 27 of the American Convention on Human Rights, Article 5, which incorporates the prohibition of torture, is recognised both in unrestricted terms and as a non-derogable right '[i]n time of war, public danger or other emergency that threatens the independence or security of a State Party'.[161] Article 5 of the African Charter does not contain any explicit limitation and the African Commission has held that the prohibition on torture is absolute.[162] Although the Charter does not contain a suspension or derogation clause, the Commission has consistently held that the Charter does not permit derogation from its obligations in states of emergency.[163]

Article 2(2) of the Convention against Torture provides that '[n]o exceptional circumstances whatsoever, whether a state of war or a threat of war, internal political instability or any other public emergency, may be invoked as a justification of torture'.[164] This provision confirms that the prohibition of torture is non-derogable in all circumstances. Ahcene Boulesbaa observes that the word 'whatsoever' is crucial in the formulation of this provision. The drafters used this word, she argues, 'to close

---

[159] UNHCR, 'Concluding Observations of the Human Rights Committee: Israel' (2003) CCPR/CO/78/ISR § 18 (emphasis added).

[160] European Convention on Human Rights, Article 15(1)(2).

[161] American Convention on Human Rights, Article 27(1)(2).

[162] *Huri-Laws* v. *Nigeria*, African Commission on Human and Peoples' Rights, Comm. no. 225/98 (2000). See also Frans Viljoen and Chidi Odinkalu, *The Prohibition of Torture and Ill-Treatment in the African Human Rights System: A Handbook for Victims and their Advocates* (OMCT Handbook Series Vol. 3, World Organisation against Torture, 2006), p. 82.

[163] Viljoen and Odinkalu, *The Prohibition of Torture*, p. 82. According to Viljoen and Odinkalu, despite the African Commission's interpretation that derogation is impermissible under the African Charter, this point is arguable due to the fact that the entitlement of states to derogate from treaties exists in customary law. See, Viljoen and Odinkalu, *The Prohibition of Torture*, p. 25.

[164] Convention against Torture, Article 2(2).

the door to a construction of the article which could lead to an interpretation that the exceptional circumstances referred to ... are exhaustive'.[165]
The draft text submitted for deliberation to the Commission on Human
Rights in 1978 by the International Association of Penal Law contained
an analogous, albeit more detailed clause. Article VI stated: 'Torture can
in no circumstances be justified or excused by a state or threat of war or
armed conflict, a state of siege, emergency or other exceptional circumstances, or by any necessity or any urgency of obtaining information, or
by any other reason.'[166] It is of interest that this clause permitted not only
no justification but also no excuse for the use of torture. In addition, this
clause emphasised the unjustifiable and inexcusable use of torture in the
kinds of situations that are currently the subject of debate. The Declaration
against Torture, as well as the original Swedish draft text on which the
Convention is based, extended the application of the 'no exceptional circumstances' provision to other cruel, inhuman or degrading treatment or
punishment.[167] During the drafting, however, a number of delegates suggested that these accompanying phrases be deleted from the provisions of
Article 2 as a whole due to the lack of a precise definition of the terms.[168]
In particular, the United States took the position that 'cruel, inhuman or
degrading treatment was a relative term and what might constitute cruel,
inhuman or degrading treatment in times of peace "might not rise to that
level during emergency situations"'.[169]

John T. Parry argues that the omission of these protections from
Article 2(2) of the Convention 'speaks volumes'.[170] He suggests that the
Convention incorporates the possibility of derogation from other forms of
ill-treatment that do not constitute torture. It follows that '[t]he possibility
of derogation must also include the possibility that violent treatment of
prisoners or others short of torture can be justifiable under some circumstances'.[171] Although he acknowledges the absolute and non-derogable
ban on torture and all other forms of ill-treatment under the Civil and
Political Rights Covenant, he nevertheless warns:

> If the [C]onvention [against Torture] is the controlling document, a state
> will simply claim that its violent conduct is not torture. If that claim is

[165] Ahcene Boulesbaa, *The UN Convention on Torture and the Prospects for Enforcement*
(The Hague: Martinus Nijhoff Publishers, 1999), p. 79.
[166] Nowak and McArthur, *The United Nations Convention against Torture*, p. 90.
[167] *Ibid.*   [168] *Ibid.*, pp. 91–2.   [169] *Ibid.*, p. 118.
[170] John T. Parry, *Understanding Torture: Law, Violence and Political Identity* (Ann Arbor:
University of Michigan Press, 2010), p. 38.
[171] *Ibid.*, p. 37.

correct under the convention, that state has at worst engaged in cruel, inhuman or degrading treatment. If the state can come up with a sufficient justification for its conduct, it has not violated the convention at all. At this point, the discussion gets bogged down in definitions, which distract attention from the conduct, its consequences, and its victims.[172]

Parry picks up on the kind of arguments that have been advanced, particularly by the United States, in order to evade the prohibition of torture in the interrogation of detainees. Parry is also correct to point out that there is a perceived link between the severity of ill-treatment and the possible justification of such ill-treatment. It is important, however, not to construct this perception as a factual incoherence in the law prohibiting torture. It is misleading to suggest that the prohibition of cruel, inhuman and degrading treatment or punishment permits derogation. Article 16 of the Convention, concerning cruel, inhuman and degrading treatment, contains a savings clause that provides: 'The provisions of this Convention are without prejudice to the provisions of any other international instrument or national law which prohibit cruel, inhuman or degrading treatment or punishment.'[173] Nowak and McArthur concur that both the savings clause and the clear reference in the Convention against Torture's preamble to the existing standards in the Universal Declaration and the Civil and Political Rights Convention suggest that too much weight should not be placed on the restriction of this provision to the prohibition of torture.[174] It should also be recalled that the Convention against Torture does not contain any explicit provision prohibiting either torture or other cruel, inhuman or degrading treatment or punishment.[175] Herman Burgers and Hans Danelius, who were involved in the drafting of the Convention, point out that the Convention against Torture 'is based upon the recognition that [such practices] are already outlawed under international law. The principal aim of the Convention is to strengthen the existing prohibition of such practices by a number of supportive measures'.[176] The argument that derogation is permitted from the prohibition of cruel, inhuman and degrading treatment or punishment is thus incorrect. There is also no limitation or restriction on the prohibition of these other forms of ill-treatment; their use is not subject to the proportionality principle or justifiable in any situation. Nowak, in his capacity as Special Rapporteur on Torture, has

[172] *Ibid.*, p. 39.
[173] Convention against Torture, Article 16(2).
[174] Nowak and McArthur, *The United Nations Convention against Torture*, p. 118.
[175] *Ibid.*, p. 23.
[176] Burgers and Danelius, *The United Nations Convention against Torture*, p. 1.

explained that the proportionality principle only applies in defining the scope of the right not to be subjected to cruel, inhuman or degrading treatment or punishment.[177] He observes:

> Inherent in the concept of [cruel, inhuman and degrading treatment or punishment] is the disproportionate exercise of police powers. The beating of a detainee with a truncheon for the purpose of extracting a confession must be considered torture if it inflicts severe pain or suffering; the beating of a detainee with a truncheon walking to and from a cell might amount to CIDT, but the beating of demonstrators in the street with the same truncheon for the purpose of dispersing an illegal demonstration or prison riot, for example, might be justified as lawful use of force by law enforcement officials.[178]

In short, the principle of proportionality is only relevant in determining whether a particular measure of law enforcement is disproportionate to the aim to be achieved. If excessive use of force is employed, it might be considered to constitute cruel, inhuman or degrading treatment or punishment. The principle of proportionality does not apply at all once a person is under the *direct* control of a law enforcement official, for example when such a person is under arrest, in custody or detention or in interrogation.[179] According to Nowak and McArthur, Article 2(2) 'provides a clear answer to all attempts aimed at undermining the absolute prohibition of torture for the sake of national security in combating global terrorism, such as the "ticking bomb scenario" or special interrogation methods introduced by Israel and the US Government in their respective counter-terrorism strategies'.[180] In General Comment 2 to Article 2 of the Convention, the Committee responds to these attempts at undermining the prohibition of torture. The Committee elaborates upon the list of 'exceptional circumstances' by including 'any threat of terrorist acts or violent crime as well as armed conflict, international or non-international'.[181] In addition, the Committee notes its deep concern and absolute rejection of 'any efforts by States to justify torture and ill-treatment as a means to protect public safety or avert emergencies in these and all other situations'.[182] To emphasise its

---

[177] Manfred Nowak, 'What Practices Constitute Torture? US and UN Standards' (2006) 28 *Human Rights Quarterly* 809, 836.
[178] UNCHR, 'Report of the Special Rapporteur on the Question of Torture, Manfred Nowak' (2005) UN Doc. E/CN.4/2006/6, para. 38.
[179] UNCHR, 'Report of the Special Rapporteur: Manfred Nowak', para. 38.
[180] Nowak and McArthur, *The United Nations Convention against Torture*, p. 89.
[181] UNCAT, 'General Comment 2', para. 5.
[182] *Ibid.*

concern, the Committee reiterates that Article 2(2) is a provision that 'must be observed in all circumstances'.[183]

Like the Human Rights Committee, the Committee against Torture does not recognise the compatibility of the defence of necessity with the prohibition on torture. In its concluding observations to Israel's first periodic report, submitted whilst the Landau Commission guidelines were in place, the Committee noted 'as a matter of deep concern that Israeli law pertaining to the defences of "superior orders" and "necessity" are in clear breach of that country's obligations under Article 2'.[184] In 2002, following the Supreme Court decision, the Committee recommended that Israel remove '[n]ecessity as a possible justification for the crime of torture' from its domestic law.[185] This position was reiterated in 2004.[186]

(6) Justifiability? Jurisprudence from the European Commission and Court

In the *Greek Case*[187] the European Commission on Human Rights, in its interpretation of torture, inhuman and degrading treatment or punishment under Article 3 of the European Convention, stated: 'The notion of inhuman treatment covers at least such treatment as deliberately causes severe suffering, mental or physical, *which, in the particular situation, is unjustifiable.*'[188] By including the concept of justifiability in the definition of torture, in this way, the Commission, as Nigel Rodley points out, appeared to be saying that deliberate ill-treatment 'might in certain circumstances be justifiable, despite the fact that the European Convention ... couched the prohibition ... in absolute terms and permitted no derogation from it'.[189] In the case of *Ireland* v. *United Kingdom*[190]

---

[183] *Ibid.*
[184] UNGA, 'Report of the Committee against Torture' UN Doc. A/49/44 (1993), para. 167. See also UNGA, 'Report of the Committee against Torture' UN Doc. A/52/44 (1997), para. 258; UNGA 'Report of the Committee against Torture' UN Doc. A/53/44 (1998), para. 238(a).
[185] UNGA, 'Report of the Committee against Torture' UN Doc. A/57/44 (2002), para. 53(i).
[186] UNCAT, 'Consideration of Reports Submitted by States Parties under Article 19 of the Convention: Israel' UN Doc. CAT/C/ISR/CO/4 (23 June 2009), para. 14.
[187] *Denmark et al.* v. *Greece (The Greek Case)* (1969) 12 Yearbook of the European Convention on Human Rights (emphasis added).
[188] *Ibid.*, p. 186 (emphasis added).
[189] Rodley, *The Treatment of Prisoners*, p. 78.
[190] *Ireland* v. *United Kingdom* (App. No. 5310/71) (Report of the Commission, 25 January 1976).

the Commission took the opportunity to address the 'misunderstanding' that had arisen as a result of its employment of 'the term "unjustifiable"'.[191] *Ireland* v. *United Kingdom* concerned an inter-state application filed by the government of Ireland against the United Kingdom for the breach of, amongst others, Article 3 of the European Convention on Human Rights following the introduction of internment in Northern Ireland.[192] With respect to Article 3, the application concerned, on the one hand, the use of physical violence against detainees in a number of places of detention and, on the other hand, the use of the so-called 'five techniques'[193] or 'interrogation in depth'.[194] The Commission, referring back to the *Greek Case*, stated that 'it did not have in mind the possibility that there could be a justification for any treatment in breach of Art. 3'.[195] The Commission corrected itself with reference to the majority considerations contained in the Parker Report. The Parker Report was published in 1972 following a government-appointed commission of inquiry into the use of the 'five techniques'. The Commission noted that whilst the government of the United Kingdom had not attempted to 'excuse or condone any acts of ill-treatment by saying that they were justified because the authorities has been dealing with a ruthless organisation', this point had, however, 'been referred to in the so-called "Parker Report"'.[196] In that regard, the Commission noted:

> the majority considered that expressions such as 'humane', 'inhuman', 'humiliating' and 'degrading' fell to be judged by a dispassionate observer 'in the light of the circumstances in which the techniques were applied, for example, that the operation was taking place in the course of urban guerrilla warfare in which completely innocent lives are at risk: that there is a degree of urgency; and that the security and safety of the interrogation centre, of its staff and of the detainees are important considerations.[197]

In response to these considerations, the Commission, referring to Article 15 of the European Convention, stated that the emergency situation that existed in Northern Ireland could not justify the use of ill-treatment under

---

[191] *Ibid.*, p. 378.
[192] For the background to this case, see William A. Schabas and Aisling O'Sullivan, 'Of Politics and Poor Weather: How Ireland Decided to Sue the United Kingdom under the European Convention on Human Rights' (2007) 2 *Irish Yearbook of International Law* 3.
[193] The 'five techniques' consisted of wall-standing in a stress position, hooding, subjection to continuous noise, sleep deprivation and reduced diet and water.
[194] Rodley, *The Treatment of Prisoners*, p. 91.
[195] *Ireland* v. *United Kingdom* (App. No. 5310/71) (Report of the Commission, 25 January 1976), p. 378.
[196] *Ibid.*, p. 379.   [197] *Ibid.*

the Convention.[198] On this point, it concluded that the prohibition under Article 3 is absolute and 'that there can never be under the Convention or under international law, a justification for acts in breach of that provision'.[199] The Commission, thus, clearly settled the question of possible justifications for the use of inhuman treatment under Article 3.

The European Court of Human Rights consistently reiterates the non-derogable nature of Article 3. It also consistently upholds the absolute nature of the prohibition of torture and inhuman or degrading treatment or punishment 'irrespective of the victim's conduct'. [200] The case of *Tomasi* v. *France* concerned the ill-treatment in custody of the applicant, a French national and a member of a Corsican political organisation, who had been arrested on suspicion of having taken part in a 'terrorist attack'.[201] The government argued that it was necessary for the Court to take into account the '"particular" circumstances obtaining in Corsica' and the fact that the applicant was suspected of involvement in a terrorist attack that had led to the death of one man and had caused grave injuries to another. The Court rejected the government's reasoning: 'The requirements of the investigation and the undeniable difficulties inherent in the fight against crime, particularly with regard to terrorism, cannot result in limits being placed on the protection to be afforded in respect of the physical integrity of individuals.'[202]

In *Chahal* v. *United Kingdom*[203] the Court, citing *Soering* v. *United Kingdom*,[204] established that the prohibition on *refoulement* is absolute and not subject to exception.[205] In this case the government argued that the deportation to India of the applicant, a Sikh activist, would pose no real risk of ill-treatment and that national security interests should, at any rate, either override the risk, or be taken into account in assessing the risk, of ill-treatment in deportation cases.[206] The Court found that the deportation of the applicant would give rise to a violation of Article 3.[207] In its

---

[198] *Ibid.*   [199] *Ibid.*
[200] *Ireland* v. *United Kingdom* (App. No. 5310/71) ECHR 18 January 1978, para. 163
[201] *Tomasi* v. *France* (App. No. 12850/87), ECHR 27 August 1992.
[202] *Ibid.*, paras. 114–15.
[203] *Chahal* v. *United Kingdom* (App. No. 22414/93) ECHR 15 November 1996.
[204] *Soering* v. *United Kingdom* (App. No. 14038/88) ECHR 7 July 1989. *Soering* v. *United Kingdom* concerned the extradition of a German national to the United States where he was likely to face death row. The case established the principle that a state may violate its obligations under Article 3 of the Convention if it exposes an individual to the risk of treatment contrary to Article 3 in a place outside its own jurisdiction.
[205] *Chahal* v. *United Kingdom*, paras. 79–80.
[206] *Ibid.*, para. 76.   [207] *Ibid.*, para. 107.

reasoning, the Court appeared to close the door on any potential justification for a breach of Article 3:

> The Court is well aware of the immense difficulties faced by States in modern times in protecting their communities from terrorist violence. However, even in these circumstances, the Convention prohibits in absolute terms torture or inhuman or degrading treatment or punishment, irrespective of the victim's conduct ... Article 3 makes no provision for exceptions and no derogation from it is permissible under Article 15 ... The prohibition provided by Article 3 against ill-treatment is equally absolute in expulsion cases ... the activities of the individual in question, however undesirable or dangerous, cannot be a material consideration.[208]

The Court subsequently upheld the principle established in *Chahal* in a number of cases.[209] In *Saadi v. Italy*,[210] decided in 2008, the Court was faced with a challenge to the absolute prohibition of *refoulement*. The Court, however, was not swayed by the notion that the 'rules of the game' had changed following the events of 11 September, requiring a rethinking of international human rights standards.[211] On the contrary, the Court reasserted this absolute principle. It held that the deportation of the applicant, Nassim Saadi, to Tunisia would constitute a breach of Article 3 of the European Convention.[212] Italy, joined by the United Kingdom, which had intervened as a third party,[213] argued that the 'standard, as outlined in *Chahal*, ought to be amended and recast in the context of individuals who pose a particular danger to the community as a whole'.[214] In particular, the United Kingdom argued that the rigidity of the principle upheld in *Chahal* 'caused many difficulties for the Contracting States by preventing them in practice from enforcing expulsion measures'; that '[t]errorism seriously endangered the right to life, which was the necessary precondition for enjoyment of all other fundamental rights', and that, in light

---

[208] *Ibid.*, paras. 79–80.

[209] Daniel Moeckli, '*Saadi v. Italy*: The Rules of the Game Have *Not* Changed' (2008) 3 *Human Rights Law Review* 534, 536.

[210] *Saadi v. Italy* (App. No. 37201/06) ECHR 28 February 2008.

[211] Fiona de Londras, 'International Decision: *Saadi v. Italy*' (2008) 102 *American Journal of International Law* 616, 620; Moeckli, '*Saadi v. Italy*' 548.

[212] *Saadi v. Italy*, para. 149.

[213] The United Kingdom intervened under Article 36(2) of the European Convention. Article 36(2) states: 'The President of the Court may, in the interest of the proper administration of justice, invite any High Contracting Party which is not a party to the proceedings or any person concerned who is not the applicant to submit written comments or take part in hearings.' See, European Convention on Human Rights, Article 36(2).

[214] de Londras, '*Saadi v. Italy*' 617.

of the threat posed by international terrorism, 'the approach followed by the Court in the *Chahal* case had to be altered and clarified'.[215] The Court remained resolute. It rejected the reasoning that the dangerousness represented by the individual to the community ought to be balanced against the risk of harm if that person were deported. In this regard, the Court asserted clearly that '[t]he concepts of risk and dangerousness in this context do not lend themselves to a balancing test because they are notions that can only be assessed independently of each other'.[216] In addition, the Court found that irrespective of the increased 'terrorist threat', as asserted by Italy and the United Kingdom, the conclusions of the *Chahal* judgment could not be called into question.[217] With respect to the *Saadi* decision, Fiona de Londras remarks that 'while it constitutes a serious rebuff to Italy's deportation policy ... perhaps the greatest significance is in relation to the United Kingdom's assertion that the *Chahal* standard is inappropriate in the context of contemporary counterterrorism'.[218] The *Saadi* decision unambiguously confirmed that, in Article 3 cases, 'state interests cannot be taken into account – there is no scope for balancing'.[219] In his concurring opinion, Judge Zupančič articulated the importance of the *Saadi* decision. He remarked that the Court's refusal to take into account the danger represented by the individual should be read 'as a categorical imperative protecting the rights of the individual. The only way out of this logical necessity would be to maintain that such individuals do not deserve human rights – the third party intervener is unconsciously implying just that to a lesser degree – because they are less human.'[220]

The question of diplomatic assurances, as a way of satisfying Article 3, was dealt with briefly in *Saadi*, but not considered applicable in that case. However, in the case of *Othman (Abu Qatada) v. United Kingdom*,[221] decided in January 2012, the Court did discuss this question at length and seemed, to some degree, to set a low threshold on their application in *non-refoulement* cases.[222] Despite its usual recital of the absolute protection afforded by Article 3, the Court determined that the return of

---

[215] *Saadi* v. *Italy*, paras. 117, 118 and 122.
[216] *Ibid.*, para. 139.   [217] *Ibid.*, para. 141.
[218] de Londras, '*Saadi* v. *Italy*' 616, 620.
[219] Moeckli, '*Saadi* v. *Italy*' 543.
[220] *Saadi* v. *Italy*, Concurring Opinion of Judge Zupančič, para. 2.
[221] *Othman (Abu Qatada) v. United Kingdom* (App. No. 8139/09) ECHR 17 January 2012.
[222] See Christopher Michaelson, 'The Renaissance of Non-Refoulement? The Othman (Abu Qatada) Decision of the European Court of Human Rights (2012) 61 *International and Comparative Law Quarterly* 750, 764.

Abu Qatada to Jordan would, due to the Memorandum of Understanding agreed between the governments of Jordan and the United Kingdom, not violate Article 3.[223] This aspect of an otherwise strong judgment[224] was articulated by the Court in dubious terms. The Court acknowledged that the practice of torture against Islamist detainees is widespread and that without diplomatic assurances there would be a real risk of the applicant being subjected to ill-treatment.[225] However, the Court was content to reconcile this with faith in the strength of bilateral relations between the United Kingdom and Jordan and in the nominated monitoring body, the Adaleh Centre for Human Rights, which together would remove the risk of ill-treatment.[226] Arguably, diplomatic assurances, however controversial, cannot be said to directly threaten the Court's absolute stance on the justifiability of torture.

In two earlier cases before the Court, neither of which was directly related to counterterrorism, the unambiguous tone of the *Saadi* decision was, arguably, less audible. In the case of *Jalloh v. Germany*[227] the Court found that the forcible administration of an emetic to cause the applicant to regurgitate evidence – a drug bubble that he had swallowed during his arrest – constituted inhuman and degrading treatment contrary to Article 3.[228] In its reasoning, the Court introduced the language of justification:

> Any recourse to a forcible medical intervention in order to obtain evidence of a crime must be convincingly *justified* on the facts of a particular case. This is especially true where the procedure is intended to retrieve from inside the individual's body real evidence of the very crime of which he is suspected. The particularly intrusive nature of such an act requires a strict scrutiny of all the surrounding circumstances. In this regard, *due regard must be had to the seriousness of the offence at issue.*[229]

The Court then stated: 'as with interventions carried out for therapeutic purposes, the manner in which a person is subjected to a forcible medical procedure in order to retrieve evidence from his body must not exceed the

---

[223] *Othman* v. *United Kingdom*, para. 207.
[224] The Court found that the applicant's deportation to Jordan would violate Article 6 due to the risk of the use of evidence obtained by torture in the trial proceedings. See *Othman* v. *United Kingdom*, paras. 280–2, 287.
[225] *Ibid.*, paras. 191–2.
[226] *Ibid.*, paras. 192–206.
[227] *Jalloh* v. *Germany* (App. No. 54810/00) ECHR 11 July 2006.
[228] *Ibid.*, para. 82.
[229] *Ibid.*, para. 71 (emphasis added).

minimum level of severity prescribed by the Court's case-law on Article 3 of the Convention.'[230] Between these two paragraphs, the Court fudges its own long-standing principles for the application of Article 3, since:

> According to the Court's well-established case-law, ill-treatment must attain a minimum level of severity if it is to fall within the scope of Article 3. The assessment of this minimum level of severity is relative; it depends on all of the circumstances of the case, such as the duration of the treatment, its physical and mental effects and, in some cases, the sex, age and state of health of the victim.[231]

Accordingly, the threshold requirement for Article 3 concerns the severity of the treatment and how this treatment affects the victim only. If the forcible medical intervention is considered to entail treatment severe enough to reach the minimum standard of Article 3, as it was in this case, then there is no need to debate the justifiability of the intervention or to take into account the seriousness of the offence involved. Whilst the Court may have been attempting to articulate the point that forcible medical intervention can in certain cases be considered justifiable, it did note, as a general point, that the forcible administration of emetics does 'pose health risks'; in this specific case, the manner in which emetics were administered, in addition, caused 'both physical pain and mental suffering'.[232] In its findings, therefore, the balancing test introduced by the Court was unnecessary:

> As regards the extent to which the forcible intervention was necessary to obtain the evidence, the Court notes that drug-trafficking is a serious offence. It is acutely aware of the problem confronting Contracting States in their efforts to combat the harm caused to their societies through the supply of drugs. However, in the present case, it was clear before the impugned measure was ordered and implemented that the street dealer on whom it was imposed had been storing the drugs in his mouth and could not, therefore, have been offering drugs for sale on a large scale.[233]

The Court goes on to state that it is not satisfied that the 'forcible administration of emetics was indispensable in the instant case to obtain the evidence'.[234] This reasoning implies that the justifiability of the procedure is relative to the offence committed. In his concurring opinion, Judge Bratza criticised the Court's reasoning. He objected to the implication that 'the gravity of the suspected offence and the urgent need to obtain

---

[230] *Ibid.*, para. 72.   [231] *Ibid.*, para. 67.
[232] *Ibid.*, paras. 78 and 82.   [233] *Ibid.*, para. 77.
[234] *Ibid.*, para. 77.

evidence of the offence ... should be regarded as relevant factors in determining whether a particular form of treatment violates Article 3'.[235] Judge Bratza pointed to the special character of the guarantees under Article 3 that apply 'irrespective of the victim's conduct' and that 'do not allow for the balancing of competing public interests against the use of treatment which attains the Article 3 threshold'.[236] Thus, he observed:

> Just as the urgent need to obtain evidence of a serious offence would not therefore justify resort to treatment which could otherwise attain that threshold, so also I consider that the threshold cannot change according to the gravity of the suspected offence or the urgency of the need to obtain evidence of the offence.[237]

In his concurring opinion, Judge Zupančič situated the ambiguous reasoning of the Court within the broader context of post 11 September. Citing *Rochin* v. *California*,[238] a case decided by the United States Supreme Court in 1952 in which the petitioner, Rochin, was subjected to a forcible emetic procedure, he remarked:

> Most worrisome in all of this, however, is the already apparent change in the *Zeitgeist* and the consequent degradation of minimal standards. What in 1952 was patently 'conduct that shocked the conscience' has in 2006 become an issue that must be extensively – and not just in this case – pondered, argued and debated.[239]

Gäfgen v. *Germany*[240] concerned allegations that the applicant, Magnus Gäfgen, had been subjected to torture during interrogation in violation of Article 3 of the European Convention. At the time of his arrest on 1 June 2002, the applicant was suspected of having kidnapped a child. On 28 July 2003 he was sentenced to life imprisonment following his conviction for extortionate abduction and murder.[241] The investigation of the kidnapping revealed that Gäfgen had suffocated the boy prior to making his demand for a ransom and, thus, prior to his arrest. When the Frankfurt police arrested Gäfgen, they were unaware that the child was already

---

[235] *Ibid.*, Concurring Opinion of Judge Sir Nicolas Bratza.
[236] *Ibid.*   [237] *Ibid.*
[238] *Rochin* v. *California*, 342 U.S. 165 (1952).
[239] *Jalloh* v. *Germany*, Concurring Opinion of Judge Zupančič.
[240] *Gäfgen* v. *Germany* (App. No. 22978/05) ECHR 30 June 2008. For the background to this case, see Florian Jessberger, 'Bad Torture – Good Torture? What International Criminal Lawyers May Learn from the Recent Trial of Police Officers in Germany' (2005) 3 *Journal of International Criminal Justice* 1059.
[241] Jessberger, 'Bad Torture – Good Torture?' 1062.

deceased. In response to Gäfgen's refusal to reveal the whereabouts of the child, he was threatened with torture.[242] On 20 December 2002 the Frankfurt am Main Regional Court convicted both the Deputy Chief of Police, Wolfgang Daschner, of having incited coercion, and the subordinate officer, of coercion.[243] The Court, however, accepted mitigating circumstances and essentially rendered 'a guilty but not to be punished' verdict.[244]

The European Court of Human Rights, in its decision on 30 June 2008, found that whilst the applicant was subjected to inhuman treatment prohibited by Article 3,[245] he had lost his victim status since the domestic courts had 'afforded the applicant sufficient redress for his treatment in breach of Article 3'.[246] In reaching this conclusion, the Court took into account the fact that the applicant had not yet been financially compensated, but it noted that such proceedings were pending.[247] The Court also noted:

> in a case such as the present one, in which the breach of Article 3 lies in a threat of ill-treatment (as opposed to actual physical ill-treatment attaining the threshold for Article 3 to apply), redress for this breach is essentially granted by the effective prosecution and conviction of the persons responsible. The Court finds that, not least in view of the wide public approval of the treatment to which the applicant was subjected, the criminal conviction of the police officers responsible, which acknowledged in an unequivocal manner that the applicant had been the victim of prohibited ill-treatment, was essential in affording him redress in a manner other than by the payment of a sum of money.[248]

The Court bases its finding of a loss of victim status, on one hand, on the fact of the prosecution and conviction of the officers responsible for Gäfgen's subjection to inhuman treatment and, on the other hand, on the domestic court's recognition of a violation of Article 3. It is less clear why the Court considered it relevant to differentiate between the threat of ill-treatment and 'actual physical treatment', particularly in light of the fact that it had already found Gäfgen's treatment to constitute inhuman treatment. In addition, it is unclear how public approval of the police officers' actions is relative in the context of the applicant's loss of victim

---

[242] *Gäfgen* v. *Germany* (2008), paras. 8–13.
[243] *Ibid.*, para. 43.
[244] Jessberger, 'Bad Torture – Good Torture?' 1066.
[245] *Gäfgen* v. *Germany* (2008), para. 70.
[246] *Ibid.*, para. 81.   [247] *Ibid.*, para. 80.   [248] *Ibid.*

status. In his dissenting opinion to this case, Judge Kalaydjieva warned that the Court's finding of the loss of victim status due merely to the prosecution of the officers responsible 'may be interpreted as legitimizing coercion as a method of obtaining evidence in criminal proceedings'.[249] It may, he argued, 'justify and encourage violations of the prohibition of torture and inhuman or degrading treatment in the name of justice'.[250] He also highlighted the danger of the domestic court's approach, which, he observed, might discourage the authorities from respecting Article 3 where the price to be paid for such violations is mitigated by the leniency of the punishment.

Gäfgen v. *Germany* was subsequently referred to the Grand Chamber, which issued its decision on 1 June 2010.[251] Before the Grand Chamber, the applicant argued that he had been subjected to torture in breach of Article 3 and that he was still a victim of that breach. The Grand Chamber, reasserting the findings of the Chamber, found that the applicant had been subjected to inhuman treatment.[252] It found, in addition, that the applicant could still claim to be a victim under Article 3; thus, there had been a violation of Article 3 of the Convention.[253] Correcting the approach taken by the Chamber, the Grand Chamber found that the various measures taken by the domestic authorities did not comply with the Court's established requirements for redress.[254] The Court based this finding on three substantive reasons. First, it noted that the imposition of 'almost token fines' and the suspension of those fines was an inadequate response to a breach of Article 3. The punishment, according to the Court, was 'manifestly inappropriate' and did not entail the necessary deterrent effect required to prevent future violations.[255] Second, the Court criticised Wolfgang Daschner's subsequent appointment as chief of police as an inadequate reflection of 'the seriousness involved in a breach of Article 3'.[256] Finally, the Court found that the failure of the domestic courts to decide on the merits of the applicant's compensation claim for more than three years gave rise to 'serious doubts about the effectiveness of the official liability proceedings'.[257]

The Court's findings in this specific case are of a more general significance. Florian Jessberger remarks that the verdict of the Frankfurt

---

[249] *Ibid.*, Dissenting Opinion of Judge Kalaydjieva.   [250] *Ibid.*
[251] *Gäfgen* v. *Germany* (App. No. 22978/05) ECHR 1 June 2010, para. 5.
[252] *Ibid.*, paras. 75, 108.   [253] *Ibid.*, paras. 130–2.
[254] *Ibid.*, para. 129.   [255] *Ibid.*, para. 124.
[256] *Ibid.*, para. 125.   [257] *Ibid.*, para. 127.

Regional Court, in the case of Daschner and the subordinate police officer

> deserves respect in its effort to balance the strict prohibition of torture under constitutional and international law, on the one hand, against the undeniable conflict with which state officials may be confronted if the use of physical or psychological violence against a suspect is, at least subjectively, the last resort to save innocent life.[258]

With the threat of terrorism in mind, he further argues that this verdict could provide guidance in the resolution of similar cases in international criminal law.[259] In this respect, whilst the use of torture is unavoidably a crime without grounds for excluding criminal responsibility under the Rome Statute of the International Criminal Court,[260] Rule 145(1)(b) of the Rome Statute could, following the example in the *Daschner* judgment, apply in sentencing the torturer.[261] Rule 145(1)(b) states: 'In its determination of the sentence pursuant to article 78, paragraph 1, the Court shall: Balance all the relevant factors, including any mitigating and aggravating factors and consider the circumstances both of the convicted person and of the crime.'[262] Kai Ambos maintains that the *Daschner* judgment represents 'a Solomonic decision which seems to strike a genial compromise between upholding the prohibition against torture – as an imperative conduct rule addressed to the state – and a certain tolerance and understanding towards the individual investigator who may not feel able to comply with this prohibition in extreme cases'.[263] He argues that a version of *Rettungsfolter* – which loosely translates as life-saving torture – may be modelled on the facts of both the *Daschner* case and Israeli ticking bomb cases to deal with narrowly defined ticking bomb situations.[264] Ambos maintains that although the prohibition of torture must be upheld 'for the maintenance of a law-abiding state's integrity and legitimacy', this does not 'do justice to the individual police officers or security agents who may

---

[258] Jessberger, 'Bad Torture – Good Torture?' 1066.

[259] *Ibid.*, 1070–3.

[260] Rome Statute, Article 31.

[261] Jessberger, 'Bad Torture – Good Torture?' 1072–3.

[262] Rome Statute, rule 145(1)(b). Article 78(1) reads: 'In determining the sentence, the Court shall, in accordance with the Rules of Procedure and Evidence, take into account such factors as the gravity of the crime and the individual circumstances of the convicted person.'

[263] Kai Ambos, 'May a State Torture Suspects to Save the Life of Innocents?' (2008) 6 *Journal of International Criminal Justice* 261, 263.

[264] *Ibid.*, 270.

find themselves in a situation where torture is the only available means to avert a serious danger for human life'.[265] He argues that this injustice can be mediated by 'granting these officials an excuse instead of a justification'.[266] Ambos is careful to point out that this solution

> does not set a general standard of behaviour or contain general rules to orient human conduct *ex ante* and *in abstracto* ... but only evaluates an individual's commission of a criminal offence *ex post* and *in concreto* with a view to its compatibility with the legal order as a whole and taking into account the extraordinary circumstances of the conduct.[267]

In its 2008 judgment the Chamber appeared to endorse the *Daschner* judgment as well as the positions taken both by Jessberger and Ambos. The Grand Chamber seemed to take a different position, insofar as it disagreed with the approach taken by the domestic court in sentencing the police officers. In particular, the Grand Chamber was concerned with the leniency of the punishment imposed upon the police officers involved, which, in its view, was a contributory factor in the state's failure to provide sufficient redress. The Court did not, however, articulate the degree of punishment that it would have considered acceptable. Rather, it specified a distinction between the actions of the police officers in the *Gäfgen* case and 'other cases concerning arbitrary and serious acts of brutality by the State agents which the latter then attempted to conceal'.[268] The Grand Chamber noted that, in such cases, the Court has in the past considered that 'the imposition of enforceable prison sentences would have been more appropriate'.[269] The Grand Chamber may have adopted the right approach in not specifying an appropriate punishment, since it was not its task to rule on the degree of guilt of the individuals concerned or to determine the appropriate sentence. From the Grand Chamber's reasoning, however, it is not clear that it considered the actions of the police officers to be legally inexcusable.

This interpretation is, arguably, answered by the Grand Chamber's assessment of whether the applicant's treatment violated Article 3. In the Chamber decision, the Court, in reaching its decision that the applicant's treatment constituted inhuman treatment, appeared to take into account the mitigating factors determined by the Frankfurt regional court:

> However, the questioning lasted for some ten minutes only and, as was established in the criminal proceedings against the police officers took

---

[265] *Ibid.*, 285.   [266] *Ibid.*   [267] *Ibid.*, 287.
[268] *Gäfgen v. Germany* (2010), para. 124.   [269] *Ibid.*

place in an atmosphere of heightened tension and emotions owing to the fact that the police officers, who were completely exhausted and under extreme pressure, believed that they had only a few hours to save J's life, elements which can be regarded as mitigating factors.[270]

The Court takes the subjective motivation and the state of mind of the police officers into account in its assessment of which limb of Article 3 to apply. In the Grand Chamber decision, the Court enumerates the intention or motivation behind the infliction of ill-treatment as a factor in its assessment of whether ill-treatment falls within the scope of Article 3.[271] Including this factor does not contradict the logic of the application of Article 3, since the Court has to weigh up whether the impugned conduct was a justifiable measure of law enforcement in order to assess whether it falls within the scope of that Article. Clearly, however, bearing Nowak's analysis in mind, once the individual is in police custody, this proportionality test no longer applies. In its assessment, the Grand Chamber states that 'having regard to the findings of the domestic courts and to the material before it is persuaded that the police officers resorted to the method of interrogation in question in the belief that J.'s life might be saved'.[272] However, the Court tempers the language of the earlier decision by stating:

> The threat took place in an atmosphere of heightened tension and emotions in circumstances where the police officers were under intense pressure, believing that J.'s life was in considerable danger. In that connection, the Court accepts the motivation for the police officers' conduct and that they acted in an attempt to save a child's life. However, it is necessary to underline that … the prohibition on ill-treatment of a person applies irrespective of the conduct of the victim or the motivation of the authorities.[273]

In this assessment, the Grand Chamber reasserts the long-standing principle of the Court that the absolute prohibition of torture and other ill-treatment applies irrespective of the conduct of the individual and, it adds, irrespective of the motivation behind the use of such ill-treatment. In so doing, the Court offers a response to those who would argue that in an analogous situation involving a ticking bomb, the use of torture or other ill-treatment might be justifiable. The fact that the Court considered the motives of the police officers at all, however, does suggest sympathy

---

[270] *Ibid.*, para. 69.
[271] *Ibid.*, para. 88.
[272] *Ibid.*, para. 95; See also *Gäfgen* v. *Germany* (2008), para. 67.
[273] *Gäfgen* v. *Germany* (2010), paras. 106 and 107.

towards their actions and it begs the question as to whether the Court's assessment was merely formulaic.

C.   The definition of torture: severity and purpose

The definition of torture and its distinction from other forms of (cruel) inhuman or degrading treatment or punishment has been a source of debate since the prohibition was first formulated in the Universal Declaration of Human Rights.[274] Recently, the Committee against Torture stated: 'In practice, the definitional threshold between ill-treatment and torture is often not clear.'[275] This perceived lack of clarity stems from demarcating the distinction between torture and other ill-treatment on the basis of an assessment of the severity of the treatment inflicted. The distinction between torture and other ill-treatment finds its most acute articulation in the purpose of the conduct.[276] The formula prohibiting torture and other-ill treatment should, as Nigel Rodley and Matt Pollard assert, 'be elastic and capable of evolving interpretation over time'.[277] Simultaneously, however, the definition of torture must be capable of coherently responding to those who attempt to evade it. The purposive element approach to the definition of torture is significant, therefore, both because it nulls the attempt at applying restrictive definitions of torture based on the methods of torture used and because it is intrinsic to the meaning of torture and, hence, to the overall integrity of the prohibition on torture.

(1)   Aggravated inhuman treatment

The European Commission, in the *Greek Case*, initiated the approach of dividing the prohibition on torture and other ill-treatment into its component parts.[278] In that case, interpreting Article 3 of the European Convention, the Commission held: 'It is plain that there may be treatment

---

[274] For a significantly more detailed discussion of the jurisprudence relevant to the definition of torture than is provided in this work, see in particular Part I of Steven Dewulf, *The Signature of Evil: (Re)Defining Torture in International Law* (Antwerp: Intersentia, 2011).

[275] UNCAT, 'General Comment 2', para. 3.

[276] Nigel S. Rodley, 'The Definition(s) of Torture in International Law' (2002) 55 *Current Legal Problems* 467; UNHCR, 'Report of the Special Rapporteur: Manfred Nowak', § 34; Nowak, 'What Practices Constitute Torture?' 809.

[277] Nigel S. Rodley and Matt Pollard, *The Treatment of Prisoners Under International Law*, 3rd edn (Oxford University Press, 2010), p. 82.

[278] *Ibid.*, p. 83.

to which all these descriptions apply, for all torture must be inhuman and degrading treatment, and inhuman treatment also degrading'.[279] On the definition of torture, the Commission concluded: 'The word "torture" is often used to describe inhuman treatment, which has a purpose, such as the obtaining of information or confessions, or the infliction of punishment, and it is generally an aggravated form of inhuman treatment.'[280] It defined inhuman treatment as treatment that 'deliberately causes severe suffering, physical or mental'.[281] It seems, therefore, that the Commission considered torture to constitute suffering that was 'more than severe'.[282] It is also possible, however, that the European Commission intended the word 'aggravated' to refer to a more serious violation due to the attendant circumstances. At any rate, the Commission did not conclude that a specific severity threshold beyond that of inhuman treatment is required for an act to constitute torture.[283] The Declaration against Torture, adopted in 1975, subsequently defined torture in Article 1(1) as the intentional infliction of severe pain or suffering for a purpose by or at the instigation of a public official.[284] In Article 1(2), it provided that '[t]orture constitutes an aggravated and deliberate form of cruel, inhuman or degrading treatment or punishment'.[285] As Rodley points out, the influence of the European Commission decision on the Declaration against Torture was understandable since Sweden and the Netherlands had instituted the complaint against Greece and were also heavily involved in the drafting of the Declaration.[286]

In the case of *Ireland* v. *United Kingdom*, the European Commission found that the use of the 'five techniques' was officially authorised and constituted an administrative practice.[287] As regards any potential breach of Article 3 of the European Convention, the Commission found that the 'five techniques', when used in combination, rendered them in breach of Article 3 and constituted not only inhuman and degrading treatment but

---

[279] The *Greek Case*, p. 186.
[280] *Ibid.*   [281] *Ibid.*
[282] Rodley and Pollard, *The Treatment of Prisoners*, p. 91.
[283] Anthony Cullen, 'Defining Torture in International Law: A Critique of the Concept Employed by the European Court of Human Rights' (2003) 34 *California Western International Law Journal* 29, 35.
[284] Declaration on the Protection of All Persons from Being Subjected to Torture, Article 1(1).
[285] *Ibid.*, Article 1(2).
[286] Rodley and Pollard, *The Treatment of Prisoners*, p. 83.
[287] *Ireland* v. *United Kingdom* (App. No. 5310/71) (Report of the Commission, 25 January 1976), p. 391.

also torture. The Commission applied the purpose of the conduct as the decisive criterion:

> Indeed, the systematic application of the techniques for the purpose of inducing a person to give information shows a clear resemblance to those methods of systematic torture which have been known over the ages. Although the five techniques ... might not necessarily cause any severe after effects the Commission sees in them a modern system of torture falling into the same category as those systems which have been applied in previous times as a means of obtaining information and confessions.[288]

The Commission thus endorsed the view in the *Greek Case* that torture constitutes purposive inhuman treatment; it did not rely on the notion of torture as an aggravated form of inhuman treatment. In *Ireland v. United Kingdom* the European Court of Human Rights took a different approach in its assessment of the 'five techniques' under Article 3. The Court found that the 'five techniques' used in combination constituted inhuman and degrading treatment but not torture:

> Although the five techniques, as applied in combination, undoubtedly amounted to inhuman and degrading treatment, although their object was the extraction of confessions, the naming of others and/or information and although they were used systematically, they did not occasion suffering of the particular intensity and cruelty implied by the word torture as so understood.[289]

The Court found the techniques to constitute inhuman treatment as they 'caused, if not actual bodily injury, at least intense physical and mental suffering to the persons subjected thereto and also led to acute psychiatric disturbances during interrogation'.[290] It considered the techniques to be degrading as 'they were such as to arouse in their victims feelings of fear, anguish and inferiority capable of humiliating and debasing them and possibly breaking their physical or moral resistance'.[291] The Court viewed the distinction between torture and other ill-treatment as deriving 'principally from a difference in the intensity of the suffering inflicted'.[292] According to the Court, 'it was the intention that the Convention, with its distinction between "torture" and "inhuman or degrading treatment", should by the first of these terms attach a special stigma to deliberate inhuman treatment causing very serious and cruel suffering'.[293] In adopting this reasoning, the Court cited Article 1(2) of the Declaration against

---

[288] *Ibid.* p. 402.
[289] *Ireland v. United Kingdom* (App. No. 5310/71) ECHR 18 January 1978, para. 167.
[290] *Ibid.*   [291] *Ibid.*   [292] *Ibid.*   [293] *Ibid.*

Torture and seemingly related the severity of the treatment to the notion of aggravated ill-treatment.[294]

The decision of the European Court in *Ireland v. United Kingdom* was subject to criticism.[295] In his separate opinion, Judge Zekia pointed out that the Commission had unanimously found that the treatment amounted to torture. He acknowledged, furthermore, that the judgment was uncontested by either the applicant or the respondent state. He was unable to justify the different finding of the Court.[296] Indeed, the Commission's decision was a unanimous one and, unlike the Court, it came to its decision having heard extensively from witnesses. Fionnuala Ní Aoláin has since concluded:

> The ... case needs to be read in the context of its time as a highly political case – a leading democracy being accused of systematic torture, in the context of a fraught internal conflict in Northern Ireland to which the British government had committed its military forces. In such a context, the decision needs to be read as much in terms of its political weight as the practices being examined.[297]

This reading implies that the Court may have allowed the potential consequences of its decision to inform the definition of torture that it employed.[298] Anthony Cullen remarks that understanding the different reasoning of the Court from that of the Commission might be illuminated by taking into account the principle of the margin of appreciation.[299] The term 'margin of appreciation' originated in cases involving Article 15 of the European Convention.[300] It refers to the 'room for manoeuvre' which the Court is prepared to accord to the state in fulfilling its obligations under the Convention.[301] The Court allows a margin of appreciation to

---

[294] *Ibid.*

[295] Raj Spjut, 'Notes and Comments: Torture under the European Convention on Human Rights' (1979) 73 *American Journal of International Law* 267, 270.

[296] *Ireland v. United Kingdom* (App. No. 5310/71) ECHR 18 January 1978, Separate Opinion of Judge Zekia.

[297] Fionnuala Ní Aoláin, 'The European Convention on Human Rights and Its Prohibition on Torture' in Sanford Levinson (ed.), *Torture: A Collection* (Oxford University Press, 2004), p. 216.

[298] Spjut, 'Torture under the European Convention on Human Rights' 271; Cullen, 'Defining Torture in International Law' 40.

[299] Cullen, 'Defining Torture in International Law' 40.

[300] Alfred William Brian Simpson, *Human Rights and the End of Empire: Britain and the Genesis of the European Convention* (Oxford University Press, 2001), pp. 1000–5.

[301] Steven C. Greer, *The Margin of Appreciation: Interpretation and Discretion under the European Convention on Human Rights* (Strasbourg: Council of Europe Publishing, 2000), p. 5.

the state in assessing what measures are 'strictly required by the exigencies of the situation' in a public emergency.[302] In the case of *Ireland* v. *United Kingdom*, the respondent state had officially derogated from its obligations in accordance with Article 15 of the European Convention.[303] Choosing to defer to the 'better position' of the national authorities 'to decide both on the presence of such an emergency and on the nature and scope of derogations necessary to avert it', the Court extended to the United Kingdom 'a wide margin of appreciation'.[304] The derogation provision of the Convention does not, however, apply to Article 3 and, accordingly, the Court does not afford the state a margin of appreciation where violations of Article 3 are concerned. However, in his separate opinion Judge O'Donoghue, criticising the findings of the Court vis-à-vis the findings of the Commission with respect to Article 3, suggested that the Court had employed the doctrine of the margin of appreciation in its assessment of the Article 3 violation:

> I am a firm upholder of the doctrine frequently approved by the Court that a margin of appreciation should be accorded to a State for its action taken in an emergency and impugned as a contravention of the Convention. In the present case, however, the invocation of this principle in favour of the respondent Government has been treated by the Court, in my opinion, as a blanket exculpation for many actions taken which cannot be reconciled with observance of the obligations imposed by the Convention.[305]

Whilst Judge O'Donoghue's criticism might appear to be directed towards the wide employment of the margin of appreciation in the case generally, he made this point in the context of his remarks on Article 3.[306]

In subsequent decisions the European Court found violations of Article 3 of the European Convention in respect of torture. However, the Court retained the high threshold of severe pain and suffering in its reasoning. In the case of *Aksoy* v. *Turkey*[307] the Court found a violation of Article

---

[302] European Convention on Human Rights, Article 15(1). See also Rosalyn Higgins, 'Derogations under Human Rights Treaties' (1976) 48 *British Yearbook of International Law* 281, 293.

[303] *Ireland* v. *United Kingdom* (App. No. 5310/71) ECHR 18 January 1978, para. 79.

[304] *Ibid.* See also, Joan Fitzpatrick, *Human Rights in Crisis: The International System for Protecting Rights During States of Emergency* (Philadelphia: University of Pennsylvania Press, 1994), p. 201.

[305] *Ireland* v. *United Kingdom* (App. No. 5310/71) ECHR 18 January 1978, Separate Opinion of Judge O'Donoghue.

[306] Cullen, 'Defining Torture in International Law' 42.

[307] *Aksoy* v. *Turkey*, (App. No. 21987/93) ECHR 26 November 1996.

3. The applicant had been subjected to Palestinian hanging (his hands were tied behind his back and he was strung up by his arms) and other ill-treatment. According to the Court, the treatment was deliberately inflicted for the purpose of obtaining information and it was 'of such a serious and cruel nature that it can only be described as torture'.[308] In the case of *Aydin v. Turkey*[309] the Court found that 'the accumulation of acts of physical and mental violence inflicted on the applicant and the especially cruel act of rape to which she was subjected amounted to torture in breach of Article 3'.[310] It added, however, that it would have 'reached this conclusion on either of these grounds taken separately'.[311] In addition to her subjection to rape, the applicant had been

> kept blindfolded, and in a constant state of physical pain and mental anguish brought on by the beatings administered to her during questioning and by the apprehension of what would happen to her next. She was also paraded naked in humiliating circumstances thus adding to her overall sense of vulnerability and on one occasion she was pummelled with high-pressure water while being spun around in a tyre.[312]

In addition to its conclusion that the applicant's treatment constituted torture, the Court found that the applicant's treatment was both deliberate and purposive.[313]

(2)   Conventional definition

The definition of torture contained in the Convention against Torture[314] was the first definition of torture to be included in an international treaty.[315] The Convention does not include the notion, contained in the Declaration against Torture, that torture constitutes an aggravated form of other-ill-treatment. This clause was deleted because the drafters felt that the wording was too vague and that 'it would bring imprecision to

---

[308] *Ibid.*, para. 64.
[309] *Aydin v. Turkey* (App. No. 23178/94) ECHR 25 September 1997.
[310] *Ibid.*, para. 86.   [311] *Ibid.*
[312] *Ibid.*, para. 84.   [313] *Ibid.*, para. 85.
[314] See n. 6 and accompanying text in Introduction.
[315] Chris Ingelse, *The UN Committee Against Torture: An Assessment* (The Hague: Kluwer Law International, 2001), p. 206. Article 2 of the Inter-American Convention to Prevent and Punish Torture also contains a definition of torture. This definition was influenced by, but is not identical to, the definition contained in the Convention against Torture. See Burgers and Danelius, *The United Nations Convention against Torture*, p. 116.

the concept of torture'.[316] Nowak and McArthur conclude that, in deleting this clause, the Convention followed the reasoning of the European Commission in the *Greek Case*, which endorsed the purposive element approach, and not the reasoning of the European Court, which relied on the severity approach.[317] Thus, they remark: 'It follows that the severity of pain or suffering, although constituting an essential element of the definition of torture, is not a criterion distinguishing torture from cruel and inhuman treatment.'[318] Article 16 of the Convention against Torture does provide: 'Each State Party shall undertake to prevent in any territory under its jurisdiction other acts of cruel, inhuman or degrading treatment or punishment *which do not amount to torture*.'[319] The emphasised words do not suggest, however, that torture is at the high end of the scale of intensity of ill-treatment. As Rodley and Pollard note, 'extreme scepticism as to the relevance of the notion of aggravation is ... called for by the fact that it was intentionally dropped from' the Convention against Torture.[320] The word 'amount' should not be understood as relating to the degree of pain or suffering; rather it should be understood as referring to the accumulation of elements that are required for an act to constitute torture. The practice of the Committee against Torture reveals that it does not draw sharp distinctions between torture and other ill-treatment based on the relative severity of the treatment. In *Dragan Dimitrijevic v. Serbia and Montenegro*[321] the complainant had been subjected to beatings whilst in detention.[322] He claimed that these acts 'were perpetrated with a discriminatory motive and for the purpose of extracting a confession or otherwise intimidating and/or punishing him'.[323] The Committee found that his treatment could 'be characterized as severe pain or suffering intentionally inflicted by public officials in the context of the investigation of a crime'. Without engaging in a discussion of the severity of the ill-treatment, the Committee found a violation of the Convention against Torture Article 2(1) in connection with Article 1.[324]

---

[316] Nowak and McArthur, *The United Nations Convention against Torture*, p. 34.
[317] *Ibid.*, p. 68.   [318] *Ibid.*, p. 69.
[319] Convention against Torture, Article 16(1) (emphasis added).
[320] Rodley and Pollard, *The Treatment of Prisoners*, p. 111.
[321] *Dragan Dimitrijevic v. Serbia and Montenegro*, Communication No. 207/2002, UN Doc. CAT/C/33/D/207/2002 (2004). See also *Jovica Dimitrov v. Serbia and Montenegro*, Communication No. 171/2000, UN Doc. CAT/C/34/D/171 2000 (2005); *Danilo Dimitrijevic v. Serbia Montenegro*, Communication No. 172/2000, UN Doc. CAT/C/35/D/172/2000 (2005).
[322] *Dragan Dimitrijevic v. Serbia and Montenegro*, paras. 2.1 and 2.2.
[323] *Ibid.*, para. 3.1.   [324] *Ibid.*, para, 5.3.

(3) Evolving standards?

In the case of *Selmouni* v. *France*[325] the Court finally addressed the high threshold of severity that it had established in the case of *Ireland* v. *United Kingdom*. The Court repeated that it was intended that the Convention attach a 'special stigma' to the term torture.[326] Citing Article 1 and Article 16 of the Convention against Torture for the first time in its jurisprudence,[327] the Court also remarked that this distinction is present in the definition of torture under the Convention against Torture. Oddly, the Court also asserted that the severity requirement in the Convention against Torture's definition of torture, like the minimum requirement for the application of Article 3 of the European Convention, 'is relative; it depends on all the circumstances of the case, such as the duration of the treatment, its physical or mental effects and, in some cases, the sex, age and state of health of the victim, etc'.[328] The Court then made its often-cited observation:

> The Court has previously examined cases in which it concluded that there had been treatment which could only be described as torture. However, having regard to the fact that the Convention is a 'living instrument which must be interpreted in the light of present-day conditions', the Court considers that certain acts which were classified in the past as 'inhuman and degrading treatment' as opposed to 'torture' could be classified differently in future. It takes the view that the increasingly high standard being required in the area of the protection of human rights and fundamental liberties correspondingly and inevitably requires greater firmness in assessing breaches of the fundamental values of democratic societies.[329]

The Court accordingly found that, in being subjected to beatings over a period of days, the applicant's treatment constituted torture.[330] This decision is recognised as having marked a change in the Court's interpretation of the severity threshold, initiated in the case of *Ireland* v. *United Kingdom*.[331] Crucially, whilst the change in approach adopted by the Court was welcome, it did not signal the end of the requirement of an elevated level of severity from the threshold of inhuman treatment. In its subsequent jurisprudence on Article 3 of the European Convention, the

---

[325] *Selmouni* v. *France* (App. No. 25803/94) ECHR 28 July 1999.
[326] *Ibid.*, para. 96.
[327] Rodley and Pollard, *The Treatment of Prisoners*, p. 105.
[328] *Selmouni* v. *France*, paras. 97–100.
[329] *Ibid.*, para. 101.   [330] *Ibid.*, para. 105.
[331] Rodley and Pollard, *The Treatment of Prisoners*, p. 105.

Court has alternated between applying a relative severity approach and a purposive element approach.[332]

In *Jalloh* v. *Germany* the Court found the treatment to which the applicant had been subjected to constitute inhuman treatment and degrading treatment.[333] In his concurring opinion, Judge Zupančič, referring to the Court's integration of the Convention against Torture definition into its case law in the case of *Selmouni* v. *France*, argued that the treatment to which the applicant had been subjected constituted torture '*stricto senso*'.[334] He based this conclusion on the fact that, although it is impossible to generalise on what constitutes severe pain and suffering, this is a question of fact to be determined by a criminal tribunal; in this case, the applicant had not been afforded the possibility to testify to the severity of his treatment. According to Judge Zupančič, '[i]n the absence of proof to the contrary ... I am constrained to maintain that the pain and suffering in this particular case were severe. Thus, we ought to speak of torture'.[335] On the one hand, Zupančič's argument does centralise the severity of the pain and suffering caused as the compelling element of the definition, although he speaks to the difficulty of objectively assessing the severity of pain and suffering. On the other hand, Zupančič's discomfort with the majority decision seems to be rooted in his recognition that the purpose of the emetic was to obtain evidence.

In *Gäfgen* v. *Germany* the Court found that the applicant's treatment 'was sufficiently serious to amount to inhuman treatment prohibited by Article 3, but that it did not reach the level of cruelty required to attain the threshold of torture'.[336] The applicant had been threatened with 'intolerable pain' if he failed to disclose the whereabouts of the child. The Court considered this threat to be 'real and immediate':[337]

> The process, which would not leave any traces, was to be carried out by a police officer specially trained for that purpose, who was already on his way to the police station by helicopter. It was to be conducted under medical supervision .... Furthermore, it is clear ... that D. intended, if necessary, to carry out that threat with the help of a 'truth serum' and that the applicant had been warned that the execution of the threat was imminent.[338]

---

[332] See İhlan v. *Turkey* (App. No. 22277/93) ECHR 27 June 2000, para. 87; *Dikme* v. *Turkey* (App. No. 20869/92) ECHR 11 July 2000, para. 95; *Denezi and Others* v. *Cyprus* (App. Nos. 25316–25321/94 and 27207/95) ECHR 23 May 2001, para. 384.

[333] *Jalloh* v. *Germany*, para. 82.

[334] *Ibid.*, Concurring Opinion of Judge Zupančič.   [335] *Ibid.*

[336] *Gäfgen* v. *Germany* (2010), para. 108.

[337] *Ibid.*, para. 103.   [338] *Ibid.*, para. 94.

Since in both cases the treatment was intentionally inflicted, for a purpose by or at the acquiescence of a public official, it is reasonable to conclude that each case satisfied three elements of the definition of torture under the Convention against Torture. In addition, since the Committee against Torture does not introduce a severity distinction between torture and other ill-treatment as such, it might be concluded that under the Convention against Torture, this case would have constituted torture under Article 1. According to the European Court, however, the required element of severity for the treatment to constitute torture was not reached. There is a logical incoherence in the Court's approach. Since Gäfgen's treatment was considered to constitute inhuman treatment, and since he was subjected to such treatment for a purpose, it would seem this his treatment amounted to torture. The Court's approach leads to the semantically unsound suggestion that there exists pain and suffering that is worse than inhuman.

(4)   Harmonising the definition

The Human Rights Committee does not offer a solution to the definitional problem. In General Comment 20 the Human Rights Committee states:

> The Covenant does not contain any definition of the concepts covered by article 7, nor does the Committee consider it necessary to draw up a list of prohibited acts or to establish sharp distinctions between the different kinds of punishment or treatment; the distinctions depend on the nature, purpose and severity of the treatment applied.[339]

The Committee leaves it uncertain as to the criteria it applies in respect of violations of Article 7 of the Civil and Political Rights Covenant. Whilst the Committee does, in some instances, categorise treatment as either torture or one of the other forms of ill-treatment, there is no evidence to suggest that it does so based on the notion of severity. The alternative to this definitional wrangling over the different levels of required severity is to adopt the purposive element approach to the definition. This approach does not dispense with the severity requirement. That requirement is stipulated in the definition of torture under the Convention against Torture and in the European Court's jurisprudence in the form of the minimal standard.

The purposive approach is also coherent with the war crime of torture under the Rome Statute. The only distinguishing element between

---

[339]   UNHCR, 'General Comment 20', para. 4.

the war crime of torture and the war crime of inhuman treatment is the purposive element.[340] Under the Rome Statute torture is defined by the Elements of Crimes as the infliction of 'severe physical or mental pain or suffering upon one or more persons ... for such purposes as: obtaining information or a confession, punishment, intimidation or coercion or for any reason based on discrimination of any kind'.[341] During the drafting of the war crime of torture under the Rome Statute, it was debated as to whether the war crime of torture should be distinguished from the war crime of inhuman treatment by adopting the severity approach of the European Court or by emphasising the purposive approach and/or the element of official capacity.[342] Knut Dörmann observes that 'the compromise found ... respects, to a large extent, the case law of the ad hoc Tribunals: it incorporates the purposive element by repeating the illustrative list of the Torture Convention, and drops the reference to official capacity'.[343] In *Bemba* Pre-Trial Chamber II of the International Criminal Court refused to confirm charges of torture as a war crime on the basis that the Prosecutor had failed to adequately demonstrate that acts had been committed for a specific purpose.[344]

Torture as a crime against humanity is defined in Article 7(2)(e) of the Rome Statute.[345] Unlike the war crime of torture, the crime against humanity of torture does not require a specific purpose to be proven.[346] Under the Rome Statute there is no crime against humanity of inhuman treatment. Since the crime against humanity of 'other inhumane acts of a similar character intentionally causing great suffering, or serious injury to body or to mental or physical health' must have a similar character – nature and gravity – to the specified crimes against humanity, then if the crime against humanity of torture had required a purposive element, any similar inhumane act would also have to entail the purposive element.[347] Rodley and Pollard suggest that the absence of the purposive element

---

[340] Rome Statute, Elements of Crimes 8(2)(a)(ii) – 1 and 8(2)(a)(ii) – 2.

[341] *Ibid.*, Elements of Crimes, War Crimes 8(2)(a)(ii) – 1, paras. 1–2.

[342] Knut Dörmann, *Elements of War Crimes under the Rome Statute of the International Criminal Court: Sources and Commentary* (Cambridge University Press, 2003), p. 45.

[343] *Ibid.*

[344] *Bemba* (ICC-01/05–01/08), Decision pursuant to Article 61(7)(a) and (b) of the Rome Statute on the Charges of the Prosecutor Against Jean-Pierre Bemba Gombo, 15 June 2009, paras. 290, 298–300.

[345] Rome Statute, Article 7(2)(e). See n. 150, above.

[346] *Ibid.*, Elements of Crime 7(1)(f). See also, *Bemba*, para. 195; William A. Schabas, *The International Criminal Court: A Commentary on the Rome Statute* (Oxford University Press, 2010), p. 215.

[347] Rodley and Pollard, *The Treatment of Prisoners*, p. 121.

may allow the 'crime against humanity of torture to embrace both torture (in its traditional purposive understanding) and inhuman treatment
(in which the purposive element may be absent or not demonstrable); this
conflation of the two notions is effected precisely because the alternative
category of inhuman treatment is not available'.[348] From this reading, the
absence of the purposive element from the crime against humanity of torture in the Rome Statute does not lead to the conclusion that the Rome
Statute drops entirely the notion of purpose in the definition of torture.

D. Conclusion

From the drafting history of the prohibition of torture in general and
torture-specific human rights treaties, it is clear that the objective of the
drafters was to provide a broad interpretation of torture so as to encom-
pass a ban on any single act of torture. The issue of possible justifications
for an act of torture was, at no point, given lengthy consideration. It
is possible that this was so because the drafters had not envisaged the
kinds of situations that arise contemporaneously in terms of the prevention of acts of terrorism. This reading corresponds to the kind of
reasoning that is proposed by those commentators who argue that the
events of 11 September 'represented an entirely new type and degree of
threat',[349] requiring a rethinking of the 'old' laws. It is more plausible,
however, that the drafters, of the various treaties and torture provisions
intended to enact a prohibition of torture that would endure this tem-
poral reasoning; that is, one that applies regardless of the exigencies of
the situation.

One rationale for the *absolute and non-derogable* prohibition of torture
under international human rights law seems to exist in the connection
between the inherent dignity of the human being and the protection of
human rights.[350] Torture, it is argued, represents a 'striking ... affront to
the dignity of the person'.[351] Article 5 of the African Charter explicitly
establishes this link between the inherent dignity of the human being,
the legal status of the human being and the prohibition of torture. The
prohibition of torture is also framed in unqualified terms because the

---

[348] *Ibid.*
[349] Joan Fitzpatrick, 'Speaking Law to Power: The War against Terrorism and Human
      Rights' (2003) 14 *European Journal of International Law* 241, 244.
[350] Universal Declaration of Human Rights, Preamble.
[351] Oscar Schachter, 'Editorial Comment: Human Dignity as a Normative Concept' (1983)
      77 *American Journal of International Law* 848, 850.

drafters recognised, sensibly, that the conduct of torture is not easily translated into a legal prohibition. Therefore, whilst the drafters did not recognise any correlation between the prohibition of torture and the possible use of torture to protect the right to life, this was not necessarily because they could not imagine any such scenario. Arguably, this connection was not made because the drafters understood that there is no causal link between the prohibition of torture and the right to life, which might place these rights in conflict,[352] and because they understood that there are complex reasons behind the perpetration of torture which make it impossible to imagine an exception for 'a good reason'. The Committee against Torture continues to hold, therefore, that 'elements of intent and purpose in article 1 do not involve a subjective inquiry into the motivations of the perpetrators, but rather must be objective determinations under the circumstances'.[353] It follows, then, that the motive of the perpetrator of torture should not, at any time, be taken into account in deciding on a violation of the prohibition of torture. Since the prohibition of torture is designed to protect the individual from deliberate and purposive inhuman treatment by the state, or state-like entity, taking into account the subjective motives behind the use of torture would render the prohibition normatively meaningless.

With the exception of the crime against humanity of torture under the Rome Statute, which eliminates the prohibited purpose requirement,[354] the common criteria according to which a violation of the prohibition on torture is assessed are the severity of the pain and suffering endured and the purpose of the conduct. Whilst severe pain and suffering is inherent to the process of torture, as established by the definition under the Convention against Torture, this element of the definition does not explain how the state acts through the instrumentality of the victim to further its interest or policy.[355] Accordingly, the criterion of purpose provides the most appropriate avenue for distinguishing torture from inhuman treatment, for assessing a violation of the prohibition of torture and, more broadly, for understanding the paradigm of torture.

---

[352] Steven C. Greer, 'Should Police Threats to Torture Suspects Always be Severely Punished? Reflections on the Gäfgen Case' (2011) 11 *Human Rights Law Review* 67, 68. Greer assumes that conflicts between the right to life and the prohibition of torture do exist in certain cases, notably the Gäfgen case.

[353] UNCAT, 'General Comment 2', para. 9.

[354] Schabas, *The International Criminal Court*, p. 167.

[355] Burgers and Danelius, *The United Nations Convention against Torture*, p. 118.

As regards the ticking bomb scenario, it is argued that torture is necessary for the purpose of obtaining information. This is explicitly listed as a prohibited purpose under the definition of torture.[356] The narrative that flows from the ticking bomb scenario, however, asks us to consider the prohibited use of torture in the light of the 'life-saving' motive of the perpetrator. This construction endeavours to disconnect torture, in the exceptional case, from 'other' forms of torture, where the purpose of torture is to intimidate or punish or where the motive of the state or perpetrator is sadistic or otherwise malevolent. This construction also ousts the victim of torture from the frame of perception. Torture, in the ticking bomb construct, has nothing to do with the relationship between the state or perpetrator and the torture victim: it is a matter of obtaining information and saving lives only. In the light of a historical and contextual examination of ticking bomb logic, it becomes evident, however, that the ticking bomb scenario frames torture in a manner that redacts the reality of torture.

---

[356] Convention against Torture, Article 1(1).

2

The ticking bomb scenario: origins, usages and the contemporary discourse

The ticking bomb scenario is at the core of the debate on torture; the use of torture is rarely defended in other circumstances.[1] Particularly since the events of 11 September, this scenario has prompted extensive inquiry into the legal, moral and practical issues surrounding the use of torture as an anticipatory means of preventing the use of unlawful violence and, thus, protecting lives. The ticking bomb scenario has come to be understood both as a matter of objective fact and as a potential actuality and, in contrast, as a deceptive and fantastical construct for considering the use and justification of torture, as it professes to describe a situation that would rarely, if ever, manifest in reality.[2] As a corollary to the practice of torture, the ticking bomb scenario pre-dates the events of 11 September. Understanding its origins and emergence lends insight into how this scenario has been objectified and absorbed as a means of thinking about and justifying the practice of torture.[3]

---

[1] The question of torture's justifiability or excusablity in kidnapping cases has arisen on occasion. For example, a 2002 German case in which a suspected kidnapper was threatened with torture by a police officer in order to find out the whereabouts of a kidnapped child was the subject of widespread debate both in Germany and internationally. The case resulted in a Grand Chamber judgment by the European Court of Human Rights. See *Gäfgen* v. *Germany* (App. No. 22978/05) ECHR 1 June 2010. See also Richard Bernstein, 'Kidnapping has the Germans Debating Police Torture', *New York Times* (10 April 2003); Florian Jessberger, 'Bad Torture – Good Torture? What International Criminal Lawyers May Learn from the Recent Trial of Police Officers In Germany' (2005) 3 *Journal of International Criminal Justice* 1059.

[2] See, generally, Association for the Prevention of Torture, 'Defusing the Ticking Bomb Scenario: Why We Must Say No To Torture, Always' (Geneva: Association for the Prevention of Torture, 2007). See also Bob Brecher, *Torture and the Ticking Bomb* (Malden: Blackwell Publishing, 2007), p. 12.

[3] The ticking bomb scenario is understood as a placeholder for 'necessity'-based arguments for an exception to the torture prohibition. It is not contended here that these kinds of arguments were first made in Algeria. The idea is not to track the history of this scenario but to use historical examples to analyse the scenario.

A.   The ticking bomb in theory and in practice

(1)   Ticking bombs in Algiers?

Whilst it is a tenuous task to attempt to provide the history of an abstract contrivance, the Algerian war does provide a good starting point because of the sustained use of the ticking bomb scenario as a legitimation for the use of torture by the French military and police.[4] During the Algerian war, and in particular during the Battle of Algiers in 1957, torture was used routinely and extensively by the French military and police in interrogation.[5] Members of Algeria's nationalist movement, the Front de Libération Nationale (FLN), as well as those considered to be associated, however remotely, with the FLN, were subjected to torture.[6] The official narrative disseminated by French officers of the Algerian war in defence of the practice of torture provides that its employment was indispensable in frustrating pending attacks by the FLN.[7] The use of torture has been widely accepted as a – if not *the* – critical factor in the overwhelming victory of the French against the FLN's insurgency campaign during the seven-month Battle of Algiers. Alistair Horne illustrates this perspective when he states that torture 'may have won a transient victory in the intelligence it produced but, in the longer run, coupled with protests abroad, it lost the war for France'.[8] Horne is unmistakably opposed to the use of torture, morally and also because it is 'ineffective and counter-productive'.[9] Notwithstanding his opposition to torture, he does accept that the use of

---

[4] The French parliament only officially endorsed the term 'Algerian war' in 1999 to describe what, from the Algerian perspective, was a 'war of national liberation' or a 'war of national independence'. See Raphaëlle Branche, 'Torture of Terrorists? Use of Torture in a "War Against Terrorism": Justification, Methods and Effects: the Case of France in Algeria, 1954–1962' (2007) 89 *International Review of the Red Cross* 543, 545.

[5] Rita Maran, *Torture: The Role of Ideology in the French–Algerian War* (New York: Praeger Publishers, 1989), p. 1; Malcolm D. Evans and Rodney Morgan, *Preventing Torture: A Study of the European Convention for the Prevention of Torture, Inhuman or Degrading Treatment or Punishment* (Oxford University Press, 1998), p. 27; Branche, 'Torture of Terrorists?' 543; Marnia Lazreg, *Torture and the Twilight of Empire: From Algiers to Baghdad* (Princeton University Press, 2008), p. 3.

[6] Darius Rejali, *Torture and Democracy* (Princeton University Press, 2007), p. 482.

[7] For example, in his memoirs General Jacques Massu defended the use of torture in Algeria on this basis. See Yves Beigbeder, *Judging War Crimes and Torture: French Justice and International Tribunals and Commissions (1940–2005)* (Leiden: Martinus Nijhoff Publishers, 2006), p. 117.

[8] Alistair Horne, 'Shades of Abu Ghraib' (2009) Nov/Dec *The National Interest* 23, 27.

[9] *Ibid.*, 29.

torture led to short-term gains because of its successful use as a means of intelligence-gathering. That said, he argues that the use of torture created an avalanche of outrage in France that contributed to French capitulation and that its use had the long-lasting effect of poisoning the system.[10] Darius Rejali challenges the traditional narrative that torture during the Battle of Algiers had been both effective as a means of gathering intelligence and indispensable to the French victory in that campaign. According to Rejali, 'the real significance of the Battle of Algiers is rhetorical'.[11] Rather than providing a powerful example of torture having worked, he identifies the Battle of Algiers as 'the startling moment when modern democracies began official torture apology'.[12]

(2) The Algerian war: legal framework

The Algerian war of independence began in the early hours of 1 November 1954 when the FLN carried out a series of coordinated attacks in northern Algeria against military and police establishments of the French colonial regime, thereby making their emergence known.[13] The war was brought to an end following the successful negotiation of Algerian independence; the Évian peace accords were signed on 18 March 1962, and the war officially ended on 3 July 1962, when France accepted Algeria's accession to independence.[14] The Algerian war, as Malcolm Evans and Rodney Morgan remark, was fought 'with unremitting brutality on both sides'.[15] The war also had a devastating political impact on France and played a sizeable role in the dissolution of the French Fourth Republic and in the subsequent creation of the Fifth Republic and its new constitution.[16] Under the French empire, Algeria, organised into three French *départements*, was tied politically, economically and socially to France and was, thus, considered as part of, or as an extension of, metropolitan France.[17] France's

---

[10] *Ibid.*, 27.
[11] Rejali, *Torture and Democracy*, p. 480.   [12] *Ibid.*
[13] Eldon van Cleef Greenberg, 'Law and the Conduct of the Algerian Revolution' (1970) 11 *Harvard International Law Journal* 37, 38; Branche, 'Torture of Terrorists?' 545.
[14] Shiva Eftekhari, 'France and the Algerian War: From a Policy of "Forgetting" to a Framework for Accountability' (2003) 34 *Columbia Human Rights Law Review* 413, 419.
[15] Evans and Morgan, *Preventing Torture*, p. 27.
[16] Oren Gross and Fionnuala Ní Aoláin, *Law in Times of Crisis: Emergency Powers in Theory and Practice* (Cambridge University Press, 2006), p. 190.
[17] Alfred W. B. Simpson, *Human Rights and the End of Empire: Britain and the Genesis of the European Convention* (Oxford University Press, 2001), p. 284. See also, Eftekhari, 'France and the Algerian War' 418.

commitment to its position in Algeria was additionally strong due to the fact that Algeria was populated by over one million inhabitants of European origin.[18] For these reasons, the French response to the conflict that erupted in 1954 was to treat it as an 'internal affair'.[19] France refused to recognise a state of war and referred to the conflict as 'an "insurrection", a "rebellion", "terrorism" or acts of "outlaws"', to which it responded by way of 'police operations' intended 'to maintain law and order'.[20] France accordingly opposed international involvement in its 'domestic affairs'.[21] Whilst Algerian nationalists did succeed in pushing the Algerian question onto the United Nations General Assembly agenda during its 10th session in 1955, the resolutions adopted by the General Assembly in 1955, 1956 and 1957 were anaemic.[22]

In response to an increase in FLN attacks, on 3 April 1955 the French parliament instituted a state of emergency and declared its application to Algeria for a period of six months. The emergency law extended expansive powers to the local authorities in Algeria and imposed limitations to fundamental rights and freedoms including restrictions on freedom of movement and control of the press and publications of any type.[23] In particular, Article 6 provided the governor general the power to detain without judicial control 'all individuals ... whose activity is deemed dangerous to security and public order'.[24] This provision was used to confine individuals to police barracks and detention centres where clandestine summary execution and torture were carried out.[25] A provision did specify that confinement would '[i]n no case ... result in the creation of

---

[18] Van Cleef Greenberg, 'Law and the Conduct of the Algerian Revolution' 39; Beigbeder, *Judging War Crimes*, p. 93.

[19] Van Cleef Greenberg, 'Law and the Conduct of the Algerian Revolution' 39. France's position was not unlike the position taken by the United Kingdom in Northern Ireland. The United Kingdom was unwilling to apply international humanitarian law 'to an internal crisis'. See, Fionnuala Ní Aoláin, *The Politics of Force: Conflict Management and State Violence in Northern Ireland* (Belfast: Blackstaff Press, 2000), p. 45.

[20] Branche, 'Torture of Terrorists?' 545.

[21] Van Cleef Greenberg, 'Law and the Conduct of the Algerian Revolution' 39; Lindsay Moir, *The Law of Internal Armed Conflict* (Cambridge University Press, 2002), p. 70.

[22] UNGA Resolution 909 (X) (25 November 1955); UNGA Resolution 1012 (XI) 15 February 1957; UNGA Resolution 1184 (XII) 10 December 1957. Stronger resolutions supporting Algeria's right to self-determination were 'consistently defeated' until 1960. See Heather A. Wilson, *International Law and the Use of Force by National Liberation Movements* (Oxford University Press, 1988), p. 66.

[23] Lazreg, *Torture and the Twilight of Empire*, p. 36; Eftekhari, 'France and the Algerian War' 418; Beigbeder, *Judging War Crimes*, p. 96.

[24] Lazreg, *Torture and the Twilight of Empire*, p. 36; Beigbeder, *Judging War Crimes*, p. 96.

[25] Beigbeder, *Judging War Crimes*, p. 96.

camps for the detained persons'.[26] This provision, however, was violated by the military and government authorities 'as early as May 1955'.[27] On 23 April 1955 a second law was passed. This law specified the law of 3 April and enlarged the judicial power of the military courts.[28] The state of emergency was extended for a further six months on 7 August 1955, although that law did recognise the possibility for the state of emergency to be lifted if the situation permitted.[29] On 16 March 1956, however, the French parliament replaced the previous emergency law with an Act extending special powers to the governor general in Algeria. Article 3 stated, '[i]n Algeria the government will have the most extensive powers to take any exceptional measure required by circumstances, in view of [the necessity of guaranteeing] the reestablishment of order, the protection of lives and property, and the protection of territory.'[30] Under this Act special powers were also extended to the military. Article 11 permitted the governor general to 'establish zones in which responsibility for maintaining order devolves to the military, which will assume the powers of police normally exercised by the civil authority'.[31] The military was, thereby, empowered to secure law and order.

With reference to the enactment of this Special Powers Act, Eldon van Cleef Greenberg observes that it 'laid a foundation for any number of atrocities carried out against the rebels, action that would have been unthinkable against common criminals'.[32] Neil MacMaster posits that the Special Powers Act 'provided the executive with an almost totalitarian mandate to introduce by administrative order any form of repressive measures it saw fit'.[33] Rita Maran similarly argues that the special powers granted 'virtually dictatorial powers' to the Republic's functionaries.[34] On 17 March 1956 two government decrees were passed. The first authorised the suspension of freedom of the press and freedom of association as well freedom of movement.[35] The second decree transferred jurisdiction

---

[26] Lazreg, *Torture and the Twilight of Empire*, p. 36; Beigbeder, *Judging War Crimes*, p. 96.
[27] Beigbeder, *Judging War Crimes*, p. 96.
[28] Lazreg, *Torture and the Twilight of Empire*, p. 37.   [29] *Ibid.*
[30] Law of 16 March 1956 [1956] JO 2591 Article 5, cited in van Cleef Greenberg, 'Law and the Conduct of the Algerian Revolution' 53. See also Lazreg, *Torture and the Twilight of Empire*, p. 37.
[31] Law of 16 March 1956 [1956] JO 2591 Article 11, cited in Lazreg, *Torture and the Twilight of Empire*, p. 37.
[32] Van Cleef Greenberg, 'Law and the Conduct of the Algerian Revolution' 53.
[33] Neil MacMaster, 'Torture: from Algiers to Abu Ghraib' (2004) 46 *Race & Class* 1, 6.
[34] Maran, *Torture: The Role of Ideology*, p. 40.
[35] Beigbeder, *Judging War Crimes*, p. 97.

over most offences and crimes from the civil courts to military tribunals.[36] On 7 January 1957 the process by which the French state in Algeria
became increasingly militarised culminated when the police powers of
the entire *départements* of Algiers were transferred by Robert Lacoste,
Resident Minister and Governor General of Algeria, to General Jacques
Massu, military commander of the 10th Paratrooper division in Algiers.[37]
The military was thereby charged with eliminating urban terrorism and
breaking the general strike planned by the FLN.[38] As Yves Beigbeder
phrases it, '[t]he army was in charge'.[39] The emergency regime, applied
from April 1955 onwards, facilitated a policy of repression that included
extensive use of methods such as torture and extrajudicial execution.[40]

With respect to the application of international human rights law to the
situation in Algeria, although France had signed the European Convention
on Human Rights when it opened for signature on 4 November 1950 and
was instrumental in its drafting, it did not ratify the Convention until 3
May 1974. During the Algerian war, therefore, France was not formally
bound by the European Convention. In this regard, Maran, referring to
the Vienna Convention on the Law of Treaties, observes that France, in
signing the European Convention, had indicated its 'intention and willingness to comply with the Convention's terms and, also, not to act to
weaken or negate its terms'.[41] She further observes, however, that this issue
was neither raised during the period of the conflict, nor were efforts made
by jurists or intellectuals to argue that the practice of torture violated the
spirit, 'if not the letter', of the Convention.[42] Maran notes that the Special
Powers Act introduced in 1956 would not in itself have contravened
France's obligations under the European Convention because Article 15
facilitates state derogation from its obligations '[i]n time of war or other
public emergency'.[43] She further remarks that Article 3 prohibiting torture is a non-derogable right under the European Convention and, whilst
the Special Powers Act did not mention or authorise torture, the practice
of torture was a consequence of the state of emergency.[44] Maran, thus,

[36] *Ibid.*   [37] Lazreg, *Torture and the Twilight of Empire*, p. 38.
[38] Beigbeder, *Judging War Crimes*, p. 101.   [39] *Ibid.*
[40] Gross and Ní Aoláin, *Law in Times of Crisis*, p. 194.
[41] Maran, *Torture: The Role of Ideology*, p. 10. Article 18 of the Vienna Convention on the
Law of Treaties states: 'A State is obliged to refrain from acts which would defeat the
object and purpose of a treaty when: (a) it has signed the treaty.' See Vienna Convention
on the Law of Treaties (adopted 22 May 1969, entered into force 27 January 1980) 1155
UNTS 331, Article 18.
[42] Maran, *Torture: The Role of Ideology*, pp. 10, 43.
[43] *Ibid.*, p. 42.   [44] *Ibid.*

suggests, that the situation may have been ameliorated had France been Party to the European Convention during the Algerian war as Algerian victims of torture would have had available a broader forum in which to assert their rights.[45]

With respect to the application of the laws of armed conflict, France had ratified the four 1949 Geneva Conventions for the Protection of War Victims without reservation on 28 June 1951 and was, therefore, bound 'to respect and to ensure respect [for the Conventions] in all circumstances'.[46] Article 3 common to the four Geneva Conventions applied, at a minimum, to the situation in Algeria.[47] Common Article 3 applies to 'armed conflict not of an international character occurring in the territory of one of the High Contracting Parties'.[48] The provisions of Common Article 3 reflect the 'elementary considerations of humanity';[49] they apply 'in all circumstances for the better protection of the victims, regardless of the legal classification of armed conflicts'.[50] Common Article 3, which applies to '[p]ersons taking no active part in the hostilities', requires the humane treatment of detainees, and it specifies the prohibition of, inter alia, '[v]iolence to life and persons, in particular murder of all kinds, mutilation, cruel treatment and torture'.[51] In the early years of the war France denied the application of Common Article 3. Since the conflict was viewed as an internal affair, France referred to it in terms of a 'return to order' and to the opposition as 'outlaws' and 'terrorists'.[52] It had no interest, therefore, in recognising a 'rebellion' as having reached the threshold of an

---

[45] *Ibid.*, p. 43.
[46] Geneva Convention for the Amelioration of the Conditions of the Wounded and Sick in Armed Forces in the Field (hereinafter First Geneva Convention), 12 August 1949, 6 UST 3114, 75 UNTS 31, Article 1; Geneva Convention for the Amelioration of the Conditions of the Wounded and Sick and Shipwrecked Members of Armed Forces at Sea (hereinafter Second Geneva Convention), 12 August 1949, 6 UST 3217, 75 UNTS 85, Article 1; Geneva Convention Relative to the Treatment of Prisoners of War (hereinafter Third Geneva Convention), 12 August 1949, 6 UST 3316, 75 UNTS 135, Article 1; Geneva Convention Relative to the Protection of Civilian Persons in Time of War (hereinafter Fourth Geneva Convention), 12 August 1949, 6 UST 3516, 75 UNTS 287, Article 1.
[47] Elizabeth Chadwick, *Self Determination, Terrorism and the International Humanitarian Law of Armed Conflict* (The Hague: Martinus Nijhoff Publishers, 1996), p. 48. See also van Cleef Greenberg, 'Law and the Conduct of the Algerian Revolution' 49.
[48] Article 3 common to the four Geneva Conventions.
[49] *Military and Paramilitary Activities in and against Nicaragua (Nicaragua v. United States of America)*, Merits, 1986 ICJ Reports (Judgment of 27 June 1986) 14, 114.
[50] Ray Murphy, 'Prisoner of War Status and the Question of the Guantánamo Bay Detainees' (2003) 3 *Human Rights Law Review* 257, 260.
[51] Article 3(1) common to the four Geneva Conventions.
[52] Van Cleef Greenberg, 'Law and the Conduct of the Algerian Revolution' 44.

armed conflict. This issue of the threshold requirement of an 'armed conflict not of an international character' had been extensively debated at the 1949 Diplomatic Conference. In the Commentaries to the four Geneva Conventions, some of the proposals discussed during the Diplomatic Conference are presented as criteria for distinguishing 'armed conflict not of an international character':

(1) That the Party in revolt against the *de jure* Government possesses an organised military force, an authority responsible for its acts, acting within a determinate territory and having the means of respecting and ensuring respect for the Convention.
(2) That the legal Government is obliged to have recourse to the regular military forces against insurgents organised as military and in possession of a part of the national territory.
(3) (a) That the *de jure* Government has recognized the insurgents as belligerents; or
    (b) that it has claimed for itself the rights of a belligerent; or
    (c) that it has accorded the insurgents recognition as belligerents for the purposes only of the present Convention; or
    (d) that the dispute has been admitted to the agenda of the Security Council or the General Assembly of the United Nations as being a threat to international peace, a breach of the peace, or an act of aggression.
(4) (a) That the insurgents have an organisation purporting to have the characteristics of a State.
    (b) That the insurgent civil authority exercises *de facto* authority over persons within a determinate territory.
    (c) That the armed forces act under the direction of the organised civil authority and are prepared to observe the ordinary laws of war.
    (d) That the insurgent civil authority agrees to be bound by the provisions of the Convention.[53]

Eldon van Cleef Greenberg points out that, in the early years of the conflict, prior to the establishment of the Provisional Government of the Algerian Republic (Gouvernement provisoire de la République Algérienne) in 1958,[54] the FLN were unsure of what status to seek. He

---

[53] Jean S. Pictet (ed.), *Commentary I Geneva Convention for the Amelioration of the Condition of the Wounded and Sick in Armed Forces in the Field* (Geneva: ICRC, 1952), p. 49.
[54] Van Cleef Greenberg, 'Law and the Conduct of the Algerian Revolution' 40.

deduces that France's treatment of the war as an internal affair might thus 'seem justifiable'.[55] On the other hand, he also recognises that the FLN exerted territorial control in Algeria and that the military wing of the FLN, the Armée de libération nationale (ALN), resembled an army on paper. He further argues, however, that '[t]he existence of large numbers of terrorists not in uniform and the "unconventional" character ... of much of the war' made it more difficult to classify the ALN as a belligerent army.[56] Common Article 3, however, does not require belligerent status, nor is its application dependent upon the fulfilment of the criteria outlined in the Commentaries. According to the Commentaries to the First, Third and Fourth Geneva Conventions, the outlined criteria are only an indication and, thus, not obligatory.[57] The Commentaries are clear that Common Article 3 'should be applied as widely as possible', since '[i]t merely demands respect for certain rules, which were already recognized as essential in all civilized countries, and enacted in the municipal law of the States in question, long before the Convention was signed'.[58] The Commentaries elucidate that Common Article 3 requires the fulfilment by the state of basic demands for humanitarian purposes, even in a situation that falls below the threshold of a non-international armed conflict:

> What Government would dare to claim before the world, in a case of civil disturbances which could justly be described as mere acts of banditry, that, Article 3 not being applicable, it was entitled to leave the wounded uncared for, to inflict torture and mutilations and to take hostages? However useful, therefore, the various conditions stated above may be, they are not indispensable, since no Government can object to respecting, in its dealings with internal enemies, whatever the nature of the conflict between it and them, a few essential rules which it in fact respects daily, under its own laws, even when dealing with common criminals.[59]

Anthony Cullen notes, however, that 'the main problem with the implementation of Common Article 3 is in the recognition of situations as

---

[55] *Ibid.*   [56] *Ibid.*, 42.

[57] Pictet, *Commentary I Geneva Convention*, p. 50. See also the Commentaries on the third and fourth Geneva Conventions, which reproduce this paragraph with minor changes. Jean S. Pictet (ed.), *Commentary III Convention Relative to the Treatment of Prisoners of War* (Geneva: ICRC, 1960), p. 36; Jean S. Pictet (ed.), *Commentary IV Convention Relative to the Protection of Civilian Persons in Time of War* (Geneva: ICRC, 1958), p. 36.

[58] Pictet, *Commentary I*, p. 50. See also the Commentaries on the third and fourth Geneva Conventions, which reproduce this paragraph with minor changes. Pictet, *Commentary III*, p. 36; Pictet, *Commentary IV*, p. 36.

[59] Pictet, *Commentary I*, p. 50. See also the Commentaries on the third and fourth Geneva Conventions, which reproduce this paragraph with minor changes. Pictet, *Commentary III*, p. 36; Pictet, *Commentary IV*, p. 36.

constituting armed conflict. In such scenarios, governments often find it less expedient to recognise it formally than to treat the conflict as a mere internal disturbance, aggressively suppressing it'.[60] Besides its unwillingness to concede to the existence of an armed conflict at all, France also resisted granting the FLN perceived legitimacy by recognising it as a Party to an armed conflict. Common Article 3 does clearly state, in this respect, that its application 'shall not affect the legal status of the Parties to the conflict'.[61] The Commentaries to the Geneva Conventions state with respect to this clause:

> This clause is essential. Without it neither Article 3, nor any other article in its place, would ever have been adopted. It meets the fear – always the same one – that the application of the Convention, even to a very limited extent, in cases of civil war may interfere with the de jure Government's lawful suppression of the revolt, or that it may confer belligerent status, and consequently increased authority upon the adverse Party. The provision ... makes it absolutely clear that the object of the Convention is a purely humanitarian one, that it is in no way concerned with the internal affairs of States, and that it merely ensures respect for the few essential rules of humanity which all civilized nations consider as valid everywhere and under all circumstances and as being above and outside war itself. Consequently, the fact of applying Article 3 does not in itself constitute any recognition by the de jure Government that the adverse Party has authority of any kind; it does not limit in any way the Government's right to suppress a rebellion using all the means – including arms – provided for under its own laws; it does not in any way affect its right to prosecute, try and sentence its adversaries for their crimes, according to its own laws.[62]

As Cullen observes, therefore, 'a plain reading of the final clause of Common Article 3 makes it clear that the application of this provision has no effect on the legal status of non-state actors and as such does not in any way prevent a *de jure* government from treating them as criminals for their participation in a non-international armed conflict'.[63] On the other hand, Jan Klabbers argues that the final clause of Common

---

[60] Anthony Cullen, *The Concept of Non-International Armed Conflict in International Humanitarian Law* (Cambridge University Press, 2010), p. 56.

[61] Article 3(2) common to Four Geneva Conventions.

[62] Pictet, *Commentary I*, p. 60. See also the Commentaries on the second, third and fourth Geneva Conventions, which reproduce this paragraph with minor changes. Jean S. Pictet (ed.), *Commentary II Convention for the Amelioration of the Condition of Wounded, Sick and Shipwrecked Members of Armed Forces at Sea* (Geneva: ICRC, 1960), p. 38; Pictet, *Commentary III*, p. 44; Pictet, *Commentary IV*, p. 43.

[63] Cullen, *The Concept of Non-International Armed Conflict*, p. 56.

Article 3 contradicts the rationale of Common Article 3. According to Klabbers:

> While Article 3 is intended to ensure that insurgents shall have some spe-
> cial status, the final sentence unequivocally rejects this special status ...
> the law has a hard time making up its mind as to how to deal with the
> insurgents and vacillates between treating them as combatants and as
> common criminals.[64]

Whilst Common Article 3 does, therefore, deliberately avoid the question of belligerent or combatant status, its humanitarian rationale of applying minimal standards is underpinned by the ambiguity concerning status. In this regard, Eldon van Cleef Greenberg points out that there is an underlying political significance in its application. He remarks:

> In a revolutionary war such as the one fought in Algeria, status is the prize
> for which the fighting is waged. Thus in spite of the plea contained in art-
> icle 3 of the Geneva Conventions to put aside (at least to some extent)
> questions of status, this politically is impossible.[65]

It might, accordingly, be deduced that French hesitancy in applying Common Article 3 is attributable to France's unwillingness to accept limitations on its action in defeating the FLN. It may also be deduced that France was resistant to the implied political significance of conferring authority on the opposition.[66]

Under Common Article 3, the International Committee of the Red Cross (ICRC) is authorised 'to offer its services to the Parties to the conflict'.[67] Although France did not (at least initially) formally apply Common Article 3, in February 1955 French Prime Minister Pierre Mendez France did authorise the ICRC to conduct a mission to Algeria, 'although with very limited room for manoeuvre' and with no express statement that the

---

[64] Jan Klabbers, 'Rebel with a Cause? Terrorists and Humanitarian Law' (2003) 14 *European Journal of International Law* 299, 303.

[65] Van Cleef Greenberg, 'Law and the Conduct of the Algerian Revolution' 70.

[66] Cullen, *The Concept of Non-International Armed Conflict*, p. 57. It should be noted that whilst the FLN did claim belligerent status, they did not make any claim to be treated as insurgents. Van Cleef Greenberg deduces that the FLN's claim to belligerent status, and the absence of a claim to be treated as insurgents, was predominantly political rather than indicative of a concern for the imposition of international restraints. See van Cleef Greenberg, 'Law and the Conduct of the Algerian Revolution' 46.

[67] Article 3(2) states that '[a]n impartial humanitarian body, such as the International Committee of the Red Cross, may offer its services to the Parties to the conflict'.

detainees were covered by an instrument of international law.[68] The ICRC offered its services again the following year, this time expressly based on Common Article 3. The French, under Prime Minister Guy Mellot's authorisation, eventually accepted the ICRC mission with the implication that it recognised Common Article 3 to be applicable to the situation in Algeria.[69] From then on the French accepted regular ICRC visits.[70] In the aftermath of the Battle of Algiers, France did slowly begin to alter its perception of the conflict.[71] In March 1958 special military internment centres were established for 'rebels taken captive in possession of weapons'.[72] Raphaëlle Branche remarks that in giving special status to these detainees, there was de facto recognition that their status was comparable to prisoner of war status, although she acknowledges, on the other hand, that General Raoul Salan, commander in chief of the French army in Algeria, explicitly denied the applicability of the Geneva Conventions to the rebels.[73] In November 1959 Salan's successor, General Maurice Challe, did describe the detainees as 'equivalent to members of an enemy army'.[74] It was not until 1961, however, that France finally acknowledged, in certain cases, the applicability of the Third Geneva Convention relative to the Treatment of Prisoners of War. France, under Charles De Gaulle, had by then yielded to Algeria's claim to the right to self-determination.[75] In addition, the Provisional Government of the Algerian Republic had demanded that Common Article 3 be applied 'as a minimum' and had actively pursued international recognition of its belligerent status.[76] The Provisional Government asserted that its forces qualified for prisoner of war status under Article 4 of the Third Geneva Convention.[77] It argued that, under Article 4(A)2, the military wing of the FLN, the ALN, fulfilled

---

[68] Branche, 'Torture of Terrorists?' 546.

[69] Van Cleef Greenberg, 'Law and the Conduct of the Algerian Revolution' 50.

[70] *Ibid.*, 67. In total, the ICRC conducted ten missions including visits to 500 places of detention.

[71] *Ibid.*, 45.   [72] Branche, 'Torture of Terrorists?' 546.

[73] *Ibid.*

[74] Allan Rosas, *The Legal Status of Prisoners of War: A Study in International Humanitarian Law Applicable in Armed Conflicts* (Helsinki: Academia Scientiarum Fennica, 1976), p. 149, cited in Branche, 'Torture of Terrorists?' 546.

[75] Algerian self-determination was proclaimed by Charles de Gaulle in September 1959. On 19 December 1960 the United Nations General Assembly recognised 'the right of the Algerian people to self-determination and independence'. See UNGA Resolution 1573 (XV) (19 December 1960). See also, Beigbeder, *Judging War Crimes*, p. 95.

[76] Van Cleef Greenberg, 'Law and the Conduct of the Algerian Revolution' 40.

[77] *Ibid.*, 56.

the conditions of an 'organised resistance movement'.[78] In addition, on 20 June 1960 the Provisional Government had acceded to the Geneva Conventions.[79]

Van Cleef Greenberg contends that the question of whether international legal norms were actually operating during the Algerian war or merely 'tagging along' is unanswerable or even irrelevant.[80] He argues, however, that 'law maintained its presence' as political factors induced conformity to legal constraints and, consequently, legal constraints shaped political behaviour.[81] In addition, he asserts that the language of the laws of armed conflict was consistently invoked as each side accused the other of breaches and 'officials ... spoke – and acted – as if they mattered'; in essence, there was 'both a recognition of their validity and a degree of compliance'.[82] Branche, on the other hand, seems to adhere to the view that international legal norms were merely catching up or tagging along. She suggests, for example, that France's limited recognition of the applicability of the Third Geneva Convention, whilst politically significant, was inconsequential in humanitarian terms:

> While the Provisional Government of the Algerian Republic could be pleased with its success, the pace of military operations had slowed

---

[78] Third Geneva Convention, Article 4(A)2 states:

> A. Prisoners of war, in the sense of the present Convention, are persons belonging to the following categories, who have fallen into the power of the enemy:
>
> ...
>
> (2) Members of other militias and members of other volunteer corps, including those of organized resistance movements, belonging to a Party to the conflict and operating in or outside their own territory, even if this territory is occupied provided that such militias or volunteer corps, including such organized resistance movements, fulfil the following conditions:
>   (a) that of being commanded by a person responsible for his subordinates;
>   (b) that of having a fixed distinctive sign recognizable at a distance;
>   (c) that of carrying arms openly;
>   (d) that of conducting their operations in accordance with the laws and customs of war.

[79] Van Cleef Greenberg, 'Law and the Conduct of the Algerian Revolution' 64, 57. Van Cleef Greenberg queries the Provisional Government's reliance on Article 4(A)2 and not on Article 4(A)3, which applies to '[m]embers of regular armed forces who profess allegiance to a government or an authority not recognised by the Detaining Power'. He reasons that the Provisional Government may have feared that this provision 'would not cover its irregular forces'.

[80] *Ibid.*, 70.   [81] *Ibid.*   [82] *Ibid.*, 71.

down considerably by that time, and the National Liberation Army ... was much weaker than before. Few ALN soldiers were going to appreciate such a change of heart when people regarded as 'suspects' or 'terrorists' – who had been by far the most numerous victims of the French troops since the outbreak of hostilities – continued to be excluded from the new concessions.[83]

In this respect, Branche contends that elements of the Algerian conflict are typical of many contemporary conflicts characterised by inequality between combatants. The Algerian adversaries were labelled as 'rebels', 'subversive' or 'terrorists', which enabled them to be placed in the position of 'outlaws' against whom a high degree of violence was permitted.[84]

The emergency regime enacted in Algeria could have coexisted with the application of the minimal standards of Common Article 3. However, French ambiguity in recognising the threshold of applicability of Common Article 3 was coupled, at any rate, with extensive breaches of Article 3's minimal standards, in particular through the practice of torture. The safety net of international human rights law, particularly the non-derogable prohibition of torture under Article 3 of the European Convention, which could, in theory, have been invoked to pressurise the French State to bring an end to the repressive measures instituted by the emergency regime, was also absent.[85] Rather than speculating, however, on how the application of Common Article 3 or international human rights law may have prevented the widespread practice of torture, the more germane point to draw from the situation in Algeria is the fact that the French authorities endeavoured to emphasise the non-status of the Algerian detainees. This denial of the applicability of Common Article 3 and other international standards and its effect, whereby the enemy was placed outside of the protection of the law, reverberates in numerous contexts, including the so-called 'war on terror'. The exclusion of certain categories of persons from the protection of the law is particularly significant to understanding how the practice of torture may be justified against those who are not deemed suitable for the protection of the law.

---

[83] Branche, 'Torture of Terrorists?' 546.
[84] Ibid., 559.
[85] For example, Fionnuala Ní Aoláin remarks that the judgment of the European Commission/Court in Ireland v. United Kingdom 'had a deterrent effect on the use of these interrogation techniques, which were the main prop of the machinery to ensure conviction for terrorist offences' in Northern Ireland. See Ní Aoláin, The Politics of Force, p. 56.

(3)   Torture during the Algerian war: the discovery of the ticking bomb

The extent of the practice of torture during the Algerian war is exemplified by the figures that account for the use of torture during the Battle of Algiers. According to Branche, by the end of the Battle of Algiers, under the orders of General Jacque Massu, Paul Teitgen, the police prefect of Algiers, had signed the arrest orders for 24,000 individuals 'most of whom (80 per cent of the men and 66 per cent of the women) were tortured'.[86] Of those individuals 3,024 disappeared, following summary execution or death in interrogation.[87] From her consultation of the archival material, Branche finds that whilst the use of torture was not officially justified in writing, it was 'suggested by the highest authorities and on the whole was both tolerated and encouraged'.[88] General Paul Aussaresses, who served in Philippeville from 1955 and who later coordinated intelligence during the first six months of the Battle of Algiers, confirms in his memoirs how successive French governments had tolerated the use of torture.[89] Marnia Lazreg extrapolates that the routine use of torture was enabled by the militarisation of the French state. This militarisation was upheld by law and effected over a period of eleven months, first, through the declaration of the state of emergency, second, through the granting of special powers to the military and, finally, through the surrender of police and administrative powers to the military.[90]

The use of torture, according to Branche, stemmed from the urgency assigned to intelligence-gathering as a means of dismantling the FLN networks within Algerian society. The war was conceptualised as 'a new kind of war' in which 'the French army undertook to wage a revolutionary war, justified by its adversary's methods'.[91] Torture thus became a kind of anticipatory punishment, used to extract intelligence from an individual who was considered necessarily guilty – 'a terrorist who knew where

---

[86] Raphaëlle Branche, *La torture et l'armée pendant la guerre d'Algérie* (Paris: Gallimard, 2001), cited in Rejali, *Torture and Democracy*, p. 482. Branche's study was informed by analysis of the military archives, which opened in 1993.

[87] *Ibid.* Rejali notes that these figures only represent those who were detained in civilian prisons and, therefore, do not include 'others whom military units tortured extrajudicially'.

[88] Branche, 'Torture of Terrorists?' 547.

[89] Paul Aussaresses, *Services Spéciaux: Algérie 1955–1957* (Paris: Perrin, 2001), p. 155: 'Quant à l'utilisation de la torture, elle était tolérée, sinon recommandée'. See also p. 153.

[90] Lazreg, *Torture and the Twilight of Empire*, p. 253.

[91] Branche, 'Torture of Terrorists?' 549.

the next bomb was'.[92] In practice, however, the justification for the use of torture to prevent imminent attacks crystallised into a more general justification of the use of torture to eradicate any threat.[93] Branche proposes that the use of torture in the interrogation of detainees may have been successful in making significant arrests and possibly even in thwarting planned attacks.[94] She contends, however, that the alleged purpose of torture for obtaining urgent information was a fantasy: 'Far from being a form of violence chosen, in an emergency, to stop a murderer, it came to be an everyday, ordinary form of violence used indiscriminately in towns or in the mountains, well away from any "terrorist" threat'.[95] She claims that the main objective of torture was communicative – torture was a political tool and was employed in order to eradicate the FLN and, by doing so, to communicate French omnipresence and power to an otherwise impenetrable Algerian population.[96] Lazreg similarly considers that the systematic use of torture was not simply a response to FLN terror as claimed.[97] Like Branche, she argues that its use resulted from revolutionary war theory developed during the 1950s by a group of demoralised military veterans of French colonial wars, particularly of the French Indochina war.[98] This theory, according to Lazreg, held that, after the Second World War, a 'new kind of war' was being fought in which conventional armies would have to adjust to guerrilla or revolutionary warfare by implementing counter-revolutionary techniques.[99] Revolutionary war theory thus informed an 'antisubversive war doctrine' whereby the 'twin principles of force and intelligence' needed to be implemented in order to gain 'total control of the population'.[100] Torture, Lazreg maintains, although not initially advocated by this theory, became 'the most elemental expression of the use of force as preventative and anticipatory punishment for "subversive" acts that may not have taken place, in addition to being a routine method of interrogation for intelligence gathering'.[101]

---

[92] *Ibid.*, 550.   [93] *Ibid.*   [94] *Ibid.*, 555.
[95] *Ibid.*, 556.   [96] *Ibid.*
[97] Lazreg, *Torture and the Twilight of Empire*, p. 15.
[98] *Ibid.* From 1947 to 1954 the French army fought in Indochina to regain French control in the face of an effective nationalist movement. The Geneva Agreement of 1954 brought the war to an end with the French having endured defeat at Dien Bien Phu in May 1954. The war was regarded by many French military leaders, who suffered loss of honour and prestige, as a humiliation that could not be repeated elsewhere. See James Joll, *Europe Since 1870: An International History* 4th edn (London: Penguin Books, 1990), p. 449.
[99] Lazreg, *Torture and the Twilight of Empire*, p. 15. See also Branche, 'Torture of Terrorists?' 548 and MacMaster, 'Torture: from Algiers to Abu Ghraib' 5.
[100] Lazreg, *Torture and the Twilight of Empire*, p. 15.   [101] *Ibid.*

Torture during the Algerian war has been comprehensively researched and numerous testimonies and biographies by French ex-military have been published.[102] In spite of the fact that ticking bomb reasoning became the justificatory logic for the extensive use of torture, no example exists of torture having been used in ticking bomb conditions.[103] Rejali remarks that 'no rank and file soldier has related an incident in which he personally, through timely interrogation, produced decisive information that stopped a ticking bomb from exploding'.[104] He further notes that even Aussaresses fails to cite a specific example of torture having been successfully used to extract *vital* information.[105] In Aussaresses' memoirs, published in 2001, he continues to defend the use of torture in Algeria.[106] Aussaresses seems to have found his justification for using torture both in the exceptionality of the situation faced in Algeria and in ticking bomb logic.[107] He describes a conversation in Philippeville, in which a police officer confronted him with a ticking bomb dilemma, as the turning point in his own attitude towards the necessity of torture:

> Imagine un instant que tu soit opposé par principe à la torture et que tu arrêtes quelqu'un qui soit manifestement impliqué dans la préparation d'un attentat. Le suspect refuse de parler. Tu n'insistes pas. Alors l'attentat se produit et il est particulièrement meurtrier. Que dirais tu aux parents de victimes, aux parents d'un enfant, par example, déchiqueté par la bombe, pour justifier le fait que tu n'aies pas utlisés tous les moyens pour faire parler le suspect?[108]

Aussaresses maintains that contemplating this 'parable' removed the last of his doubts. He concluded that nobody had the right to pass judgement

---

[102] Neil MacMaster, 'The Torture Controversy (1998–2002): Towards a "New History" of the Algerian War?' (2002) 10 *Modern and Contemporary France* 449, 451. Rejali provides a list of recent autobiographies by interrogators and torturers. See Rejali, *Torture and Democracy*, p. 749 at n. 5.

[103] MacMaster, 'Torture: from Algiers to Abu Ghraib' 7; Branche, 'Torture of Terrorists?' 550; Rejali, *Torture and Democracy*, p. 545.

[104] Rejali, *Torture and Democracy*, p. 481.   [105] *Ibid.*, p. 491.

[106] See generally, Aussaresses, *Services Spéciaux*. For the English translation, see Paul Aussaresses (tr. Robert L. Miller), *The Battle of the Casbah* (New York: Enigma Books, 2002).

[107] Aussaresses, *Services Spéciaux*, p. 30.

[108] *Ibid.*, p. 31: 'Imagine a situation in which you are opposed in principle to the use of torture and you have arrested an individual who is clearly involved in the preparation of an attack. The suspect refuses to talk. You do nothing. As a result, a particularly deadly attack ensues. What would you say to the parents of the victims, for example, to the parents of a child, mutilated by the bomb, to justify the fact that you failed to do whatever possible to make the suspect talk?' (author's translation).

on their actions and that even if his duties would lead him to do very unpleasant things, he would never regret having done them:

> Une brève méditation sur cette parabole m'enleva mes derniers scrupules. J'en conclus que personne n'aurait jamais le droit de nous juger et, que même si mes fonctions m'amenaient à faire des choses trés désagréables, je ne devrais jamais avoir des regrets.[109]

In his memoirs, Ausseresses' description of torture and of summary execution is far removed from the police officer's dilemma. He recounts that the first individual whom he subjected to torture died during interrogation having said nothing.[110] The torture of another individual, a bomb manufacturer who died under interrogation, confirmed information that had already been gathered during a house search.[111] Aussaresses describes torture in the interrogation unit in Algiers, 'la Villa de Tourelles', as having been systematically used on those prisoners who refused to talk, which, he says, was often the case.[112] According to Aussaresses, the information extracted under torture was used in the discovery of arms, munitions or explosives caches or in making new arrests.[113] His memoirs clarify that torture was employed not as a necessary tactic to prevent imminent attacks but as a routine method of intelligence-gathering.[114] Aussaresses does relate one incident in which Fernand Iveton, an employee at a gasworks and a member of the Parti Communiste Algérien, was caught in possession of a bomb.[115] A second bomb, which he had planted at the gasworks, had not been discovered. Aussaresses describes how this second bomb malfunctioned and, as a result, did not detonate.[116] He does not relate, however, that Teitgen, who was opposed to the use of torture and later resigned in protest at its use, was pressured to have Iveton tortured into revealing the location of the bomb.[117] In his account to Horne, Teitgen stated: 'But I refused to have him tortured. I trembled the whole afternoon. Finally, the bomb did not go off. Thank God I was right. Because if you

---

[109] *Ibid.*   [110] *Ibid.*, p. 44.

[111] *Ibid.*, p. 157. See also William E. Schulz (ed.), *The Phenomenon of Torture: Readings and Commentary* (Philadelphia: University of Pennsylvania Press, 2007), p. 139.

[112] Aussaresses, *Services Spéciaux*, p. 147.

[113] *Ibid.*

[114] MacMaster, 'The Torture Controversy' 452.

[115] Aussaresses, *Services Spéciaux*, p. 85.

[116] *Ibid.*, p. 86.

[117] Franz Kaltenbeck, 'On Torture and State Crime' (2003) 24 *Cardozo Law Review* 2381, 2390. In 1957 Teitgen resigned in protest at the use of torture in Algeria. See Rejali, *Torture and Democracy*, p. 165.

once get into the torture business, you're lost.'[118] Significantly, in an interview in *Le Monde* in 2000, Massu, who until that time had continued to defend the use of torture on the basis of necessity,[119] expressed his regret at the use of torture in Algeria, admitted that it had not been useful or necessary and acknowledged that things could have been done differently.[120] Lazreg concludes that it is not possible to verify the apologists' claim that torture saves lives because this was not the purpose of using torture in Algeria; rather it was used 'to obtain any piece of information that had a bearing on the war'.[121] The number of individuals tortured as well as the various analyses of its systematic practice in Algeria demonstrate that torture was routinely used both for ordinary intelligence-gathering and, more broadly, as a weapon of control in a complex war. The reality of the practice of torture in Algeria shatters the illusion that torture was ineluctable because of ticking bombs.

Rejali credits Jean Lartéguy, a French writer, war journalist and former paratrooper, with having invented the ticking bomb scenario in his novel *Les Centurions*.[122] Published in 1960 as the Algerian war dragged on, *Les Centurions* revolves around the actions of a beleaguered group of French paratroopers, veterans of the Second World War and of the French colonial war in Indochina, who resolve to do whatever is necessary to win their next war – the Algerian war.[123] In one of the novel's pivotal closing scenes, during the fictional two-day-long Battle of Algiers, an Algerian dentist, Arouche, is captured.[124] It is discovered that Arouche, suspected to be part of a bombing campaign, likely knows the whereabouts of fifteen bombs set to explode the following morning, at the start of the general strike, in various European shops in the city.[125] Esclavier, a French army

---

[118] Alistair Horne, *A Savage War of Peace: Algeria 1954–1962* (New York Review of Books, 2006), p. 204; Horne, 'Shades of Abu Ghraib' 27. See also Kaltenbeck, 'On Torture' 2392. It is worth noting that Teitgen had himself been tortured by the Gestapo during the Second World War.

[119] Edward Peters, *Torture* (Philadelphia: University of Pennsylvania Press, 1999), p. 177.

[120] Beigbeder, *Judging War Crimes*, p. 117. See also MacMaster, 'The Torture Controversy' 452.

[121] Lazreg, *Torture and the Twilight of Empire*, p. 253.

[122] Rejali, *Torture and Democracy*, p. 546.

[123] Jean Lartéguy, *Les Centurions* (Paris: Presses de la Cité, 1960). For a short summary of the novel, see David O'Connell, 'Jean Lartéguy: A Popular Phenomenon' (1972) 45 *The French Review* 1087, 1089.

[124] Lartéguy, *Les Centurions*, p. 401.

[125] *Ibid.*: 'Arouche est le responsable du réseau bombes d'Alger. Du moins, tous les reseignements que je viens d'avoir à l'instant le laissant supposer. Demain matin, au moment où commencera la grève générale, quinze bombes éclateront dans différents magasins

captain who is ordered to prevent these attacks at any price, interrogates Arouche under the constant pressure of a clock striking in the background.[126] Esclavier, having failed to reason with the resolute Arouche by relating his own experience of torture at the hands of the Germans during the Second World War, reluctantly tortures him. When Arouche is stretchered away in the early hours of the morning, he has confessed everything. None of the bombs detonate.[127] It is probably more correct to state that Lartéguy adapted to fiction a polished version of the justification that was already circulating amongst French police and military officers in Algeria.[128] Rejali's point, however, is that the Lartéguy narrative prevailed. *Les Centurions* was a bestseller 'to be found on every railway bookstall'.[129] The novel, according to Philip Dine, is 'a particularly important site of literary mystification'.[130] Dine describes *Les Centurions* as having perpetuated the myth of the heroic paratrooper, a myth that was used to escape the complex social and political realities of the war.[131] Rejali considers *Les Centurions* to have provided a more palatable version of events than the reality that France was not willing to face. In contrasting this fictional depiction of torture with the factual practice of torture during the Algerian war, Rejali perceives *Les Centurions* to have 'supplied the scenario that substituted the symbolic violence of the ticking bomb

européens de cette ville. Il ne faut à aucun prix que ces bombes explosent, et Arouche connaît les endroits où elles ont été posées.'

[126] *Ibid.*, pp. 402–6.

[127] *Ibid.*, p. 406: 'Quand, au petit matin, on emporta le dentiste sur une civière, il avait tout dit; aucune des quinze bombes n'explosa.'

[128] As early as 1955 reports emerged in France that torture was being practised in Algeria. See James D. Le Sueur, 'Torture and the Decolonisation of French Algeria: Nationalism, "Race" and Violence during Colonial Incarceration' in Graeme Harper (ed.), *Colonial and Postcolonial Incarceration* (London: Continuum, 2001), pp. 161–2. The French public's attention was really captured and a debate on torture sparked, however, when in 1958 Henri Alleg's account of his torture, following his arrest by General Massu's 10th Paratrooper Division, was published in France. Alleg was a French national and a well-known editor of the communist newspaper *Alger Republicain*. Alleg wrote *La Question* whilst he was still in detention. It became an immediate bestseller and the first book to be banned in France since the eighteenth century. See Henri Alleg (tr. John Calder), *The Question* (London: John Calder Publishers, 1958).

[129] Philip Dine, *Images of the Algerian War: French Fiction and Film, 1954–1992* (Oxford: Clarendon Press, 1994), p. 29. *Les Centurions* was adapted as the Hollywood film *Lost Command*, which, although not commercially successful, was widely distributed in France. See Philip Dine, 'Anglo-Saxon Literary and Filmic Representations of the French Army in Algeria' in Martin S. Alexander, Martin Evans and J. F. V. Keiger (eds.), *The Algerian War and the French Army, 1954–62: Experiences, Images, Testimonies* (New York: Palgrave Macmillan, 2002), pp. 137, 142.

[130] Dine, *Images of the Algerian War*, p. 42.   [131] *Ibid.*, p. 27.

scenario for the messy, wholesale process of torture during the Algerian war'.[132] In this articulation, he identifies the hyperrealism of the ticking bomb scenario. He speculates that, in the aftermath of the Algerian war, the memory of heroic, professional torture to save lives was created, providing a re-narration of events that, in effect, endeavoured to provide a historical amnesia of the routine use of torture. After Algeria, Rejali observes, 'reality embraced art'.[133] In identifying this account of torture as a fiction, he questions how it, and not the real account of torture, has managed to prevail.[134]

(4)   Ticking bombs after Algeria

After the Algerian war the ticking bomb scenario appeared sporadically in academic literature and in the media. In 1973 Michael Walzer cited a ticking bomb scenario as an example of the problem of 'dirty hands' decision-making in politics.[135] In Walzer's analysis of the problem of 'dirty hands', he argues that it is necessary to oversee the moral culpability of the politician who dirties his hands and to assess the moral value

---

[132] Rejali, *Torture and Democracy*, p. 546.   [133] *Ibid.*, p. 547.

[134] *Ibid.* This blurring of fact and fiction, identified by Rejali, was repeated in the aftermath of 11 September, most conspicuously, in the Fox Network television series *24*. This series, which first aired in the United States in 2001 and continued for eight seasons, dramatises a 24-hour period in which a fictional Counterterrorism Agency and the series hero, counterterrorism agent Jack Bauer, must race against the clock to unravel and prevent an impending act of terrorism. Bauer regularly tortures – successfully – in his efforts to prevent the attacks, to the extent that the use of torture often dominates the show's plot. See Adam Green, 'Normalizing Torture: One Rollicking Hour At a Time', *The New York Times* (22 May 2005) 34. The depiction of torture and ticking bombs in *24* paralleled both the debate on torture in ticking bomb situations and the disclosures of the policies and practices of the United States administration with respect to the use of torture. Arguably, this was not so much uncanny as deliberate. In an interview, the show's executive producer, Joel Surnow, informed Jane Mayer that 'the series is ripped out of the Zeitgeist of what people's fears are – their paranoia that we are going to be attacked', and 'it makes people look at what we are dealing with'. Surnow also informed Mayer that faced with an impending attack, torture would be 'the right thing to do'. The interweaving of reality and fiction represented by *24* was starkly recognised when in 2006 a meeting was organised by the non-governmental organisation Human Rights First, between a United States military official and the series' creative team. The objective of the meeting was to ask the show's creators to tone down the use of torture, due to the adverse influencing effect that it was having on cadets in training. See Jane Mayer, 'Whatever It Takes: The Politics of the Man behind *24*' *The New Yorker* (19 February 2007) 66.

[135] Michael Walzer, 'The Problem of Dirty Hands' (1973) 2 *Philosophy and Public Affairs* 160. This article is also included in Sanford Levinson (ed.), *Torture: A Collection* (Oxford University Press, 2004), p. 61.

of his decision-making. Walzer inherited the expression 'dirty hands' from Jean Paul Sartre's play *Les Mains Sales* (Dirty Hands). In the play, the Communist leader Hoerderer asks, 'I have dirty hands right up to the elbows. I have plunged them in filth and blood. Do you think I can govern innocently?'[136] Walzer does not consider that it is possible to govern innocently, nor does he consider the public to suppose that they are governed innocently. He believes that, in politics, dirty hands are inevitable. More than that, he considers dirty hands to be, at times, required. This approach is rooted in Machiavelli's *realpolitik* of ruling and the exercise of power. Machiavelli conceived that it was necessary to learn how 'to be not always good' in order to succeed 'amongst so many who are evil'.[137] Walzer grapples with the moral dilemma that results from getting one's hands dirty whilst doing 'the right thing'. He makes a distinction between what it means to do the right thing in government and what it means to act immorally in government: '[A] particular act of government may be exactly the right thing to do in utilitarian terms and yet leave the man who does it guilty of a moral wrong.'[138] According to Walzer, doing the right thing in a certain situation, even if it means relinquishing one's moral innocence, may be the requirement of office. He exemplifies this moral dilemma with a ticking bomb scenario. In Walzer's ticking bomb scenario, a political leader is faced with the decision to order 'the torture of a captured rebel leader [in a prolonged colonial war] who knows or probably knows the location of a number of bombs hidden in apartment buildings around the city, set to go off within the next twenty-four hours'.[139] Walzer claims that the politician, having dirtied his hands through the commission of this moral crime, although it may have been the right thing to do, must acknowledge and bear this guilt to provide evidence that he is a moral politician: 'If he were a moral man and nothing else, his hands would not be dirty; if he were a politician and nothing else, he would pretend that they were clean'.[140] Walzer's overriding concern is with how 'we' ought to regard this otherwise moral politician who, by torturing, has transgressed his own moral code, and 'ours', 'for the sake of the people who might otherwise die in the explosions'.[141] For Walzer, ordering torture in such an instance is an example of the unavoidable reality, identified by Machiavelli, that politics requires immoral decision-making. Walzer

---

[136] Walzer, 'The Problem of Dirty Hands' 161.
[137] Machiavelli (tr. C. E. Donald), *The Prince* (Ware: Wordsworth Editions, 1997), p. 59.
[138] Walzer, 'The Problem of Dirty Hands' 161.
[139] *Ibid.*, 167.   [140] *Ibid.*   [141] *Ibid.*

rejects the Machiavellian account of the politician with dirty hands because Machiavelli's concern was only with the prudential judgement of the political leader. He did not consider the state of mind, or the penalties due to a politician with dirty hands.[142] Walzer is also not persuaded by the approach of Max Weber. Weber's politician is a tragic hero, who 'does bad in order to do good' but acts with 'an ethic of responsibility'.[143] Having dirtied his hands, he pays the price for his choices through his inward suffering. For Walzer, this inward suffering does not satisfy society's need to judge the politician's actions or to witness the tragic hero's suffering.[144] The approaches of Machiavelli and of Weber fail to convince Walzer because, in both cases, there is no room for imagining the politician's penance or punishment.[145] Walzer prefers the approach taken by Albert Camus in his play *The Just*.[146] Based in Moscow in 1905, *The Just* concerns a group of five individuals whose determination to fight the tyranny and injustice of the Tsarist regime leads them to believe that they are justified in carrying out acts of terrorism, as they resolve to die for their actions, by facing execution.[147] Walzer recognises a crucial difference between the actions of Camus' assassins and the politician who dirties his hands. In the latter case, 'moral rules are broken for reasons of state, and no one provides the punishment'.[148] Walzer might prefer the 'just assassins' approach 'because it requires us at least to imagine a punishment or penance that fits the crime'; [149] however, he admits that there is no way to ensure accountability when official disobedience is at issue. In his proposal for an extra-legal approach to the ticking bomb scenario, Oren Gross encounters the same problem of accountability. With the extra-legal measures model, Gross attempts to develop upon Weber's ethic of responsibility and Walzer's moral politician by providing a mechanism by which the culpability of the torturer may be decided. According to Gross, this question must be decided by the public:

---

142 *Ibid.*, 176.
143 Max Weber, 'Politics as a Vocation' in Hans Heinrich Gerth and Charles Wright Mills (eds.), *From Max Weber: Essays in Sociology* (London: Routledge, 1948), pp. 77, 127; Walzer, 'The Problem of Dirty Hands' 176.
144 Walzer, 'The Problem of Dirty Hands' 178.   145 *Ibid.*, 179.
146 Albert Camus, 'The Just' in Albert Camus, *Caligula and Other Plays* (London : Penguin Books, 1984), p. 163.
147 *Ibid.*, p. 163. A number of the characters in the play represent real members of the socialist revolutionary organisation Narodnaya Volya, which was responsible for the assassination of Alexander II in 1881. See Walter Lacquer, *Terrorism: A Study of National and International Political Violence* (Boston, MA: Little, Brown and Company, 1977), p. 12.
148 Walzer, 'The Problem of Dirty Hands' 179.   149 *Ibid.*

It is ... up to the people, as the sovereign, to determine whether the values, principles, rules, and norms that were violated by such actions are so important, and the social commitment to them so strong, as not to accept any deviation from them. If this is the conclusion that is reached, then the actor must accept whatever sanctions may be imposed on her by the community. Her motivations for violating the law may have been noble, but the final assessment of her deeds (and the concomitant legal implications of such violations) is in the hands of the public.[150]

Although Gross purports to extend the analysis beyond that of Weber and Walzer, in essence his endorsement of an 'ethic of responsibility' is not altogether unlike the conclusion reached by Walzer. Walzer determines that it is only the public who can keep check on the moral decision-making of the officially disobedient state official: 'Without the executioner ... there is no one to set the stakes or maintain the values except ourselves, and probably no way to do either except through philosophical reiteration and political activity.'[151] Walzer warns that, in setting the moral stakes and in maintaining moral values, the public risks dirtying their own hands 'and then we must find some way of paying the price ourselves'.[152] Gross' assessment differs insofar as he places great weight on the public ratification aspect as part of his overall model. Yet, like Walzer, Gross' mechanism for assuring both official disclosure and public involvement is vague.

In one of his earlier writings Henry Shue discussed the morality of torture compared to the morality of killing. He presented a ticking bomb scenario as a potential case in which torture might be justified:

[I]t cannot be denied that there are imaginable cases in which the harm that could be prevented by a rare instance of pure interrogational torture would be so enormous as to outweigh the cruelty of the torture itself, and, possibly, the enormous potential harm which would result if what was intended to be a rare instance was actually the breaching of the dam which would lead to a torrent of torture. There is a standard philosopher's example which someone always invokes: suppose a fanatic, perfectly willing to die rather than collaborate in the thwarting of his own scheme, has set a hidden nuclear advice to explode in the heart of Paris. There is no time to evacuate the innocent people or even the movable art treasures – the only hope of preventing tragedy is to torture the perpetrator, find the

---

[150] Oren Gross, 'Chaos and Rules: Should Reponses to Violent Crises Always Be Constitutional?' (2003) 112 *Yale Law Journal* 1011, 1118.
[151] Walzer, 'The Problem of Dirty Hands' 180
[152] *Ibid.*

> device and deactivate it. I can see no way to deny the permissibility of tor-
> ture in a case *just like this*.[153]

Shue qualified his argument that torture would be permissible in a case 'just like this' by adding, 'there is a saying in jurisprudence that hard cases make bad law, and there might well be one in philosophy that artificial cases make bad ethics'.[154] Shue was clearly unconvinced by the realism of the hypothetical that he had proposed. He pointed out that his hypo-thetical assumed untenable circumstances and background conditions, and he warned of the 'metastatic tendency' of torture to spread beyond the isolated or rare case.[155] Shue's overall argument provided that tor-ture is morally worse than killing by virtue of the fact that the torture victim is entirely powerless and at the mercy of the torturer.[156] He made his objection to the use of torture clear by stating that the prohibition against torture should be strengthened, not relaxed. His argument con-cluded, however, on an ambiguous note. He reasoned that an individual who felt justified in committing an act of torture should face prosecution and that '[i]f the situation approximates those in the imaginary examples in which torture seems possible to justify, a judge can surely be expected to suspend the sentence'.[157]

Walzer's argument that a case for 'just' torture might exist is made on the back of a primary concern with the problem of dirty hands in politics. He provides no critique of the scenario that he uses to illustrate the dilemma of dirty hands. Nor does he engage in a discussion of the legal and polit-ical issues of using torture in such situations. He does make it clear that the stakes would have to be considerably high for torture to be justified, although he is unable to provide an avenue for accountability. Walzer's approach to the question of using torture in ticking bomb situations is to view the question entirely through the prism of morality – 'our' morality. He condenses the complexity of torture into the torturer or politician's moral dilemma, eschewing, thereby, the broader political and social con-text of torture. This approach reverberates in the contemporary debate, whereby the use of torture in the ticking bomb scenario is accepted prima facie as a question pertaining to morality. Shue's approach is also uncrit-ically predicated on the morality of torturing in such a situation. Shue, in his oscillation between an absolute regard for the prohibition of torture and recognition of a possible justification of torture in the rare instance,

---

[153] Henry Shue, 'Torture' (1978) 7 *Philosophy and Public Affairs* 124, 141. As will be dis-cussed later in the chapter, Shue has since renounced this position.
[154] *Ibid.*   [155] *Ibid.*, 142.   [156] *Ibid.*, 130.   [157] *Ibid.*, 143.

illustrates the superficial and vexing question posed by the ticking bomb scenario. In that sense he also provides an insight into the kind of reasoning that exploded in the aftermath of 11 September. Shue indicates a leniency towards the use of torture in certain exceptional cases, although his proposal is tentative and, like Walzer, mindful that the stakes would have to be incredibly high. Whilst both Walzer and Shue were writing conceptually, it is likely, in Walzer's case, that he had in mind colonial conflicts such as the Algerian war, in which torture was used ostensibly to prevent impending attacks.[158] Shue explicitly connects the Algerian war to his argument. Stating that partial justifications for torture are already in circulation, Shue cites Roger Trinquier, a counter-insurgency theorist and proponent of the use of torture in ticking bomb-like cases, who served as second in command to General Massu during the Algerian war.[159]

(5)   The Landau Commission of Inquiry

In 1987 the Israeli government established a 'Commission of Inquiry into the Methods of Investigation of the General Security Service (GSS) Regarding Hostile Terrorist Activity'.[160] The Commission of Inquiry was established in order to make recommendations and proposals regarding the methods and procedures to be used in interrogation 'taking into account the unique needs of the struggle against Hostile Terrorist Activity'.[161] During the first twenty years of the occupation of the West Bank and Gaza, serious allegations had been made against the Israeli authorities concerning the use of force in the interrogation of Palestinian detainees; these allegations were 'consistently denied'.[162] The establishment of the Commission of Inquiry followed the revelation that an Israeli army officer had been convicted of security offences on the basis of a confession extracted under coercion in interrogation.[163]

---

[158]   It is clear from Walzer's later work that he was well versed on the question of torture during the Battle of Algiers. See Michael Walzer, *Just and Unjust Wars* (New York: Basic Books, 1977), p. 204.

[159]   Shue, 'Torture', 124, n. 2.

[160]   'Excerpts of the Report of the Commission of Inquiry into the Methods of Investigation of the General Security Service Regarding Hostile Terrorist Activity' (hereinafter Excerpts of the Report) (1989) 23 *Israel Law Review* 146.

[161]   *Ibid.*

[162]   David Kretzmer, *The Occupation of Justice: The Supreme Court of Israel and the Occupied Territories* (Albany: State University of New York Press, 2002), p. 136.

[163]   *Ibid.*

The Commission of Inquiry found that, since the early 1970s, 'the GSS had used force in interrogation and had systematically lied when challenged in court'.[164] The Commission stated that, whilst the GSS method of giving false testimony in court 'deserved utter condemnation', the methods of interrogation used were 'largely to be defended, both morally and legally'.[165]

The report of the Commission of Inquiry is an extraordinary account of official discourse regarding the possible justification of the use of torture.[166] According to the Commission, the goal of the GSS is 'to collect information about terrorists and their modes of organisation and to thwart and prevent the perpetration of terrorist acts whilst they are still in a state of incubation'.[167] The Commission reasoned that there were three possible options available to them in dealing with the interrogation methods of the GSS. The first was to leave the GSS in a 'twilight zone which is outside of the realm of the law ... freed from the bonds of the law and ... permitted deviations from the law'. This option was rejected by the Commission with the rhetorical reasoning that '[i]f the GSS, with its immense latent power, is not to be subject to the rule of law in its interrogations, who will determine its way in that regard?'[168] The Commission concluded that this approach risked a descent into the 'despotism of a police state'.[169] The second option to be rejected by the Commission was that of the 'hypocrites', whereby the law of the land would be maintained whilst turning a 'blind eye' to the practices of the GSS in interrogation.[170] The Commission decided that the better option was to establish guidelines to regulate the use of special interrogation methods. This approach was viewed by the Commission as the 'truthful road of the rule of law'. The Commission deduced that to achieve its goal of thwarting acts of terrorism by conducting effective interrogation of suspects, the use of pressure was necessary in order 'to overcome an obdurate will not to disclose information and to overcome the fear of the person under interrogation that harm will befall him from his own organisation, if he does reveal information'. [171] The Commission reasoned that '[t]he effective interrogation of terrorist suspects is impossible without the use of means of pressure' and that this pressure 'should principally take the form of non-violent psychological pressure through a vigorous and extensive interrogation, with the use of

---

[164] *Ibid.*   [165] 'Excerpts of the Report' 148.
[166] Evans and Morgan, *Preventing Torture*, p. 42.
[167] 'Excerpts of the Report', 157.
[168] *Ibid.*, 182.   [169] *Ibid.*, 183.   [170] *Ibid.*   [171] *Ibid.*, 184.

stratagems including acts of deception. However, when these do not attain their purpose, the exertion of a moderate measure of physical pressure cannot be avoided'.[172] According to the Commission, 'the pressure must never reach the level of physical torture or maltreatment of the suspect or grievous harm to his honour which deprives him of his human dignity.'[173] As Yuval Ginbar identifies, however, the Commission may have qualified this in its earlier reference to an 'imagined' ticking bomb scenario.[174] The Commission referred to 'an extreme example of real torture, the use of which would perhaps be justified in order to uncover a bomb about to explode in a building full of people'.[175] According to the Commission, the use of 'moderate physical pressure' was justifiable, morally and legally, as a 'lesser evil', under the defence of necessity.[176] The Commission's decision to authorise the GSS to use 'moderate physical pressure' was underpinned by ticking bomb logic. The Commission took a broad view of the imminence requirement for the defence of necessity to be triggered in a ticking bomb-like situation: 'And indeed, when the clock wired to the explosive charge is already ticking, what difference does it make, in terms of the necessity to act, whether the charge is certain to be detonated in five minutes or in five days?'[177] The Commission took the view, therefore, that the use of 'moderate physical pressure' would be justified to get any information that could contribute to foiling potential acts of terrorism:

> [T]he information which an interrogator can obtain from the suspect, about caches of explosive materials in the possession or the knowledge of the suspect, about acts of terrorism which are about to be perpetrated, about the members of a terrorist group to which he belongs, about the headquarters of terrorist organizations inside the country or abroad, and

---

[172] *Ibid.*

[173] *Ibid.*, 187. Ginbar notes that this translation differs from the Hebrew text. He observes that the word 'never' does not appear in the Hebrew text, rather the translation reads as 'must not' or 'prohibited'. See Yuval Ginbar, *Why Not Torture Terrorists? Moral, Practical, and Legal Aspects of the 'Ticking Bomb' Justification for Torture* (Oxford University Press, 2008), p. 175, n. 30.

[174] *Ibid.*, p. 175.   [175] 'Excerpts of the Report' 174.

[176] *Ibid.*, 170–4, 184. At the time of the publication of the Landau report, the Defence of Necessity was provided for in Section 22 of the Penal Law: A person may be exempted from criminal responsibility for an act or omission if he can show that it was done or made in order to avoid consequences which could not otherwise be avoided and which would have inflicted grievous harm or injury on his person, honour or property, or on the person or honour of others whom he was bound to protect or on property placed in his charge: Provided that he did no more than was reasonably necessary for that purpose and that the harm caused by him was not disproportionate to the harm avoided.

[177] 'Excerpts of the Report' 174.

about terrorist training camps – any such information can prevent mass killing and individual terrorist acts which are about to be carried out.[178]

The Commission appears to have concluded that the imminence of the threat to be avoided determines the level of pressure to be applied. In its broad interpretation of a ticking bomb scenario, 'moderate physical pressure' is permissible; in the extreme example, torture might be justified.

With respect to the application of international human rights law and international humanitarian law, the Commission of Inquiry noted that the 'State of Israel is not formally bound by these Conventions'.[179] At any rate, since the Commission argued that 'moderate physical pressure' did not constitute torture or other ill-treatment, it did not consider its recommendations to be in violation of the prohibition on torture and other ill-treatment in international human rights law. With respect to the protections afforded by international humanitarian law, the Commission of Inquiry endorsed the official position of the government that while the Fourth Geneva Convention was not formally applicable, Israel would abide by its humanitarian provisions.[180] The Commission cited Article 31 of the Fourth Geneva Convention, which states: 'No physical or moral coercion shall be exercised against protected persons, in particular to obtain information from them or from third parties.'[181] The ICRC Commentary to this provision provides that 'coercion is forbidden for any purpose or motive whatever'.[182] The Commission of Inquiry noted, however:

> This provision should be read with Art. 5 of the Convention, which deprives a person who is under definite suspicion of activities hostile to the security of the State, or who is engaged in such activities, of the rights and privileges under the Convention, to the degree that the granting of such rights harms the security of the State. Nevertheless, such persons are entitled to humane treatment.[183]

---

178   *Ibid.*, 172.   179   *Ibid.*, 179.
180   *Ibid.*, 181. See also Kretzmer, *The Occupation of Justice*, p. 33.
181   Fourth Geneva Convention, Article 31.
182   Pictet, *Commentary IV*, p. 220.
183   'Excerpts of the Report' 181. Article 5 of the Fourth Geneva Convention states:

> Where in the territory of a Party to the conflict, the latter is satisfied that an individual protected person is definitely suspected of or engaged in activities hostile to the security of the State, such individual person shall not be entitled to claim such rights and privileges under the present Convention as would, if exercised in the favour of such individual person, be prejudicial to the security of such State.
> Where in occupied territory an individual protected person is detained as a spy or saboteur, or as a person under definite suspicion of activity hostile to the security

It is not clear whether the Commission was referring to paragraph 1 or 2 of Article 5. In either case, it is clear from the Commentary on Article 5 that, under this provision, torture remains prohibited.[184] The commentary to paragraph 1 explicates that forfeiture of rights under the provision is limited essentially to 'the right to correspond, the right to receive individual or collective relief, the right to spiritual assistance from ministers of their faith and the right to receive visits from representatives of the Protecting Power and the International Committee of the Red Cross'; the security of the state would, thus, not limit the protection of the person from physical or moral coercion.[185] Paragraph 2 only concerns the forfeiture of rights of communication. The Commentary also clarifies that 'Article 5 can only be applied in individual cases of an exceptional nature, when the existence of specific charges makes it almost certain that penal proceedings will follow'.[186] Nevertheless, the Commission seems to have interpreted this provision as providing for a general derogation from Article 31.

The Commission of Inquiry's recommendations were adopted by the government. The second part of the Commission's report, which established the guidelines and constraints for GSS interrogation methods, has never been published.[187] It was recommended, however, that this part of the report be regularly reviewed by a ministerial committee. With respect to the Commission of Inquiry's recommendations, David Kretzmer remarks, '[t]he Commission apparently assumed that if the use of force were strictly regulated it could be contained and "excesses" would be prevented'.[188] In the years following the publication of the Commission of Inquiry Report, it became clear, as Kretzmer notes, that practices amounting to torture had become widespread in the interrogation of Palestinian detainees.[189] Mordechai Kremnitzer writes, in this respect:

> In the years that followed the publication of the Landau Commission Report, the use of these methods increased substantially, mainly due to the growth in the number of Palestinians interrogated by the GSS after the outbreak of the Palestinian uprising in the Occupied Territories in

> of the Occupying Power, such person shall, in those cases where absolute military security so requires, be regarded as having forfeited rights of communication under the present Convention.
> In each case, such persons shall nevertheless be treated with humanity.

[184] Pictet, *Commentary IV*, p. 57.
[185] *Ibid.*   [186] *Ibid.*
[187] Kretzmer, *The Occupation of Justice*, p. 137.
[188] *Ibid.*   [189] *Ibid.*

1987. At its peak, the number of people who were detained and interrogated reached thousands per year. Moreover, it was common for the GSS
interrogators to knowingly go beyond the directives set by the Landau
Commission Report and the ministerial committee.[190]

Ginbar describes the methods authorised by the Commission as having
been used 'on an industrial scale'.[191] The Commission of Inquiry's recommendations were not overturned, however, until a judgment was issued
by the Supreme Court in 1999.[192]

Unsurprisingly, the conclusions of the Commission of Inquiry were
criticised by national and international non-governmental organisa-
tions.[193] In addition, since Israel had ratified both the Covenant on Civil
and Political Rights and the Convention against Torture, it was subject to
monitoring by the relevant treaty bodies. In its concluding observations
to Israel's State Party Report in 1994, the Committee against Torture criticised the Commission of Inquiry's report for 'creating conditions leading
to the risk of torture or other cruel, inhuman or degrading treatment'.[194]
In 1997 the Committee again criticised the guidelines of the Commission
of Inquiry as in violation of the Convention. In particular, it noted:

> [T]he methods of interrogation, which were described by
> non-governmental organisations on the basis of accounts given to them
> by interrogatees and appear to be applied systematically, were neither
> confirmed nor denied by Israel. The Committee must therefore assume
> them to be accurate. Those methods include: (1) restraining in very
> painful conditions, (2) hooding under special conditions, (2) sounding
> of loud music for prolonged periods, (4) sleep deprivation for prolonged
> periods, (5) threats, including death threats, (6) violent shaking and, (7)
> using cold air to chill, and are, in the Committee's view breaches of Article

---

[190] Mordechai Kremnitzer and Re'em Segev, 'The Legality of Interrogational Torture: A
Question of Proper Authorization or a Substantive Moral Issue?' (2000) 34 *Israel Law
Review* 509, 513.

[191] Ginbar, *Why Not Torture Terrorists?*, p. 182.

[192] *The Public Committee against Torture in Israel et al.* v. *Government of Israel et al.*, HCJ
5100/94.

[193] The examples are too numerous to cite. B'Tselem, however, produced the first report
criticising the conclusions of the Commission of Inquiry and concluding that meth-
ods of ill-treatment constituting torture were being carried out in a widespread and
routine manner by members of the GSS. See Stanley Cohen and Daphna Golan, 'The
Interrogation of Palestinians During the Intifada: Ill-Treatment, "Moderate Physical
Pressure" or Torture?' (Jerusalem: B'Tselem, 1991); Stanley Cohen and Daphna Golan,
'The Interrogation of Palestinians During the Intifada: Follow Up to March 1991
B'Tselem Report' (Jerusalem: B'Tselem, 1992).

[194] UNGA, 'Report of the Committee against Torture' UN Doc. A/49/44, (1993) para.
168(a).

16 and also constitute torture as defined in Article 1 of the Convention. This conclusion is particularly evident where such methods of interrogation are used in combination, which appears to be the standard case.[195]

In its concluding observations to Israel's report in 1998, the Human Rights Committee noted that the guidelines issued by the Commission of Inquiry 'can give rise to abuse' and that the methods that the government of Israel had admitted to using, namely, 'handcuffing, hooding, shaking and sleep deprivation', constituted a violation of Article 7. It also reiterated the non-derogable nature of the prohibition of torture.[196]

The authorisation of the practice of coercion in interrogation by an ostensibly liberal democratic state also sparked academic debate about the legal, moral and practical implications of the Commission's decision. S. Z. Feller criticised the report for its legal and practical defects. He was particularly critical of the Commission's interpretation that the necessity defence could be stretched to include 'a possible future danger'.[197] In addition, he argued that the notion of 'moderate physical pressure' was likely to be rendered immoderate when used on a suspect aware of the limited extent to which such pressure could be applied.[198] Mordechai Kremnitzer condemned the conclusions of the report in despairing terms: 'It is difficult to live with the Landau report. One is tempted to shake oneself free of it, to awaken as if from a bad dream and say: perhaps it never was.'[199] Kremnitzer considered the Commission's conclusions to be inconsistent with Israeli and international law.[200] He was wholly critical of the Commission's improper reliance on the defence of necessity.[201] He reasoned, furthermore, that 'what the Commission describes as "moderate physical pressure" which does not reach the point of torture or degrading treatment is none other than degrading treatment or torture'.[202] In Kremnitzer's view, there are deontological reasons, such as the inviolability of human dignity, as well as consequentialist reasons, such as the danger of slippery slopes and of harming the innocent, which inform the

---

[195] UNGA, 'Report of the Committee against Torture' UN Doc. A/52/44, (1997), para. 257. See also UNGA, 'Report of the Committee against Torture' UN Doc. A/53/44, (1998), para. 338.

[196] UNHRC, 'Concluding Observations of the Human Right Committee: Israel' (18 August 1998) UN Doc. CCPR/C/79/Add. 93, para. 19.

[197] S. Z. Feller, 'Not Actual "Necessity" but Possible "Justification"; Not "Moderate" Pressure but Either "Unlimited" or "None at All"' (1989) 23 *Israel Law Review* 201, 207.

[198] *Ibid.*

[199] Mordechai Kremnitzer, 'The Landau Commission Report – Was the Security Service Subordinated to the Law, or the Law to the "Needs" of the Security Service?' (1989) 23 *Israel Law Review* 216, 278.

[200] *Ibid.*, 255.   [201] *Ibid.*, 233.   [202] *Ibid.*, 252.

prohibition on torture.[203] For those reasons, he stated, 'I would avoid permitting torture ... even in circumstances of concrete and immediate threat
to human life.'[204] The reaction to the Commission's recommendations
was not, however, entirely condemnatory. Alan Dershowitz's response
was to disapprove of the legal means by which the Landau Commission
had justified its conclusions. Dershowitz described the Commission's
conclusions as problematic, not because the Commission had essentially
authorised the use of torture, but because it had done so through reliance
on the defence of necessity: 'The great virtue of the Landau Commission
report is that it raises to the surface a conundrum that few democracies
ever openly confront. The vice of the report is that it purports to resolve
that conundrum by reference to a legal doctrine that is essentially lawless
and undemocratic.'[205]

The three options that the Landau Commission considered in reaching its eventual conclusions are loosely analogous to the way in which
the contemporary debate is structured. The first option of allowing the
security services to deviate from the law corresponds, for example, to
Gross' extra-legal measures model, although Gross is adamant that such
deviations must not be permitted or considered permissible a priori. By
insisting on the candour of the official who tortures and on public scrutiny of the official's actions, Gross attempts, in addition, to avoid what
the Commission referred to as the 'descent into despotism'.[206] The second
option – described by the Commission as the hypocrite's way – is arguably comparable to the position taken by those, like Kremnitzer, who
defend the absolute prohibition of torture for moral and legal reasons,
whilst knowing that torture is being practised despite an absolute ban.
The obvious rebuke to this comparison is that those who defend the absolute prohibition do so because they believe that the prohibition should be
implemented and enforced, thus bringing an end to the practice of torture. Finally, the third option, selected by the Commission and dubbed
the 'truthful road of the rule of law', is, in essence, not dissimilar to
Dershowitz's approach in advocating for the use of torture warrants. In
fact, Dershowitz developed the torture warrant idea in reaction to what
he considered to be the flaws within the Commission's approach.[207]

---

[203] *Ibid.*, 248–54.   [204] *Ibid.*, 272.

[205] Alan M. Dershowitz, 'Is it Necessary to Apply Physical Pressure to Terrorists and to Lie
about it?' (1989) 23 *Israel Law Review* 192, 200.

[206] 'Excerpts of the Report' 183.

[207] Alan Dershowitz, 'Tortured Reasoning' in Sanford Levinson (ed.), *Torture: A Collection*
(Oxford University Press, 2004), p. 259.

(6)   Landau in practice

Between 1987, when the Landau Commission of Inquiry issued its guide-lines on interrogations by the General Security Services, and 1999, when the Supreme Court overturned the system established by the Commission of Inquiry,[208] a number of petitions were made to the Supreme Court concerning the use of physical force during GSS interrogation.[209] In its consideration of these petitions, the Court did not address the fundamental legal position taken by the Commission of Inquiry, namely that the defence of necessity could form the basis for the use of 'moderate physical pressure' by the GSS in interrogation; rather it deferred its decision and, in so doing, 'created an ambiguous legal position in which the Guidelines were neither sanctioned nor condemned'.[210] During this period, the Court was presented with a number of cases in which the petitioner would request an interim injunction ordering that the GSS bring to an end the use of torture in interrogation.[211] In many cases such interim injunctions were ordered,[212] and in other cases the request for an interim injunction was rejected.[213] Of the injunctions that were granted, Ginbar observes:

> [I]n the vast majority of cases where the Court issued interim injunctions to halt the torture, the State did not object ... because torture was used routinely rather than limited to cases where it was deemed absolutely vital; and, at any rate, by the time the case was considered, the GSS would have had ample time – in some cases weeks – to interrogate the detainee to its satisfaction.[214]

In two cases, *Bilbeisi* and *Hamdan*, the Court initially ordered an interim injunction; later, however, each injunction was rescinded at the request of the state.[215] In both cases the Court based its decision to annul the interim injunction on the fact of the state's suspicion, substantiated by the Court, that the petitioners possessed vital information

---

[208] Ginbar, *Why Not Torture Terrorists?*, p. 202.

[209] *Public Committee* v. *Israel*, para. 17.

[210] Eyal Benvenisti, 'The Role of National Courts in Preventing Torture of Suspected Terrorists' (1997) 8 *European Journal of International Law* 596, 597.

[211] Ginbar, *Why Not Torture Terrorists?*, p. 194. Ginbar notes that the term 'torture' was used only by the petitioners and by the Court only when citing the petitioners.

[212] *Ibid.*, p. 195; Benvenisti, 'The Role of National Courts' 598.

[213] Ginbar, *Why Not Torture Terrorists?*, p. 195.

[214] *Ibid.* See also Benvenisti, 'The Role of National Courts' 598.

[215] Yuval Ginbar, 'Legitimizing Torture: The Israeli High Court of Justice Rulings in the Bilbeisi, Hamdan and Mubarak Cases: An Annotated Sourcebook' (Jerusalem: B'Tselem, 1997), p. 4.

that could save lives.[216] David Kretzmer remarks of these cases that
'[r]evocation of the interim injunctions ... necessarily implied that the
use of force in interrogation could be legal'.[217] In the *Mubarak* case the
petitioner argued, and the state admitted, that his interrogation involved
his hands being shackled behind his back in a painful position, hooding, subjection to loud music and sleep deprivation.[218] These methods of
interrogation 'had been used, intermittently, for almost a month'.[219] The
state argued that the use of these methods was incidental to the interrogation and, thus, not physical pressure as such.[220] The Court accepted
the state's arguments, although it remarked that shackling in a painful position was unlawful. The petition for an interim injunction was
rejected.[221] According to Kretzmer, the 'Court's timidity' in these cases
resulted from the difficult situation in which the Court was placed:

> During 1996, when the three decisions were handed down, there was
> a series of suicide bombings in which a large number of civilians were
> killed and many more were injured. In each of the cases the Court heard
> evidence by senior members of the General Security Services who were
> adamant that they could not obtain the information necessary to frus-
> trate further attacks unless they were permitted to use the interrogation
> methods allowed by the Landau Commission. The covert message was
> clear: if it tied the hands of the investigating authorities, *the Court* would
> be held responsible for any future terrorist attacks.[222]

(7)   The Landau model under judicial scrutiny

In 1999 the Supreme Court, sitting as the High Court of Justice, finally
ruled on the legality of the use of certain methods of interrogation
approved by the Landau Commission of Inquiry on the basis of the defence
of necessity.[223] The Court, sitting with an expanded bench of nine judges,
delivered its opinion that certain methods of interrogation authorised
by the Commission did not comply with Israeli law.[224] The Court determined, first, that the GSS were authorised to conduct interrogations.[225] It
then considered the scope of the GSS authority to interrogate and whether

---

[216] *Ibid.*, pp. 7, 13.
[217] Kretzmer, *The Occupation of Justice*, p. 140.
[218] *Ibid.*, p. 139. Ginbar, *Why Not Torture Terrorists?*, p. 196.
[219] Ginbar, *Why Not Torture Terrorists?*, p. 196.
[220] Ginbar, 'Legitimizing Torture', pp. 16–17.   [221] *Ibid.*, p. 17.
[222] Kretzmer, *The Occupation of Justice*, p. 140 (original emphasis).
[223] Kremnitzer and Segev, 'The Legality of Interrogational Torture' 518.
[224] *Public Committee* v. *Israel*.   [225] *Ibid.*, para. 20.

this authority encompassed the use of physical means in the course of the interrogation.[226] The Court noted that 'a reasonable investigation is necessarily one free of torture, free of cruel, inhuman treatment of the subject and free of any degrading handling whatsoever'.[227] It determined that these prohibitions are absolute and leave no room for exception or balancing.[228] The Court subsequently examined a number of methods of interrogation – 'shaking'; 'crouching on the tips of ... toes for five minute intervals'; 'the "Shabach" method', which consists of 'the cuffing of the suspect, seating him on a low chair, covering his head with an opaque sack (head covering) and playing powerfully loud music in the area'; and 'sleep deprivation'.[229] The Court determined that all of these methods surpassed the requirements of a reasonable investigation and, thus, exceeded the limits of the general power to conduct interrogations.[230] The Court subsequently addressed the question of whether the permissibility of the use of such interrogation methods might be inferred, in advance, from the defence of necessity.[231] The Court rejected this inference:

> In the Court's opinion, a general authority to establish directives respecting the use of physical means during the course of a GSS interrogation cannot be implied from the 'necessity' defence. The 'necessity' defence does not constitute a source of authority ... This defence deals with deciding those cases involving an individual reacting to a given set of facts; it is an ad hoc endeavor, in reaction to an event ... Thus, the very nature of the defence does not allow it to serve as the source of a general administrative power.[232]

Having established that the nature of the necessity defence proscribes its use as a source of authority to make use of physical means during interrogation, the Court reasoned that such authority must be prescribed by law and must, thus, be determined by the legislative branch:[233]

> Endowing GSS investigators with the authority to apply physical force during the interrogation of suspects suspected of involvement in hostile terrorist activities, thereby harming the latters' dignity and liberty, raise basic questions of law and society, of ethics and policy, and of the Rule of Law and security. These questions and the corresponding answers must

---

[226] *Ibid.*, para. 21.   [227] *Ibid.*, para. 23.
[228] *Ibid.*   [229] *Ibid.*, paras. 24–31.
[230] *Ibid.*, para. 32. See also Ginbar, *Why Not Torture Terrorists?*, p. 204; Kremnitzer and Segev, 'The Legality of Interrogational Torture' 521.
[231] *Public Committee* v. *Israel*, paras. 33, 35. See also Kremnitzer and Segev, 'The Legality of Interrogational Torture' 522.
[232] *Public Committee* v. *Israel*, paras. 33, 36.   [233] *Ibid.*, para. 37.

be determined by the Legislative branch. This is required by the principle
of the Separation of Powers and the Rule of Law, under our very understanding of democracy.[234]

The Court concluded that should the legislature enact such legislation,
it would have to conform to Israel's Basic Law: Human Dignity and
Liberty.[235] To date, no such legislation has been introduced.

In its concluding remarks, the Court explained the difficulty it had
faced in arriving at its decision:

> Deciding these applications weighed heavy on this Court. True, from the
> legal perspective, the road before us is smooth. We are, however, part of
> Israeli society. Its problems are known to us and we live its history. We are
> not isolated in an ivory tower. We live the life of this country. We are aware
> of the harsh reality of terrorism in which we are, at times, immersed. Our
> apprehension is that this decision will hamper the ability to properly deal
> with terrorists and terrorism ... We are, however, judges. Our brethren
> require us to act according to the law.[236]

Clearly, the difficultly was not with the complexity of the substantive
issue. As Kremnitzer and Re'em Segev observe, 'the Court analyzed the
issue in a way that made the ruling look simple and inescapable'.[237] The
decision was a difficult one because of the reported success of the interrogation methods authorised by the Commission of Inquiry in preventing
acts of terrorism. As a consequence of its decision, it may be argued that
the Court saw itself as a potential source of blame for tying the hands of
interrogators in the case of future acts of terrorism.[238] In this sense, the
Court's decision, as pointed out by some commentators, was a courage-
ous one.[239]

(i)   The ticking bomb exception

Whilst the Court determined that, in the absence of specific legislation,
the use of physical means of interrogation is unlawful under Israeli law,

---

[234] Ibid.
[235] Ibid., para. 39. See also Amnon Reichman and Tsvi Kahana, 'Israel and the Recognition
of Torture: Domestic and International Aspects' in Craig Scott (ed.), Torture as Tort:
Comparative Perspectives on the Development of Transnational Human Rights Litigation
(Oxford: Hart Publishing, 2001), p. 632 (for an analysis of the decision and two alternative interpretations of this 'address to the legislature').
[236] Public Committee v. Israel, para. 40.
[237] Kremnitzer and Segev, 'The Legality of Interrogational Torture' 529.
[238] Ibid.; Kretzmer, The Occupation of Justice, p. 140.
[239] Kremnitzer and Segev, 'The Legality of Interrogational Torture' 531; Kretzmer, The
Occupation of Justice, p. 140.

in the course of its reasoning, the Court also took the position that the necessity defence might be available *ex post facto* to a GSS interrogator who is criminally indicted:

> [W]e are prepared to presume, as was held by the Inquiry Commission's Report, that if a GSS investigator – who applied physical interrogation methods for the purpose of saving human life – is criminally indicted, the 'necessity' defence is likely to be open to him in the appropriate circumstances.[240]

The Court referred to ticking bomb situations as possible 'appropriate circumstances' in which the necessity exception is likely to arise. According to the Court, in such situations, the imminent nature of the act, rather than the immediacy of the danger, fulfils the requirements under the defence of necessity:

> [T]he immediate need ... refers to the imminent nature of the act rather than that of the danger. Hence, the imminence criteria is satisfied even if the bomb is set to explode in a few days, or perhaps even after a few weeks, provided the danger is certain to materialize and there is no alternative means of preventing its materialization. In other words, there exists a concrete level of imminent danger of the explosion's occurrence.[241]

The Court, thereby, established that the use of interrogation methods, declared unauthorised by the Court, might be justified under the necessity defence in 'appropriate circumstances' such as ticking bomb situations.[242] Like the Commission of Inquiry, the Court defined a ticking bomb situation in loose terms. Moreover, the Court did not explicitly state that the methods of interrogation under discussion constituted torture or other-ill-treatment as defined in international law. In addition, having cited the absolute prohibition of torture in the earlier part of the decision, the Court neglects to assess the moral and legal validity of its assumption with respect to the defence of necessity in the light of international standards. As Ginbar remarks, 'when discussing the [ticking bomb situation], international law simply vanishes'.[243] In fact, as Kremnitzer and Segev point out, the '[t]he premise underlying this assumption must be that the use of these measures might be justified from a moral and therefore also legal point of view'.[244]

---

[240] *Public Committee v. Israel*, para. 34.
[241] *Ibid.*
[242] Kremnitzer and Segev, 'The Legality of Interrogational Torture' 554.
[243] Ginbar, *Why Not Torture Terrorists?*, p. 206.
[244] Kremnitzer and Segev, 'The Legality of Interrogational Torture' 557.

The Court did not discuss the implications of this reasoning, although it did make clear that the details would fall to the discretion of the Attorney General: 'The Attorney General can instruct himself regarding the circumstances in which investigators shall not stand trial, if they claim to have acted from a feeling of "necessity".'[245] Following the judgment, the Attorney General issued a document outlining the guidelines according to which he would instruct himself in such cases.[246] The document, according to Ginbar, states that the defence of necessity 'would not apply to any "measure of interrogation the use of which constitutes 'torture' within the meaning of the Convention against Torture"'.[247] For Kremnitzer and Segev the document is no more than 'a general restatement of the statutory conditions of the necessity defense'.[248] However, the Attorney General explains in the document that the decision not to prosecute will depend on a number of factors including 'the command-levels which authorised the act, their involvement in the decision and the reasoning during the act'.[249] Itamar Mann and Omar Shatz describe the document as a 'blueprint for necessity management'.[250] As a consequence of the Attorney General's self-instruction, a 'bureaucratic mechanism' for the authorisation of torture was created: 'according to the Israeli government's current position, torture can be authorised ex-ante by high ranking officials. Yet it remains an illegal, even if un-prosecuted practice'.[251] That torture can be authorised by high-ranking officials was confirmed by the GSS in November 2006, when it published a 'clarification' of its position confirming that 'permission to use special measures during interrogations may only be granted by the GSS'.[252]

(8) 'Enhanced interrogation' in the 'war on terror'

On 14 September 2001 then President of the United States, George W. Bush, declared a national emergency in the United States 'by reason of the

[245] *Public Committee* v. *Israel*, para. 38.
[246] Kremnitzer and Segev, 'The Legality of Interrogational Torture' 541; Itamar Mann and Omer Shatz, 'The Necessity Procedure: Laws of Torture in Israel and Beyond, 1987–2009' (2010) 6 *Unbound: Harvard Journal of the Legal Left* 59, 72.
[247] Ginbar, *Why Not Torture Terrorists?*, p. 208.
[248] Kremnitzer and Segev, 'The Legality of Interrogational Torture' 541.
[249] Cited in Ginbar, *Why Not Torture Terrorists?*, p. 208. See also Mann and Shatz, 'The Necessity Procedure' 72.
[250] Mann and Shatz, 'The Necessity Procedure' 72.   [251] *Ibid.*, 89.
[252] Cited in Ginbar, *Why Not Torture Terrorists?*, p. 208. See also Mann and Shatz, 'The Necessity Procedure' 75.

terrorist attacks at the World Trade Center, New York and the Pentagon, and the continuing and immediate threat of further attacks on the United States'.[253] On 20 September 2001, in a televised address to a joint session of Congress, the president launched the 'war on terror'.[254]

In November 2001 Bush issued an executive order that provided for the establishment of military commissions to try any non-US citizen believed to be a member or former member of Al-Qaeda or otherwise engaged in 'acts of international terrorism'.[255] The issuance of this executive order was rationalised on the basis of the 'danger to the safety of the United States and the nature of international terrorism':[256]

> Having fully considered the magnitude of potential deaths, injuries, and property destruction that would result from potential acts of terrorism against the United States, and the probability that such acts will occur, I have determined that an extraordinary emergency exists for national defense purposes, that this emergency constitutes an urgent and compelling government interest, and that issuance of this order is necessary to meet the emergency.[257]

The order stipulated that individuals detained subject to it 'shall be ... treated humanely'.[258] The authorisation of 'exclusive jurisdiction' to the military commissions[259] was coupled with a policy of removing detained suspects from the protections afforded by international law.[260] In February 2002 a memorandum filed by President Bush concluded that the Geneva Conventions did not apply to the conflict with Al-Qaeda, that Common Article 3 applied neither to Al-Qaeda or Taliban detainees and that members of Al-Qaeda and the Taliban did not qualify as prisoners of war.[261] In regard to the treatment to be afforded to detainees, the memorandum provided:

> our values as a Nation ... call us to treat detainees humanely, including those who are not entitled to such treatment ... As a matter of policy, the

---

[253] Proclamation 7463 of 14 September 2001.

[254] The White House, Office of the Press Secretary, 'Address to a Joint Session of Congress and the American People', 20 September 2001.

[255] Exec. Order No. 222 66 Fed. Reg. 57833 (16 November 2001), cited in Karen J. Greenberg and Joshua L. Dratel, *The Torture Papers: The Road to Abu Ghraib* (Cambridge University Press, 2005), p. 26.

[256] *Ibid.*, p. 26.   [257] *Ibid.*, pp. 25, 26.   [258] *Ibid.*

[259] *Ibid.*, pp. 25, 28.

[260] Ginbar, *Why Not Torture Terrorists?*, p. 228.

[261] George Bush, Memorandum for the President *et al.*, 2 February 2002, cited in Greenberg and Dratel, *The Torture Papers*, pp. 134–5.

> United States Armed Forces shall continue to treat detainees humanely
> and, to the extent appropriate and consistent with military necessity, in a
> manner consistent with the principles of Geneva.[262]

The unavoidable implication of the President's statement was that there existed detainees who were not legally entitled to be treated humanely, which, as Ginbar observes, was 'a sweeping and innovative position'.[263] A further implication of the president's memorandum was the notion that humane treatment, and tacitly the prohibition on torture and other ill-treatment, could be subjugated to the principle of military necessity.[264]

In August 2001 Jay S. Bybee, in a memorandum to Alberto Gonzales, then Counsel to the President of the United States, provided legal advice on the conduct of interrogations under the Convention against Torture as implemented by Section 2340–2340A of Title 18 of the United States Code.[265] Section 2340A of the United States Code provides federal criminal jurisdiction over anyone who commits or attempts to commit torture extraterritorially if 'the alleged offender is a national of the United States' or if 'the alleged offender is present in the United States, irrespective of the nationality of the victim or alleged offender'.[266] Section 2340(1) defines torture as an 'act committed by a person acting under the color of law specifically intended to inflict severe physical or mental pain or suffering (other than pain or suffering incidental to lawful sanctions) upon another person within his custody or control'.[267] According to Bybee, 'the adjective "severe" conveys that the pain or suffering must be of such a high level of intensity that the pain is difficult for the subject to endure.'[268] On that basis, he concluded that for the treatment to constitute torture, physical pain 'must be of an intensity akin to that which accompanies serious physical injury such as death or organ failure'; mental pain, he argued, 'requires suffering not just at the moment of infliction but it also requires long-lasting psychological harm'.[269] Bybee also implied that other ill-treatment was not absolutely prohibited. According to Bybee, the Convention against Torture 'establishes a category of acts that are not to be committed and that states must endeavor to prevent, but that states

---

[262] Ibid.
[263] Ginbar, Why Not Torture Terrorists?, p. 232.   [264] Ibid.
[265] Jay S. Bybee, Memorandum for Alberto R. Gonzales, 'Standards of Conduct for Interrogation under 18 U.S.C. §§ 2340–2340A, 1 August 2002, cited in Greenberg and Dratel, The Torture Papers, p. 172 (hereinafter the Bybee Memorandum).
[266] 18 U.S.C § 2340A(a)(b).   [267] 18 U.S.C § 2340(1).
[268] The Bybee Memorandum, p. 176.   [269] Ibid., p. 213.

need not criminalize, leaving those acts without the stigma of criminal penalties'.[270]

In order to violate Section 2340A, Bybee argued, a defendant would have to act with the specific intent to cause severe pain and suffering:

> [E]ven if the defendant knows that severe pain will result from his actions, if causing such harm is not his objective, he lacks the requisite specific intent even though the defendant did not act in good faith. Instead, a defendant is guilty of torture only if he acts with the express purpose of inflicting severe pain or suffering on a person within his custody or physical control.[271]

In addition, Bybee concluded, first, that the 'application of Section 2340A to interrogations undertaken pursuant to the President's Commander-in-Chief powers may be unconstitutional' and, second, that even if interrogation methods were in violation of Section 2340A, defences such as necessity or self-defence 'could provide justifications that would eliminate any criminal liability'.[272] Through this restricted definition of torture, the qualification of the prohibition based on the specific intent requirement of the definition, the suggestion that the president could, at any rate, order torture and the suggestion that legal defences might be available to interrogators, the Bybee memorandum emptied the prohibition of torture of any value. Moreover, the Bybee memorandum was used as the legal basis for the authorisation of interrogation methods.[273] In December 2002, Donald Rumsfeld, then Secretary of Defense, approved of a number of counter-resistance techniques, including stress positions, to be used in the interrogation of detainees at the Guantánamo Bay detention facility.[274] It is now known that the techniques of interrogation, authorised by Rumsfeld, also migrated to Iraq and, specifically to Abu Ghraib prison.[275]

Following the disclosure of the Abu Ghraib photographs in April 2004,[276] in June 2004, the Bybee memorandum, which had been leaked

---

[270] *Ibid.*, p. 185.   [271] *Ibid.*, p. 175.   [272] *Ibid.*, p. 213.

[273] Manfred Nowak, 'What Practices Constitute Torture? US and UN Standards' (2006) 28 *Human Rights Quarterly* 809, 812.

[274] William J. Haynes, General Counsel, Memorandum for Secretary of Defense, 27 November 2002, cited in Greenberg and Dratel, *The Torture Papers*, pp. 236, 237.

[275] Jordan J. Paust, 'Above the Law: Unlawful Executive Authorizations Regarding Detainee Treatment, Secret Renditions, Domestic Spying, and Claims to Unchecked Executive Power' (2007) 2 *Utah Law Review* 345, 348.

[276] Nowak, 'What Practices Constitute Torture?' 815.

to the press,[277] was withdrawn.[278] In December 2004 it was replaced with a memorandum written by Daniel Levin, then Acting Assistant Attorney General, which superseded 'the August 2002 Memorandum in its entirety'.[279] The Levin memorandum rejected Bybee's interpretation of 'severe mental pain and suffering',[280] but did not substantially broaden the statutory definition.[281] Rather it interpreted severe to mean 'intense and of extended duration'.[282] Thus, it continued to hold that the intensity of pain or suffering is the distinguishing criterion for an act to constitute torture.[283] The Levin memorandum did not discuss other forms of ill-treatment and thus, like the Bybee memorandum, left the impression that 'only torture is absolutely prohibited under US law'.[284] According to the Levin memorandum, it was not useful to precisely define 'specific intent'.[285] The memorandum did, however, expressly distinguish between specific intent and motive: 'There is no exception under the statute permitting torture to be used for a "good reason". Thus, a defendant's motive (to protect national security, for example) is not relevant to the question whether he has acted with the requisite specific intent under the statute.'[286] Levin considered it unnecessary to deal with the question of the president's constitutional authority to authorise torture and of the possible availability of defences to torture:

> Because the discussion in that memorandum concerning the President's Commander-in-Chief power and the potential defenses to liability was – and remains – unnecessary, it has been eliminated from the analysis that follows. Consideration of the bounds of any such authority would be inconsistent with the President's unequivocal directive that United States personnel not engage in torture.[287]

The memorandum consequently skirted the substantive claims made by the Bybee memorandum on these two issues.[288] As evidenced by the

---

[277] Alfred W. McCoy, *A Question of Torture: CIA Interrogation: From the Cold War to the War on Terror* (New York: Metropolitan Books, 2006), p. 144.

[278] John R. Crook (ed.), 'Contemporary Practice of the United States Relating to International Law' (2005) 99 *American Journal of International Law* 479.

[279] Daniel Levin, Acting Assistant Attorney General, Memorandum for James B. Comey, Deputy Attorney General (30 December 2004) (hereinafter Levin Memorandum).

[280] *Ibid.*, p. 2.

[281] David Luban, 'Liberalism, Torture, and the Ticking Bomb' (2005) 91 *Virginia Law Review* 1425, 1457.

[282] Seth F. Kreimer, '"Torture Lite," "Full Bodied" Torture, and the Insulation of Legal Conscience' (2005) 1 *Journal of National Security Law and Policy* 187, 199.

[283] Nowak, 'What Practices Constitute Torture?' 815.   [284] *Ibid.*

[285] Levin Memorandum, p. 16.   [286] *Ibid.*, p. 17.   [287] *Ibid.*, p. 2.

[288] Harold Hongju Hoh, 'Can the President Be Torturer in Chief?' (2005) 81 *Indiana Law Journal* 1145, 1151.

president's directive, the memorandum cited the president's statement on the United Nations International Day in Support of Victims of Torture in June 2004: 'America stands against and will not tolerate torture. We will investigate and prosecute all acts of torture ... in all territory under our jurisdiction ... Torture is wrong no matter where it occurs, and the United States will continue to lead the fight to eliminate it everywhere.'[289] The Levin memorandum suggested, therefore, that analysis of the underpinning legal reasoning was unnecessary because the president opposed torture.[290] As Ginbar remarks, 'this appears more like a claim that the President can be trusted not to exercise his authority to order torture than that he lacks such authority'.[291] Ultimately, therefore, the Levin memorandum appeared to support the Bybee memorandum's claim that the president has the ultimate authority to decide.[292]

Manfred Nowak observes that whilst the Bybee memorandum was withdrawn, the interrogation techniques authorised on the basis of its flawed legal analysis 'remained in force and continued to be applied in practice'.[293] However, on 31 December 2005 the Detainee Treatment Act was passed, introducing uniform standards for the interrogation of persons under the detention of the Department of Defense.[294] According to Section 1002(a), 'no person in the custody or under the effective control of the Department of Defense or under detention in a Department of Defense facility shall be subject to any treatment or technique of interrogation not authorized by and listed in the United States Army Field Manual on Intelligence Interrogation'.[295] A new Army Field Manual was issued in September 2006.[296] The manual provides, on a number of occasions, for the prohibition of torture and other cruel, inhuman and degrading treatment.[297] In addition, it specifically prohibits a number of interrogation methods including, but not limited to, sexual humiliation; hooding; beatings, electric shocks or other forms of physical pain; 'waterboarding'; the use of military dogs; inducing hypothermia or heat injury;

---

[289] Levin Memorandum, p. 2, n. 7.
[290] Luban, 'Liberalism, Torture, and the Ticking Bomb' 1457.
[291] Ginbar, *Why Not Torture Terrorists?*, p. 232. See also Hoh, 'Can the President Be Torturer in Chief?' 1151.
[292] Ginbar, *Why Not Torture Terrorists?*, p. 232.
[293] Nowak, 'What Practices Constitute Torture?' 816.
[294] Detainee Treatment Act, Pub. L. No. 109–148, Tit. X, 119 Stat. 2739 (2005). See also Nowak, 'What Practices Constitute Torture?' 816.
[295] Detainee Treatment Act, section 1002(a).
[296] Headquarters, Department of the Army, *Human Intelligence Collector Operations* FM 2-22.3 (FM 34–52) (Washington, 6 December 2006).
[297] *Ibid.*, ss. 4–41, 5–73, 5–74, 6–20, 6–23.

mock executions; and dietary restriction.[298] The Detainee Treatment Act of 2005 also provides in Section 1003(a) that '[n]o individual in the custody or under the physical control of the United States Government, regardless of nationality or physical location, shall be subject to cruel, inhuman, or degrading treatment or punishment'.[299] The Act provides, however, for a legal defence to US officials and agents involved in the detention and interrogation of detainees who risk civil action or criminal prosecution:

> [I]t shall be a defense that such officer, employee, member of the Armed Forces, or other agent did not know that the practices were unlawful and a person of ordinary sense and understanding would not know the practices were unlawful. Good faith reliance on advice of counsel should be an important factor, among others, to consider in assessing whether a person of ordinary sense and understanding would have known the practices to be unlawful. Nothing in this section shall be construed to limit or extinguish any defense or protection otherwise available to any person or entity from suit, civil or criminal liability, or damages, or to provide immunity from prosecution for any criminal offense by the proper authorities.[300]

The Military Commissions Act introduced in 2006 amended this good faith defence to cover 'actions occurring between September 11, 2001, and December 30, 2005'.[301]

M. Cherif Bassiouni describes the Bush administration as having 'developed a policy of institutionalized torture'.[302] He argues that, whilst the making of legal policy in the United States is the prerogative of the legislature, the 'torture-enabling policy' instituted by the Bush administration 'was in some respect a subversion of the legislative powers of Congress'.[303] He recognises, therefore, that the policy was not authorised pursuant to legislation, as such. However, he maintains that through its interpretation of the law, the Bush administration 'simply re-wrote the law'.[304] Owing to

---

[298] *Ibid.*, s. 5–75.
[299] Detainee Treatment Act, section 1003(a). This general ban on cruel, inhuman or degrading treatment or punishment is limited, in section 1003(d) to: cruel, unusual, and inhumane treatment or punishment prohibited by the Fifth, Eighth, and Fourteenth Amendments to the Constitution of the United States, as defined in the United States Reservations, Declarations and Understandings to the United Nations Convention Against Torture and Other Forms of Cruel, Inhuman or Degrading Treatment or Punishment done at New York, December 10, 1984.
[300] Detainee Treatment Act, s. 1004(a).
[301] Military Commissions Act of 2006 Pub. Law No. 109–366 120 STAT 2600.
[302] M. Cherif Bassiouni, *The Institutionalisation of Torture by the Bush Administration: Is Anyone Responsible?* (Antwerp: Intersentia, 2010), p. 2.
[303] *Ibid.*, p. 109.   [304] *Ibid.*

the issuance of a number of governmental memoranda, Bush administration policies were enabled, approving of practices that would ordinarily be illegal.[305] Bassiouni characterises this policy as 'a hub-like conspiracy'[306] and 'subterfuge'.[307] He further contends that these 'torture-enabling' policies were allowed to stand as a consequence of inaction from the legislative and judicial branches:

> Even though the subterfuge was transparent to so many, it was not met with much if any opposition by the Legislative branch, or for that matter by the Judicial branch, whose role in this case would not have been to oppose government policy, but to simply interpret it as being in violation of the Constitution and laws of the United States. The failure of these two branches of government to carry out their constitutional responsibilities is what allowed the Executive branch to abuse its power and subvert the law.[308]

Bassiouni explains the failure of the legislative and judicial branches as a consequence of the ineffectiveness of 'the constitutional framework of checks and balances within the American political system'.[309]

Ginbar characterises the policies and practices of the US government with respect to the prohibition of torture as 'quasi-legalized torture'.[310] He employs the prefix 'quasi' because, he argues, there is an insufficient 'full-proof basis' to demonstrate 'a real, or a full, model of legalised torture':[311]

> No laws have so far been promulgated explicitly allowing the brutalization of terrorist suspects, nor have any courts explicitly interpreted existing US legislation as so allowing. Nor yet have any courts directly improved any such interpretation of the law by the government, or for that matter any acts of torture in the interrogation of terrorist suspects.[312]

Ginbar identifies four reasons in support of his view that torture was 'quasi-legalized'. First, the memoranda written by government lawyers broadly interpreting the provisions concerning the constitutional authority of the president and, thus, arguing that torture could be legally sanctioned, became 'official (albeit confidential) policy'.[313] Second, interrogation methods – 'some of which have been described as torture by international human rights monitoring mechanisms, the ICRC and international experts, at least with the accumulation of time

[305] *Ibid.*   [306] *Ibid.*, p. 2.   [307] *Ibid.*, p. 109.
[308] *Ibid.*   [309] *Ibid.*, p. 140.
[310] Ginbar, *Why Not Torture Terrorists?*, p. 226.
[311] *Ibid.*, pp. 225–6.   [312] *Ibid.*, p. 225.   [313] *Ibid.*

and methods' – were approved by the US Secretary of Defense; the CIA was authorised to use such techniques whilst holding detainees in secret detention.[314] Third, the Detainee Treatment Act, passed in 2005, and the Military Commissions Act, passed in 2006, effectively exempt 'past torturers (not so named) from criminal liability, thus adding a total-immunity dimension'.[315] Fourth, 'the US administration has consistently interpreted this legislation and relevant international legal provisions, as allowing the use of methods which …. may amount to torture.'[316] Since Ginbar published his text, the Obama administration has rejected the policies and practices of 'enhanced interrogation' implemented by the Bush administration.[317] Obama has, however, remained committed to a no prosecution policy with respect to agents who acted under the official authorisation of the Bush administration.[318] In that sense, Ginbar's analysis continues to apply.

The torture-relevant policies pursued in the aftermath of 11 September in the United States were predicated on the efforts to manipulate the torture prohibition coupled with the pursuit of emergency rationale centred on the need to obtain information about impending attacks.

B.   Debating torture

(1)   *The ticking bomb construct*

Whilst the ticking bomb scenario is central to the debate on torture, it is also argued that it is an artificial construct, unlikely to manifest in reality and an inappropriate basis on which to construe a moral or legal justification for torture. Shue, in a revision of the ambiguous position that he had taken with respect to the ticking bomb scenario in 1978, argues that imaginary examples like the ticking bomb hypothetical are misleading insofar as they both idealise and abstract.[319] Such constructs, he argues, are idealised through the addition of positive features that make them more concrete than is likely under real circumstances. They abstract from reality insofar as the negative features are removed in order to make the example better than reality: 'Idealisation adds sparkle, abstraction

---

[314]   *Ibid.*, p. 226.   [315]   *Ibid.*, pp. 226, 252–5.   [316]   *Ibid.*, p. 226.
[317]   Exec. Order No. 13491, 74 Fed. Reg. 4893 (27 January 2009).
[318]   See n. 87 and accompanying text in Introduction.
[319]   Henry Shue, 'Torture in Dreamland: Disposing of the Ticking Bomb' (2006) 37 *Case Western Reserve Journal of International Law* 231.

removes dirt.'[320] Shue argues that the ticking bomb scenario idealises by claiming that 'the right man' is in custody and that he will promptly and accurately disclose information under torture.[321] It further idealises by claiming that torture will only be used in this 'rare, isolated case'.[322] According to Shue, the ticking bomb scenario abstracts from the reality that torture requires institutional competence – proper administration, thus, trained torturers.[323] Shue concludes by taking 'the most moderate position on torture ... feasible in the real world ... Never, ever, exactly as international law indisputably requires'.[324] Similarly, David Luban argues that the ticking bomb 'cheats its way around ... [the] difficulties by stipulating that the bomb is there, ticking away, and that officials know it and know they have the man who planted it'.[325] He points out that these exact circumstances will seldom arise.[326]

These arguments may embrace some compelling points that do expose the flaws of the hypothetical. It has become clear, however, that they are incapable of wholly disposing of the ticking bomb scenario as a justification for torture. In reference to Shue, Gross challenges the idea that the ticking bomb scenario is entirely artificial:

> They are real, albeit rare. Ignoring them completely, by rhetorically relegating them to the level of 'artificial', is utopian or naïve, at best. There is a difference between ignoring completely the truly catastrophic cases and focusing our attention elsewhere when designing general rules and policies. We can address the real conundrums presented by such cases in other ways.[327]

Gross is attentive here to the dangers of drawing policy from an artificial or extremely rare case, but, equally, he is unwilling to use this as a general motive to avoid preparation for the catastrophic case. Whilst Shue does not deny the potential occurrence of such a scenario, he does not believe that torture should be used in such a situation: '[i]f the perfect time for torture comes, and we are not prepared to prevent a terroristic catastrophe, we will at least know that we have not sold our souls and we have not

---

[320] *Ibid.*   [321] *Ibid.*, 233.   [322] *Ibid.*

[323] *Ibid.*, 237. This argument does not necessarily strengthen the case against ticking bomb rationale. For example, Rejali writes that most torturers do not report receiving formal training. See Rejali, *Torture and Democracy*, p. 28.

[324] Shue, 'Torture in Dreamland' 238.

[325] Luban, 'Liberalism, Torture, and the Ticking Bomb' 1442.   [326] *Ibid.*

[327] Oren Gross, 'The Prohibition on Torture and the Limits of the Law' in Sanford Levinson (ed.), *Torture: A Collection* (Oxford University Press, 2004), p. 234.

brutalised the civilisation.'[328] The hypothetical remains because, even if it can be proven to be historically inexistent (intelligence obstacles aside), it cannot be empirically proven to be impossible. Moreover, it is the hypothetical that sustains the debate. As Luban highlights, '[e]veryone argues the pros and cons of torture through the ticking time bomb'.[329] Luban characterises the ticking time bomb as seductive, misrepresentative, bewitching.[330] He does not deny the real life potentiality of the time-bomb scenario, but he is wary of its deceit. Like Shue and others, he considers 'ticking bomb stories' to be 'built on a set of assumptions that amount to intellectual fraud'.[331] Yet his uneasiness with the ticking bomb rationale extends beyond its having implicit oversights. Luban does not engage and discuss the merits, pros and cons of the ticking bomb scenario because he views it as flagging a liberal ideology of torture: '[t]icking bomb stories depict torture as an emergency exception, but use intuitions based on the exceptional case to justify institutional practices and procedures of torture.'[332] His concern is that the ticking bomb scenario is, inherently, access to a liberal discussion of exception to the torture prohibition, and ultimately to torture as a practice. He observes that 'the ticking bomb begins by denying that torture belongs to liberal culture, and ends by constructing a torture culture'.[333]

A gap exists between talking about torture in the exceptional circumstance through ticking bomb logic and talking about the reality of torture – its practice. Luban posits that the ticking bomb is much more welcome in liberal discussion than talking about the actual practice of torture:

> [E]ven though absolute prohibition remains liberalism's primary teaching about torture, and the basic liberal stance is empathy for the torture victim, a more permissive stance remains an unspoken possibility, the Achilles heel of absolute prohibitions. As long as the intelligence needs of a liberal society are slight, this possibility within liberalism remains dormant, perhaps even unnoticed. But when a catastrophe like 9/11 happens, liberals may cautiously conclude that … it is 'Time to Think About Torture'.[334]

For Luban, the prohibition of torture is absolute in the liberal democracy only to the extent that absolute does not contradict the state's intelligence

---

[328] Shue, 'Torture in Dreamland' 239.
[329] Luban, 'Liberalism, Torture, and the Ticking Bomb', 1440.
[330] *Ibid.*, 1441.   [331] *Ibid.*, 1440.   [332] *Ibid.*, 1427.
[333] *Ibid.*   [334] *Ibid.*, 1439.

needs. There is, therefore, an inherent vulnerability in the prohibition vis-à-vis liberalism. This vulnerability is usually suppressed, but when there is a need for intelligence the demand for exceptional use of torture arises; torture becomes thought about and debated. The ticking bomb portrays this vulnerability in a liberally acceptable way: a 'highly stylised and artificial way',[335] with the ticking bomb scenario crystallising all of the ideas that liberalism employs to justify permissiveness:

> The liberal ideology insists that the sole purpose of torture must be intelligence gathering to prevent the catastrophe; that torturing is the exception, not the rule so that it has nothing to do with state tyranny; that those who inflict the torture are motivated solely by the looming catastrophe, with no tincture of cruelty; that torture in such circumstances is, in fact, little more than self-defense; and that, because of the association of torture with the horrors of yesteryear, perhaps one should not even call harsh interrogation 'torture'.[336]

As such, the debate on torture attempts to make torture acceptable in the liberal democracy through the ticking bomb scenario. Luban appreciates this scenario as little more than an escape route from the reality of torture. He argues that ticking bomb logic creates a culture of torture that is far from liberal.[337] In her response to Alan Dershowitz's torture warrant proposal, Elaine Scarry makes a similar point. She considers it necessary to confront the ticking bomb dilemma because of its frequent invocation not just by academics but also by policy-makers. She is sceptical, however, that the ticking bomb can provide 'an accurate understanding of torture' and argues, rather, that it 'opportunistically provides a flexible shield whose outcome is a systematic defense of torture'.[338]

Luban argues that the ticking bomb scenario is proffered to force the liberal prohibitionist to undo a principled approach and to admit that torture is justifiable in this scenario. Having loosened one's moral guard against the prohibition's breach, the individual is stripped of the moral high ground and is on a par with the torture apologist.[339] According to Luban, '[d]ialectically, getting the prohibitionist to address the ticking bomb is like getting the vegetarian to eat just one little oyster because it has no nervous system. Once she does that – gotcha!'[340] Rejali views the

---

[335] *Ibid.*   [336] *Ibid.*   [337] *Ibid.*, 1453.

[338] Elaine Scarry, 'Five Errors in the Reasoning of Alan Dershowitz' in Sanford Levinson (ed.), *Torture: A Collection* (Oxford University Press, 2004), p. 281.

[339] Luban, 'Liberalism, Torture, and the Ticking Bomb' 1440.

[340] *Ibid.*, 1427.

ticking bomb scenario as a kind of test. He argues that this scenario provides an avenue for the reassertion of 'manliness' in the democratic society by feeding 'on a long-felt, common anxiety that democracy has made us weak and there are no real men anymore'.[341] In the face of a threat that takes advantage of democracy's perceived 'weaknesses', stepping up to the mark is, therefore, seen as essential.[342] Jeremy Waldron argues that it is difficult to defend any moral absolute, including the absolute torture prohibition, in a society that squirms at the idea of holding such absolutes. He comments that '[e]xtreme circumstances can make moral absolutes look ridiculous', and in an effort to not seem unrealistic, even deontologists can be quick to cast off absolute values.[343] In other words, overt pressure to accept less than absolute is combined with a more esoteric impulse to resist absolutes.

Matthew Hannah contends that the ticking bomb scenario is a 'discursive construction' that explains, to a significant extent, both the United States' administration policy since the events of 11 September and the American public's tolerance of that policy.[344] He argues that the ticking bomb scenario becomes the yardstick for official and public understanding of the threat posed by terrorism and, in this ticking bomb guise, the threat is considered to be an unacceptable one, thus making torture seem like a reasonable response: 'The ticking-bomb scenario prompts a reimagining of the landscape of everyday life as suffused with an unacceptably high level of risk.'[345] Hannah regards the ticking bomb scenario as having become the touchstone for interpreting the inflated threat of terrorism – 'anytime, anywhere' – a threat that is considered too much to bear. He concedes that this rationalisation of the ticking bomb might better explain the complacency of the public (regarding the practice of torture) than it does the Bush administration's motives (for having debated and authorised torture).[346] He considers it to nevertheless offer a plausible account for the latter, given the dearth of alternative explanations.[347] Whilst Hannah's point, that there is insufficient explanation as to why the ticking bomb scenario is invoked by policy-makers, may be valid, his argument gives the ticking bomb scenario an objective value – arising solely from

---

[341] Rejali, *Torture and Democracy*, p. 548.   [342] *Ibid.*
[343] Jeremy Waldron, 'Torture and Positive Law: Jurisprudence for the White House' (2005) 105 *Columbia Law Review* 1681, 1712.
[344] Matthew Hannah, 'Torture and the Ticking Bomb: The War on Terrorism as a Geographical Imagination of Power/Knowledge' (2006) 96 *Annals of the Association of American Geographers* 622, 623.
[345] *Ibid.*   [346] *Ibid.*   [347] *Ibid.*

the inflated threat of terrorism – and, thus, he disbands responsibility by presenting the ticking bomb scenario back to the authorities as justification for its actions.

If arguing the artificiality of the ticking bomb scenario provides one ill-fated attempt to crush the debate, the discussion on torture's efficacy affords another. On the question of whether or not torture works, there is inevitable deadlock.

(i)   Lessons from history?

Throughout the history of the practice of torture, the reliability of evidence, confessions or information extracted under torture has been the subject of doubt. In Ancient Greece torture was practised against those without legal status – slaves and foreigners.[348] In Ancient Rome the use of torture was, in early Roman law, restricted to slaves accused of a crime. Later, slaves acting as witnesses were subjected to torture, albeit with severe restrictions. Gradually, however, the practice of torture expanded and was used against 'freemen' in the case of treason and increasingly in other cases 'determined by imperial order'.[349] With respect to the practice of torture in Roman law, Peters observes:

> [E]mperors, orators and jurists all recognised the problem of evidence extracted by torture, although such concerns seem to have been the limit of their concern for the practice. Like the Greeks, the Romans recognized in treason, and in servile or low social status, adequate causes for the continuation of practices that they themselves knew were highly unreliable.[350]

It may thus be inferred that, in practising torture, the extraction of evidence was not the sole purpose of torture; rather the status of the accused was at issue. The actual reliability of torture was, therefore, less important than the perception that evidence was obtained through the use of torture. The effectiveness of torture, as a result, was not necessarily reliant upon the procedures or methods used but upon 'a jurisprudence that was designed to give greater assurance to its reliability'.[351]

From approximately 1250 to the late 1800s judicially administered torture for the purpose of obtaining confession was a routine part of criminal legal procedure in the Western legal tradition.[352] A confession made

---

[348] Peters, *Torture*, p. 14.   [349] *Ibid.*, p. 18.
[350] *Ibid.*, p. 34.   [351] *Ibid.*, p. 35.
[352] John H. Langbein, 'The Legal History of Torture' in Sanford Levinson (ed.), *Torture: A Collection* (Oxford University Press, 2004), p. 93.

under torture was considered involuntary and only became official once it had been repeated in the courtroom; however, in the event of an accused recanting such an involuntary confession, torture would once again be administered.[353] Yet, as John Langbein remarks, '[a]gainst the coercive force of the engines of torture, no safeguards were ever found that could protect the innocent and guarantee the truth. The agony of torture created an incentive to speak, but not necessarily to speak the truth'.[354] Langbein asserts that judicial torture survived for centuries in spite of its defects because criminal procedure was 'inextricably dependent on the tortured confession'.[355] This suggests that judicial torture was not necessarily prac- tised because of its effectiveness; rather, criminal procedure was unable to function without coerced confessions. In 1764, as the abolition of judicial torture from European criminal codes was gaining momentum, Cesare Beccaria published a treatise in which he condemned the practice of tor- ture. In particular, he challenged the rationale that torture constituted an efficacious method of eliciting truth or confession and of establish- ing guilt.[356] In what became 'the last learned defence of judicial torture in European history', Pierre François Muyart de Voughlans, Conseiller au Grand-Conseil in France, responded to Beccaria's claims. In a treatise published in 1780 he argued, 'it is without doubt that experience has made plain that one may use [torture] with success in particular cases where it is authorized by this law'.[357] Muyart's defence of judicial torture did not hold much sway, however. In the same year Louis XVI abolished torture from French criminal procedure.[358]

(ii)   Does torture work?

More than two centuries later the subject of torture's effectiveness is still debated. The terms of the debate have shifted, however, since the singular contemporary concern is with using torture for the purpose of extracting information and not practising torture for the purpose of establishing guilt or of obtaining confession or evidence. The distinction is significant. The ticking bomb hypothetical purports to concern a rare and exceptional case in which the only relevant factor is accessing the required information. Ostensibly, then, the status of the suspect is not at issue, as it was in Ancient Greece and in the Roman Empire, where the

---

[353] *Ibid.*, p. 96.   [354] *Ibid.*, p. 97.   [355] *Ibid.*
[356] Cesare Beccaria (tr. David Young), *On Crimes and Punishments* (Indianapolis: Hackett Publishing Company, 1986), p. 31.
[357] Cited in Peters, *Torture*, p. 72.   [358] *Ibid.*, p. 73.

idea of torture as abhorrent or inhuman was of less account. The tight strictures of the hypothetical also portray it as unlikely that a system of intelligence-gathering would become dependent upon the use of torture, in the way that criminal procedure became dependent upon confessions obtained through torture in late medieval and early modern law. At root, however, the question remains the same: Does torture work? Arguably, though, this question is now considerably more decisive. The problem, as Sanford Levinson and others have pointed out, is that this question is practicably unanswerable because there exists no methodologically or ethically sophisticated means of conclusive investigation.[359]

One argument persists in defence of torture's potential efficacy. If torture is as inefficient as claimed, why is it so frequently debated and commonly practised? Richard Posner describes as 'a plea in avoidance' objections to torture based on the rationale that it is an ineffective method of interrogation.[360] In somewhat contradictory terms, he reasons that although torture may be a 'clumsy and inefficient method of interrogation' and although it should be generally avoided because of its 'frequent inefficacy', 'it is hard to believe that it is always and everywhere ineffectual; if it were, we would not have to spend so much time debating it'.[361] Levinson concedes that there are numerous instances in which torture did not work.[362] He asserts, however, '[i]f we could be confident that torture *never* worked, then there would in fact be nothing to debate.'[363] He deduces that insistence on torture's definitive inefficaciousness is implausible, and he suggests that the evidence of torture's efficacy is in the existence of the prohibition itself: 'If, after all, there were no genuine lure of the Sirens, Ulysses would scarcely have needed to tie himself to the mast.'[364] Posner notes that there are other motives behind the use of torture, such as 'extracting false confessions, intimidating the population or particular subgroups, and sadism'; however, he quickly dismisses the idea that the prevalence of these 'uses' of torture might indicate torture to be 'a completely inefficacious method of obtaining true information'.[365] According

---

[359] Sanford Levinson, '"Precommitment" and "Postcommitment": The Ban on Torture in the Wake of September 11' (2003) 81 *Texas Law Review* 2013, 2029.

[360] Richard A. Posner, 'Torture, Terrorism, and Interrogation' in Sanford Levinson (ed.), *Torture: A Collection* (Oxford University Press, 2004), p. 294.

[361] *Ibid.*

[362] Levinson, '"Precommitment" and "Postcommitment"' 2030.

[363] Sanford Levinson, 'Slavery and the Phenomenology of Torture' (2007) 74 *Social Research* 149, 155.

[364] Levinson, '"Precommitment" and "Postcommitment"' 2030.

[365] Posner, 'Torture, Terrorism, and Interrogation', p. 294.

to Posner, 'this is very unlikely, the practice is too common'.[366] This point is echoed by Alan Dershowitz: '[i]t is precisely because torture sometimes does work and can sometimes prevent major disasters that it still exists in many parts of the world and has been totally eliminated from none.'[367] Philip Rumney responds to Dershowitz (and by extension to Posner and Levinson) by suggesting that Dershowitz 'makes a leap by simply assuming that torture exists around the globe for a rational reason, that is, as a means of preventing terrorism or criminality'.[368] In making this leap, Dershowitz and others adopt a benevolent view of the motivations behind torture, and they avoid exploring the political, social and cultural factors that predetermine the use of violence.[369] Eric Staub identifies a number of cultural–societal characteristics that lead to torture. Among them he includes 'a history of devaluation of a subgroup of society and discrimination against this subgroup', 'respect for authority' and the existence of 'an ideology that designates an enemy'.[370] Superficially, these characteristics appear to correlate more accurately to authoritarian states; however, as Luban has highlighted, the 'seemingly innocent' ticking bomb scenario creates a liberal ideology of torture.[371] Posner, Levinson and Dershowitz all raise a significant issue at the heart of the psychology of the ticking bomb. In the ticking bomb scenario the question of whether torture works is crucial; if the assumption that torture does not work is 'a plea in avoidance', it can equally be said that the assumption that torture must work is a kind of psychological defence. For if torture does not work, then the discursive landscape alters and the question of why torture is so frequently debated and practised becomes more difficult to face.

To reinforce the belief that torture must work, commentators argue that sufficient evidence exists to demonstrate that it does work. Dershowitz

---

[366] *Ibid.*

[367] Alan M. Dershowitz, *Why Terrorism Works: Understanding the Threat, Responding to the Challenge* (Yale University Press, 2002), p. 138.

[368] Philip N. S. Rumney, 'Is Coercive Interrogation of Terrorist Suspects Effective? A Response to Bagaric and Clarke' (2006) 40 *University of San Francisco Law Review* 479, 488.

[369] Eric Staub, 'Psychology and Torture' in William F. Schulz (ed.), *The Phenomenon of Torture: Readings and Commentary* (Philadelphia: University of Pennsylvania Press, 2007), p. 204.

[370] *Ibid.*, pp. 204–5.

[371] *Ibid.*, p. 209. See also Ronald Crelinsten, 'How to Make a Torturer' in William F. Schulz (ed.), *The Phenomenon of Torture: Readings and Commentary* (Philadelphia: University of Pennsylvania Press, 2007), p. 210 (identifying the political and social characteristics that make a polity, democratic or otherwise, more likely to use torture, with particular emphasis on the 'war on terror').

contends, in this respect, that '[t]here are numerous instances in which torture has produced self-proving, truthful information that was necessary to prevent harm to civilians'.[372] By way of example, he cites the case of Abdul Hakim Murad, a commercial pilot who was convicted in the United States in 1998 on charges of conspiracy to bomb twelve United States commercial airliners in Southeast Asia. For information about Murad's case, Dershowitz relies on articles published in *The Washington Post* in 2001.[373] Murad was arrested on 7 January 1995 in Manila, following the discovery of bomb-making material in his apartment.[374] He was held in custody until mid-April, during which time he was interrogated and allegedly subjected to torture.[375] During his interrogation Murad confessed to his involvement in a number of planned attacks including the so-called Boyinka plot for which he was later convicted in the United States.[376] Writing about his torture, Dershowitz states, 'after successfully employing this procedure [of tactical interrogation] they turned him over to the American authorities, along with the lifesaving information they had beaten out of him'.[377] If Murad's case exemplifies a ticking bomb scenario, it is worth examining the forensics of the case. When we do, we find that there was no bomb actually ticking and that the duration of his torture was sixty-seven days; factors that qualify the 'successfulness' of this example.[378] There is, however, a more fundamental problem with Dershowitz relying on Murad's case. Stephanie Athey remarks that press reports detailing Murad's case have misrepresented and distorted the facts, condensing them down to a 'purpose-driven parable': 'From story to story, aspects of Murad's physical ordeal, his arrest and his plans are amplified and embroidered; other details are recast and removed.'[379] In this regard, Dershowitz reports that it was through the use of torture that the planned attacks were thwarted. He does not recount the fact, explained in one of *The Washington Post* articles to which he refers, that critical evidence, containing all of the

---

[372] Dershowitz, *Why Terrorism Works*, p. 137.
[373] Matthew Brzenziki, 'Bust and Boom' *The Washington Post* (30 December 2001) W09; Doug Struck, 'Borderless Network of Terror: Bin Laden Followers Reach Across the Globe' *The Washington Post* (23 September 2001) A01.
[374] Struck, 'Borderless Network of Terror'; Stephanie Athey, 'The Terrorist we Torture: The Tale of Abdul Hakim Murad' (2007) 24 *South Central Review* 73, 75.
[375] Athey, 'The Terrorist we Torture' 75.
[376] Struck, 'Borderless Network of Terror'.
[377] Dershowitz, *Why Terrorism Works*, p. 137.
[378] Brecher, *Torture and the Ticking Bomb*, p. 26.
[379] Athey, 'The Terrorist we Torture' 77.

information about the planned attacks, was seized at Murad's apartment.[380] According to Athey:

> Stories that attributed the 'break' in the case to torture flatly ignore the evidence said to be found in Murad's apartment. In addition to bomb-making equipment and evidence that tracked co-conspirators, a computer there was said to hold photos and aliases, airline names, flight numbers and timer detonation settings ... If the evidence at the scene was what the police said it was, swift use of routine tools of investigation could have or did deliver more useful intelligence more quickly than the tools of torture.[381]

Dershowitz's example is convenient but inaccurately represented. The example has been cited and supported, however, by Levinson and Mirko Bagaric and Julie Clarke, to name but a few, without critical engagement.[382]

In addition to Dershowitz's example, Levinson, Bagaric and Clarke also rely on the Israeli case and on the Algerian war for corroboration of the effectiveness of torture.[383] Levinson references the Israeli High Court of Justice judgment in 1999 in which it was stated that GSS interrogation procedures had 'in the past ... led to the thwarting of murderous attacks'.[384] Bagaric and Clarke rely on an article by Eric Posner and Adrian Vermeule in which the authors focus on evidence from Israel that 'coercive interrogation' works.[385] This evidence, which Posner and Vermeule admit to be 'anecdotal', constitutes the Landau Commission of Inquiry report, statements made during the 1999 judgment and a contention, made in the Israeli state report to the United Nations Committee against Torture, that 'GSS investigations had foiled 90 planned terrorist attacks, including suicide bombings, car bombings, kidnaps and murders'.[386] With respect to the Algerian war, Levinson relies on an essay reviewing a

---

[380] Brzenziki, 'Bust and Boom'; Athey, 'The Terrorist we Torture' 81; McCoy, *A Question of Torture*, p. 112.

[381] Athey, 'The Terrorist we Torture' 81.

[382] Sanford Levinson, 'Contemplating Torture: An Introduction' in Sanford Levinson (ed.), *Torture: A Collection* (Oxford University Press, 2004), p. 34; Mirko Bagaric and Julie Clarke, *Torture: When the Unthinkable is Morally Permissible* (Albany: State University of New York Press, 2007), p. 55.

[383] Levinson, 'Contemplating Torture', p. 34; Bagaric and Clarke, *Torture*, p. 54.

[384] Cited in Levinson, 'Contemplating Torture', p. 34.

[385] Bagaric and Clarke, *Torture*, p. 54. Eric A. Posner and Adrian Vermeule, 'Should Coercive Interrogation be Legal?' (2005) 84 *Chicago Public Law and Legal Theory Working Paper* 1, 13.

[386] Posner and Vermeule, 'Should Coercive Interrogation be Legal?' 13.

number of books on the Algerian war published in the *New York Review of Books*.[387] On the question of whether torture was effective, Levinson says, '[a]las if the books under review are reliable, the answer seems to be yes'.[388] Bagaric and Clarke also reference this essay but, in addition, they refer to General Aussaresses' memoirs to find examples of 'effective torture'.[389] With respect to the Israeli case, it is difficult to assess the actual success of coercive interrogation in preventing ticking bombs because such evidence is publically unavailable.[390] It is worth reiterating, however, that the Landau Commission of Inquiry took a broad and elastic view of what would constitute a ticking bomb. It is also worth noting that if the objective of authorising the GSS to use 'moderate physical pressure' was to thwart planned or imminent attacks, GSS interrogators did not limit its use to such cases. Torture became routine.[391]

(iii) Back in Algiers

Reliance on the Algerian war for evidence of the effectiveness of torture in ticking bomb situations is also problematic. Notably, one of the books reviewed in the essay cited by Levinson and Bagaric and Clarke was Branche's study of torture during the Algerian war. Branche argues that torture was used as a routine method of intelligence-gathering and as a tool of repression and intimidation. Although she does express the possibility that intelligence may have been extracted resulting in the thwarting of a planned attack, she does not argue that torture was generally or effectively used as method of preventing imminent attacks, as, according to Branche, this was not the purpose of torture in Algeria. Rejali calls into question the assessment that the use of torture during the Algerian war, and particularly during the Battle of Algiers, was the key to preventing impending attacks and to dismantling the FLN. Rejali contends that the French army defeated the FLN both because it exhibited overwhelming force in a contained area and because of its efficient informant system.[392] He identifies three factors that account for General Massu's victory in the Battle of Algiers. First, he considers the arrest of nearly 'one-third of an entire city quarter in just nine months' to have created a feeling of terror

---

[387] Adam Shatz, 'The Torture of Algiers', *The New York Review of Books* (21 November 2002) 53.
[388] Levinson, 'Contemplating Torture', p. 34.
[389] Bagaric and Clarke, *Torture*, p. 54.
[390] Rumney, 'Is Coercive Interrogation of Terrorist Suspects Effective?' 489.
[391] Kremnitzer and Segev, 'The Legality of Interrogational Torture' 519.
[392] Rejali, *Torture and Democracy*, p. 480.

that is difficult to discount.[393] According to Rejali, French strategy was not to target FLN bombers but to 'identify and disable anyone who was even remotely associated with the FLN'.[394] Second, he argues that 'selective persistent violence' acted as 'a powerful deterrent ... few would risk appearing even remotely associated with the FLN'.[395] Finally, he highlights the significance of the efficient informant system that allowed the French to make critical arrests.[396] Rejali portrays the system of torture in Algeria as far from effective. He notes that, in using torture, ordinary and more effective methods of investigation were discouraged whilst investigators engaged in 'competitive brutality'.[397] However much the use of torture may have contributed to the overall strategy of repression and, consequently, to France's victory in the Battle of Algiers, the Algerian case does not demonstrate the effectiveness of torture in ticking bomb situations. From his research on the use of torture in Algeria, Rejali observes, '[i]nterrogators rarely cite specific personal successes at retrieving valuable information through torture. No one cites his role in preventing a ticking bomb from going off. Such rumoured successes always happen elsewhere and are things interrogators have only heard of'.[398]

(iv)   Does it matter if torture works?

Rejali argues that pain cannot be scientifically measured, that torture does not come with restraints, that the conducting of professional torture rapidly declines and that other methods of information-gathering, such as public cooperation, work better.[399] From his analysis of scientific and social scientific accounts of torture's efficacy, Rejali holds that information extracted under torture can mislead, especially when the victim is innocent or holds a grudge.[400] With respect to the ticking bomb scenario, he deems the likelihood of efficacy to be even more improbable. Due to the time limit, the torturer cannot use techniques that increase the pain slowly. According to Rejali, '[r]eal torture – not the stuff of television – takes days, if not weeks'.[401] In addition, he argues that the time limit stretches resources in verifying information gleaned from torture.[402] Finally, he maintains that committed 'believers' do not break easily under torture.[403]

Rather than disproving the efficacy of torture, this manner of assembling the odds against its efficacy actually demonstrates that

[393] Ibid., p. 483.   [394] Ibid., p. 482.   [395] Ibid., p. 483.
[396] Ibid.   [397] Ibid., pp. 446–86.   [398] Ibid., p. 489.
[399] Ibid., pp. 446–58.   [400] Ibid., pp. 460–3.   [401] Ibid., p. 474.
[402] Ibid., p. 475.   [403] Ibid., p. 476.

the question as to whether torture works is complex and probably unanswerable. This approach might also be interpreted as defensive. At any rate, the limited success of torture generally is unlikely to concern those who argue for the use of torture in the ticking bomb scenario, because, in this one catastrophic case, torture might just work. Bagaric and Clarke represent this form of reasoning: 'If thousands of lives were at stake, even a 20 percent likelihood that torture would be effective would justify its use.'[404] They argue that the efficacy aspect of the debate has become 'a distracting and superficial numbers game – with the winner supposedly being the side that can provide the most number of examples to support its contention'.[405] Their own examples are catalogued, they assert, not 'to claim victory on this issue, but rather to illustrate how easily the numbers game is played'.[406] The purpose of analysing examples of torture's alleged effectiveness is not, however, to partake in a numbers game. On the contrary, this kind of analysis demonstrates that uncritically examined examples are misleading. Moreover, as the example of the Algerian war illustrates, analysis of these cases demonstrates the way in which fixation upon the effectiveness of torture whitewashes the complexity of the phenomenon of torture.

The debate on the efficacy of torture cannot resolve in an endgame. There is too much conjecture and not enough hard and definitive evidence for conclusiveness. In his earlier study of torture in Iran, Rejali argued that torture apologists ought to shoulder the burden of proving the efficacy of torture.[407] Perhaps Rejali made this point, tongue in cheek, safe in the knowledge that such proof is probably unattainable. It is more likely that he was critiquing the improper or imprecise 'evidence' of torture's efficacy used by torture apologists in arguing their case. In his later work Rejali states, '[a]pologists often assume that torture works, and all that is left is the moral justification. If torture does not work, then their apology is irrelevant. Deciding whether one *ought* or *ought not* to drive a car is a pointless debate if the car has no gas'.[408] The danger with such an assertion, however, is the weight that it appears to place on the importance of knowing whether or not torture works.

---

[404] Bagaric and Clarke, *Torture*, p. 61.
[405] *Ibid.*, p. 58.   [406] *Ibid.*
[407] Darius Rejali, *Torture and Modernity: Self, Society and State in Modern Iran* (Boulder: Westview Press, 1994), p. 175.
[408] Rejali, *Torture and Democracy*, p. 447 (original emphasis).

(2)   Torture in exceptional circumstances and the liberal democracy

On the question of torture's justifiability in certain circumstances, Slavoj Žižek says:

> Ok, we can well imagine that in a specific situation, confronted with the proverbial 'prisoner who knows' and whose words can save thousands, we would resort to torture – even (or, rather precisely) in such a case, however, it is absolutely crucial that we do not elevate this desperate choice into a universal principle; following the unavoidable brutal urgency of the moment, we should simply do it. Only in this way, in the very inability or prohibition to elevate what we had to do into a universal principle, do we retain the sense of guilt, the awareness of the admissibility of what we have done.[409]

Žižek is opposed to the kind of essays that, whilst not advocating torture outright, do introduce the subject as 'a legitimate topic of debate'. In particular, he refers to those essays that advocate some form of legal regulation of torture in the 'ticking bomb' situation.[410] He contends that such essays are 'even more dangerous than an explicit endorsement of torture'.[411] He disagrees with debating torture because this allows torture to be considered whilst those considering it retain 'a pure conscience'.[412] The debate, according to Žižek, 'changes the background of ideological presuppositions and options much more radically than [torture's] outright advocacy'.[413]

Žižek's approach has been condemned as hypocritical in two ways: first, for pointing to the dilemma and then failing to confront it, and, second, for seemingly accepting the use of torture in these ticking bomb cases but preferring to disengage from any debate around the issue, legal or otherwise. Levinson, for example, characterises Žižek's approach as similar 'to the "don't ask, don't tell" policy adopted by the Clinton Administration with regard to gays and lesbians in the military'.[414] Of Žižek's writing, Louis Michael Seidman remarks, 'even some of the best work ... is marked by a palpable sense of unease about really coming to grips with the problem'.[415] For Steven Lukes the questions are why we should be entitled to a pure conscience and why this pure conscience should take priority over

---

[409] Slavoj Žižek, *Welcome to the Desert of the Real* (London: Verso, 2002), p. 103.

[410] *Ibid.*   [411] *Ibid.*   [412] *Ibid.*, p. 104.   [413] *Ibid.*

[414] Levinson, '"Precommitment" and "Postcommitment"' 2042; Levinson, 'Contemplating Torture', p. 23.

[415] Louis Michael Seidman, 'Torture's Truth' (2005) 72 *University of Chicago Law Review* 881, 883.

facing up to hard questions.[416] Whilst Žižek does appear to adopt a dirty
hands approach to the dilemma, and his approach is perhaps contradictory, it should be understood within the broader context of his work.[417]
Žižek criticises Jonathan Alter and Dershowitz for their positions on the
subject of using torture to obtain information. Alter argued in 2001 that
whilst torture could not be legalised as it is 'contrary to American values',
'court-sanctioned psychological interrogation ... [and] transferring some
suspects to ... less squeamish allies' is necessary.[418] Dershowitz argues
that, whilst he is not in favour of the use of torture, torture warrants
should be introduced in 'ticking bomb' circumstances: 'If we are to have
torture, it should be authorised by law.'[419] Žižek describes Alter's views as
obscene and hypocritical,[420] and he describes Dershowitz's approach as
'extremely dangerous; it gives legitimacy to torture and, thus, opens up
the space for more illicit torture'.[421] Rather than reading Žižek as unwilling to engage in the debate, I suggest that he is unwilling to talk about
torture *in this way*. This is illustrated in his comments on Dershowitz's
reaction to the debate about whether Abu Zubaydah, at that time suspected second-in-command of Al-Qaeda, should be tortured. Žižek
remarks, '[i]f ever there were an ultimate ethical fiasco of liberalism, this
was it'.[422] Dershowitz did not approve of the torture of Abu Zubaydah,
first, because this was 'not a clear case of the ticking bomb situation', and,
second, because 'torturing him would not yet be legal'.[423] The problem
for Dershowitz was not the measures to which Zubaydah would be subjected but the fact that these measures were not authorised by law. For
Žižek, therein lies the 'ethical fiasco'. Dershowitz legitimised a discussion
around the torture of Zubaydah and, thereby, he fictionalised Zubaydah's
actual situation by implying that legitimacy of action requires law.[424]
Dershowitz did not approve of Zubaydah's torture, insofar as he did not
agree that Zubaydah would meet the criteria to invoke an exception to the
torture prohibition. If he had met these criteria, Dershowitz would still
not approve as the torture would be illegal.

---

[416] Steven Lukes, 'Liberal Democratic Torture' (2006) 36 *British Journal of Political Science* 1.
[417] Whilst arguing that the discussion of torture should not be engaged, he nevertheless
        winds up entering the debate and even introduces 'slippery slope' arguments. His pos-
        ition also seems to accept somewhat uncritically the premise of the torture debate, i.e.
        the ticking bomb.
[418] Jonathan Alter, 'Time to Think about Torture' *Newsweek* (5 November 2001).
[419] See Alan M. Dershowitz, 'Is there a Torturous Road to Justice?' *Los Angeles Times* (8
        November 2001).
[420] Žižek, *Welcome to the Desert of the Real*, p. 102.
[421] *Ibid.*, p. 103.   [422] *Ibid.*, p. 105.   [423] *Ibid.*   [424] *Ibid.*

Žižek's overall point is that he has no wish to engage in a torture debate for that debate simply masks the reality in which torture is happening. For Žižek, the torture discourse is in fact the liberal lie which shields and simultaneously supports the reality in which torture will be resorted to by the liberal democracy irrespective of the legal landscape. Whilst arguments over justifiability and non-justifiability, regulation and non-regulation curdle, the fiction that legal, moral and practical justification or non-justification must somehow be worked out first is bolstered. All the while, what is being scorned is the existence of an absolute prohibition on torture, and what is being missed is the reality that 'there is no longer any need to cover administrative measures with the legal big Other'.[425]

Whilst Žižek's reference to the 'proverbial prisoner who knows' could suggest a 'don't ask, don't tell' attitude and an unwillingness to confront the dilemma, in the context of his overall critique a broader point can be extrapolated. With respect to liberal ideology, Žižek writes that whilst one might agree that one has all the freedoms that one wants, this 'feel[ing] free' is only because 'we lack the very language to articulate our unfreedom'.[426] He continues:

> Today, all the main terms we use to designate the present conflict – 'war on terrorism', 'democracy and freedom', 'human rights' and so on, are false terms, mystifying our perception of the situation instead of allowing us to think it. In this precise sense, our 'freedoms' themselves serve to mask and sustain our deeper unfreedom.[427]

In this vein, the torture debate provides the veneer of freedom and allows liberal thinking to believe that society hosts an open debate on a prohibition precious to democratic values. What is in fact occurring is disguised, and, thus, slips beneath the radar of perceptibility. Žižek is not agreeable to the fact that this veneer of freedom allows for the maintenance of pure conscience; it is simply part of the pretence. The ticking bomb as the crystallisation of the liberal ideology of torture presents a dichotomy: torture or terrorism. The underlying logic of the ticking bomb is that this hypothetical presents a choice. However, it is a 'forced choice: you're free to decide, on condition that you make the right choice'.[428]

Echoing Žižek, Richard Weisberg, who has also been accused of adopting a 'don't ask, don't tell' approach,[429] clarifies that he does not take issue

---

[425] *Ibid.*, p. 106. [426] *Ibid.*, p. 2. [427] *Ibid.* [428] *Ibid.*, p. 3.
[429] Richard H. Weisberg, 'Loose Professionalism, or Why Lawyers Take the Lead on Torture' in Sanford Levinson (ed.), *Torture: A Collection* (Oxford University Press, 2004), p. 300.

with the legal community discussing torture per se; rather he is opposed to those discussions that rationalise the practice. Weisberg reasons that the justification of torture both encourages and sustains its practice:

> I am not suggesting that those who ... begin to rationalize torture necessarily favour the practice; what I am saying is that the lessons of history are clear in demonstrating that such rationalizations not only help the practice to thrive but often provide ... the main reasons for its baleful success.[430]

Weisberg, like Žižek, describes the effect that rationalising torture has in legitimising its practice. There are differences in the contextual, or theoretical, backgrounds from which they both depart. Weisberg is concerned with the rationalisation of aberrational practices in the context of an emergency, and he contends that torture apology may in fact be the catalyst for the practice of torture:

> Apologists for torture cannot be absolutely sure that an American variation on the practice actually exists in any widespread way. Thus what looks – sadly enough – like an apologetics for torture actually also stands as a potential goad to decision-makers to adopt or expand a practice that may currently be no more than a blip on the radar screen.[431]

For Žižek the use of torture in the aftermath of 11 September did not require rationalisation or torture apology. Žižek recognises that a state of emergency, in the form of the 'war on terror', had already replaced the normal state of affairs, and, as such, he considered the prohibition of torture to be already under threat.[432]

C. Conclusion

In endeavouring to trace the trajectory of the ticking bomb scenario, the legacy of the Algerian war is prominent. During this conflict, torture, although not explicitly authorised, was routinely and extensively practised. Considered 'outlaws' or 'terrorists', individuals subjected to torture were deprived of a status and entered a 'rights-free zone'.[433] The ticking bomb became a general, and as Aussaresses' case illustrates, a personal

---

[430] *Ibid.*, p. 300. [431] *Ibid.*, p. 303.
[432] Žižek, *Welcome to the Desert of the Real*, pp. 106–7.
[433] Harold Koh, 'America's Offshore Refugee Camp' (1994) 29 *Richmond Law Review* 139, 140–1, cited in Joan Fitzpatrick, 'Speaking Law to Power: The War against Terrorism and Human Rights' (2003) 14 *European Journal of International Law* 241, 242.

justification for the practice of torture. In reality, however, torture was practised routinely to gather ordinary intelligence and, according to Branche, Lazreg and Rejali, amongst others, to repress the FLN and to intimidate the local population. After the Algerian war, the ticking bomb scenario was the subject of sporadic debate. This debate intensified following the publication of the Landau Commission's recommendations in Israel in 1987 and, particularly, in the aftermath of the events of 11 September. In both cases the ticking bomb scenario supplied the logic for the authorisation of practices constituting torture.

The torture debate engendered by the ticking bomb scenario fails to provide an accurate understanding of torture. Such an understanding of torture is more accurately revealed by the actual practice of torture; however, a precise analysis of state practices of torture tends to fall outside the frame of the ticking bomb scenario. The torture debate is unable to articulate torture in real terms, for in doing so it would, as Žižek's analysis makes clear, expose its own fiction. The debate feasts on the notion that torture is incompatible with liberalism and inimical to democracy and only in this one exceptional instance is it legitimate to consider the use of torture. The refrain that the practice of torture is barbaric, abhorrent, an 'affront to human dignity'[434] and contrary to international law and liberal democratic principles and values accompanies almost all commentary on the subject of torture in ticking bomb scenarios.[435] Between this discussion of the exceptional use of torture and the recital of legal and moral principles that condemn the use of torture exists the reality of the practice of torture. In the debate, this reality becomes mystified. Justifications for the use of torture in ticking bomb scenarios survive on shaky premises: first, that such a hypothetical situation is likely to materialise and, second, that torture will work in such a situation. However, although the examples proffered to support such contentions are misleading, neither contention can entirely be discounted. In that sense, the question posed by the ticking bomb is unanswerable. More importantly, however, this question is irrelevant. The following chapter proposes an alternative frame for considering the juridical and political space out of which this ticking bomb scenario arises.

---

[434] Sanford Levinson, 'In Quest of a "Common Conscience": Reflections on the Current Debate About Torture' (2005) 1 *Journal of National Security Law and Policy* 231, 232.

[435] Bagaric and Clarke offer a unique perspective when they argue that torture is not anti-democratic. They contend that if democracy 'means majoritarianism ... then a lawfully elected government can obviously through its normal democratic political process legalize torture'. See Bagaric and Clarke, *Torture*, p. 63.

3

State of exception

A. Emergencies and torture

It is generally recognised that states of emergency imperil the protection of human rights[1] and 'challenge the state's commitment to govern through law'.[2] International human rights law treaties make explicit provision for states to manage periods of crisis. The International Covenant on Civil and Political Rights, the European Convention on Human Rights and the American Convention on Human Rights all make provision for public emergencies by permitting states to lawfully derogate from certain human rights obligations for the purposes of defending the state during emergency and thus restoring it to a state of normalcy. From a human rights perspective, derogation is, therefore, exceptional, temporary and necessary only for the restoration of normalcy.[3] The designation of certain enumerated rights, including the prohibition on torture, as non-derogable is intended to prevent states from abusing their power by violating fundamental rights during such public emergencies. Joan Fitzpatrick observed, with respect to the violation of non-derogable rights, that 'emergencies often entail deprivation of fundamental rights of the population ... Ironically, this appears to be particularly true of non-derogable rights, those that supposedly can never be suspended, even in time of public emergency threatening the life of the nation'.[4] She further noted that '[t]orture is frequently practiced by emergency regimes ... and tends to be associated with other human rights abuses characteristic of emergencies, such as incommunicado detention, disappearances,

---

[1] Joan Fitzpatrick, *Human Rights in Crisis: The International System for Protecting Rights During States of Emergency* (Philadelphia: University of Pennsylvania Press, 1994), p. 1.
[2] Victor V. Ramraj, 'No Doctrine More Pernicious? Emergencies and the Limits of Legality' in Victor V. Ramraj (ed.), *Emergencies and the Limits of Legality* (Cambridge University Press, 2008), p. 4.
[3] CCPR General Comment No. 29 CCPR/C/21/Rev 1/Add. II, 31 August 2001, paras. 1 and 2.
[4] Fitzpatrick, *Human Rights in Crisis*, p. 35.

administrative detention, and secret trials in which confessions form the primary evidence of guilt'.[5] In a sense, then, the practice of torture might be explained by the lowering of legal safeguards against its practice in a state faced with crisis or as a knock-on effect of a state derogating from human rights provisions that otherwise protect the liberty and security of the individual.[6] However, such an analysis does not help to make sense of those contexts in which the use of torture is pursued, or justified, as a policy for the ostensible purpose of obtaining intelligence or information. Nor does this analysis apply to the debate on the use of torture in ticking bomb situations as the outright concern of this debate is exception to the torture prohibition.

The practice of torture in a state of emergency, and indeed generally, is always evidence of the 'limits of legality'.[7] In this regard, Winston P. Nagins and Lucie Atkins state: 'As torture is conduct that cannot be officially sanctioned by law, it is also conduct that seeks, operationally, to trump law. In this sense, torture challenges the very idea of law itself.'[8] The challenge posed by the practice of torture to the rule of law is analogous, therefore, to the more general test to the rule of law presented by states of emergency.

Legal scholarship, which mirrors legal tradition on the question of states of emergency, tends to consider the state of emergency dichotomously as, on the one hand, a juridical problem that must be constitutionally or legislatively mandated or, on the other hand, a political problem that ought to be dealt with extra-legally but with consequences in the sphere of law.[9] This dichotomous approach to the question of states of emergency is replicated in the debate on torture by the torture warrant proposal and the extra-legal measures model respectively. In his theorisation of the state of exception, Giorgio Agamben perforates this binary conception of the state of emergency. Agamben's analysis can, accordingly, be employed to deconstruct these proposals to regulate or accommodate torture.

[5] *Ibid.*, p. 36.
[6] Amnesty International, for example, has warned that when the legal barriers are lowered in states of emergency, torture frequently rears its head. See, for example, Amnesty International, 'USA Human Dignity Denied: Torture and Accountability in the War on Terror' (London: Amnesty International, 2004), p. 7.
[7] Ramraj, 'No Doctrine More Pernicious?', p. 3.
[8] Winston P. Nagin and Lucie Atkins, 'The International Law of Torture: From Universal Proscription to Effective Application and Enforcement' (2001) 14 *Harvard Human Rights Journal* 87, 90.
[9] Giorgio Agamben (tr. Kevin Attell) *State of Exception* (University of Chicago Press, 2005), p. 22.

(1)   The relevance of the state of exception

The events of 11 September and the subsequent policies established by the government of the United States, coupled with the expansion of emergency powers at both national and international level,[10] have accelerated discussion as to how a democracy ought to respond to the threat of violent crises.[11] The solution to this problem is not obvious. The question of how to define 'emergency' remains unresolved, as does the issue of squaring emergency powers with the rule of law.[12] The emergencies debate has often remained within the confines of the traditional approach to emergencies. Opinion has divided, for example, between those who argue for the legal containment and control of states of emergency through mechanisms such as an emergency constitution[13] and those who argue for some form of deference to executive decision-making in states of emergency.[14] One of the striking features of this emergencies debate is the absence of a theoretical framework from which to understand states of exception. Agamben asserts, in this regard, that there exists 'no theory of the state of exception in public law', and that this is so because 'jurists and theorists of public law seem to regard the problem more as a *quaestio facti* than as a genuine juridical problem'.[15] The inexistence of a theory of the state of exception becomes even more problematic with Agamben's assertion that the state of exception 'tends increasingly to appear as the dominant paradigm of government'.[16] Nasser Hussain similarly argues that 'the concept of emergency and its relation to the norm' is under-theorised. He argues that this 'neglect is curious ... given the constitutive role emergency plays alongside the rule of law in the concept of modern sovereignty'.[17] Hussain's point, like Agamben's, is not that the whole subject of emergencies has been neglected. Rather, he contends that it is the constitutive

---

[10] Oren Gross and Fionnuala Ní Aoláin, *Law in Times of Crisis: Emergency Powers in Theory and Practice* (Cambridge University Press, 2006), p. 1.

[11] Michael Ignatieff, *The Lesser Evil: Political Ethics in an Age of Terror* (Princeton University Press, 2004), p. vii.

[12] Gross and Ní Aoláin, *Law in Times of Crisis*, pp. 6–7.

[13] Bruce Ackerman, 'The Emergency Constitution' (2004) 113 *The Yale Law Journal* 1029.

[14] Eric A. Posner and Adrian Vermeule, *Terror in the Balance: Security, Liberty and the Courts* (New York: Oxford University Press, 2007). Richard A. Posner, *Not a Suicide Pact: The Constitution in a Time of National Emergency* (New York: Oxford University Press, 2007).

[15] Agamben, *State of Exception*, p. 1.   [16] *Ibid.*, p. 2.

[17] Nasser Hussain, *The Jurisprudence of Emergency: Colonialism and the Rule of Law* (Ann Arbor: University of Michigan, 2003), p. 16.

relationship formed by emergency between modern law and sovereignty, and thus modern power, that has received scant attention.[18] In theorising the state of exception, Agamben recalls Carl Schmitt's pronouncement of the sovereign as 'he who decides on the exception',[19] by which Schmitt, according to Agamben, established the 'essential congruity between the state of exception and sovereignty'.[20] Schmitt criticises the liberal constitution's regulation of the exception. Sceptical that the exception derives wholly from the norm,[21] he argues that the exception requires a decision and that this extends to the sovereign unlimited authority, specifically, the ability to suspend 'the entire existing order'.[22]

Schmitt's formulation of the exception has been condemned for its authoritarian implications. Schmitt was a German legal theorist and a critic of the Weimar Republic. He joined the National Socialist Party in 1933.[23] His writings, whilst influential, are understandably controversial. William Scheuerman argues that Schmitt has been received in the English-speaking world in two ways:

> Whereas some scholars have been satisfied with an apologetic discussion of Schmitt's ideas and their relationship to National Socialism, others criticize his views but succeed in doing so only by caricaturing them. The apologists downplay Schmitt's Nazi activities and the role he played in legitimizing a dictatorial alternative to the crisis-ridden Weimar Republic during the early 1930s, while the caricaturists obscure central elements of Schmitt's account and unwittingly provide intellectual fodder for Schmitt's defenders.[24]

In this context, it is debated whether Schmitt's ruminations on the exception represent a critique of liberal constitutionalism, particularly the German constitutional tradition,[25] and a warning of its weaknesses, or whether it prescriptively espouses the end of democracy.[26]

---

[18] *Ibid.*
[19] Carl Schmitt (tr. George Schwab), *Political Theology: Four Chapters on the Concept of Sovereignty* (University of Chicago Press, 2005), p. 5.
[20] Agamben, *State of Exception*, p. 1.
[21] Schmitt, *Political Theology*, p. 6.   [22] *Ibid.*, p. 12.
[23] William E. Scheuerman, *Carl Schmitt: The End of Law* (Boston, MA: Rowman & Littlefield Publishers, 1999), p. 1.
[24] *Ibid.*
[25] Carlo Galli, 'Carl Schmitt's Antiliberalism: its Theoretical and Historical Sources and its Philosophical and Political Meaning' (2000) 21 *Cardozo Law Review* 1597, 1599.
[26] Oren Gross, 'The Normless and Exceptionless Exception: Carl Schmitt's Theory of Emergency Powers and the "Norm/Exception" Dichotomy' (2000) 21 *Cardozo Law Review* 1825, 1826. Hannah Arendt describes Carl Schmitt's writing as theories about the end of

Notwithstanding the controversy to which Schmitt's writings and politics lead, his writings have contemporary relevance.[27] His definition of the sovereign, whilst divisive, is, as William Rasch points out, not by any means 'anachronistic'.[28] His theories on the exception persist to the extent that parallels have been drawn between these theories and American administrative law,[29] the Bush administration's theory of executive power and, specifically, its policy on torture.[30]

Adrian Vermeule argues that American administrative law contains built-in 'black and grey holes' and that these exceptions are both inevitable and irremovable. He describes American administrative law, in this sense, as 'substantially Schmittian'.[31] Sanford Levinson describes Schmitt as the 'legal philosopher who provides the best understanding of the legal theory of the Bush Administration'.[32] In that vein, Christopher Kutz compares the theoretical roots, and weaknesses, of the constitutional theory of presidential authority, advocated in the aftermath of 11 September, to Schmitt's investigation of the relationship between states of emergency and political authority.[33] Scheuerman contends that the Bush administration interpreted the limitations of the legal regime for responding to terrorism in the spirit of Schmitt 'as evidence for the necessity of a fundamentally *norm-less* realm of decision-making in which the executive possesses full discretionary authority'.[34] In the Bybee memorandum,

---

democracy and legal government. See Hannah Arendt, *The Origins of Totalitarianism* (New York: Harcourt Books, 1968), p. 339.

[27] Scheuerman, *Carl Schmitt*, p. 1.

[28] William Rasch, 'From Sovereign Ban to Banning Sovereignty' in Matthew Calarco and Steven DeCaroli (eds.), *Sovereignty and Life* (Stanford University Press, 2007), pp. 92, 96.

[29] Adrian Vermeule, 'Our Schmittian Administrative Law' (2009) 122 *Harvard Law Review* 1095, 1149.

[30] See, for example, Christopher Kutz, 'Torture, Necessity and Existential Politics' (2007) 95 *California Law Review* 235, 238; William E. Scheuerman, 'Carl Schmitt and the Road to Abu Ghraib' (2006) 13 *Constellations* 108, 118–20.

[31] Vermeule, 'Our Schmittian Administrative Law' 1107.

[32] Sanford Levinson, 'Preserving Constitutional Norms in Times of Permanent Emergencies' (2006) 13 *Constellations* 59. See also Jason Ralph, 'The Laws of War and the State of the American Exception' (2009) 35 *Review of International Studies* 631, 633 (arguing that Schmitt's concept of the exception helps in the interpretation of aspects of the Bush administration policy in the 'war on terror').

[33] Kutz, 'Torture, Necessity and Existential Politics' 268.

[34] Scheuerman, 'Carl Schmitt and the Road to Abu Ghraib' 118. See also William E. Scheuerman, 'International Law as Historical Myth' (2004) 11 *Constellations* 537 (wherein he remarks, 'anyone familiar with Schmitt's work on international law occasionally finds herself wondering whether the White House playbook for foreign policy might not have been written by Schmitt or at least by one of his followers').

Scheuerman finds the 'unambiguous message' that international and domestic law, including statutory provisions on torture, are to be considered unconstitutional if in conflict with the president's discretionary power.[35] In other words, it would be unconstitutional to limit the president's authority to authorise torture.[36]

There are four interlinked ways in which the state of exception correlates with the question of torture in exceptional circumstances. First, whilst Agamben's critics protest his claim that the exception is not treated by jurists as a genuine juridical problem, the continued debate as to whether states of emergency should be regulated by law, or be left unregulated, supports the assertion that a theory of the state of exception remains elusive.[37] Absent this theory, the question of exceptional torture is debated in the same terms as the emergencies debate. Second, when Agamben claims that the state of exception is increasingly the dominant paradigm of government, he is not referring to the consequences of specific temporary emergency measures.[38] Rather, he is proposing that the state of exception is, in fact, the originary structure of the juridical order.[39] Agamben is, therefore, concerned with the consequences more generally for the legal order,[40] in which the exception erodes the determinacy of the norm.[41] Third, Schmitt's emphasis on the decision on the exception must be borne in mind where exceptional torture is concerned because, as an absolute norm, there is no normative basis for an exception to the prohibition; only a decision on the exception could override the prohibition. Finally, Schmitt's criticism of the exception under the liberal constitution, taken

---

[35] Scheuerman, 'Carl Schmitt and the Road to Abu Ghraib' 119. See also Jay S. Bybee, Memorandum for Alberto R. Gonzales, 'Standards of Conduct for Interrogation under 18 U.S.C. §§ 2340–2340A, 1 August 2002, cited in Karen J. Greenberg and Joshua L. Dratel (eds.), *The Torture Papers: The Road to Abu Ghraib* (Cambridge University Press, 2005), pp. 202–7; Levinson, 'Preserving Constitutional Norms' 70.

[36] Levinson, 'Preserving Constitutional Norms' 70.

[37] See Vik Kanwar, 'Book Review: Giorgio Agamben, State of Exception' (2006) 4 *International Journal of Constitutional Law* 567, 573. Kanwar argues that Agamben does not bring this debate any closer to resolution. This criticism, however, oversteps the problem with which Agamben is concerned. He does not seek resolution in a regulation/ non-regulation, inside/outside dichotomy. In fact, it is in this dichotomy that Agamben finds evidence for his claim that the state of exception has not been treated as a genuine juridical matter. This point will be elaborated upon below.

[38] Bas Scholten, 'Defending Our Legal Practices: A Legal Critique of Giorgio Agamben's State of Exception' (2009) 1 *Amsterdam Law Forum* 113, 114.

[39] Agamben, *State of Exception*, p. 2.

[40] Scholten, 'Defending Our Legal Practices' 114.

[41] Daniel McLoughlin, 'In Force without Significance: Kantian Nihilism and Agamben's Critique of Law' (2009) 20 *Law and Critique* 245, 257.

at face value, proves instructive to the contemporary challenge of prohibiting torture in the liberal democracy. The state of exception connects,
therefore, to the question of torture in exceptional circumstances, despite
the fact that the prohibition on torture is an absolute and non-derogable
norm in international law. In the contemporary debate on torture, claims
to exceptionality persist. Moreover, it is apparent that the practice of
torture in a number of liberal democracies is the result of state policies
of torture. Bearing this in mind, what effect does the reiteration of the
absolute prohibition of torture have? Should claims to exceptionality be
understood as nothing more than the inevitable response to new threats?
Should the practice of torture in countering terrorism be understood as
abuse of the law? In this regard, Paul Kahn argues that as long as torture
exists as a state practice of violence (and he opines that there is an intuitive knowledge that this torture is almost inevitable),[42] it is fruitless to
pronounce it as illegal or even as contrary to the rule of law; this, he says,
is self-explanatory. According to Kahn, it is unproductive to treat torture
from this perspective of illegality because this does not reach an understanding of the way in which torturous violence 'creates and sustains political meaning'.[43] He pursues such an understanding by inquiring into
the forces that operate in, what he describes as, the space of sovereignty
beyond law – 'the space of the exception'.[44] It is clear that even the absolute prohibition on torture is not insulated from abuse in the response to
violent crises. Whether or not law has, or ought to have, the capacity to
provide this insulation underpins the torture debate.

B.   Carl Schmitt's sovereign exception

Agamben attributes Schmitt with having made the most 'rigorous attempt
to construct a theory of the state of exception'.[45] His definition of sovereignty has, furthermore, been noted as the '*locus classicus* of contemporary discussions of sovereignty'.[46] It is therefore logical to take Schmitt's
theory of the exception and his subsequent, and corroborative, definition
of sovereignty as the starting point for examining the state of exception.

---

[42] Paul W. Kahn, *Sacred Violence: Torture, Terror, and Sovereignty* (Ann Arbor: University
      of Michigan Press, 2008), p. 172.
[43] *Ibid.*, p. 4.   [44] *Ibid.*, p. 89.
[45] Agamben, *State of Exception*, p. 32.
[46] Andrew Norris, 'Sovereignty, Exception, and Norm' (2007) 34 *Journal of Law and Society*
      31, 32.

(1) Dictatorship

The exception was central to Schmitt's understanding of sovereignty.[47] He remarked, in that regard, that 'it is precisely the exception that makes relevant the subject of sovereignty, that is, the whole question of sovereignty'.[48] Schmitt derived his theory on the exception from his study on dictatorship.[49] In this study, Schmitt traced the history of dictatorship with the aim of conveying its juridical content.[50] Dictatorship, to Schmitt, exists in the suspension of law.[51] He distinguished between two forms of dictatorship – the commissarial and the sovereign, which Agamben recognises as the opposition between constitutional and unconstitutional dictatorship.[52] The commissarial dictatorship is the constitutionally authorised suspension of the legal order, in a state of emergency, for the purposes of restoring order to safeguard that constitution; the sovereign dictatorship uses crisis to overthrow the existing constitutional order with the intention of establishing a new order.[53] In the commissarial dictatorship, whilst the constitution is suspended in its application, it nevertheless remains in force by virtue of its being suspended by a 'concrete exception'; the exception retains its juridical content because the norm is suspended in order that its realisation can be brought about with the restoration of order.[54] Thus, '[t]he exception is ... defined by the norm'.[55] In the sovereign dictatorship, it is the constituent power of the sovereign that binds the exception to the juridical order. Schmitt argues, therefore, that in both the commissarial and the sovereign forms of dictatorship the exception is connected to the legal order.[56] He strives to establish this

---

[47] Gross, 'The Normless and Exceptionless Exception' 1831.

[48] Schmitt, *Political Theology*, p. 6.

[49] Carl Schmitt, *Die Diktatur: Von den Anfängen des modernen Souveränitätsgedankens bis zum proletarischen Klassenkampf* (Berlin: Duncker & Humblot, 2006).

[50] Grigoris Ananiadis, 'Carl Schmitt and Max Adler: The Irreconcilability of Politics and Democracy' in Chantal Mouffe (ed.), *The Challenge of Carl Schmitt* (London: Verso, 1999), p. 122.

[51] Agamben, *State of Exception*, p. 32.

[52] *Ibid.*, p. 8. Elucidating this distinction in order to make 'the concept of dictatorship "finally accessible to jurisprudential consideration"' was the intended outcome of his study. See Agamben, *State of Exception*, p. 34.

[53] Ananiadis, 'Carl Schmitt and Max Adler', p. 122.

[54] Agamben, *State of Exception*, p. 33.

[55] Gross, 'The Normless and Exceptionless Exception' 1835.

[56] Agamben, *State of Exception*, p. 34.

relationship in order to make the distinction between the exception and anarchy or chaos.[57]

Schmitt's immediate reference for his theory on the exception was Article 48 of the Weimar Constitution, established in 1918.[58] Article 48 vested in the Reich president both the authority to use the armed forces to compel a federal state to fulfil its constitutional obligations and to take the necessary steps to restore public security and order in the event of its disturbance or endangerment, with the intervention of the armed forces if required. Under Article 48, the president could suspend, in whole or in part, the fundamental rights provided for in Articles 114, 115, 117, 118, 123, 124 and 153.[59] Article 48 was theoretically safeguarded by the provision that measures taken by the president could be revoked by the Reichstag.[60] Article 48 stipulated, furthermore, that a law would be passed to specify the 'conditions and limitations under which this presidential power was to be exercised'.[61] This law was never passed.[62] As a consequence, Agamben notes, the president's emergency powers remained

---

[57] Schmitt, *Political Theology*, p. 12; Agamben, *State of Exception*, p. 33.

[58] Schmitt, *Die Diktatur*, p. 212.

[59] Article 48 of the Weimar Constitution stated:

> If a state does not fulfil the duties incumbent upon it under the national Constitution or laws, the President of the Reich may compel it to do so with the aid of the armed forces.
>
> If the public safety and order in the German Reich are seriously disturbed or endangered, the President of the Reich may take the measures necessary to the restoration of the public safety and order, and may if necessary intervene with the armed forces. To this end he may temporarily suspend in whole or in part the fundamental rights established in Articles 114 (inviolability of the person), 115 (inviolability of domicile), 117 (secrecy of communications), 118 (freedom of opinion and expression thereof), 123 (freedom of assembly), 124 (freedom of association), and 153 (inviolability of property).
>
> The President of the Reich must immediately inform the Reichstag of all measures taken in conformity with sections 1 or 2 of this Article. The measures are to be revoked upon the demand of the President of the Reich or the Reichstag.
>
> In cases where delay would be dangerous, the state government may take for its territory temporary measures of the nature described in section 2. The measures are to be revoked upon the demand of the President of the Reich or the Reichstag.
>
> A national law shall prescribe the details.

> Cited in Clinton Rossiter, *Crisis Government in the Modern Democracies* (Princeton University Press, 1948), p. 31.

[60] Rossiter, *Crisis Government*, p. 31. See also Gross and Ní Aoláin, *Law in Times of Crisis*, pp. 84–5.

[61] Article 48, cited in Rossiter, *Crisis Government*, p. 31; Agamben, *State of Exception*, p. 14.

[62] Rossiter, *Crisis Government*, p. 32.

indeterminate.[63] Clinton Rossiter has remarked that Article 48 'became the foundation for all sorts and degrees of constitutional dictatorship'.[64] Oren Gross and Fionnuala Ní Aoláin assert that, by the end of the Weimar Republic, Article 48 had 'been used as practically the exclusive legal source for governmental action, with the ordinary legislative and administrative processes virtually suspended'.[65]

Schmitt considered Article 48 – if applied 'correctly' – in a favourable light, as adequate to deal with crises.[66] George Schwab states that, 'according to [Schmitt's] view, interpreting the provisions of the constitution in a manner that strengthened the state's raison d'être, assuring citizens of order and stability would enable the constitutional order of the state to function normally'.[67] Schwab contends that Schmitt sought an expansive interpretation of Article 48 whereby presidential action would not be restricted in restoring order.[68] This correlates with Schmitt's scepticism of the authority of the norm. Schmitt understood the emergency provision of the Weimar Constitution to correspond to the commissarial form of dictatorship.[69] Whether, as in Gross' words, Schmitt 'embraces' this form of exception[70] or whether he viewed it as juridically unavoidable is debatable. Schmitt was, nevertheless, mindful of Article 48's potential for abuse.[71] At any rate, in distinguishing between the commissarial dictatorship and the sovereign dictatorship, Schmitt created a false dichotomy. In his efforts to establish the link between the exception and the juridical order, he underestimated that the commissarial dictatorship was, in fact, a precursor to the sovereign dictatorship and to totalitarianism:

> The state of exception in which Germany found itself during the Hindenburg presidency was justified by Schmitt on a constitutional level by the idea that the president acted as the 'guardian of the constitution'; but the end of the Weimar Republic clearly demonstrates that, on the contrary, a 'protected democracy' is not a democracy at all, and that the paradigm of constitutional dictatorship functions instead as a transitional phase that leads inevitably to the establishment of a totalitarian regime.[72]

[63] Agamben, *State of Exception*, p. 14.
[64] Rossiter, *Crisis Government*, p. 32.
[65] Gross and Ní Aoláin, *Law in Times of Crisis*, p. 85.
[66] George Schwab, 'Introduction' in Schmitt, *Political Theology*, p. xliv.
[67] *Ibid.*, p. xlv.   [68] *Ibid.*, p. xlvi.   [69] *Ibid.*, p. xlv.
[70] Gross, 'The Normless and Exceptionless Exception' 1840. Gross argues that Schmitt embraces this form of dictatorship in *Die Diktatur* but abandons it in *Political Theology* in favour of the sovereign dictatorship.
[71] Schwab, 'Introduction' in Schmitt, *Political Theology*, p. xlv.
[72] Agamben, *State of Exception*, p. 15.

(2) The sovereign and the exception

Schmitt's definition of sovereignty derived from this prior study of dicta-torship in which he outlined his theory of the exception.[73] His definition of sovereignty comprises, first, the decision on what constitutes an excep-tion[74] and, second, what decision to take on that exception:[75] the sovereign 'decides whether there is an extreme emergency as well as what must be done to eliminate it'.[76] David Dyzenhaus explains this definition as mean-ing 'sovereign authority accrues to one who has the power to make an effective decision, both about whether there is an emergency and how best to respond to it'.[77] Schwab adds that this definition also subsumes the 'ability to decide whether order and stability have been restored and normality regained'.[78] Schmitt draws an analogy between the exception in jurisprudence and the miracle in theology.[79] In so doing, he transfers to the sovereign 'the functions theology attributed to the miracle'.[80] It is, therefore, instructive to point out that, in appointing the sovereign as the decider, rather than establishing the sovereign as God, Schmitt is stating the sovereign decision as determinant.[81] Daniel McLoughlin remarks in this regard that 'for Schmitt … the authority to decide on the norm is cru-cial for the life of the law, and as such, the decision is as much a part of the law as the norm'.[82] For Schmitt, the exception did not refer to 'every police emergency measure or emergency decree'.[83] Nor did the exception only describe an event, as such; rather, it evoked the limit of the legal order in

---

[73] *Ibid.*, p. 35.

[74] Schmitt, *Political Theology*, p. 6.

[75] Tracy B. Strong, 'Foreword: The Sovereign and the Exception: Carl Schmitt, Politics, Theology, and Leadership' in Schmitt, *Political Theology*, p. xiii. There is a divergence of opinion on the interpretation and translation from the German, which Strong discusses. Whilst the interpretation is important for pinpointing Schmitt's political leaning, for the purposes of this basic outline of Schmitt's definition of sovereignty it is not necessary to engage that discussion. Schwab's translation is, therefore, considered appropriate.

[76] Schmitt, *Political Theology*, p. 7.

[77] David Dyzenhaus, 'The Compulsion of Legality' in Victor V. Ramraj (ed.), *Emergencies and the Limits of Legality* (Cambridge University Press, 2008), p. 40.

[78] Schwab, 'Introduction' in Schmitt, *Political Theology*, p. xliv.

[79] Schmitt, *Political Theology*, p. 36.

[80] Lutz Koepnick, *Walter Benjamin and the Aesthetics of Power* (University of Nebraska Press, 1999), p. 43.

[81] Tracy B. Strong, 'Foreword' in Carl Schmitt, (tr. George Schwab), *The Concept of the Political* (University of Chicago, 2007), p. xiv.

[82] McLoughlin, 'In Force without Significance' 247.

[83] Schmitt, *Political Theology*, p. 12. This is the distinction between the fictitious state of exception and the real state of exception.

extreme emergency where the sovereign decision suspends the law.[84] It is in this sense that Schmitt understood the exception as a 'general concept in the theory of the state'.[85]

In his theory of sovereignty, Schmitt abandoned the distinction between the commissarial and sovereign dictatorship and replaced it with the primacy of the decision. It is thus the decision, rather than norms of the realisation of law or the distinction between constituted and constituent power, that inscribes the exception within the juridical order.[86] The sovereign decision transcends the norm in the exception by suspending the law: 'The decision frees itself from all normative ties and becomes in the true sense, absolute. The state suspends the law in the exception on the basis of its right of self-preservation.'[87] The exception, which results from the decision, is characterised by 'principally unlimited authority, which means the suspension of the entire existing order'.[88] The exception, Schmitt wrote, nevertheless remains 'accessible to jurisprudence because both the norm and the decision remain within the framework of the juristic'.[89] Schmitt's conceptualisation of the exception at this point complicates the traditional relationship between the norm and the exception. He argued that it is the exception that confirms the rule; that is to say, the normal is in essence constituted by the exception:

> The exception is more interesting than the rule. The rule proves nothing; the exception proves everything. It confirms not only the rule but also its existence, which derives only from the exception. In the exception the power of real life breaks through the crust of a mechanism that has become torpid by repetition.[90]

Gross asserts that it is at this point that Schmitt's theory diverges from previous discussion of emergencies:

> The traditional discourse, dating as far back as the Roman republic, regards the issue of emergencies through a dichotomized world view in which the normal case, the ordinary state of affairs, is separated and clearly distinguished from the exceptional case ... Moreover, this classical model of thinking about emergencies has considered such phenomena to be sporadic, temporary, and exceptional against the background of an otherwise uninterrupted normalcy. Schmitt calls into question

---

[84] McLoughlin, 'In Force without Significance' 247.
[85] Schmitt, *Political Theology*, p. 5.
[86] Agamben, *State of Exception*, p. 35.
[87] Schmitt, *Political Theology*, p. 12.
[88] *Ibid.*   [89] *Ibid.*, p. 13.   [90] *Ibid.*, p. 15.

this approach by reversing the relationship between normal and the
exceptional cases.[91]

Gross considers this reversal of norm and exception to be instructive
as a descriptive exercise, but he does not accept the normative solution
proposed by Schmitt to the problem of emergencies. Gross argues that,
in Schmitt's account, 'the exception is no longer merely normless, it is
also exceptionless'.[92] According to Gross, Schmitt no longer embraces the
commissarial dictatorship; rather, he is defending the sovereign dictatorship insofar as he abandons entirely the 'notion of the norm and replaces it
with the exception'.[93] He further contends that Schmitt continues to speak
in terms of the distinction between norm and exception, as a rhetorical
device, to disguise the authoritarian implications of his new position.[94]

In fact, Schmitt's position had not altered from that which he presented
in his study on dictatorship insofar as he continued to defend his primary
position – the juridical significance of the exception. The distinction that
Schmitt makes between commissarial and sovereign dictatorship is not a
distinction based on nature but on degree.[95] That which operated those distinctions is replaced in the sovereign theory of exception by the decision
that suspends the norm. The exception is governed not by the law but by the
political authority of the sovereign, whose authority nevertheless derives
from the law. The sovereign 'stands outside the normally valid legal system',
but 'he, nevertheless, belongs to it, for it is he must decide whether the constitution needs to be suspended in its entirety'.[96] In his writings, Schmitt
strives to emphasise this continued relation with the juridical order, which
he established in the study of dictatorship, because, for him, the exception
cannot denote lawlessness. In a situation in which the law is suspended,
according to Schmitt, 'it is clear that the state remains, whereas law recedes.
Because the exception is different from anarchy and chaos, order in the juristic sense still prevails even if it is not of the ordinary kind'.[97]

By binding the sovereign to the exception through the decision, Schmitt
therefore identified the decision on the exception as the clearest manifestation of state authority. Undoubtedly, this normative solution to the
exception is authoritarian:

> The sovereign produces and guarantees the situation in its totality. He has
> the monopoly over this last decision. Therein resides the essence of the

[91] Gross, 'The Normless and Exceptionless Exception' 1829.
[92] *Ibid.*, 1841.   [93] *Ibid.*, 1840.   [94] *Ibid.*
[95] Agamben, *State of Exception*, p. 35.
[96] Schmitt, *Political Theology*, p. 7 (emphasis added).   [97] *Ibid.*

state's sovereignty which must be juristically defined correctly, not as
the monopoly to coerce or rule, but as the monopoly to decide. The exception reveals most clearly the essence of the state's authority. The decision
parts here from the legal, and (to formulate it paradoxically) authority
proves that to produce law it need not be based on law.[98]

In having the monopoly over the last decision, the sovereign is endowed
with the authority to decide not only on the exception but also on what
constitutes the normal situation.

The decision is crucial to Schmitt's theory of the exception. It is also
crucial to his criticism of the liberal constitution. Schmitt argued that a
legal norm cannot wholly provide for an exception. In deciding that a real
exception exists, therefore, the decision cannot originate entirely from
the norm:[99] 'Like every other order, the legal order rests on a decision and
not on a norm.'[100] As mentioned, Schmitt was not referring to any emergency situation for which the norm can predict exception. The exception,
to him, is a situation of extreme emergency that 'can at best be characterised as a case of extreme peril, a danger to the existence of the state, or the
like'.[101] He consequently challenged the very idea that the exception can
be accounted for within the norm, where '[t]he precise details of an emergency cannot be anticipated, nor can one spell out what may take place in
such a case, especially when it is truly a matter of an extreme emergency
and of how it is to be eliminated'.[102] He is questioning, in other words,
how the unknown can be enumerated. Schmitt suggests that, in such an
extreme emergency situation, the liberal constitution, which denies the
sovereign decision, is immobilised: 'From the liberal constitutional point
of view, there would be no jurisdictional competence at all.'[103] This implies
that the sovereign decision is necessary in the exception; its absence
obscures the authority to deal with the exception: 'The most guidance the
constitution can provide is to indicate who can act in such a case. If such
action is not hampered by checks, as is the case in a liberal constitution,
then it is clear who the sovereign is.'[104] Schmitt challenged the idea that
the liberal constitution could regulate the exception through suspension
of the legal order without descending into juristic chaos. According to
Schmitt, '[t]he tendency of liberal constitutionalism to regulate the exception as precisely as possible means, after all, the attempt to spell out in
detail the case in which law suspends itself'.[105] He asked, '[f]rom where

[98] *Ibid.*, p. 13.   [99] *Ibid.*, p. 6.   [100] *Ibid.*, p. 10.
[101] *Ibid.*, p. 6.   [102] *Ibid.*   [103] *Ibid.*, p. 7.
[104] *Ibid.*   [105] *Ibid.*, p. 14.

does the law obtain this force, and how is it logically possible that a norm is valid except for one concrete case that it cannot factually determine in any definitive manner?'[106] It is evident that Schmitt did not recognise the liberal constitution's regulation of the exception as anything more than an absence of authority and, as such, a precursor to lawlessness.

C.   The gods and the giants

(1)   The Benjamin/Schmitt debate

Schmitt's theorising of the exception and, in particular, his pronouncement of the sovereign as 'he who decides on the exception' is critical to Agamben's engagement with the state of exception.[107] So too is the work of Walter Benjamin. Agamben traces the debate between Schmitt and Benjamin to serve as a foil for his thesis on the state of exception.[108] Agamben reads Schmitt's theory of sovereignty as a response to Benjamin's 'Critique of Violence', published a year previous to the first publication of Schmitt's *Political Theology*.[109]

Whilst Schmitt strived to preserve the link between the exception and the juridical order to ensure that the law always maintains the monopoly of 'violence',[110] Benjamin aimed to 'ensure the possibility of a violence ... that lies absolutely "outside" ... and "beyond" ... the law and that, as such, could shatter the dialectic between lawmaking violence and law-preserving violence'.[111] This violence originates in human action entirely devoid of the law and its purpose is to break the cycle of the violence that creates law and the violence that maintains that law:

> A gaze directed only at what is close at hand can at most perceive a dialectical rising and falling in the lawmaking and law-preserving forms of violence. The law governing their oscillation rests on the circumstances that

---

[106] *Ibid.*
[107] Giorgio Agamben (tr. Daniel Heller-Roazen), *Homo Sacer: Sovereign Power and Bare Life* (Stanford University Press, 1998), pp. 11–12.
[108] Agamben, *State of Exception*, p. 35.   [109] *Ibid.*, p. 53.
[110] The word employed by Benjamin is *Gewalt*. As Louis Wolcher explains, 'for Benjamin, the essence of law is *Gewalt*, a German term that denotes power, authority, dominion, might, force and violence, and that is often used to refer to official or authorised means of domination'. Wolcher further notes that whilst the word violence does not fully capture the meaning of *Gewalt*, there is no single word in English that captures Benjamin's meaning any better. See Louis Wolcher, *Law's Task: The Tragic Circle of Law, Justice and Human Suffering* (Aldershot: Ashgate 2008), p. 33.
[111] Agamben, *State of Exception*, p. 53.

all law-preserving violence, in its duration, indirectly weakens the law-making violence it represents, by suppressing hostile counter-violence ... This lasts until either new forces or those earlier suppressed triumph over the hitherto lawmaking violence and thus found a new law, destined in its turn to decay. On the breaking of this cycle maintained by mythic forms of law, on the suspension of law with all the forces on which it depends as they depend on it, finally therefore on the abolition of state power, a new historical epoch is founded.[112]

Benjamin describes the 'law-destroying'[113] violence required to break this cycle as divine, pure or revolutionary violence;[114] a form of violence that he assumes is 'capable of validly and definitively discriminating between the just and the unjust'.[115] He does not offer any indication of the nature of divine violence or how it is to be identified.[116] In fact, he specifically denies that it can be recognised in any concrete case: 'Less possible and also less urgent for humankind, however, is to decide when unalloyed violence has been realised in particular cases.'[117] Louis Wolcher notes that whilst Benjamin exposes 'the terrible truth of universal historical violence by denying it any kind of rational ... justification', he 'cannot resist nurturing a desire for the appearance of a Messianic principle of division that would be beyond reproach'.[118] Benjamin's belief that a right or just action may be divinely recognisable allowed him to propose the possibility that human beings may be justified in their use of revolutionary violence.[119]

In absolute contrast to Schmitt, whose sovereign sustains both law-making and law preservation, Benjamin breaks the sovereign free from this cycle: 'But all mythic, law-making violence, which we may call "executive", is pernicious. Pernicious too, is the law-preserving, "administrative", violence that serves it. Divine violence ... may be called "sovereign" violence.'[120] As stated by Agamben, Schmitt responds to Benjamin's assurance of a pure violence beyond law by leading this violence back to the juridical order: 'According to Schmitt, there cannot be a pure violence – that is a violence absolutely outside the law – because

---

[112] Walter Benjamin (tr. Edmund Jephcott), 'Critique of Violence' in Marcus Bullock and Michael W. Jennings (eds.), *Walter Benjamin: Selected Writings, Vol. I, 1913–1926* (Cambridge, MA: The Belknap Press, 1996), p. 251.

[113] *Ibid.*, p. 249.   [114] *Ibid.*, p. 252.

[115] Wolcher, *Law's Task*, p. 34.

[116] Agamben, *Homo Sacer*, p. 63.

[117] Benjamin, 'Critique of Violence', p. 252; See also Wolcher, *Law's Task*, p. 34.

[118] Wolcher, *Law's Task*, p. 34.   [119] *Ibid.*, p. 35.

[120] Benjamin, 'Critique of Violence', p. 252.

in the state of exception it is included in the law through its very exclusion.'[121] Agamben reads, therefore, the exception as Schmitt's response to Benjamin, who strives to ensure the separation between violence and law by affirming the existence of an anomic space for human action. In order to tactically dispose of Benjamin's figure of pure, 'law-destroying' violence, Schmitt replaces his previous distinction between constituent and constituted power with the sovereign decision that suspends the law. Agamben deciphers that where Benjamin remarks upon the 'ultimate undecidabilty of all legal problems', Schmitt responds with the sovereign decision that conjoins anomie and the juridical law.[122] For Benjamin, it is impossible to recognise, by means of a decision, the situation in which pure violence has been realised. Schmitt, however, renders the sovereign decision as necessary in the extreme case, precisely because of the difficulty in ascertaining when this extreme case exists.[123] Sam Weber identifies, in both Benjamin and Schmitt, a 'methodological extremism'; they are both concerned with employing the extreme case in order to bring conceptual clarity to the normal,[124] as Schmitt puts it, 'not because of a romantic irony for the paradox, but because the seriousness of an insight goes deeper than the clear generalisations inferred from what ordinarily repeats itself'.[125] From this mutual employment of the extreme case, however, Benjamin and Schmitt diverge in their descriptions of sovereignty.[126] Benjamin, responding to Schmitt's theory of sovereignty, which gives the sovereign the last word on the state of exception by means of the decision,[127] alters the relationship between the state of exception and the juridical order by excluding the exception from the juridical order through the figure of the secularised baroque sovereign:[128] 'Whereas the modern concept of sovereignty amounts to a supreme executive decision on the part of the prince, the baroque concept emerges from a discussion of the state of emergency, and makes it the most important function of the prince to exclude this.'[129] For Benjamin, the state of exception is not

---

[121] Agamben, *State of Exception*, p. 54.
[122] *Ibid.*   [123] *Ibid.*, p. 55.
[124] Samuel Weber, 'Taking Exception to Decision: Walter Benjamin and Carl Schmitt' (1992) 22 *Diacritics* 5, 7.
[125] Schmitt, *Political Theology*, p. 15.
[126] Agamben, *State of Exception*, p. 55. Agamben makes this observation from his reading of Weber. See Weber, 'Taking Exception to Decision' 12.
[127] Weber 'Taking Exception to Decision' 10.
[128] Agamben, *State of Exception*, p. 55. See also Weber, 'Taking Exception to Decision' 12.
[129] Walter Benjamin, cited in Weber, 'Taking Exception to Decision' 12.

a miracle to be attributed to the sovereign; it is a catastrophe.[130] And the figure of the baroque sovereign is not the 'decider', analogous with God; the sovereign is human and incapable of decision.[131] Agamben concludes from his reading of the debate between Benjamin and Schmitt that where Schmitt relies on the decision to complete the relationship between sovereign power and the state of exception, Benjamin denies the sovereign the ability to decide and, thereby, divides this relationship.[132]

> This drastic redefinition of the sovereign function implies a different situation of the state of exception. It no longer appears as the threshold that guarantees the articulation between an inside and an outside, or between anomie and the juridical context, by virtue of a law that is in force in its suspension; it is rather, a zone of absolute indeterminacy between anomie and law, in which the sphere of creatures and the juridical order are caught up in single catastrophe.[133]

(2)   Exception as rule

This debate becomes even more relevant with Benjamin's statement, in his eighth thesis on the concept of history, that the exception has become the rule:

> The tradition of the oppressed teaches us that the 'state of emergency' in which we live is not the exception but the rule. We must attain to a conception of history that accords with this insight. Then we will clearly see that it is our task to bring about a real state of emergency, and this will improve our position in this struggle against fascism.[134]

In 1940, when Benjamin made this observation, the Third Reich was functioning as a sovereign dictatorship. The state of exception proclaimed in 1933 had, however, not been repealed and there was no attempt to replace the existing order. In Agamben's words, the exception and the rule had become indecidable. Benjamin, observing that the exception had become the rule, therefore challenges the assumptions of Schmitt's theory of the exception. In this regard, Agamben notes, '[s]overeign decision is no longer capable of performing the task that *Political Theology* assigned it; the rule which now coincides with what it lives by, devours itself'.[135]

---

[130] Agamben, *State of Exception*, p. 56.
[131] *Ibid.*, p. 57.   [132] *Ibid.*, p. 55.   [133] *Ibid.*, p. 57.
[134] Walter Benjamin (tr. Harry Zohn), 'On the Concept of History' in Howard Eiland and Michael W. Jennings (eds.), *Walter Benjamin: Selected Writings, Vol. IV, 1938–1940* (Cambridge, MA: The Belknap Press, 2003), p. 392.
[135] Agamben, *State of Exception*, p. 58.

Schmitt attempts at every stage to give the exception juridical content through the sovereign's decision to suspend the law, but Benjamin contends that the distinction between exception and rule no longer exists.

The debate between Benjamin and Schmitt manifests as a struggle over the anomie that constitutes the state of exception. Schmitt endeavours to ensure the exception a juridical context. Benjamin, on the other hand, argues that the true state of exception takes an anomic form devoid of law.[136] Agamben reads the debate between Benjamin and Schmitt as a struggle between the gods and giants on the nature of being. Whilst Schmitt continuously attempts to lodge the exception, and thus violence, within the juridical order by means of the divine decision, Benjamin constantly responds by assuring pure violence a space outside of law for human action. Agamben concludes that the state of exception is not a space of either sovereign violence or pure violence: '[T]hen the structure of the state of exception is even more complex than we have glimpsed it up to now, and the positions of the two sides that struggle in and for it are even more tightly woven into each other.'[137] In fact, for Agamben, the state of exception is neither simply the sovereign suspension of the juridical order nor is it a space of human action devoid of law. Rather, the state of exception is itself the foundation of the juridical order.

D. Agamben's state of exception

Agamben is concerned with the 'no-man's land', or state of exception, that he identifies 'between public law and political fact, and between the juridical order and life'.[138] He maintains that it is necessary to fathom the ambiguity of the state of exception in order to distinguish between the political and the juridical, and between law and authority. Agamben's ambition is to reach a platform from which it is possible to decipher the meaning of political action. In addition, his investigation is an attempt to rectify the fact that no theory of the state of exception exists in public law. The text opens with the question – '[q]uare siletis juristae in munere vestro?: why are you jurists silent about that which concerns you?' According to Agamben, jurists and theorists of public law are silent due to their contention that the state of necessity cannot take a juridical form, necessity being the basis on which the exception is founded. In other words, they tend not to consider the state of exception 'as a genuine juridical problem', but rather as a question of fact, following the dictum necessitas legum non

---

[136] *Ibid.*, p. 59.   [137] *Ibid.*, p. 60.   [138] *Ibid.*, p. 1.

habet (necessity has no law).[139] Agamben concedes that it is intrinsically difficult to provide a theory of the state of exception; the state of exception is not only difficult to theorise, it eludes definition because it exists 'at the limit between law and politics'.[140]

Agamben identifies the complex relationship that exists between the state of exception, political authority and the juridical order as the obstacle to reaching a theory of the state of exception. He asks, on the one hand, in what terms should exceptional measures be understood when they are employed by a political authority during political crisis? On the other hand, in what terms should the exception be understood when it is employed by the law, for example through the suspension of the constitution? In the first case, the authority to impose exceptional measures is politically derived but, because these measures are of legal consequence, they must also be understood in juridical terms. In the second case, he asks, more generally, what it means for the law to suspend itself:

> [I]f exceptional measures are the result of periods of political cri-
> sis and, as such, must be understood on political grounds and not
> juridico-constitutional grounds, then they find themselves in the para-
> doxical position of being juridical measures that cannot be understood
> in legal terms, and the state of exception appears as the legal form of what
> cannot have legal form. On the other hand, if the law employs the excep-
> tion – that is the suspension of law itself – as its original means of refer-
> ring to and encompassing life, then a theory of the state of exception is the
> preliminary condition for any definition of the relation that binds and, at
> the same time, abandons the living being to the law.[141]

Agamben makes it clear that the state of exception with which he is concerned is not a distinct body of law or type of law. Rather, it places the juridical order on hold and in so doing defines the limits of the law.[142] He describes the state of exception as the 'dominant paradigm of government in contemporary politics'; a response to the 'unstoppable progression of what has been called a global civil war'.[143] The state of exception, he argues, has transformed from a temporary and exceptional measure to a technique of government and it appears 'as a threshold of indeterminacy between democracy and absolutism'.[144] In describing the state of exception as the dominant paradigm of government in contemporary politics, Agamben deliberately negates the existence of the traditionally understood declared state of exception, which by its very nature is temporary.

---

[139] *Ibid.*   [140] *Ibid.*   [141] *Ibid.*
[142] *Ibid.*, p. 4.   [143] *Ibid.*, p. 2.   [144] *Ibid.*, p. 3.

The notion of the state of exception as limited in time and in space is the fiction that Agamben seeks to expose. To him such a state of exception is non-existent. It has been replaced by the notion of state security: 'In conformity with a continuing tendency in all of the Western democracies, the declaration of the state of exception has gradually been replaced by an unprecedented generalisation of the paradigm of security as the normal technique of government.'[145]

Two considerations are essential to Agamben's analysis – the state of exception as a creation of the democratic–revolutionary tradition and not the absolutist tradition and the state of exception as 'fictitious' or political, where a vocabulary of war is maintained metaphorically to justify recourse to extensive government powers.[146]

(1)   Locating the state of exception

Agamben differentiates between the different modes of accommodating the state of exception in Western legal tradition. He identifies Germany and France as having legal traditions that regulate the state of exception through the text of the constitution or through a law.[147] Provision is made for the declaration of a state of emergency, thus allowing states to remain within the law whilst suspending certain rights. Humphreys points to the existence of the derogations regime in international human rights law 'as a "concession" to the "inevitability of exceptional state measures in times of emergency, and also as means to somehow control these"'.[148] On the other hand, other states such as Italy, Switzerland, England[149] and the United States do not regulate the state of exception explicitly.

In the end, Agamben concludes that the mode of accommodation of the state of exception is relatively unimportant insofar as it does not define the existence of the resort to the state of exception: 'On the level of the material constitution something like a state of exception exists in all the above mentioned orders, and the history of the institution shows that its development is independent of its constitutional or legislative formalization.'[150]

[145] *Ibid.*, p. 14.
[146] Stephen Humphreys, 'Legalising Lawlessness: On Giorgio Agamben's State of Exception' (2006) 17 *European Journal of International Law* 677, 679.
[147] Agamben, *State of Exception*, p. 10.
[148] Humphreys, 'Legalising Lawlessness' 679.
[149] By England, Agamben is presumably referring to the United Kingdom.
[150] Agamben, *State of Exception*, p. 10.

The existence of the state of exception is not preconditioned by its positivist specification.

This division within the legal traditions, Agamben observes, is mirrored in the literature. Some scholars favour an accommodation approach in which the state of exception is included constitutionally or legislatively 'within the sphere of the juridical order'.[151] Certain among those who adhere to this perspective 'understand the state of exception to be an integral part of positive law because the necessity that grounds it acts as an autonomous source of law'; others view the state of exception as the state's right to its own preservation.[152] In contrast, it is also argued that the law cannot regulate that which has no normative content. These scholars consider the state of exception, and the necessity that grounds it, to be factual and thus outside of the juridical framework, although the state of exception may have consequences for and within the law.[153]

Agamben, however, dismisses both of these approaches as an unsatisfactory explanation of the state of exception.[154] He argues that such a simplistic oppositional approach – inside/outside – is an inadequate explanation for the state of exception. Pertinently, he questions how, concerning the first approach, the juridical order could contain that which it suspends and in so doing include lawlessness within it: 'If the state of exception's characteristic property is a (total or partial) suspension of the juridical order, how can such a suspension still be contained within it? How can anomie be inscribed within the juridical order?'[155] With respect to the latter approach, which considers the state of exception as fact unconnected to the law, he deliberates on how the law can fail to provide in that situation where it is most needed: 'And if the state of exception is instead only a factual situation, and is as such unrelated or contrary to law, how is it possible for the order to contain a lacuna precisely where the decisive situation is concerned?'[156] Agamben seeks, therefore, to define the meaning of this lacuna.

In pointing to what he sees as the essential misinterpretation of the meaning of the state of exception, Agamben forces examination of that which, by its very nature, eludes investigation. In grappling with the notion of either anomie or a lacuna in the law, he comes to the conclusion that neither lawlessness nor a loophole explains the state of

---

[151] *Ibid.*, p. 23.   [152] *Ibid.*   [153] *Ibid.*
[154] Humphreys, 'Legalising Lawlessness' 679.
[155] Agamben, *State of Exception*, p. 23.   [156] *Ibid.*

exception. He rules out a black or white approach to its positioning and, in fact, admits that it is the grey area of intersection between the two approaches where the state of exception is located. In other words, the state of exception is neither purely juridical nor purely extra-legal. It is exclusively neither:

> In truth, the state of exception is neither external nor internal to the jur-
> idical order, and the problem of defining it concerns precisely a threshold,
> or a zone of indifference, where inside and outside do not exclude each
> other but rather blur with each other. The suspension of the norm does
> not mean its abolition, and the zone of anomie that it establishes is not (or
> at least claims not to be) unrelated to the juridical order.[157]

Agamben conceives of the exception as a form of exclusion of the individual case from the rule. In being excluded from the rule, this does not mean that the connection to the rule is severed. The very existence of the rule preconditions its suspension, and in suspension, the exclusion confirms the existence of the rule. According to Agamben, '[t]he rule applies to the exception in no longer applying, in withdrawing from it'.[158] He further elaborates that the state of exception, contrary to Schmitt's conception, is 'not the chaos that precedes order' but the result of the suspension of order. The suspension of order does more than just exclude the exception, Agamben notes; in accordance with the Latin explanation of exception, *excipere*, the exception is *taken outside* of the order.[159]

(2)   State of necessity

As mentioned at the outset of this section, Agamben maintains that the resistance to theorising the state of exception is rooted in reliance on the belief that necessity grounds the state of exception, which public law tends to consider extracted from the juridical realm. The problem with defining the state of exception extends to the definition of necessity. In that regard, Agamben notes:

> The attempt to resolve the state of exception into the state of necessity
> thus runs up against as many and even more serious aporias of the phe-
> nomenon that it should have explained. Not only does necessity ultim-
> ately come down to a decision, but that on which it decides is, in truth,
> something undecidable in fact and law.[160]

---

[157] *Ibid.*   [158] Agamben, *Homo Sacer*, p. 18.
[159] *Ibid.*   [160] Agamben, *State of Exception*, p. 30.

The 'decision' is whether or not the norm should be abridged at a particular time or, more accurately, whether or not a particular case should be released from 'literal application'.[161]

Bolstering the argument against the simplistic resolution of the state of exception's connection to the juridical order through the state of necessity is Agamben's identification of the subjectivity of the state of necessity.[162] He cites Giorgio Balladore-Pallieri, writing in 1970, who observed that '[t]he concept of necessity is an entirely subjective one, relative to the aim that one wants to achieve'.[163] Balladore-Pallieri observed that 'the recourse to necessity entails a moral or political (or, in any case, extrajudicial) evaluation, by which the juridical order is judged and is held to be worthy of preservation or strengthening even at the price of its possible violation. For this reason, the principle of necessity is, in every case, always a revolutionary principle'.[164] In this reasoning, necessity demonstrates that the norm exists through its violation.

Attempts to explain the state of exception through the state of necessity as the source of law are vilified by the consideration both of necessity's relation to the particular case and of its subjectivity, of its unrelatedness to fact and to law. The state of necessity is not a source of law. As Agamben demonstrates, it occupies an opening in the juridical order. The state of necessity thus represents 'a space without law', where law is suspended, and the 'state of exception appears as the opening of a fictitious lacuna in the order for the purpose of safeguarding the existence of the norm and its applicability to the normal situation'.[165] This lacuna does not manifest as a gap in the law; it is other than the law insofar as the law is observed in its breach: 'That is, the state of exception separates the norm from its application in order to make its application possible. It introduces a zone of anomie into the law in order to make the effective regulation [*normazione*] of the real possible.'[166]

(3)   Force of law

Having pinpointed the state of exception as a zone of anomie built into the juridical order, Agamben turns to elaborate upon the function of this lawlessness in relation to the norm and on what the separation of norm

---

[161] *Ibid.*, p. 25.   [162] *Ibid.*, p. 30.
[163] Giorgio Balladore-Pallieri, *Dritto Costituzionale* (Milan: Giuffrè, 1970), p. 168, cited in Agamben, *State of Exception*, p. 30.
[164] *Ibid.*   [165] Agamben, *State of Exception*, p. 31.   [166] *Ibid.*, p. 36.

from application means. To do this, he employs the notion of force-of-law. The state of exception, he claims, posits law as in force but not applied. Accordingly, '[t]he state of exception is an anomic space in which what is at stake is a force of law without law', and this is depicted as the force of the emptiness of law.[167] In a sense, by colonising that space that has, in the state of exception, become empty of operating law, through the separation of norm and application, the state authority (for example) becomes the force behind a law that is suspended: 'The state of exception is the opening up of a space in which application and norm reveal their separation and a pure force-of-law realizes (that is, applies by ceasing to apply [*dis-applicando*]) a norm whose application has been suspended',[168] and the exception has become the norm.

(4)   Normalcy, exception and empty space

Agamben describes the juridical system of the West as a 'double structure, formed by two heterogeneous yet coordinated elements'.[169] These elements are, in short, the state of normalcy, the 'normative and juridical', and the state of lawlessness, 'the anomic and metajuridical'.[170] As Agamben has shown, normalcy requires the state of exception in order to be applied. Conversely, the state of exception can only exist in the suspension of normalcy. In his description of this dialectic between the normative and the anomic, Agamben evokes an image of a parasitic symbiosis because of which 'the ancient dwelling of law is fragile and, in straining to maintain its own order, is always already in the process of ruin and decay'.[171] It is, he argues, the state of exception that maintains this structure and allows it to function, binding together the juridical and the political, fictional though the hold may be. However, he warns that 'when they tend to coincide in a single person, when the state of exception, in which they are bound and blurred together, becomes the rule, then the juridico-political system transforms itself into a killing machine'.[172]

It is in this space – where a delicate balance, no more than a fictional dialectic, is maintained through the state of exception, which in itself is no more than 'an empty space, a human action with no relation to law [which] stands before a norm with no relation to life' – that 'we live'.[173]

Agamben's effort to realise a theory of the state of exception takes him through an analysis of Schmitt's theory, which fastens the state of

---

[167] *Ibid.*, p. 39.   [168] *Ibid.*, p. 40.   [169] *Ibid.*, p. 86.
[170] *Ibid.*   [171] *Ibid.*   [172] *Ibid.*   [173] *Ibid.*

exception to dictatorship and which attempts to inscribe the state of exception, and its consequences, within the juridical order. Agamben falsifies this conception of the exception, stating that it 'is not defined as a fullness of powers, a pleromatic state of law, as in the dictatorial model, but as a kenomatic state, an emptiness and standstill of the law'.[174] His discrediting of Schmitt's theory of the exception provokes the question of what, then, it is that constitutes a state of exception. Agamben argues that previous attempts to rationalise the state of exception as existing either solely within the law or solely outside of the law are flawed. For the state of exception, grounded in the state of necessity, like the state of necessity, is both a juridical concept and an extra-legal concept, necessarily and factually. The state of exception is localised at the intersection of law and politics, where it opens up a zone of indistinction, prescribed by law but devoid of law. In this zone of anomie, the state of exception is driven by the force of political action assuming and activating the suspension of law. In this act, the political gives realisation to the norm that has been suspended, but in the absence of that norm's implementation. The norm that has been taken out of function, through the political act, simultaneously captures and abandons its subject. The political, as a result, decides through law on the fate of the living being.

E.   Conclusion

Agamben's theorisation of the state of exception is instructive on the question of torture for two interconnected reasons. First, his theory provides a frame for conceptualising the act of torture. Second, his interrogation of traditional approaches to accommodating the exception and his subsequent dismissal of the traditional topographical approach to the exception provides the analytical tool to unpack proposals that attempt to regulate or accommodate torture in conformity with the rule of law.

The act of torture constitutes a paradigm of the state of exception as theorised by Agamben. Torture is necessarily an exceptional practice, insofar as, in order for torture to be perpetrated, there must be an exception to the norm. This exception, on the one hand, can, and should, be understood as a violation of the norm. However, when the exception is tolerated, justified, institutionalised or quasi-legalised, its meaning becomes even more essential to grasp. To grasp the meaning of exceptional torture, a rethinking of the relationship between norm and violation is required.

[174] *Ibid.*, p. 48.

This is so, not because it is incorrect to describe torture as a violation of the norm, but because exceptional torture retains a connection to the juridical order. This connection is established in the suspension of the norm; the application of the norm is withdrawn and replaced by the political act that has the force of law. The act of torture, so understood, does not constitute a legal black hole. The norm is not abolished. However, the victim of torture is excluded from the protection of the norm whilst, simultaneously, captured within the state's notion of order. Thus, the act of torture reduces its victim to a position of inescapable rightlessness in the face of the constituted power of the state. The factual reality, therefore, is not that there is an exception, in the literal sense, from the rule in the particular case, rather the exception takes on normative force. It is in this sense that the exception becomes the norm.[175]

It is this relationship between the law and the exception that the ticking bomb scenario masks. The attempt by Alan Dershowitz to bring the ticking bomb exception into the legal order through the torture warrant proposal, and by Oren Gross to exclude this exception through the extra-legal model, cannot escape this posited space of exceptional torture. The torture warrant procedure strives to cabin the exceptional use of torture inside the juridical order. The extra-legal measures model endeavours to secure torture a space outside of the juridical order as something external. Neither of the proposed solutions manages to explain how the suspension of the norm prohibiting torture can be brought into conformity with the rule of law. The theoretical problem with both of these proposed solutions lies in their failure to account for the suspension of the norm. Dershowitz, for his part, advocates that the judiciary assume the decision on whether an exception to the torture prohibition is necessary in a ticking bomb situation. This judicial determination of the exception is necessary for the exceptional use of torture to comply with the rule of law.[176] Whilst insisting that the exception is, through the torture warrant procedure, made compatible with the rule of law, Dershowitz neglects to explain by what legal procedures this judicial determination is made. It is unlikely that this is an oversight. In reality, the torture warrant procedure is judicial in name only since the decision, to be made by the judge, is in fact administrative.[177] Gross' model attempts to sever the activation of the

---

[175] Agamben, *Homo Sacer*, p. 18.

[176] John T. Parry, 'Torture Warrants the Rule of Law' (2008) 71 *Albany Law Review* 885, 889.

[177] Yuval Ginbar, *Why not Torture Terrorists? Moral, Practical, and Legal Aspects of the 'Ticking Bomb' Justification for Torture* (Oxford University Press, 2008), p. 190.

exception from the legal order, although it recognises a potential place for the law in deciding on the validity of the public official's decision to torture. Gross insists that the norm remains in force even whilst the public official perpetrates the act of torture: 'Legal principles, rules and norms continue to apply throughout the exception and can serve as appropriate benchmarks by which to assess both the legality of, and the appropriate response to, actions taken by public officials in times of emergency.'[178] From Gross' perspective, the public official who tortures is operating outside of the law. The meaning of 'outside the law' in this context is unclear, however; is torture outside of the law illegal torture? Since the ex post ratification procedure should decide this question, the public official who decides to torture is neither acting legally or illegally but extra-legally. The logical incoherence in Gross' model exists in the fact that although the norm remains, as Gross would have it, it does not remain in force in the particular situation.

As the following chapter will demonstrate, the rule of law cannot bring torture under its control, as Dershowitz advocates, nor can the rule of law separate itself from torture, in the way that Gross claims. Rather than showing how the use of torture in the ticking bomb case might be regulated or accommodated, the deconstruction of these proposals actually highlights how narratives are woven to accommodate the ticking bomb scenario.

---

[178] Oren Gross, 'Extra-Legality and the Ethic of Political Responsibility' in Victor V. Ramraj (ed.), *Emergencies and the Limits of Legality* (Cambridge University Press, 2008), p. 63.

4

Legal, extra-legal or illegal? The academic debate on the use of torture in exceptional circumstances

There are three different academic perspectives that have been set forth in regard to the question of torture's justifiability in exceptional circumstances. These perspectives reflect the moral, legal and practical arguments that underpin the academic torture debate. For our purposes, these perspectives are termed the qualified torture prohibition, the pragmatic absolute torture prohibition and the absolute torture prohibition respectively. The first position holds that torture may be necessary in exceptional circumstances and should be judicially sanctioned.[1] The second position supports the preservation of an absolute ban on torture but argues that it may be necessary to violate the prohibition in exceptional circumstances.[2] The third position maintains that the absolute prohibition against torture is inviolable under any circumstance.[3]

These perspectives are discussed and deconstructed with a dual objective: first, of elucidating the relationship between the law and the exception, as represented by the ticking bomb scenario, and, second, of clarifying why the ticking bomb scenario is a fallacious frame for this debate.

[1] For the representative 'torture warrant' proposal, see Alan M. Dershowitz, *Why Terrorism Works: Understanding the Threats, Responding to the Challenge* (New Haven: Yale University Press, 2002), pp. 158–9; Alan M. Dershowitz, 'Tortured Reasoning' in Sanford Levinson (ed.), *Torture: A Collection* (Oxford University Press, 2004), p. 257. Sanford Levinson provides a conditional approach to Dershowitz's torture warrant proposal, which is also examined. See Sanford Levinson, '"Precommitment" and "Postcommitment": The Ban on Torture in the Wake of September 11' (2003) 81 *Texas Law Review* 2013, 2043.

[2] For the extra-legal measures model proposal, see Oren Gross, 'Chaos and Rules: Should Reponses to Violent Crises Always Be Constitutional?' (2003) 112 *Yale Law Journal* 1011, 1097; Oren Gross, 'Are Torture Warrants Warranted? Pragmatic Absolutism and Official Disobedience' (2004) 88 *Minnesota Law Review* 1481; Oren Gross, 'The Prohibition on Torture and the Limits of the Law' in Sanford Levinson (ed.), *Torture: A Collection* (Oxford University Press 2004), p. 229; Oren Gross, 'Extra-Legality and the Ethic of Political Responsibility' in Victor V. Ramraj (ed.), *Emergencies and the Limits of Legality* (Cambridge University Press, 2008), p. 60.

[3] For Jeremy Waldron's idea that the prohibition of torture represents a legal archetype, see Jeremy Waldron, 'Torture and Positive Law: Jurisprudence for the White House' (2005) 105 *Columbia Law Review* 1681.

A. Qualified torture prohibition

Proponents of a qualified or conditional torture ban argue that there are exceptional situations that necessitate the use of torture to prevent the loss of innocent life. These exceptional circumstances should not be dealt with in a legal vacuum; rather, the use of torture in the exceptional case should be legislatively or judicially monitored. Advocates of a conditional torture ban view their position as a necessary response to a challenge that must be addressed. The question of torture cannot be simply left to work itself out in a 'twilight zone';[4] it is an issue that requires open and frank debate. In arguing the qualified prohibition position, proponents tend to highlight the primacy of the rule of law both in confronting this challenge and in its ultimate regulation.

(1) The torture warrant

Alan Dershowitz is one of the more prominent advocates of the qualified prohibition on torture. Dershowitz supports the introduction of a torture warrant system to judicially supervise torture in ticking bomb cases. He views the current ban in place on the use of torture as laden with hypocrisy and deniability.[5] To support this contention, he argues that non-lethal torture is, at any rate, in use by the United States and its allies and, furthermore, that even lethal torture would be used in an imminent 'mass terrorism' attack, with public support. He asks whether it would not be normatively better to regulate such acts of torture by means of a torture warrant, which would provide 'accountability, record-keeping, standards and limitations'.[6] For Dershowitz, this represents an important policy question about how a democracy should 'make difficult choice-of-evil decisions in situations for which there is no good resolution'.[7]

Dershowitz regards the ticking bomb dilemma in the democratic state as exhibiting a tripartite conflict:

(a) The practice of torture below the radar screen of accountability means that there is no legitimation of the practice, but its use expands;

---

[4] 'Excerpts of the Report of the Commission of Inquiry into the Methods of Investigation of the General Security Service Regarding Hostile Terrorist Activity' (hereinafter Excerpts of the Report), (1989) 23 *Israel Law Review* 146, 182.
[5] Dershowitz, 'Tortured Reasoning' 265.
[6] *Ibid.*, 266.   [7] *Ibid.*, 258.

(b) the practice of torture is regulated, thus legitimising the practice but adding accountability and perhaps reducing its severity and frequency;

(c) nothing is done, preventable acts of terrorism occur and the public subsequently demands the further constraint of liberty.[8]

These are the options which must be weighted against each other in finding a definitive solution to the torture problem. Dershowitz's tripartite conflict implicitly centralises the use of torture as the compelling variable in the ticking bomb case; that is to say, he supposes that if torture is not used, preventable acts of terrorism will occur. In other words, his concern starts with the management of the practice rather than with an examination of the practice itself.

(i) Judicial versus extra-legal torture

Dershowitz first argued for the introduction of the torture warrant in Israel in the late 1980s. The Landau Commission of Inquiry had at that time authorised the General Security Services to use 'moderate physical pressure' in interrogation.[9] With respect to the effectiveness of the Commission of Inquiry's recommendations, Dershowitz observes that some acts of terrorism that may have killed many civilians were undoubtedly prevented by the use of 'moderate physical pressure', but he further contends that the impact of saving these lives on basic human rights was costly. In assessing the situation that resulted from the Commission of Inquiry's recommendations, Dershowitz came to the realisation that the 'extraordinarily rare situation of the hypothetical ticking bomb terrorist was serving as a moral, intellectual, and legal justification for the pervasive *system* of coercive interrogation, which though not the paradigm of torture, certainly bordered on it'.[10] According to Dershowitz, a policy based on the defence of necessity, which he describes as 'a "state of nature" plea', should not provide a surrogate to legislative or judicial means in dealing with a long-term problem: 'It is ironic ... that in an effort to incorporate the interrogation methods of the GSS into "the law itself", the Commission selected the most lawless of legal doctrines – that of necessity – as the prime candidate for coverage.'[11] Dershowitz found it problematic that the means chosen by the Landau Commission did not

---

[8] *Ibid.*, 267.   [9] 'Excerpts of the Report' 182.
[10] Dershowitz, 'Tortured Reasoning' 258–9.
[11] *Ibid.*, 260.

represent a democratic means insofar as it consisted in the unnecessary continuous besmirching of the rule of law:

> A state agency faced with systematic problems over a long period of time has options available to it other than civil disobedience – other than the deliberate decision to violate the rule of law repeatedly. These options may not be completely satisfactory, but they are democratic options: namely, to seek a change in the law, an exemption from the law's strictures, or a change in its own responsibilities.[12]

The torture warrant was, therefore, Dershowitz's alternative to a policy based on the defence of necessity.

In formulating the 'torture warrant' proposal, Dershowitz reasoned that permission to use non-lethal torture should be limited exclusively to the 'compelling but rare' ticking bomb case with advanced judicial approval.[13] The goal of this proposal is to limit the use of torture to the smallest degree possible, all the while creating public accountability for its use:

> Since judges would not be willing to issue any such warrants, such a requirement would eliminate, or severely limit, any resort to torture. Under our current hypocritical approach, we declare torture illegal and yet most countries in the world employ it under the table and without accountability. My proposed procedure would make that hypocritical approach more difficult to justify.[14]

Dershowitz makes two claims here. First, he contends that judges would be unwilling to issue torture warrants unless they were confronted with that rare, compelling case, and, second, he asserts that because of the existence of the warrant system, there would be no justification for torturing extra-legally, without having sought a warrant. In regard to the first point, he maintains that the majority of judges would require compelling evidence before issuing a warrant because, in so doing, they would be departing from constitutional norms. He argues, additionally, that even if judges were to rarely turn down a request, this would still lead to less torture as compared to a lawless system in which torture occurs without accountability. Dershowitz admits to the possibility that individual agents might nonetheless torture without a warrant, but is unconcerned as they would have 'no excuse'.[15] The torture warrant would not compromise civil

---

[12] Alan M. Dershowitz, 'Is it Necessary to Apply 'Physical Pressure' to Terrorists – and to Lie about it?' (1989) 23 *Israel Law Review* 192, 197.

[13] Dershowitz, 'Tortured Reasoning' 259.

[14] Alan M. Dershowitz, 'Terrorism and Torture', *The Irish Times* (10 January 2003), p. 15.

[15] Dershowitz, *Why Terrorism Works*, pp. 158–9.

liberties but in fact maximise them insofar as, in these ticking bomb cases, torture would otherwise be practised without accountability, and thus presumably in ever-widening circumstances.[16] A 'formal, visible, accountable, and centralized system' would be logically 'easier to control than an ad-hoc, off the books, and under-the-radar-screen nonsystem'.[17] In addition to limiting the general practice of torture, he argues that the formal requirement of a judicial torture warrant would diminish the amount of violence actually directed against the suspect in interrogation.[18]

The judiciary and not individual interrogators should enforce these rules and maintain the balance between the need for security and the imperatives of liberty: 'The essence of a democracy is placing responsibility for difficult choices in a visible and neutral institution like the judiciary.'[19] Dershowitz maintains that the Israeli Supreme Court, in its decision in 1999, erred in leaving open the possibility for individual members of the security services to raise the defence of necessity:

> [U]nless a democratic nation is prepared to have a proposed action governed by the rule of law, it should not undertake, or authorise, that action. As a corollary, if it needs to take the proposed action, then it must subject it to the rule of law. Suggesting that an after-the-fact 'necessity defence' might be available in extreme cases is not an adequate substitute for explicit advanced approval.[20]

Dershowitz does concede that the major drawback with the torture warrant system is that it legitimises a repugnant practice. He reasons, however, that 'it is better to legitimate and control a *specific* practice that will occur than to legitimate a *general* practice of tolerating extra-legal actions so long as they operate under the table of scrutiny and beneath the radar screen of accountability'.[21]

(ii) Outdated laws

Dershowitz's advocacy of judicially monitored torture is embedded in his view that the nature of warfare has changed profoundly since the Second World War, as the proliferation of weapons of mass destruction, which 'in the hands of suicide terrorists with no fear of death and no home address have rendered useless the deterrent threat of massive

[16] Dershowitz, 'Tortured Reasoning' 259.
[17] Dershowitz, *Why Terrorism Works*, p. 158.
[18] *Ibid.*
[19] Dershowitz, 'Tortured Reasoning' 264.
[20] *Ibid.*   [21] *Ibid.*, 272.

retaliation'.[22] He maintains that it is the potential occurrence and prevention of such 'mega-acts' that increases the pressure in the torture debate.[23] Dershowitz also contends that the current law contains a 'vast black hole', which has freed governmental action from the constraints of the rule of law. This black hole, he argues, accounts for the existence of the United States detention facility at Guantánamo Bay and other, secret detention sites, as well as the practice of extraordinary rendition. It follows then that changing the old laws is necessary for the protection of human rights and democratic accountability:

> Laws must change with the times. They must adapt to new challenges. That has been the genius of the common law ... What is needed is a new set of laws, based on the principles of the old laws of war and human rights – the protection of civilians – but adapted to the new threats against civilian victims of terrorism.[24]

Beyond his suggestion that these outdated laws require amendment to cater for the new reality, Dershowitz does not provide much substantive legal analysis. It is not clear exactly how this torture warrant system and the rules governing the methods to be used in interrogation would be designed as legislation. It is equally unclear how a system of torture warrants introduced into the United States legal system would conform with the United States' obligations under international law.

In terms of circumventing the United States' constitutional safeguards, he argues:

> Those who have valuable, real-time information will be interrogated, and – short of the absolute law against 'torture' – there are few, if any, rules governing the nature of permissible interrogation when the object is not to elicit 'incrimination confessions' for purposes of criminal prosecution, but rather to obtain 'preventive intelligence' for the purpose of pre-empting future terrorist attacks.[25]

In this regard, he considers that interrogation techniques including the use of truth serum and torture are not substantively prohibited in the United States Supreme Court's interpretation of the Fifth Amendment privilege against self-incrimination. He argues that the Supreme Court interprets the exclusionary rule as prohibiting only the introduction of the evidence

---

[22] Alan M. Dershowitz, 'Should we Fight Terror with Torture' *The Independent* (3 July 2006), p. 1.
[23] Dershowitz, *Why Terrorism Works*, p. 138.
[24] Dershowitz, 'Should we fight terror with torture', p. 1.   [25] *Ibid.*

from such methods in a criminal trial against the person on whom the methods were used. In order to make the interrogational torture practicable, the argument follows, the suspect can be given 'use immunity', which would satisfy the rule against self-incrimination.[26] The suspect can thus be compelled to answer questions under duress and the only issue to be established is the level of compulsion that can be constitutionally applied. Truth serum, in his opinion, can be lawfully used as it (i) does not violate the privilege against self-incrimination – the suspect has been given immunity so he has no such privilege, or (ii) his right of bodily integrity. To argue this latter point, he relies on a case in which a drunk-driver was involuntarily injected to remove blood for alcohol testing. He opines that there is certainly no constitutional distinction between an injection to remove a liquid and an injection to insert a liquid.[27] For Dershowitz, the due process clauses of the Fifth and Fourteenth Amendments are the only potential constitutional barriers to the permissibility of torture in ticking bomb cases. However, he pronounces these to be 'general and sufficiently flexible to permit an argument that the only process "due" a terrorist suspected of refusing to disclose information necessary to prevent a terrorist attack is the requirement of probable cause and some degree of judicial supervision'.[28]

Dershowitz suggests that the absolute prohibition on torture in the ticking bomb case may be based more on historical and aesthetic considerations than on moral or logical ones.[29] He attempts, therefore, to extrapolate a more contemporary moral theory to fit the ticking bomb scenario. In his formulation of a model of judicial torture, he adopts a 'constrained' utilitarianism to support the legal and practical arguments:

> The simple cost–benefit analysis for employing such non-lethal torture seems overwhelming: it is surely better to inflict nonlethal pain on one guilty terrorist who is illegally withholding information needed to prevent an act of terrorism than to permit a large number of innocent victims to die. Pain is a lesser and more remediable harm than death; and the lives of a thousand innocent people should be valued more than the bodily integrity of one guilty person.[30]

Dershowitz is not content to rest with a 'simple-minded, quantitative case utilitarianism', which he criticises as having 'no inherent limiting principle'

---

[26] Alan M. Dershowitz, 'Is there a Torturous Road to Justice', *Los Angeles Times* (8 November 2001).

[27] *Ibid.*   [28] Dershowitz, *Why Terrorism Works*, p. 135.

[29] *Ibid.*, p. 148.   [30] *Ibid.*, p. 144.

and as 'morality by numbers'.[31] He suggests that in order to construct a version of act or case utilitarianism with principled brakes, constraints should be borrowed from rule utilitarianism or from other moral principles. He refers to the prohibition against deliberately punishing the innocent as one such example.[32] In other words, Dershowitz attempts to introduce principled controls to his utilitarian assessment in order to argue a more moral perspective that would prevent the descent down 'slippery slopes' into lethal torture or torture of the innocent. He remarks, 'if nonlethal torture were legally limited to convicted terrorists who had knowledge of future massive terrorist attacks, were given immunity, and still refused to provide the information, there might still be objections to the use of torture, but they would have to go beyond the slippery slope argument'.[33]

(2)   Torture warrant with conditions

Sanford Levinson adopts Dershowitz's torture warrant proposal. He is unconvinced of the realism of the absolute ban in force. The prohibition of torture, according to Levinson, 'appears to have what may be describable as "expressive" or "aspirational" dimensions that serve to make it a less than completely reliable guide to the actual behaviour even of the states that have ratified it – at least with regard to the absoluteness of its prohibition'.[34] Given the widespread practice of torture, he does not consider

---

[31] *Ibid.*, p. 146.   [32] *Ibid.*   [33] *Ibid.*, p. 147.

[34] Levinson, '"Precommitment" and "Postcommitment"' 2018. To support this point, Levinson cites Oona Hathaway who, in her study of compliance with human rights treaties, finds that non-compliance is common. See Oona A. Hathaway, 'Do Human Rights Treaties Make a Difference?' (2002) 111 *Yale Law Journal* 1870. Hathaway has also researched the effects of treaties prohibiting torture. Amongst other observations, she finds that countries that ratify treaties outlawing torture do not necessarily have better torture practices than those that do not ratify. However, Hathaway does not conclude from this research that non-compliance is evidence of the utter ineffectiveness of the prohibition of torture or of international law, more generally:

> The Convention against Torture has not brought an end to states' horrific abuse of their own citizens. Far from it ... Violations of both the letter and spirit of the law are rampant. Yet while the Convention is not a panacea, neither is the problem of torture beyond the reach of international law. Although the Convention has not achieved its lofty goals, it has contributed to the now almost universal view that torture is an unacceptable practice. By facing up to the Convention's successes and its failures, we can begin to learn how to harness the real but limited power of international law to continue to change the world for the better.

See Oona A. Hathaway, 'The Promise and Limits of the International Law of Torture' in Sanford Levinson (ed.), *Torture: A Collection* (Oxford University Press, 2004). pp. 199, 210.

'the law-on-the-books' approach to considering the absolute torture prohibition to represent what 'societies are likely to do when a perceived
crunch comes'.[35] Like Dershowitz, Levinson believes that the events of 11
September represented such a decisive point. As a consequence of his concern that torture was being practised by the United States either directly
or through engagement with other states that practice torture,[36] Levinson
maintained, '[i]t is vitally important that we discuss what is being done in
our name'.[37]

Levinson reaches agreement with Dershowitz, having dismissed other
approaches that have been put forward in response to this discussion: he
is unconvinced by arguments that consider torture to be always inefficacious; he does not agree with an approach that would see the commitment
to the prohibition dismissed altogether; he does not favour the definitional tactic whereby it is argued that certain techniques or treatment
being applied do not constitute torture; and he does not concur with a
'don't ask, don't tell' or dirty hands approach.[38] Levinson is sympathetic
to aspects of the latter position; however, he is critical of its failure to deal
with the ex post legal aspect of using torture. He points to the 'practical
difficulty' of having torture victims, who, 'if they are left to live', may
wish to invoke criminal proceedings to sue for civil damages.[39] In this ex
post environment, he envisages problems with enforcing the prohibition
on torture in the courtroom where jurors would find it difficult to con-
vict and, moreover, sentence a torturer who they believe has tortured an
unattractive victim to safeguard nationalist interests. This would consequently lead to an 'underenforcement of the norm against torture'.[40]

Levinson views the torture warrant, therefore, as providing the method
by which torture can be used with a minimum effect of legitimising
torture:

> One should certainly address the possibility that the requirement of a
> warrant, coupled with strict liability and severe punishment for any tor-
> turous activity that occurs without such a warrant, would generate less
> deviation from the basic precommitment against torture and other inhu-
> mane and degrading actions imposed on the vulnerable by a powerful
> state.[41]

---

[35] Levinson, '"Precommitment" and "Postcommitment"' 2019.
[36] Ibid., 2052. Levinson's text was written before the revelations from Abu Ghraib and the
watershed that followed. At that time there was no substantive proof that agents of the
United States were engaging in torture or in practices such as extraordinary rendition.
[37] Ibid., 2050. [38] Ibid., 2028–42. [39] Ibid., 2043.
[40] Ibid., 2048. [41] Ibid., 2045.

Levinson envisages that with a strict liability torture warrant procedure, the torturer would be subject to the ex post absolute enforcement of the prohibition should torture occur without the agent having first secured such a warrant. This would lessen the possibility of unintentionally developing a two-tier situation of torture legitimisation by, on the one hand, legitimising some torture through the introduction of a warrant procedure and, on the other hand, legitimation of some occurrences of torture in the prosecution of extra-legal torture.

In order to minimise the occurrence of torture warrants and to enhance the credibility of the torture warrant procedure, Levinson argues that certain conditions must exist. First, all torture warrants should be publicly disclosed, with written opinions subject to scrutiny. He recognises that such written opinions may not be able to specify all of the evidence that the judge would have at their disposal in deciding on the issuance of the warrant.[42] Second, the individual subject to the torture warrant request should be brought before the judge so that the judge would have to recognise their own complicity in the torture and, thus, be denied any detachment from the act. He suggests that the judges in question might undergo torture in order to experience exactly what the victim of torture would be condemned to, should a warrant be issued. Levinson is wary of the difficulty with enforcing complicity of the judges. He notes that certain judges who hold an absolute objection to the practice might refuse to be complicit. In that regard, he points to Justice Scalia's remark that in capital punishment cases the judge is complicit in the act to the extent that if they hold a moral obligation against the act, then they should not preside over the case. Levinson holds that the judge would be similarly complicit with the torture warrant. Finally, 'just compensation' for the violation of the individual's right not to be tortured should be introduced. Aware that the suggestion might cause offence, given the context, Levinson emphasises the role that these compensatory payments might play in restricting instances of torture. He proposes that all those against whom a torture warrant is issued should receive a significant compensatory payment, and that this payment should be increased in cases where those tortured did not have significant information to provide the authorities.[43]

B.   Pragmatic prohibition of torture

A second model on torture argues that the absolute prohibition of torture should be upheld with the realisation that, in exceptional cases, public

---

[42] *Ibid.*, 2048.   [43] *Ibid.*, 2049

officials will step outside of the legal framework – act extra-legally – by employing torture to acquire information in order to prevent an impending act of unlawful violence. This position contains two competing aspirations. Proponents want to uphold the sacrosanct prohibition – the absolute individual and societal right to be free from torture. Simultaneously, they want to protect society from acts of terrorism and defend the right to life of the victims of such acts. This position best illustrates the tension that exists between the moral compulsion to never defend torture and submission to the pressure to respond to the ticking bomb hypothetical. The preference for an extra-legal approach is motivated by an opposition to any form of judicial regulation of torture. The pragmatic prohibitionist would rather operate outside of the law. Slavoj Žižek encapsulates the tension of the pragmatic prohibition position; rather than talking about what to do in ticking bomb situations, and rather than regulating torture in these cases, should the situation arise, 'we should simply do it'.[44] Žižek's response is at one end of the pragmatic scale: he refuses to engage in a discussion on the management of this issue. Gross' extra-legal measures model provides a mechanism that combines an official disobedience approach with a system for accountability, thus extending the analysis into a means for attaining ex post ratification of official disobedience.

(1)   The extra-legal measures model

The pragmatic torture prohibition strives to accommodate exceptional circumstances alongside the absolute legal prohibition. In contrast to the qualified torture prohibition, which seeks to accommodate the prohibition within the law, this position seeks to accommodate the exception extra-legally. The extra-legal measures model negotiates a middle ground between the moral and legal nature of the torture prohibition based on the concept of pragmatic absolutism. This pragmatic absolutist perspective attempts to navigate between, on the one hand, surrendering the legal prohibition on torture to the ticking bomb hypothetical and, on the other hand, upholding the torture ban 'no matter what'. Combining this pragmatic absolutism with a theory of official disobedience with accountability, Gross aspires to carve out a space that neither ignores nor denies the exigencies created by the existence of an emergency. The model is composed of a two-tier process. First, the public official, confronted with a 'catastrophic case', must respond to the 'obvious question' and decide whether to step outside the legal framework and breach

[44]   Slavoj Žižek, *Welcome to the Desert of the Real* (London: Verso, 2002), p. 103.

the prohibition on torture. Subsequently, the public must respond to the 'tragic question' by judging the actions of the official through a procedure of ex post ratification. Central to the framework of this model is, on the one hand, the public official's candour and 'ethic of responsibility' in disclosing the violation of the norm and, on the other hand, the public's 'ethic of responsibility' in the democratic ratification or decision-making process.

Gross believes that moral compromise is inevitable, at least in times of crisis:

> The Extra-Legal Measures model is disconcerting. It forces us to look to what may be the darkest corners of our national life. We would rather not look there. We would prefer to be led to believe that 'we are known for humanitarian treatment' and that we, as a society, are above moral reproach. That is, however, a luxury we cannot afford in such times.[45]

In negotiating the tension between 'absolutely no torture' and the prevention of impending acts of terrorism, Gross draws on an extra-legal model that blends pragmatic absolutism with official disobedience. As he puts it, this model permits the 'maintenance of rules' but also provides for 'highly circumscribed, but effective, escape mechanisms'.[46] Quite unlike Žižek's approach, Gross is inclined towards the development of a framework for addressing the hard question provided by the catastrophic case. He posits that there may be circumstances that require stepping outside the constitutional order, potentially violating its principles and norms, so as to tackle grave dangers and threats.

Simply put, Gross is persuaded by the belief that the use of torture may, in some cases, not only be inevitable but also morally imperative:

> To deny the use of preventative interrogational torture even when, for example, there is good reason to believe that a massive bomb is ticking in a mall is as coldhearted as it is to permit torture in the first place. It is coldhearted because in true catastrophic cases the failure to use preventive interrogational torture will result in the death of many innocent people.[47]

Like Dershowitz, he is motivated by a 'realist' perspective; he maintains that in a real 'ticking bomb' situation, investigators would apply torture to get the required information to thwart the attack, and he believes that they should do this:

---

[45] Gross, 'Chaos and Rules' 1128.   [46] *Ibid.*, 1097.
[47] Gross, 'The Prohibition on Torture', p. 237.

> After all … most of us believe that most, if not all, government agents, when faced with a genuinely catastrophic case, are likely to resort to whatever means they can wield – including preventative interrogational torture – in order to overcome the particular grave danger that is involved. And most of us hope they will do so.[48]

In contradistinction to Dershowitz, Gross does not believe that torture in such an instance should be *legally* sanctioned. His objective is, in fact, to disconnect the moral and legal spheres.[49] Accordingly, Gross formulates a model that, in essence, places the exceptional use of torture in a space external to the juridical order.[50] However, he denies that his model establishes 'a space of juridical vacuum': 'Legal principles, rules and norms continue to be applicable throughout the exception and can serve as appropriate benchmarks by which to assess both the legality of, and the appropriate response to, actions taken by public officials in times of emergency.'[51] For Gross, this exceptional use of torture does not remain unrelated to law both because he suggests that the extra-legal action of the public official actually constitutes a violation of the norm, as opposed to a suspension of the norm, and because he insists on the role of law in monitoring the resort to the exception, albeit after the fact. The extra-legal measures model is, he insists, designed to 'preserve, rather than undermine, the rule of law'.[52]

(i) Official disobedience

The extra-legal measures model caters for the extra-legal action of public officials, confronted with a catastrophe such as a ticking bomb. In such cases, public officials must make a judgement as to whether torture should be applied to the suspect to extract information, and they must do so in the knowledge that they are acting extra-legally. Gross is optimistic that the fully enforced legal prohibition against torture would act as a deterrent to public officials who might resort to using torture in such a situation.[53] The difficult choice between the prospective promotion of the greatest good for the greatest number of people and the respect for a legal, political, social or moral principle also serves to create an element of uncertainty

---

[48] *Ibid.*, p. 249; Gross, 'Chaos and Rules' 1098.
[49] Gross, 'Are Torture Warrants Warranted?' 1487.
[50] Giorgio Agamben (tr. Kevin Attell), *State of Exception* (University of Chicago Press, 2005), pp. 22–3.
[51] Gross, 'Extra-Legality and the Ethic of Political Responsibility', p. 63.
[52] *Ibid.*, p. 62.
[53] Gross, 'The Prohibition on Torture', p. 246.

that raises the cost for the public official of choosing an extra-legal course of action.[54] The decision-making burden rests solely on the shoulders of the public official who has no legal approval for this action; there is no one to hide behind.[55] The cost of deviation is raised whilst there is a simultaneous emphasis on 'strong commitment to rule abidingness, in general, and to strict adherence to the absolute ban on torture, in particular'.[56] With regard to the consequences of choosing to torture, the public official may be deterred by the possibility of facing criminal, civil or impeachment proceedings.[57] Beyond the domestic ramifications, there may also be international implications insofar as the public official may be subjected to criminal and civil proceedings in jurisdictions outside of their own, and there is the additional possibility of international criminal prosecution.[58]

(ii)   Ex post ratification

Gross' extra-legal model requires the public official to openly and publicly acknowledge having committed an act of torture. The public must then engage in a process of appraisal, through whatever democratic means are available, in order to decide how to judge the actor's official disobedience.[59] The public must essentially decide whether the actor ought to be 'punished and rebuked, or rewarded and commended for her actions'.[60] In the former instance, the public may demonstrate their commitment to upholding the principle violated, that is to say, they may judge that the public official was unjustified in breaching the prohibition against torture, and the official may, as a result, have to make legal and political reparations. Gross argues that in the constitutional, accountable and individual rights-based democratic society, the public would be wary of any attempt by the government to justify or excuse its illegal action, even if this action is taken in the interests of the public.[61] A further safeguarding aspect of this ratification process exists in the fact that the public would probably have more information available to them about the case in an *ex post facto* environment. In addition, the ratification would occur under calmer and more rational circumstances, and '[t]he higher the moral and legal

---

[54] Gross, 'Chaos and Rules' 1023.
[55] Gross, 'The Prohibition on Torture', p. 243.
[56] Gross, 'Are Torture Warrants Warranted?' 1522.
[57] Gross, 'Chaos and Rules' 1099.
[58] Gross, 'The Prohibition on Torture', p. 247.
[59] Gross, 'Chaos and Rules' 1099.
[60] *Ibid.*, 1112.   [61] *Ibid.*, 1123.

interests infringed on, the less certain the actor should be of the probability of securing ratification'.[62] As David Dyzenhaus observes, Gross' model is, therefore, entirely dependant upon 'genuine democratic deliberation' actually taking place in response to the official's extra-legal action.[63]

Gross suggests a number of means by which the public official might escape punishment for having violated the prohibition:

> Legal modes of ratification include, for example, the exercise of prosecutorial discretion not to bring criminal charges against officials accused of violating the law, jury nullification where criminal charges are brought, mitigation of penalties and sanctions that are imposed on the official when she is found liable ... for violating the law and executive pardoning or clemency where criminal proceedings result in conviction.[64]

There is an obvious problem with such an approach to ratifying the official's actions. If Gross' insistence on the continued formal application of the norm, despite the extra-legal action of the public official, is accepted, it is, nevertheless, difficult to imagine how the norm does not risk erosion due to its violation being excused: 'if the consequences are such that official resort to illegal action is usually excused rather than punished, one might worry that official illegality will become the norm – a kind of precedent – when officials deem there to be an emergency.'[65] Gross contends that the uncertainty of, and potential cost to, the public official who is involved in acting extra-legally would provide a deterrent effect.[66] This reasoning sits uneasily, however, with Gross' own recognition that 'the exception ... has merged with the rule'.[67]

(iii) Ethic of responsibility

The ex post ratification process, which engages the responsibility of each member of society in whose name terrible things have been done, is essential to Gross' extra-legal model. Gross defers to Martha Nussbaum's distinction between 'the obvious question' and 'the tragic question' in situations of choice.[68] The 'obvious question' asks 'what shall we do?' It

[62] Gross, 'The Prohibition on Torture', p. 244.
[63] David Dyzenhaus, 'The Compulsion of Legality', in Victor V. Ramraj (ed.), *Emergencies and the Limits of Legality* (Cambridge University Press, 2008), pp. 33, 41.
[64] Gross, 'Extra-Legality and the Ethic of Political Responsibility', p. 65.
[65] Dyzenhaus, 'The Compulsion of Legality' p. 41.
[66] Gross, 'Extra-Legality and the Ethic of Political Responsibility', p. 75.
[67] Oren Gross, 'What "Emergency" Regime?' (2006) 13 *Constellations* 74, 85.
[68] Martha Nussbaum, 'The Costs of Tragedy: Some Moral Limits of Cost–Benefit Analysis', (2000) 29 *Journal of Legal Studies* 1005, 1005; Gross, 'Chaos and Rules' 1101.

concerns the utilitarian working out of the right thing to do in a particular situation. According to Nussbaum, sometimes our choices engage an additional question – the 'tragic question'. The 'tragic question' confronts a distinct difficulty from that which exists in responding to what may be a difficult choice. It registers the question as to whether 'any of the alternatives open to us [are] free from serious moral wrongdoing'.[69] Insofar as the 'tragic question' has public consequences, it therefore requires public deliberation; such moral dilemmas are not just for individual appraisal.[70]

Gross insists that underlying and inherent to his extra-legal measures model is 'an ethic of responsibility' not only on the part of the executive or public official but also on the public.[71] This 'ethic of responsibility' is an effort to respond to Nussbaum's 'tragic question'. The extra-legal measures model distinguishes between the 'obvious question' and the 'tragic question'. Gross interprets the 'obvious question' as the ascertainment of 'the right thing to do from a pragmatic standpoint' – the maximisation of good for the greatest number of people. The 'tragic question', according to Gross, inquires into the 'assessment of the legal, political, social, and moral implications of such actions'.[72] In the ticking bomb scenario, the 'obvious question' is whether or not to torture. The public official must answer this question. The 'tragic question' probes the moral value of this decision and, therefore, requires public disclosure and public discussion. Gross argues that there is a general tendency only to address the obvious question. Others, he argues, conflate the two questions, imbuing the actions taken by governmental officials with moral value. Gross accords great importance to the consideration of both questions because, as he notes, '[e]ven when counter-emergency actions are deemed necessary under the obvious question, such actions may still be considered unjustified or nonexcusable from a moral or legal perspective, as they run afoul of a community's fundamental principles and values'.[73] Nussbaum's approach, which Gross follows, thus diverges from that of Max Weber, who viewed the moral dilemma, resulting from the politician having made a particular decision, as the politician's moral dilemma. According to Gross, Walzer's model also fails to inquire beyond the 'obvious question'. However, what distinguishes Walzer from Gross on the issue of judging the official's action is not Walzer's failure to consider accountability; it is his recognition of the fiction of accountability.

---

[69] Nussbaum, 'The Costs of Tragedy' 1005–7.
[70] *Ibid.*, 1011.   [71] Gross, 'Chaos and Rules' 1099
[72] *Ibid.*, 1101.   [73] *Ibid.*

(iv) Emergencies

Gross asserts that the 'exception [to the otherwise ordinary state of affairs] is no longer invisible'.[74] As a consequence, he has developed the extra-legal measures model that seeks to demonstrate how a constitutional democracy should respond to violent challenges, a discourse that has been rigorously debated since the events of 11 September. His concern is with finding a constitutional balance between maintaining democratic values, without turning the constitution into a 'suicide pact', and responding to emergency, without transforming the state into an authoritarian regime.[75] Gross is critical of traditional models for accommodating emergency. He observes that faced with violent threats, 'democratic nations tend to race to the bottom as far as the protection of human rights and civil liberties, indeed of basic and fundamental legal principles, is concerned'.[76] The rush to legislate results in the introduction of emergency powers and counterterrorism measures that, whilst dressed up as exceptional, seep in to the system, blurring the line between normalcy and exception. The extra-legal model may be understood as Gross' attempt to minimise the damage created by a state of emergency. He argues that dispensing with the law in these cases is a preferable course of action than the alternative, which involves continuously bending the law to accommodate emergencies, thus undermining the rule of law.

Gross' preference for this model over a judicial mechanism is influenced by his desire to keep the judicial system clean in times of crisis. He argues that extra-legal action frees the courts from the dangers inherent in the restriction of the exercise of rights when faced with serious threats, such as the ticking bomb scenario. The extra-legal measures model 'permits the judicial branch to fulfil its role as protector of individual rights without having to fear that by doing so it compromises the security of the state'.[77] Although he admits that the official disobedience of governments and public officials may create political precedents, Gross is assured that by annexing this hard case from the realm of the judiciary, the ordinary legal system would be protected both from 'the permeation of such precedents into times of peace and normalcy' and from involvement in the murky waters of the fight against terrorism.[78]

The rationale for the formulation of the extra-legal model can thus be summarised as comprising a dual motivation: the protection of the legal

---

[74] *Ibid.*, 1016.   [75] *Ibid.*, 1028, 1029.   [76] *Ibid.*, 1019.
[77] *Ibid.*, 1121.   [78] *Ibid.*, 1130, 1133.

system from the deleterious effects of fighting terrorism with dirty hands and the concurrent attempt to develop a pragmatic method for dealing with real crises.

In addition, Gross' opposition to a judicial model is motivated by reluctance to place this hard question into the hands of judges. He maintains that 'when faced with national crises, the judiciary tends to "go to war". Judges, like the general public and its political leaders, "like to win wars" and are sensitive to the criticism that they impede the war effort'.[79] In other words, Gross is not convinced that the judiciary could remain dispassionate in the ticking bomb case.

Gross is not sold by the ticking bomb argument per se. He is careful to underscore the dangers in basing law on such artificial cases. Gross, however, is equally mindful of the danger of failing to recognise that catastrophic cases 'are real, albeit rare'.[80] Consequently, he argues that whilst a qualified ban on torture has a high cost, so too does an absolute ban. He maintains that the challenge posed by the ticking bomb situation is ignored at our peril as this may lead to the legal system being interpreted as unrealistic and inadequate. Damage to certain norms and to the legal system more generally may result 'as the ethos of obedience to law may be seriously shaken and challenges emerge with respect to the reasonableness of following these norms'.[81] This explains his pragmatic position.

Gross is insistent, however, on the imperative of maintaining an absolute legal ban. First, he argues that whether one holds either an absolute or a conditional position on the use of torture, a legal ban on preventative interrogational torture should be advocated. Second, he reasons that an absolute legal ban is important, as a general policy should not be established with respect to exceptional cases and because it is important symbolically to uphold the prohibition. According to Gross, 'even if one believes that an absolute ban on torture is unrealistic, as a practical matter, there is independent value in upholding the myth that torture is absolutely prohibited'.[82] Third, he regards the absolute legal prohibition as a necessary strategy of resistance in order to contain the use of torture and to slow down the rush to resort to torture practices even in truly exceptional cases. Fourth, he thinks that balancing tests that place the use of torture in competition with other values should be rejected. Finally, he

[79] *Ibid.*, 1034.
[80] Gross, 'Are Torture Warrants Warranted?' 1503.
[81] Gross, 'The Prohibition on Torture', p. 237.
[82] *Ibid.*, p. 234.

considers it necessary to uphold the absolute legal prohibition to prevent 'slippery slopes'.[83]

Gross argues that '[a] categorical legal prohibition on torture is also desirable in order to uphold the symbolism of human dignity and the inviolability of the human body'.[84] Even if one believes that an absolute ban is pragmatically impossible, it is, nevertheless, worth upholding the ban for independent reasons:

> Such a position provides obvious notice that fundamental rights and values are not forsaken whatever the circumstances, and that cries of national security, emergency, and catastrophe do not trump individual rights. The more entrenched a norm is – and the prohibition of torture is among the most entrenched norms – the harder it will be for government to convince the public that violating that norm is necessary.[85]

There are other educational benefits of maintaining an absolute legal ban on torture. In this regard, Gross argues that it is not only domestically appropriate but that it additionally 'sends a strong unequivocal message to countries around the world that such practices are impermissible'.[86] Another argument introduced to defend legal absolutism follows the reasoning that the maintenance of an unqualified prohibition places the government on the moral high ground in fighting terrorism. He notes that '[e]ven in the post-September 11 world, terrorism's most critical threat to democratic regimes lies in provoking the target nations to overreact and employ authoritarian measures, such as interrogational torture'.[87]

C.   Absolute torture prohibition

The absolute position is represented by the torture prohibition's protection under international law. Freedom from torture is a non-derogable right under international and regional human rights treaty law. Torture is prohibited under international humanitarian law and is a codified crime in international criminal law. Moreover, it is widely recognised as having a customary status under international law and as representing a peremptory norm of international law. However, these legal qualifications are challenged by both political and moral arguments in confrontation with the exceptional case. Those who hold an absolutist position argue,

---

[83] *Ibid.*, p. 235.   [84] Gross, 'Are Torture Warrants Warranted?' 1504.
[85] *Ibid.*   [86] *Ibid.*, 1505.   [87] *Ibid.*

from an ethical perspective, that torture is immoral and inconsistent with democratic society;[88] torture is inherently wrong, 'an evil that can never be justified or excused'.[89] Absolutists further argue, from a perspective that, arguably, collapses consequentialist reasoning into absolutism, that torture imposes a great cost not only on the tortured but also on the torturer and on society itself.[90] At the core of the absolutist perspective is the refutation of the end justifies the means rationale as an argument for torturing a suspect in order to save lives.

(1)   Torture prohibition as an archetype

As a legal response to the challenge posed by the ticking bombs scenario and the debate on the justifiability of torture, Jeremy Waldron, defending a legal absolute position, has developed a theory that conceives that the prohibition of torture represents a legal archetype. Waldron defends the absolute prohibition on torture not only intrinsically, but also because he conceives of the torture prohibition as having an extrinsic function in representing the separation of law from brutality and law from force. In contrast to the approaches of Dershowitz and Gross, Waldron believes that it is exactly in circumstances such as the post 11 September environment that the law prohibiting torture must be tightened, rather than loosened. He is unconvinced by both the proliferation of the ticking bomb hypothetical and the pressure to relax principled moral standpoints. According to Waldron, the prohibition on torture cannot easily be cast aside because it does not exist in a vacuum; rather, it is underpinned by long-standing normative values. Not only does the prohibition proscribe torture, it stretches across the law acting as a reference point for all acts that lie on the brutality spectrum.

Waldron argues that the prohibition of torture epitomises a legal archetype that operates not only as a rule but also as an underpinning feature of the legal system, in the Dworkinian sense, as a policy, a principle or a norm.[91] He argues that the rule against torture is archetypal of more than a general hostility to the practice of torture; it is representative of a certain policy that governs the relation between law and force, and the force with which law rules. In this regard, he asserts:

---

[88]   Marcy Strauss, 'Torture' (2004) 48 *New York Law School Law Review* 201, 254.
[89]   Gross, 'The Prohibition on Torture', p. 229.
[90]   Strauss, 'Torture' 254.
[91]   Waldron, 'Torture and Positive Law' 1722.

Law is not brutal in its operation. Law is not savage. Law does not rule
through abject fear and terror, or by breaking the will of those whom it
confronts. If law is forceful or coercive, it gets its way by nonbrutal methods which respect rather than mutilate the dignity and agency of those
who are its subjects ... the rule against torture ... is vividly emblematic of
our determination to sever the link between law and brutality, between
law and terror, and between the law and the enterprise of breaking someone's will.[92]

The revelations about abusive treatment of prisoners under American
control in Abu Ghraib and other prisons combined with the realisation
of the larger policy context of these revelations, namely the United States'
executive efforts to restrict the meaning and the application of the prohibition against torture, provoked Waldron to develop this legal archetype
theory. He expresses dismay not only at the fact that the use of torture is
flourishing in the 'security state' but also that its use is being defended.[93]
Waldron is concerned about the policy implications of the 'definitional
shenanigans', which he views as a comprehensive attempt to gut commitment to the legal norm.[94] He is additionally absorbed by the jurisprudential effect of this treatment of the torture question and the more general
issue of upholding 'the integrity of the law'.[95]

Waldron is far from convinced that the events of 11 September have
changed everything, necessitating a relaxation of the law or a restrictive
interpretation of the definition of torture. He argues, on the contrary, that
it is precisely to cater for these circumstances, in which the use of torture
would be 'most tempting', that the different domestic and international
law prohibitions have been enacted. According to Waldron, '[i]f the prohibitions do not hold fast in those circumstances, then they are of little
use in any circumstance'.[96]

In contemplating the legal prohibition of torture, Waldron makes the
distinction between two different approaches to legal interpretation,
namely *malum prohibitum* and *malum in se*. The former governs the
interpretation of a legal provision introducing a prohibition 'into what
was previously a realm of liberty'.[97] In other words, if the rule had not
been enacted, there would be no offence and anything not explicitly prohibited by the regulation would remain as free as before. With the *malum
in se* approach, on the other hand, the positive law enacting the prohibition does not *establish* the wrongfulness of the act. The prohibition

---

[92] *Ibid.*, 1727.   [93] *Ibid.*, 1686.   [94] *Ibid.*, 1709.
[95] *Ibid.*, 1687.   [96] *Ibid.*, 1686.   [97] *Ibid.*, 1692.

merely provides in certain terms for something that was already impermissible. To distinguish *malum in se* from *malum prohibitum*, it is necessary, Waldron points out, to locate a legally recognisable normative background, for example, 'a shared moral sense or ... some form of higher or background law: natural law, perhaps, or international law'.[98]

Waldron applies these models of interpretation to the prohibition of torture. He argues that the United States' Anti-Torture Statute[99] cannot be interpreted according to the *malum prohibitum* model, as this statute was not enacted in a vacuum. Rather its enactment was a legal obligation under the Convention against Torture, as well as a statutory recognition of the spirit of the criminal law. As Waldron puts it, the Anti-Torture Statute 'gave definition to an existing and legally recognised sense of the inherent wrongness of torture'.[100] In the same way, the prohibition on torture did not just turn up, so to speak, when international treaties gave it positive legal recognition. The Convention against Torture and the International Covenant on Civil and Political Rights 'represent a consensual acknowledgement of deeper background norms that are binding on nations, *anyway*, treaty or no treaty'.[101]

Waldron points out that the prohibition on torture has been given various protections, albeit positive law protections, to prevent it from revision, redefinition and repeal. He cites, for example, the prohibition's status as a peremptory norm of international law and its non-derogable status under the European Convention on Human Rights. However, he points out that even these devices are subject to manipulation. Therein Waldron locates the crux of the issue. In times of crisis, legal norms become subject to political and moral deconstruction.[102]

(i)   Absolutism and the hypothetical case

Waldron states that '[i]n these troubled times, it is not hard to make the idea of an absolute torture prohibition, or any absolute look silly, as a matter of moral philosophy'.[103] However, he levels criticism at moral absolutists who relax their values in the face of crisis, observing that '[e]ven among those who are not already Bentham-style consequentialists, most are moderates in their deontology. They are willing to abandon even cherished absolutes in the face of ... catastrophic moral horror'.[104] Waldron's

---

[98] *Ibid.*   [99] 18 U.S.C. §2340 (2000).
[100] Waldron, 'Torture and Positive Law' 1693.
[101] *Ibid.*, 1693 (emphasis added).
[102] *Ibid.*, 1712.   [103] *Ibid.*, 1713.   [104] *Ibid.*

response to the ticking bomb scenario is to set the limit at torture. He reasons that most people would draw the line somewhere. For example, he maintains that few people would condone the rape of the 'terrorist's' relatives. He is not convinced by this 'picking and choosing' of absolutes. If there is a line to be drawn, he argues, he would see it drawn in the human rights tradition.[105]

Beyond his distrust of any fickleness in defending absolutes, Waldron is critical of the hypothetical itself. He criticises Dershowitz for taking it, with its high stakes, as the starting point in thinking about torture, reasoning that such hypotheticals, once let loose, could convince anyone to justify almost anything. He also observes that, in reality, torture is not used to elicit information about the exact circumstance of the hypothetical; rather, it is used as a broader piecing-together, information-gathering technique. Overall, he finds the hypothetical itself to be deeply corrupt because, he maintains, it is used 'deliberately to undermine the integrity of certain moral positions'.[106] Not only that but it fails to tell the whole story:

> The hypothetical asks us to assume that the power to authorise torture will not be abused, that intelligence officials will not lie about what is at stake or about the availability of the information, that the readiness to issue torture warrants in one case (where they may be justified by the sort of circumstances Dershowitz stipulates) will not lead to their extension to other cases (where the circumstances are even less compelling), that a professional corps of torturers will not emerge who stand around looking for work, that the existence of a law allowing torture in some cases will not change the office politics of police and security agencies to undermine and disempower those who argue against torture in other cases, and so on.[107]

(ii) The legal archetype

Conscious of the potential for a corruptive interpretation of the torture prohibition and aware of the power of the hypothetical to devalue the absolute moral position, Waldron sets about establishing a legal mechanism for defending the absolute. This legal archetype theory originates in a twofold criticism of legal positivism. First, it reiterates Ronald Dworkin's critique of the failure of legal positivism to give adequate consideration to anything but the rules. Second, it criticises the failure of legal positivism to treat the law as a system in the sense that doctrines, laws and precedents hang together. This failure, he argues, results in the overall sense in

---

[105] *Ibid.*, 1715. [106] *Ibid.* [107] *Ibid.*, 1716.

which laws connect being lost, leading, consequently, to the overlooking of the spirit and principle of the law. Waldron argues that within the 'cluster of laws' that constitute a system, there sometimes exists one provision which 'by virtue of its force, clarity and vividness expresses the spirit that animates the whole area of law'.[108] This is Waldron's archetype.

This archetype is a particular provision 'which has a significance going beyond its immediate normative content, a significance stemming from the fact that it sums up or makes vivid to us the point, purpose, principle, or policy of a whole area of law'.[109] The archetype has a foundational or background function, in a Dworkinian 'principle' sense, in any given legal system.[110] However, archetypes work differently to Dworkin's 'principle' as they extend to the foreground acting as rules and precedents, and they sum up the spirit of a whole body of the law beyond their own positive legal requirements.

According to Waldron, the prohibition of torture embodies 'something very important in the spirit and the genius of our law' which 'we mess with ... at our peril'.[111] The prohibition on torture, in and of itself, or considered collectively, in terms of the various international, regional and domestic prohibitions, amounts to a legal archetype. This ought to be weighed into to any considerations that would amend, limit or define the prohibition out of existence. The rationale for torture's consideration as an archetype is found in the prohibition's position at the interface of law and human dignity. Whilst uniting these two aspects, it amputates law from brutality.[112]

To determine the archetypal status of the torture prohibition, Waldron puts forward a two-tier test. This comprises, first, establishing that a particular principle or policy pervades the body of law, and second, establishing that the prohibition is representative of that policy or principle. In United States constitutional jurisprudence, Waldron finds that a policy of non-brutality pervades, and it is of this policy that the prohibition is archetypal. He finds evidence for this in an examination of Eighth Amendment as well as procedural and due process jurisprudence, where the prohibition on torture is the reference point for deciding other cases that lie

---

[108] *Ibid.*, 1722.   [109] *Ibid.*, 1723.

[110] Ronald Dworkin articulates a principle as 'a standard that is to be observed, not because it will advance or secure an economic, political, or social situation deemed desirable but because it is a requirement of justice or fairness or some other dimension of morality'. See Ronald Dworkin, *Taking Rights Seriously* (London: Duckworth, 1977), p. 22.

[111] *Ibid.*, p. 1749.   [112] *Ibid.*, p. 1727.

on the brutality spectrum. Mention of the torture prohibition is not a reminder that torture is prohibited but, in a sense, a cautionary reference point that explains other more common or pervasive prohibitions.[113]

Waldron proceeds to examine and to adjudicate the rule against torture as an archetype of international humanitarian law and of international human rights law. He argues that it should be considered 'an archetype of international law as such, or of the way international law operates'.[114] In this regard, he refers to the status of the torture prohibition as a norm of *jus cogens*.[115]

Waldron argues that the ban on torture also operates as an archetype of the rule of law. The fact that state agents are prohibited from torturing is a function of law in a state that does not condone brutality. Broadly speaking, to Waldron the torture prohibition represents law's control over the exercise of power, a control which should not be easily forfeited:

> In this way, a state subject to law becomes not just a state whose excesses are predicable or whose actions are subject to forms, procedures and warrants; it becomes a state whose exercise of power is imbued with this broader spirit of the repudiation of brutality ... the prohibition on torture is archetypal of the project of bringing power under this sort of control.[116]

The status of the prohibition on torture as an archetype consequently endows it with a responsibility beyond the protection against its own violation. Other law is dependent upon the integrity of the prohibition. If torture is the reference point for finding that certain other acts are unconstitutional or illegal, what happens when the act of torture itself becomes justifiable? Do less serious crimes or acts of brutality become acceptable or at the very least also the subject of a 'lesser evil' debate? Waldron argues that loosening the absolute prohibition on torture would have a domino effect on how we think about our acts of ill-treatment:

> Our beliefs – that flogging in prisons is wrong, that coerced confessions are wrong, that pumping a person's stomach for narcotic's evidence is wrong, that police brutality is wrong – may each be a little uncertain and shaky, but the confidence we have in them depends partly on analogies we have constructed between them and torture or on a sense that what is wrong with torture gives us some insight into what is wrong with these other evils. If we undermine the sense that torture is absolutely out of the

---

[113] *Ibid.*, p. 1730.   [114] *Ibid.*, p. 1747.
[115] *Ibid.*, p. 1722.   [116] *Ibid.*, p. 1742.

question, then we lose a crucial point of reference for sustaining these other less certain beliefs.[117]

Waldron maintains that the destabilisation of an archetype affects the morality of the law more generally. The basis for the surrounding law may become questionable. Waldron asks, for example, whether the torture warrant system would make it harder to justify the exclusionary rule for involuntary confessions. Without the reference point of the archetype each of the surrounding provisions would be exposed to a reliance on its own resources and, Waldron says, 'each will be only as resilient ... as the particular arguments that can be summoned in its favour. It will lose the benefit of the archetype's gravitation force'.[118]

D.   Conclusion

The three positions outlined in this chapter provide alternate descriptions of how the law ought to speak to the exception. Dershowitz advocates that the law should include an exception to the torture prohibition in ticking bomb circumstances. Gross concludes that the law should remain absolute and that an exception to it should be taken extra-legally and, thereafter, dealt with through a system of ex post ratification. Waldron denies any framework for exceptionality to the law prohibiting torture, arguing that the prohibition represents the point at which force and law are separated. In other words, the torture prohibition must exclude exception. Dershowitz, with the torture warrant procedure, asks us to believe that torture in ticking bomb situations can be regulated with precision in conformity with the rule of law. Gross asks us to consider the possibility for torture to be practised, in an exceptional case, extra-legally and without any deleterious effects on the rule of law. Waldron prompts a reconsideration of the object and purpose of the absolute prohibition of torture and its inter-relationship with the rule of law.

Dershowitz and Gross accept the ticking bomb scenario as a basis for thinking about exceptional torture; through their proposals, they attempt to mould a picture of exceptional torture that adapts to this framework. Their proposals implicitly assume that the ticking bomb threat exceeds the application of the absolute torture prohibition under international law. They do not contemplate the possibility that the prohibition of

---

[117]   *Ibid.*, p. 1736.   [118]   *Ibid.*, p. 1748.

torture was drafted and developed in order to combat the use of torture in exactly the kinds of situations that the ticking bomb scenario
claims to represent. Historical amnesia and contextual abstraction are
also inherent in their proposals. Dershowitz goes to great lengths to dis-
credit the necessity defence as the basis for the justification of torture.
In his discussion of the Israeli case, however, he fails to recognise ana-
logies between that case and his own torture warrant proposal. In this
regard, Yuval Ginbar remarks that a system of torture warrants operated,
in effect, during the Landau period in Israel.[119] During this period the
Israeli Supreme Court continuously rejected requests for interim injunctions in individual cases where torture was being applied. In so doing,
the Court 'consistently allowed the continuation of torture whenever the
State insisted that there was a need for it, even weeks after it had begun'.[120]
Although unacknowledged by Dershowitz, the Landau experience offers
an illustrative counterpart to the stylised version of reality represented
by the torture warrant proposal. Similarly, Gross fails to situate historical lessons within his model. In fact, Gross and Fionnuala Ní Aoláin
refer to the Israeli Supreme Court's endorsement of prosecutorial discretion in potential ticking bomb cases, in *Public Committee against Torture
in Israel et al. v. the Government of Israel et al.*, as an example of the ex
post ratification procedure for the extra-legal measures model.[121] Again,
however, Gross does not discuss the similarity between his model and
the actual system currently in place in Israel where the extra-legal use of
torture is practised and legitimated on the basis of the necessity defence,
absent of the accountability mechanisms he supports. These proposals
dissolve on a close analysis, and it becomes clear that they only provide a
fictional solution to an artificially framed problem.

By contrast, Waldron, whilst not directly submerging himself in the
ticking bomb debate, broadens the frame by flooding the picture with a
reminder of the historical and contextual significance of the ban on torture. Waldron speaks to the strategic importance of the ban on torture in
order to highlight how it should represent a rupture between law and violence. Waldron's approach is itself strategic. He does not attempt to 'win'

---

[119] Yuval Ginbar, *Why not Torture Terrorists? Moral, Practical, and Legal Aspects of the
'Ticking Bomb' Justification for Torture* (Oxford University Press, 2008), p. 194.
[120] *Ibid.*, p. 199.
[121] Oren Gross and Fionnuala Ní Aoláin, *Law in Times of Crisis: Emergency Powers in
Theory and Practice* (Cambridge University Press, 2006), p. 137, noted in Ginbar, *Why
not Torture Terrorists?*, p. 201.

the argument on the basis of a morally convincing defence of the absolute prohibition. Whilst it is clear that Waldron conceptualises the torture
prohibition as a moral absolute, he seems to believe that the ticking bomb
scenario cannot be solved through such an ethical debate. As the ticking
bomb scenario as a basis for the justification of torture crumbles under
analysis, it is, however, this ethical debate that appears to form the basis
on which the torture debate rests.

5

Torture prohibition and the torture debate:
moral aspects

When W. L. and P. E. Twining published Jeremy Bentham's writings on torture in 1973, they pointed out that the prohibition of torture had been left largely ignored in philosophical writings. They attribute this to a general acceptance of torture as morally indefensible and 'as so obviously "beyond the Pale", except possibly in extreme circumstances, as not to warrant sustained discussion'.[1] Torture, they contend, is assumed not to raise many conceptual or ethical issues. While rational analysis of the subject of torture is impeded by its 'powerful emotive associations', they argue, 'if there is to be headway with a theory of individual rights ... then the philosophical basis for claiming that there is a fundamental, and perhaps absolute, right not to be tortured requires uninhibited critical analysis'.[2]

It is, however, the application of this fundamental right in 'extreme circumstances' that renders the subject of torture ethically vexing, and, arguably, it is precisely because of the question of torture's justifiability in extreme circumstances that there is a poverty of rational analysis. The umbilical link between torture and the ticking bomb scenario is inherently restraining as it claims to engage torture only in exceptional circumstances and, yet, it renders the problem of torture holistically and conceptually uncertain. If, as it is alleged, there are certain purposes to which torture can ethically be applied, what is it that makes torture wrong in the first place? Can the torture prohibition be ethically carved as a response to the conflicts to which it is perceived to meet? Because of the current political landscape in which torture is now 'thinkable' (for example, as a counterterrorism measure or in the ticking bomb scenario), conceptual and ethical clarity is doubly impeded. Where rational analysis

---

[1] W. L. and P. E. Twining, 'Bentham on Torture' (1973) 24 *Northern Ireland Legal Quarterly* 305, 315.
[2] *Ibid.*

exists, it is rational analysis within a debate that is already inescapably emotive.

The ticking bomb torture debate positions the wrongfulness of torture in all circumstances against its rightfulness in exceptional cases and, thereby, challenges the universal prohibition. The ethics of this torture debate is often considered to mirror the classical ethical dilemma between absolutism and consequentialism, where the moral emphasis on and between what one is doing, in the former case, and what will happen, in the latter case, gives rise to an irresolvable moral dilemma.[3] The debate is composed, however, of more than an irresolvable clash *between* these concepts. There are deontologists and consequentialists on both sides. As Jeremy Wisnewski and R. D. Emerick point out, there 'are an astonishing number of diverse positions that one can take when it comes to torture'.[4] When reduced, the debate challenges the meaning of rights and, moreover, a human being's right to have rights. It views the ticking bomb as creating a conflict between rights – the suspect's right not to be subjected to torture and the right to life of the potential victims. Whether the moral measurement used is deontological, a just war analysis or a 'lesser evil' balancing test, the crucial questions *appear* to be: Which right is trump? Which is the 'lesser evil'? In its current guise, there is no foreseeable conclusion to the ethical debate. Its cyclical nature (due to its composition by apparently incompatible opposing moral views) has dogged the subject of torture for centuries. When Beccaria denounced judicial torture in the eighteenth century, Bentham was compelled to respond with a utilitarian justification of torture in limited circumstances. When the torture debate was rekindled in the aftermath of the events of 11 September, a flurry of contrasting moral opinions flooded both the academic and the public discourse.

It is possible, however, to challenge the existence of a conflict between the prohibition of torture and the right to life in the first place. What the ticking bomb scenario is asking is whether an alleged 'terrorist' can be

---

[3] Paul W. Kahn, *Sacred Violence: Torture, Terror, and Sovereignty* (Ann Arbor: University of Michigan Press, 2008), p. 88. Kahn considers this conflict between deontological and consequentialist thought to mask a more elemental conflict between love for a particular community on the one hand and moral universalism on the other. According to Kahn, love, and not morality, informs one's commitment to the community; the hypothetical tests this commitment. See also Thomas Nagel, 'War and Massacre' in Joram Graf Haber (ed.), *Absolutism and Its Consequentialist Critics* (Boston, MA: Rowman & Littlefield Publishers Inc. 1994), pp. 217, 218–19.

[4] J. Jeremy Wisnewski and R. D. Emerick, *The Ethics of Torture* (London: Continuum, 2009), p. 9.

tortured for the protection of the life of others. This question sets up a moral conflict, or clash of rights, between the right to be free from torture and the right to life. If this ostensible conflict between rights can be exposed as an artificial construction, then the connection between torture and saving lives is severed. In terms of rights and their *raison d'être*, this exercise is necessary since in imagining a conflict between the prohibition on torture and the right to life, there is a perversion of the human rights discourse. It is foreseeable, however, that even if no logical connection can be found between these rights in moral conflict, the ticking bomb problem will not dissipate. In reality, the context of terrorism, the emotional reaction that insists that everything possible must be done to inhibit acts of terrorism and the historical proof that states might do anything to prevent terrorism, sustains this torture debate. In the ticking bomb debate, the hypothetical transcends human rights-speak, not just by compelling an emotional response but also by inducing confusion whereby, still committed to the rule of law, one is nevertheless forced to envisage overriding values, moral and legal, in support of just that one instance of violence.[5] What is proposed here is that this 'conflict' of rights exposes the real conundrum of the ticking bomb scenario. It posits that there are places of political action that law cannot reach.

Yet the ticking bomb conundrum cannot be resolved through moral inquiry alone;[6] the absolute prohibition has already fixed torture's moral status. The history of the prohibition is informative on this point. The torture prohibition emerged not only because of a process of modernisation and liberalisation but also because of complex shifts of state power and because of human rights concerns with that power. On the one hand, if we accept that the Universal Declaration of Human Rights fulfils the 'Enlightenment promise of emancipation and self-realisation',[7] then it follows that the prohibition of torture fulfils the project of individual emancipation from the barbarism of torture. On the other hand, the prohibition of torture inscribed in the Universal Declaration compensates for the incompleteness of the Enlightenment's project of abolition, which failed to foresee that torture, abolished from the judicial system, nevertheless remained an instrument of state power. Twentieth-century totalitarianism bore witness to this oversight; the human rights movement corrected

---

[5] Kahn describes the ticking bomb as presenting a worldview wherein political violence beyond law must be imagined and wherein our commitments straddle both law and the political violence of the state of exception. See Kahn, *Sacred Violence*, p. 92.

[6] *Ibid.*, p. 169.

[7] Costas Douzinas, *The End of Human Rights* (Oxford: Hart Publishing, 2000), p. 2.

it. In that sense, the torture prohibition must be understood as more than an aspirational moral prohibition as it encapsulates the prohibition on the political exercise of this power. Within the prohibition on torture understood in this way, however, one finds the paradox or aporia that Costas Douzinas identifies at the heart of human rights. Human rights, descendent from political liberalism, constructs a state power built in the image of individuals as absolute rights-holders, whilst simultaneously defending these same rights-holders from that state power. They are 'the weapon of resistance to state omnipotence and an important antidote to the inherent ability of sovereign power to negate the autonomy of individuals in whose name it came into existence'.[8] Or as Paul Kahn argues, human rights law is unable to find a space in which to operate, free of the politics that it is intended to regulate.[9] Political liberalism has trouble explaining the nature of rights in this internal fissure.[10] The torture debate, for the most part, has failed to grapple with its meaning.[11] Those who do approach this problem attempt to reconcile the competition between force and right through conceptions of political morality.

A.   The ethical debate

(1)   An enlightened debate?

The legal history of torture has been well researched and documented, from its emergence in Greek and Roman law, to its reappearance in the medieval law of proof, through to its abolition from European criminal law and to its modern history.[12] The ethical torture debate takes, as its

---

[8] *Ibid.*, p. 20.

[9] Kahn, *Sacred Violence*, p. 56.

[10] Douzinas, *The End of Human Rights*, p. 3.

[11] Kahn, *Sacred Violence*, p. 77. Kahn laments the failure of arguments in the debate to understand the relationship between law and sovereignty in the modern state. In a notable exception to the dearth of such analysis, Kahn examines torture within this relationship. Kahn also describes the writing of Oren Gross as an interesting exception.

[12] For a history of torture from Greek and Roman law to the present, see Edward Peters, *Torture* (Philadelphia: University of Pennsylvania Press, 1999). For a legal history of torture from medieval times to the eighteenth century, see John H. Langbein, *Torture and the Law of Proof: Europe and England in the Ancien Régime* (University of Chicago Press, 2006). For a comparison of the legal history of medieval European torture to the coercive nature of American plea bargaining, see John H. Langbein, 'Torture and Plea Bargaining' (1978) 46 *University of Chicago Law Review* 3. For an application of the lessons of the history of medieval European torture law to the contemporary torture debate, see John H. Langbein, 'The Legal History of Torture' in Sanford Levinson (ed.), *Torture: A Collection* (Oxford

starting point, the abolition of 'judicial torture'[13] from European criminal codes in the latter half of the eighteenth century.[14] During the so-called Enlightenment period, a shift in emphasis occurred whereby torture, previously considered principally from a judicial perspective, became a matter of 'enlightened' moral concern.[15] This is notable in the literature of, among others, Voltaire,[16] Montesquieu[17] and Cesare Beccaria,[18] whose famous 'moral protest' of torture, according to Edward Peters, formed part of 'the foremost treatise on penal reform produced by the Enlightenment'.[19]

The Enlightenment period of abolition provides both obvious and interesting reasons for considering the moral aspects of torture; obvious because abolition marked the beginning of the liberal conception of torture and interesting because of the many competing abolition narratives that have been put forward to explain judicial abolition.[20]

University Press, 2004), p. 93. For a history of judicial torture, or the torture warrant system, in England and Scotland, see David Hope, 'Torture' (2004) 53 *International Comparative Law Quarterly* 807. For a more general history, see also Nigel S. Rodley, *The Treatment of Prisoners under International Law* 2nd edn (Oxford University Press, 1999), p. 7; James Ross, 'A History of Torture' in Kenneth Roth and Minky Worden (eds.), *Torture: A Human Rights Perspective?* (New York: Human Rights Watch 2005), p. 3.

[13] John H. Langbein describes the system of judicial torture as 'part of the ordinary criminal procedure, regularly employed to investigate and prosecute routine crime before the ordinary courts'. Judicial torture was the use of 'physical coercion by officers of the state in order to gather evidence for judicial proceedings'. See Langbein, *Torture and the Law of Proof*, p. 3.

[14] Langbein records that Prussia abolished judicial torture in 1754; Saxony in 1770; Poland and Austrian Bohemia in 1776; France in 1780; Tuscany in 1786; the Austrian Netherlands (Belgium) in 1787; and Sicily in 1789. See Langbein, *Torture and the Law of Proof*, p. 10.

[15] Peters, *Torture*, p. 64.

[16] Montesquieu's protest against the use of torture can be found in Book VI, Chapter XVII of *The Spirit of the Laws*. See Charles De Secondat Montesquieu (Baron de), *The Spirit of the Laws: Vol. I* (New York: Hafner Publishing Company, 1949), p. 91.

[17] Voltaire, 'Torture and Capital Punishment' in William F. Schulz, *The Phenomenon of Torture: Readings and Commentary* (Philadelphia: University of Pennsylvania Press, 2007), p. 36.

[18] Cesare Beccaria (tr. David Young), *On Crimes and Punishments* (Indianapolis: Hackett Publishing Company, 1986). An excerpt can be found in William F. Schulz (ed.), *The Phenomenon of Torture: Readings and Commentary* (Philadelphia: University of Pennsylvania Press, 2007), p. 34.

[19] Peters, *Torture*, p. 264.

[20] That is not to say that torture was not debated during other periods of history. Indeed, its existence in Roman law provoked much debate about the uses that torture served, its efficacy and the injustice of torturing the innocent. See Peters, *Torture*, pp. 18–39. See also *The Theodosian Code, Book 9, Title 35*, cited in Peters, *Torture*, p. 212; *The Diges of Justinian, Book 48, Title 18*, cited in Peters, *Torture*, p. 215; *The Code of Justinian, Book 9, Title 41*, cited in Peters, *Torture*, p. 224; *Augustine: The City of God, XIX.6*, cited in Peters,

(2)   Abolition narratives

The abolition of judicial torture is generally considered to have been spurred on by moral outrage against its practice, which led, consequently, to judicial reform. Langbein, however, describes the traditional historical explanation of the abolition of torture as a 'fairy-tale'.[21] The explanation for the disappearance of judicial torture, concludes Langbein, is 'neither publicistic nor political, but jurisitic'.[22] Langbein's account dismisses the explanation that a shock to the conscience, spurred on by the moral condemnation of Voltaire, Beccaria and other Enlightenment thinkers, shaped a liberal public opinion and encouraged European monarchs to usher torture out of the judicial system.[23] He argues, plausibly, that this account of abolition does not compute since many of their arguments against torture had been known for centuries.[24] He adduces torture's abolition to have resulted from the development of a system of free judicial evaluation of evidence that dispensed with the dependency on confession evidence and, therefore, on the law of proof: 'The true explanation for the abolition of torture is that by the age of abolition, torture was no longer needed. The system of proof which had required the use of torture was dead.'[25]

Michel Foucault, in his seminal work on the changing nature of power and punishment in the second half of the eighteenth century, attributes the development of a more 'humane' punishment, not only to the development of moral sensibility concerning the act of punishment, but, primarily, to a shift in the technology of power, from the exertion of power and punishment on the body to an exercise of societal control over the body through, for example, the prison system:

> If the law must now treat in a 'humane' way an individual who is 'outside nature' (whereas the old justice treated the 'outlaw' inhumanely), it is not

---

Torture, p. 229. It is also not to say that the pre-Enlightenment history of torture is not informative. With respect to the history of medieval European legal torture, Langbein has shown that its lessons are applicable to the current debate on torture. He argues that investigation under torture in modern circumstances is unlikely to circumvent the failures of medieval judicial torture with respect to the reliability of information, torturing the innocent and avoiding 'slippery slopes'. According to Langbein, '[h]istory's most important lesson is that it has not been possible to make coercion compatible with truth'. See Langbein, 'The Legal History of Torture', p. 101.

[21] Langbein, Torture and the Law of Proof, p. 10.
[22] Ibid., p. 4.   [23] Ibid., p. 64.   [24] Ibid., p. 65.   [25] Ibid., p. 4.

on account of some profound humanity that the criminal conceals within him, but because of a necessary regulation of the effects of power.[26]

Foucault does not suggest that all forms of torture disappeared following the abolition of judicial torture. He does argue that the use of 'public rituals of torture' was replaced by a new technology of power,[27] the aim of which lies beyond the immediate exertion of physical control over the body through the administration of physical pain:

> Physical pain, the pain of the body itself, is no longer the constituent aim of the penalty. From being an art of unbearable sensations punishment has become an economy of suspended rights. If it is still necessary for the law to reach and manipulate the body of the convict, it will be at a distance, in the proper way, according to strict rules, and with a much 'higher' aim.[28]

Foucault was referring to the massive overhaul that transformed European judicial and penal processes from a system that relied on judicial physical punishment, in the form of judicial torture and the spectacle, to a system with the 'higher aim' of disciplinary control. Foucault, in this sense, is certainly correct to suggest that, at least on the books, in this new 'age of sobriety in punishment', torture is not part of European legal systems.[29] However, whilst judicial torture was no longer deemed essential 'to the maintenance of sovereign power', it is not Foucault's claim that the practice of torture was completely abolished.

More recently, Kahn has argued that the 'humanisation' of criminal law, including the abolition of penal torture in the period of the French Revolution was not merely driven by sympathy and Enlightenment ideals of doubt, reason and objective investigation; rather, it was spurred on by a shift in the relationship between the subject and the sovereign – 'not a rejection of pain but a relocation of the locus of sacrifice'.[30] Kahn conceptualises penal torture as having embodied the relationship between the subject and the sovereign. He contends that the law represented the word of the sovereign and that crime was, therefore, akin to treason.[31] Through torture, the sacral presence of the sovereign was inscribed upon the body of the subject whose criminal actions served to deny the

---

[26] Michel Foucault, (tr. Alan Sheridan), *Discipline and Punish: The Birth of the Prison* (London: Penguin Books, 1977), p. 92.
[27] Talal Asad, 'On Torture or Cruel, Inhuman and Degrading Treatment' (1996) 63 *Social Research* 1081, 1085.
[28] Foucault, *Discipline and Punish*, p. 11. [29] *Ibid.*, p. 14.
[30] Kahn, *Sacred Violence*, p. 44. [31] *Ibid.*, p. 30.

presence, or authority, of the sovereign.[32] Torture acted then to destroy opposition to the sovereign; the subject's confession was reaffirmation. In that way, the torture of the subject induced that subject's sacrifice to the sovereign. Kahn draws a theological parallel: crime was not indifferent to sin; torture was a kind of repentance through confession.[33] The relocation of sovereign authority from the king to the people did not eliminate the sacral nature of sovereignty or the demand for sacrifice. It did, however, dispel the need to display sovereign power on the body: 'The scaffold loses its purpose when sovereignty already dwells within the individual citizen.'[34] According to Kahn, with the transfer of sovereign power, the nature of sacrificial violence became an all pervasive 'ordinary condition of life'.[35] Modernity's generalisation of sacrificial violence became the practice of political violence through democratic participation.[36]

Peters argues that whilst the abolition of torture was likely related to a growing moral appreciation of human dignity in Enlightenment thought, as a blanket explanation this is too simplistic. He critiques the general acceptance and proliferation of this explanation by Enlightenment historians. Like Langbein and Foucault, Peters purports that there are other explanations, among them legal and social ones, for abolition, such as a shift in the judicial evaluation of proof, as well as a shift in the power and practices of the state and the individual's relation to the state.[37]

These alternative accounts as to the removal of judicial torture from the European criminal codes shatter the perception that the abolition of torture was due entirely to ethical concerns with the practice. Whilst the dominant narrative for the explanation of judicial abolition is that of Enlightenment humanitarian progressivism, this explanation appears to oversimplify a complex phenomenon. With this in mind, it seems practical to suggest that morality alone can explain neither the abolition of judicial torture, nor the contemporary prohibition on torture and the current debate. It is, nevertheless, the moral discourse of a heightened concern with values and the rights of the individual as an explanation for torture's abolition that prevailed and that has continued to represent the dominant discourse with respect to the torture prohibition.

Beccaria's denunciation of judicial torture and Bentham's late 1770's writings on the question are similar in that they both adopt a utilitarian

---

[32] *Ibid.*, pp. 25, 30.   [33] *Ibid.*, p. 30.   [34] *Ibid.*, p. 34.
[35] *Ibid.*, p. 35.   [36] *Ibid.*, p. 36.   [37] Peters, *Torture*, p. 86.

perspective.[38] They differ, however, as Beccaria's condemnation takes on a tone of moral protest wholly condemning the usages to which judicial torture is put, whereas Bentham calculates that torture serves a purpose in two specific cases where accomplices are sought in respect of serious crimes. The comparison between Beccaria and Bentham serves to highlight that, if moral outrage was the motivating factor for the abolition of torture, in the philosophical writings of some this moral outrage was limited.

(3)   Beccaria on torture

When Beccaria published *On Crimes and Punishments* in 1764,[39] the movement for the abolition of torture from the criminal law in Europe was underway to the extent that, by 1800, provisions for torture in the criminal codes of Europe were almost dispensed with.[40] Beccaria's text was among a growing body of literature that adopted an Enlightenment critique of torture, and is considered to have almost certainly been influential on this accelerated legislative reform.[41] Beccaria's text prompted Pierre François Muyart de Vouglans to write a refutation in 1766, defending the use of judicial torture, as part of a treatise on French criminal law dedicated to Louis XVI. Muyart de Vouglans' refutation, which proved ineffective, is the last known defence of judicial torture in European history.[42]

In an introductory note to the reader, added as a response to criticism of his treatise, Beccaria describes torture laws as 'an emanation of the most barbarous ages'.[43] He denunciates torture for the purposes of extracting confession, of reconciling contradictions in the statement of the accused, of naming accomplices, of extracting admission to additional crimes and of purging infamy.[44] Whilst Beccaria's views concerned the judicial use of torture, his writing envelops a more general critique of torture. Beccaria's views on torture, and his views on crimes and punishment more generally, combine a utilitarian outlook, whereby society's main goal should

---

[38] Francis Hutcheson is considered to be the first to have clearly stated the principle of utility. According to Hutcheson, utility provides that 'that action is best, which procures the greatest happiness for the greatest numbers; and that, worst, which, in like manner, occasions misery', cited in John Rawls, *A Theory of Justice* (Cambridge, MA: The Belknap Press, 1971), p. 22, n. 9.

[39] Beccaria, *On Crimes and Punishments*.

[40] Peters, *Torture*, p. 74.

[41] *Ibid.*, p. 99.   [42] *Ibid.*, p. 73.

[43] Beccaria, *On Crimes and Punishments*, p. 1.   [44] *Ibid.*, p. 29.

be 'the greatest happiness shared among the greatest number',[45] with an anti-utilitarian, justice or even natural law perspective derived from 'the general principles'[46] and 'the interests of humanity'.[47]

Beccaria describes the reasons for the use of judicial torture as 'ridiculous'.[48] He struggled to come to terms with the conundrum of using torture to resolve a crime if the guilt of the accused was certain enough to warrant torture in the first place. On the other hand, if torture had to be inflicted to resolve the crime, this would mean that the guilt or innocence of the citizen was undetermined:

> [E]ither the crime is certain, or it is not; if it is certain, then no other punishment is suitable for the criminal except the one established by law, and torture is useless because the confession of the accused is unnecessary; if the crime is uncertain, one should not torment an innocent person, for, in the eyes of the law, he is a man whose misdeeds have not been proven.[49]

Beccaria thereby identifies the conceptual flaw at the heart of judicial torture for the purpose of ascertaining confession. This argument has further implications; it points to the disregard that torture has, in effect, upon due process and, particularly, the presumption of innocence. Writing in a post-September 11 context, John T. Parry, citing Franz Kafka, echoes Beccaria and succinctly captures the incongruity of torture:

> The domination effected by torture plays out in several ways. Intense pain warps and destroys human perception and personality. Even more, torture uses, inverts and destroys, the trappings of civilization. Thus, torture mocks the law, using punishment to gather evidence to justify the punishment already inflicted, rather than using evidence already gathered to justify punishment. When torture becomes an official policy, the victim's suffering and pain lose legal relevance, and they become further isolated just when they most need the law's protections.[50]

Beccaria then turns to critique the nature of the act of torture. This critique resonates with the concept of personal integrity, and even the prohibition on self-incrimination. He remarks, 'one confuses all natural relationships in requiring a man to be the accuser and the accused at the same time and in making pain the crucible of truth, as though the criterion of truth lay in the muscles and fibers of a poor wretch'.[51] He argues,

---

[45] *Ibid.*, p. 5.   [46] *Ibid.*   [47] *Ibid.*, p. 6.
[48] *Ibid.*, p. 30.   [49] *Ibid.*, p. 29.
[50] John T. Parry, 'Escalation and Necessity: Defining Torture at Home and Abroad' in Sanford Levinson (ed.), *Torture: A Collection* (Oxford University Press, 2004), p. 153.
[51] Beccaria, *On Crimes and Punishments*, p. 29.

furthermore, that 'this is a sure way to acquit robust scoundrels and to condemn weak but innocent people'.[52] Beccaria stresses his concern with the dangers of torturing the innocent,[53] and he also condemns torture as an enquiry after truth. He contends that torture is a poor means of resolving the contradictions of the accused and of attaining truth. Torture heightens the potential for uncertainty and self-contradiction: 'as though contradictions which are common enough among calm men, would not be multiplied in the turbulent mind of someone completely absorbed in the thought of saving himself from imminent danger.'[54] Torture impedes the investigation for truth:

> The examination of someone accused of a crime is undertaken in order to learn the truth, but, if truth is difficult to discover in the bearing, the gestures, and the expression of a calm man, all the less will one find it in a man in whom the convulsions of pain have distorted all the signs by which the truth reveals itself on the faces of most men in spite of themselves. Every violent action confounds and annihilates the tiny differences in objects by which one may sometimes distinguish the truth from falsehood.[55]

Beccaria compares torture to the practice of ordeals by fire and water. The only difference that he notes between the two practices is that the outcome of torture depends on the will of the accused whilst the ordeals are solved by an external validation. However, Beccaria dispels this apparent difference in noting that torture does not allow for the exercise of free will: 'Speaking the truth amid convulsions and torments is no more a free act than staving off the effects of fire and boiling water except by fraud.'[56] Whilst the comparison that Beccaria draws upon here is somewhat unconvincing, since the ordeals were considered to represent divine justice – judgements from God[57] – it is his overall thesis that torture repels truth and perverts the will of the torture victim that is noteworthy. Beccaria is not only concerned with torture because he considers it not to work but also because he considers it unjust.

On the whole, Beccaria's writing on torture shifts between utilitarian calculation of the efficacy of torture, deeming it ineffective, and an Enlightenment-inspired recognition of the right of the individual to personal integrity.[58] Beccaria's writing has an additional tone. In his

---

[52] *Ibid.* [53] *Ibid.* [54] *Ibid.*, p. 30.
[55] *Ibid.*, p. 31. [56] *Ibid.*, p. 30. [57] Peters, *Torture*, p. 42.
[58] David Young considers that the central points of Beccaria's treatise are the ineffectiveness of torture and the natural right of self-defence. See Young's commentary in Beccaria, *On Crimes and Punishments*, p. 92, n. 12.

opposition to judicial torture, his challenge to the power of the judiciary, and the individual's relation to this power, is also evident. Beccaria asks, '[w]hat right, then, other than the right of force, gives a judge the power to inflict punishment on a citizen while the question of his guilt or innocence is still in doubt?'[59]

(4)   Bentham's utilitarian framework

In 1973 W. L. and P. E. Twining published Jeremy Bentham's previously undisclosed writings on the subject of torture.[60] Bentham documented his thoughts on torture more than a decade after Beccaria had published his treatise.[61] At that stage, the movement for the abolition of torture was very advanced.[62] Bentham is considered to have been inspired by the utilitarian thinking of Beccaria, who he references in his formulation of the doctrine of utility. He refers directly to Beccaria's treatise and asserts his agreement with Beccaria 'almost without exception'.[63] Although he considered his own defence of torture in certain cases to bear no relation to that which Beccaria condemned, he disagreed with Beccaria on one fundamental issue. Bentham found reason to justify the use of torture in some circumstances for practical purposes based on utility.[64] He arrived at this conclusion having reconsidered his own beliefs on torture:

> If a few years ago any one had foretold to me that in any case I should be in the least disposed to approve of anything to which the name of Torture could with any sort of propriety be applied, I should have thought he had done me a great Injustice. That it should enter into the heart of an Englishman[65] to harbour a single word in favour of a practice abolished within a few years in several of the most absolute governments in Europe,

---

[59] Beccaria, *On Crimes and Punishments*, p. 29.
[60] Twining and Twining, 'Bentham on Torture' 307.
[61] It should be pointed out that Bentham himself chose not to publish his writings on torture. Rod Morgan suggests that this might be so because Bentham recognised the inconsistencies in his work. Rod Morgan, 'The Utilitarian Justification of Torture: Denial, Desert and Disinformation' (2000) 2 *Punishment & Society* 181, 192. This is indeed possible. Bentham's writings warrant analysis, however, because they clearly resonate with the current debates. In addition, whether or not Bentham was content with his own conclusions on torture, it is obvious that he was intuitively opposed to absolute prohibition.
[62] Twining and Twining, 'Bentham on Torture' 305.
[63] *Ibid.*, 309.   [64] *Ibid.*
[65] Unlike Europe, England's law of proof was not dependent on judicial torture.

may of all things seem singularly strange and unexpected. But in the course of a scrupulous examination a man learns to render himself proof against the delusive power of words, and to correct the first impressions of *sentiment* by the more extensive considerations of *utility*.[66]

Bentham's late eighteenth-century observations provide an early, essentially moral, framework for cost–benefit analysis of torture. Whilst this framework is, in the contemporary context, more complex, the heart of Bentham's argument remains – there are limited situations in which torture may be used to answer a particular purpose and the potential for torture to maximise happiness exists in these particular usages.

Bentham identifies, and seeks to remove, certain prejudices about torture. First, he claims that there are circumstances in which the use of torture is both customary and considered acceptable. By way of example, he characterises the pinching of a child in order to compel that child to desist from doing something as torture.[67] Second, he considers torture to be less of an infliction than other comparable punishment. In comparing the duration of imprisonment and the intensity of torture, he weighs in the latter as more favourable.[68] Third, he argues that the distinction between torture and punishment lies in the circumstance of fulfilling the purpose of torture. Once that purpose is fulfilled, torture, if not abused, has 'succeeded' and ceases. It is more difficult with punishment, on the other hand, to know how much is needed to yield measurable results.[69] In other words, there is a greater risk to over-punish.[70]

Bentham provides two cases in which he considers torture to represent the 'lesser evil'. In both cases the purpose of torture is intelligence-gathering.[71] In the first case there is, according to Bentham, minimal danger of torture being misapplied:

> The first is where the thing which a Man is required to do being a thing which the public has an interest in his doing, is a thing which for a certainty is in his power to do; and which therefore so long as he continues to suffer for not doing he is sure not to be innocent.[72]

---

[66] Twining and Twining, 'Bentham on Torture' 308, (emphasis added).
[67] *Ibid.*, 310. Bentham's definition of torture emphasised the purpose of torture. Unlike the current legal definition, he is not concerned with the severity of the pain inflicted. Hence, he speaks of pinching a child as an example of torture.
[68] *Ibid.*   [69] *Ibid.*, 311.
[70] Morgan, 'The Utilitarian Justification of Torture' 187.
[71] Twining and Twining, 'Bentham on Torture' 323.
[72] *Ibid.*, 312.

In the second, rare case the danger of torture being misapplied outweighs the danger of it not being applied at all:

> The second is where a man is required what probably though not certainly it is in his power to do; and for the not doing of which it is possible that he may suffer, although he be innocent; but which the public has so great an interest in his doing that the danger of what may ensue from his not doing it is a greater danger than even that of an innocent person's suffering the greatest degree of pain that can be suffered by Torture, of the kind and in the quantity permitted to be employed. Are there in practice any cases that can be ranked under this head? If there be any, it is plain there can be but very few.[73]

Bentham believed torture to be admissible only in these specific cases. He limited the application of these exceptions, within an otherwise general support for the abolition of judicial torture, to cases in which the accomplices to serious crimes needed to be found in the interests of the public. He considered arson and 'some of the most mischievous kinds of murder such as assassination for hire' to represent such crimes.[74]

Bentham subjected both of these exceptional cases to a list of rules in order to prevent the employment of torture 'to an improper degree, or in improper Cases'.[75] The rules in the first case stipulate that there must be sufficient proof that the accused has the required information; that the case involve imminent danger so as to require torture; in less urgent cases, less severe torture should be administered; the benefit of torture must outweigh the application of torture; the duration of torture should be limited by law; the pain must be measured to fulfil the purpose of torture only; and wrongful suffering should be compensated.[76] The second case requires that the situation be exigent and that the safety of the entire state be endangered. In addition, great care, and oversight, is required in deciding in whom to place the power to order, and not abuse, the application of torture.[77]

In the first case the interests of the individual are trumped by those of the public. The necessary component is the power of the individual to satisfy the interests of the public by fulfilling the purpose of the torture; for so long as they refuse to do so, they are necessarily guilty. Bentham's rules in this case do permit some margin of error with regard to the guilt of the individual. In the second 'rare' case the individual's guilt has not been established; however, the interests of the public outweigh even the interests of an innocent person.

---

[73] *Ibid.*   [74] *Ibid.*, 325.   [75] *Ibid.*, 313.
[76] *Ibid.*, 313–14.   [77] *Ibid.*, 315.

Bentham's two cases suggest that he is willing to defend both an institutionalised practice of torture and exceptional acts of torture; he does not distinguish between the two.[78] At first glance, his cases appear to be rooted in act-utilitarianism or case-utilitarianism; however, since Bentham applies a number of rules to his two cases – in order to protect against the torture of the innocent and to protect against the use of torture to an improper degree – it could be argued, at least for the first case, that he applies rule-utilitarian rationale.

(i)   The rare case

Whilst Bentham acknowledges the propensity for the practice of torture to be abused,[79] he only applies one rule to this particular issue:

> The power of employing it ought not to be vested in any hands but as such as from the business of their office are best qualified to judge of that necessity: and in the dignity of it perfectly responsible in case of their making an ill use of so terrible a power.[80]

Since this rule is applied only to a 'rare' case, clearly Bentham regarded the exceptional case to be more liable to abuse and error than an institutionalised practice of torture. Bentham does not clarify wherein the rules of each case would be regulated, but one might extrapolate that, in the former case of institutionalised practice, the rules would be legislated for and judicially monitored, whereas in the latter case the power to decide the rare case might emanate from a source liable to abuse this power, most likely a reference to the powers of the magistrate. He stipulates, therefore, that '[i]n *whatever* hands the power is reposed, as many and as efficacious checks ought to be applied to the exercise of it as can be made consistent with the purpose for which it is conferred'.[81] Bentham is seemingly wary of governmental abuse of the power to torture. With respect to the execution of the law by the magistrate, Bentham is equally cautious. He associates the power to order torture with the potential for tyranny. He remarks: 'The danger is then that the magistrate when armed with such effectual powers may give execution to laws repugnant to the interest as well as to [the] affections of the people.'[82]

Bentham is, however, somewhat ambivalent in deciding at what point caution is required. On the one hand, he admits to the rare use of torture 'where the safety of the whole State may be endangered'.[83] On the other

---

[78] *Ibid.*, 349.   [79] *Ibid.*, 311.   [80] *Ibid.*, 315.
[81] *Ibid.* (emphasis added).   [82] *Ibid.*, 336.   [83] *Ibid.*, 315.

hand, he later states that the power given to the magistrate to execute the law is open to abuse such that this power should be limited to cases pertaining to crimes against individuals, withholding it 'in the case perhaps of most which are offences against the State, at least if such offences are against the government'.[84] This ambiguity aside, Bentham certainly saw the utility of torture in the fight against 'ordinary' crime, but he seems less likely to sign off on torture used to fight 'political crime':

> Those whom it is found necessary to prescribe under the names of rebels, libellers, or sowers of sedition, may in fact be the best friends and defenders of the people: against these the hand of the government may be too strong. But incendiaries, assassins, highwaymen and housebreakers are under every government, be the government what it may, the standing enemies of the people: against these the hand of government can never be too strong.[85]

He warns of the particular danger that arises in conflict situations where torture has the potential to be used wrongfully as an instrument of tyranny by the state:

> Under the head of Rebellion we have shown how apt in these cases might and right are to be at variance: and how easily it may happen that a man by the sole impulse of the most virtuous principles will be driven into courses the good or evil tendency of which can be determined only by the event, but which the law according to the interpretation that is and must be made of it, can in the meantime do no otherwise than treat as criminal. The danger will always be great that torture if allowed in these cases, may be made subservient to the establishment of usurpation, or which comes to the same thing a government repugnant to the interests and affections of the great body of people.[86]

W. L. and P. E. Twining conclude that Bentham explicitly excludes the use of torture in cases of offences against the government, even in times of war or extreme emergency.[87] Bentham's caution chillingly anticipates the emergence of torture as an 'engine of the State' in the twentieth century,[88] particularly in the light of the fact that torture was pervasively authorised and justified to quell enemy and resistance movements in Stalinist Russia and Nazi Germany. This suggests that Bentham leaves a very small margin of incidence for the application of torture in his second case.

---

[84] *Ibid.*, 336.   [85] *Ibid.*, 337.
[86] *Ibid.*   [87] *Ibid.*, 351.
[88] Peters, *Torture*, p. 101.

(ii)   Contemporary application

More than two centuries after Bentham penned his thoughts on the utility of torture, his analysis remain pertinent. So where would Bentham stand with respect to the use of torture in ticking bomb cases? W. L. and P. E. Twining opine that Bentham, faced with a ticking bomb scenario, would have had a clear position in justifying the use of torture.[89] They find evidence for this assertion in an example that Bentham gives to demonstrate the utility of torture. In Bentham's scenario it is strongly suspected that a number of people are suffering violence equivalent to torture. Bentham asks:

> For the purposes of rescuing from torture those hundred innocents, should any scruple be made of applying equal or superior torture, to extract the requisite information from the mouth of one criminal, who having it in his power to make known the place where at this time the enormity was practising or about to be practised, should refuse to do so. To say nothing of wisdom, could any pretence be made so much as to the praise of blind and vulgar humanity, by the man who to save one criminal, should determine to abandon a 100 innocent persons to the same fate?[90]

It is unlikely that this example is sufficient to suggest that Bentham would support the authorisation of torture in countering terrorism or in so-called ticking bomb situations. It represents a rare case, and he has in mind a felony and not political crime.[91] As noted above, Bentham is concerned about the state's potential to abuse the power to torture. In calculating the interests of the public, he weighs the utility of torture against its potential for misuse and appears to conclude that torture is not useful in situations in which government political interests are invested. In addition, his caution against governmental use of torture in situations of rebellion appears to be independent of the rightfulness or wrongfulness of the actions of the rebellious forces. Given this, it is equally plausible to argue that Bentham would not favour the torture of enemies of the state. Rod Morgan similarly concludes that Bentham was less likely to justify torture in response to political or politically motivated crimes, 'precisely the crimes against which torture is most likely to be used in the late 20th century'.[92] As Morgan cautions, however, Bentham's utilitarian justification should not be overstretched to suit contemporary discussion.[93]

[89] Twining and Twining, 'Bentham on Torture' 347.
[90] *Ibid.*   [91] *Ibid.*
[92] Morgan, 'The Utilitarian Justification of Torture' 192.
[93] *Ibid.*

Modern consequentialist arguments in favour of torture in ticking bomb circumstances comprise a Bentham-like consideration of costs and benefits,[94] and certain central aspects of Bentham's reasoning continue to generate debate. For example, in Bentham's first scenario there is an implied equation that the definite guilt of the torture victim combined with failure to confess under torture further confirms guilt. Within this formulation, Bentham understands the torture victim, through their guilt, as having the power to stop the torture.[95] It is in this sense that Bentham relates torture to punishment. He considers torture to represent successive punishment for the successive offence of failing to submit to the purpose of torture by providing intelligence: 'The delinquent ceases to be punished when he ceases to offend.'[96] In recent times, failure to confess is rarely argued to represent simple proof of guilt. Bentham's overall formulation in the first case – the preventative power of the victim – remains, however, implicit in the debate.

In 1978 Henry Shue described this as 'torture that satisfies the constraint of possible compliance'.[97] The torture victim knows the purpose of the torture, they have it in their power to perform an action that will fulfil this purpose, and this in turn will lead to the permanent cessation of the torture. In such a situation the torture might be considered not to constitute an assault upon the defenceless; the victim of torture retains 'one last portion of control over his or her fate'.[98] Shue is wary of this approach for four primary reasons. First, he recognises the inexistence of such a compliance constraint when the purpose of torture is terroristic – to intimidate persons other than the individual torture victim.[99] Second, he argues that interrogational torture is rarely limited in its purpose to obtaining information; no constraint can exist where compliance is preceded by intimidation or sadism.[100] Moreover, there are, according to Shue, obvious difficulties with distinguishing when the victim has fully complied, that is, knowing when to stop the torture. Finally, the constraint of possible

---

[94] See, for example, Mirko Bagaric and Julie Clarke, *Torture: When the Unthinkable is Morally Permissible* (Albany: State University of New York Press, 2007); Mirko Bagaric and Julie Clarke, 'Tortured Responses (A Reply to Our Critics): Physically Persuading Suspects Is Morally Preferable to Allowing the Innocent to Be Murdered' (2006) 40 *University of San Francisco Law Review* 1; Mirko Bagaric and Julie Clarke, 'Not Enough (Official) Torture in the World? The Circumstances in Which Torture is Morally Justifiable' (2005) 39 *University of San Francisco Law Review* 581.

[95] Twining and Twining, 'Bentham on Torture' 323.   [96] *Ibid.*, 324.

[97] Henry Shue, 'Torture' (1978) 7 *Philosophy and Public Affairs* 124, 131.

[98] *Ibid.*   [99] *Ibid.*, 132.   [100] *Ibid.*, 134.

compliance means nothing to a 'dedicated enemy' whose objective is not to collaborate, but to resist or feign compliance.[101] Cumulatively, Shue's unpacking of the constraint of possible compliance renders this an unreliable constraint at best, and at worst, an existential impossibility, since the constraint can only effectively exist in situations where the victim is willing to provide information; in such situations, torture would not be necessary in the first place.

Shue's examination of the constraint of possible compliance remains wanting, however. One might argue, for example, that there are situations in which pure interrogational torture is required to obtain necessary information and, in such a case, the 'dedicated enemy's' unwillingness to betray the cause does not eradicate the possibility for them to comply. In fact, it is just as absurd to speak of torture with a constraint of possible compliance as it is to assume that failure to confess proves guilt, since, once torture is threatened, the possibility of compliance, as a free act, disappears. It is the torture that governs compliance rather than the individual's free will. Like Bentham, Shue posits, at least in the abstract, that the act of torture, under certain limited circumstances, offers the victim some power through their knowledge – thus guilt – to stop the torture at any point. In both cases it is, in fact, questionable whether the power to stop the torture is actually the victim's.

(5)   Beccaria v. Bentham

Bentham's arguments depart from Beccaria's with respect to the torture of a suspect to discover accomplices. Bentham defends torture in this instance, provided that it is known that accomplices were involved in the first place, a point on which he judges Beccaria to be unclear.[102] Bentham, unlike Beccaria, regards torture as an effective means of discovering the truth,[103] although he does appear to have some doubts:

> In the gout or under the misfortune of a broken limb a man will bear up against a very great degree of pain. In a putrid or hectic Fever a man will sink under a much less degree of pain. Add to this that in the case of an evil like Torture is seen to result immediately from the will of another, and that other present, the sentiment of anger mixing itself with the sensation of pain will have a peculiar tendency to give force to obstinacy.[104]

---

[101] *Ibid.*, 136.
[102] Twining and Twining, 'Bentham on Torture' 330.
[103] *Ibid.*   [104] *Ibid.*, 316.

From this account, he considers torture to have the potential to debilitate, through anger and pain, by comparison to other forms of less acute punishment, thereby undermining his own argument with respect to the power of the individual to stop the torture through compliance. Nevertheless, he trusts torture's efficacy in 'men of ordinary mould'.[105] In addition, Bentham considers torture to be admissible in discovering accomplices not because it is punishment of the suspect for another's crimes, as Beccaria suggests, but because the suspect in withholding information continues to offend.[106] Lastly, Bentham judges torture to constitute a more efficacious means of finding the accomplices than other investigative means suggested by Beccaria.[107]

The principle of utility engaged by Bentham assesses every action according to its tendency to augment or diminish the happiness of the interested party, be that the individual or the community.[108] In line with this philosophy, Bentham's defence of torture rests solely on a utilitarian calculation of its overall benefit for the community. At no point does he factor in consideration of the torture victim.

Since Bentham considers natural law theories to be founded in sentiment and sensibility, and thus, illogical[109] – '[n]atural rights is simple nonsense: natural and imprescriptable rights, rhetorical nonsense – nonsense upon stilts'[110] – it seems peculiar, therefore, that he does not make any reference to Beccaria's resort to a moral tone in his condemnation; Beccaria composed his denunciation of torture through arguments based both in utility and in the idea of the individual's own right to self-defence or personal integrity. Bentham interpreted that Beccaria had closed the door on torture only with respect to the five cases under examination: 'That there are no other cases in which the use of it can be justified, is more than he asserts.'[111] Yet Beccaria touches upon the idea that there is something intrinsically wrong with torture. On this reading, it is not evident

---

[105] Ibid.
[106] Beccaria, On Crimes and Punishments, p. 33; Twining and Twining, 'Bentham on Torture' 330.
[107] Beccaria, On Crimes and Punishments, p. 33; Twining and Twining, 'Bentham on Torture' 332.
[108] Jeremy Bentham, An Introduction to the Principles of Morals and Legislation (New York: Dover Philosophical Classics, 2007), p. 2.
[109] Ibid., p. 17, n. 1. See also Alasdair MacIntyre, A Short History of Ethics (London: Routledge, 1967), p. 233.
[110] Jeremy Bentham, 'Anarchial Fallacies' in John Bowring (ed.), The Works of Jeremy Bentham: Vol. II (Edinburgh: William Tait, 1859), p. 498.
[111] Twining and Twining, 'Bentham on Torture' 328.

that Beccaria's denunciation of torture applies to cases of judicial torture only.

It is possible that Bentham read Beccaria's moral tone not as based in sentiment, but rather as part of the calculation. After all, Beccaria is most defiant on the question of torture's efficacy in obtaining truth and this may suggest that he viewed the perversion of the suspect's natural inclination not to incriminate oneself under torture as a drawback to the ascertainment of truth only, and not as a wrong independent of the consequences. This explanation is somewhat inadequate, however, as Beccaria describes this perversion as a confusion of all natural relationships.

Whereas Beccaria and Bentham converge in their calculation of the utility of torture, they disagree on its having utility in that one instance where accomplices to serious crimes are sought. One reading of Beccaria's denunciation of torture portrays him as having specified that which contemporary moral absolutists consider the intrinsic factor that makes torture wrong – the violation of personal integrity. Bentham, on a first reading, might seem to offer a more depressing account. However, Bentham's utilitarianism should not be read as an infallibly calculated defence of torture. Whilst Bentham considered torture admissible in certain cases, he puts limits on the scope of these cases. One of the more noteworthy limits is the power ascribed to governments to use torture as a political instrument of power. This limit becomes all the more important in the light of torture's reappearance as an instrument of totalitarian and authoritarian power and as a counterterrorism strategy in the twentieth century. In addition, many of Bentham's utilitarian arguments in favour of the institutionalisation of torture do not predict possible contradicting utilitarian arguments. Bentham, for example, does not explain how torture can be limited to cases of serious crime only. Nor does he explain to any persuasive degree how the suspect's guilt may be unreservedly determined.[112] Undoubtedly, Bentham has continued relevance and not just with respect to the ticking bomb torture debate. The kidnapping case, which led to the European Court of Human Rights decision in *Gäfgen* v. *Germany*, resonates uncomfortably with Bentham's case for exceptionality.[113]

Beccaria and Bentham provide a historical account for and against the use of judicial torture. To an extent, their respective tracts bolster the argument that torture, in the late eighteenth century, came to be considered in the light of moral progress. On the other hand, these tracts suggest

---

[112] Morgan, 'The Utilitarian Justification of Torture' 188.
[113] *Gäfgen* v. *Germany* (App. No. 22978/05) ECHR 1 June 2010.

that there was more to the abolition of judicial torture than is accounted for by the argument based on moral outrage.

B.   Can the ticking bomb suspect be tortured? The contemporary debate

(1)   Ethical arguments for and against the use of torture

In the contemporary torture debate the problem of the ticking bomb is constructed as an ethical dilemma, with arguments for and against the use of torture couched in ethical terms. The dilemma of torturing the ticking bomb suspect revolves around questions of torture's inherent immorality; torture's immorality vis-à-vis lawful killing; the immorality of not torturing; and the consequences of both torturing and not torturing. The ethical debate is cyclical, with no definitive answer. Underlying the debate is the structure of a moral conflict between the prohibition of torture and the right to life.

Fritz Allhoff contends that most moral theories, with the exception of Kantianism, could conceivably license torture in ticking bomb cases.[114] The implications of that case, he further argues, are 'sufficient to derail entire moral theories', including Kantianism.[115] The inference of this statement is that the ticking bomb scenario saddles the torture prohibition with a blind spot that an absolutist perspective cannot reach and that all other moral theories treat as rendering torture morally possible. Kahn argues, on the other hand, that the ticking bomb scenario cannot properly be addressed through morality: 'we lose our bearings with the hypothetical because it destabilizes whatever moral perspective we take.'[116] For Kahn the question posed by the ticking bomb scenario is unanswerable through conceptions of the right or the good; the normative background is rather the relationship between violence and the state and the further relationship between the state and the individual in regard to this violence.[117] In order to investigate these approaches, it is useful to outline the various arguments for and against torture in ticking bomb circumstances. These arguments are presented in the typical deontological/ teleological fashion: moral absolutism, non-absolutist deontology and

---

[114] Fritz Allhoff, 'A Defense of Torture: Separation of Cases, Ticking Time-Bombs, and Moral Justification' (2005) 19 *International Journal of Applied Philosophy* 243, 248.
[115] *Ibid.*, 258.
[116] Kahn, *Sacred Violence*, p. 80.   [117] *Ibid.*, p. 81.

various forms of consequentialism. That said an argument defending one position or another may contain both deontological and consequentialist sub-arguments. The arguments are thus rather more nuanced than a simplistic 'the ends do not justify the means' versus 'the ends justify the means' or Kant versus Bentham framework captures.[118]

(2) The Kantians

Those who defend the prohibition on torture independent of the consequences in ticking bomb cases often do so from either a principled or practical moral absolutist perspective; either torture *would* never be justified or torture *should* never be justified. This position, in line with international law, holds the torture prohibition to be inviolable. Two concepts that derive from the ethics of Immanuel Kant provide the basis for a defence of the torture prohibition without exception.[119] First, Kant prescribed the existence of certain moral imperatives as categorical.[120] A categorical imperative is a duty-based theory that consists of a rule that has no exceptions. This is a rule that has independent value in relation to other rules. The consequences of obeying a categorical imperative are not at issue; the rule is unwavering. Kant is most often interpreted as having placed emphasis on sticking to the rule, regardless of the consequences. Christopher Tindale's more generous interpretation reads Kant as having stipulated that since 'we have no control over the consequences ... we should not act in the moral realm with the false confidence that we do'.[121] It is not that consequences do not matter; rather, they are something that

---

[118] Jean Bethke Ehlstain, 'Reflection on the Problem of Dirty Hands' in Sanford Levinson (ed.), *Torture: A Collection* (Oxford University Press, 2004), p. 78. Ehlstain remarks that the ticking bomb scenario usually probes the question, 'So where do you stand? With Kant or Bentham?' According to Ehlstain, he finds himself standing with neither.

[119] Of course, it is not necessary to be a Kantian in order to hold absolute values. In response to Oren Gross' statement that 'all but unabashed Kantians recognize the difficulties for an absolutist position presented by extreme cases', Christopher Tindale remarks '[w]hile never a Kantian, unabashed or otherwise, I remain committed to the absolutist position on this issue, even in the face of extreme cases'. See Christopher Tindale, 'Tragic Choices: Reaffirming Absolutes in the Torture Debate' (2005) 19 *International Journal of Applied Philosophy* 209, 210. See also Oren Gross, 'The Prohibition on Torture and the Limits of the Law' in Sanford Levinson (ed.), *Torture: A Collection* (Oxford University Press, 2004), p. 231.

[120] Immanuel Kant (tr. James W. Ellington), *Grounding for the Metaphyics of Morals: On a Supposed Right to Lie Because of Philanthropic Concerns* (Indianapolis: Hackett Publishing Company, 1993).

[121] Tindale, 'Tragic Choices' 216.

cannot be determined and, thus, are extrinsic to the intrinsic rightness or wrongness of the rule in question.[122] In Kant's conception, the individual is a free and equal rational being whose good will compels the fulfilment of duty. The categorical imperative requires the individual to will its universalisation: 'Act only on that maxim whereby you can at the same time will that it should become a universal law.'[123] Thus, the individual 'legislates the law he obeys'.[124] As Douzinas points out, in order to do this, the individual must assume that this imperative is universally shared by a community like-minded in reason and ego.[125] Bound to Kant's formulation of the categorical imperative is his requirement that the individual always be treated as an end and never merely as a means.

According to Tindale's interpretation of the categorical imperative, Kant 'effectively challenges the causal link between the torture and its successful outcome, forcing us to focus on the act of torture itself and its justification irrespective of any imagined consequences which are completely unpredictable'.[126] Focusing on the act of torture itself, the moral absolutist therefore argues the inviolability of human dignity and individual bodily integrity. In line with Kant's maxim that the individual cannot be used as a means to an end, the absolutist refuses to place human dignity in the balance even when confronted with the ticking bomb case. For the absolutist, both the point of departure and of conclusion in debating torturing is the act of torture itself. This is so because torture in and of itself is so corrupting that it earns categorical rejection.

In her defence of an absolutist position, Marcy Strauss indirectly demonstrates how slipping away from a Kantian or absolutist position in order to pursue that causal link between torture and the prevention of harm should, in fact, force a retreat back to an absolutist position. Strauss provides the example of a nuclear bomb set to detonate in a number of hours in a city. The suspect is tortured to no avail. The suspect's child is then tortured and the suspect breaks. Strauss states:

> A nation that intentionally and brutally harms an innocent child has clearly lost its moral bearings ... The temptation to forfeit our most precious values is always most pressing in times of emergency and war. Yet, it is at precisely those times when it is most important to maintain our moral compass. Only an absolute ban on torture without exception will

[122] Tamar Schapiro, 'Kantian Rigorism and Mitigating Circumstances' (2006) 117 *Ethics* 32, 34.
[123] Kant, *Grounding for the Metaphyics of Morals*, p. 42.
[124] Douzinas, *The End of Human Rights*, p. 346.   [125] *Ibid.*
[126] Tindale, 'Tragic Choices' 216.

enable this nation to resist the impulse to ignore critical core values in
favour of an elusive security.[127]

Strauss' argument, as a reason to denounce torture, is slightly disconcert-
ing. By using the emotive example of torturing a child to emphasise why
the prohibition must be adhered to, she leaves the impression that the torture of the suspect might be justifiable by comparison. Yet her argument,
that torture *should* never be justified, is significant in emphasising the
Kantian point that once the rule is negated and the moral realm of consequentialism entered, moral control is lost and a moral vacuum is created.

For David Sussman, the framing of the question shifts. He asks what
it is about torture that makes it so wrong as to warrant unconditional
denunciation: 'What is it about torture that sets it apart even from killing, maiming or imprisoning someone, such that circumstances that
might justify inflicting such harm would not even begin to justify torture?'[128] He is not convinced that utilitarian reasoning alone can get to the
heart of its inherent immorality.[129] According to Sussman, torture 'bears
an especially high burden of justification, greater in degree and different in kind from even that of killing'.[130] He is careful to point out that
he does not consider a wrongful act of torture to be by definition worse
than wrongful acts of maiming and killing. The act of torture, Sussman
maintains, emphasises the utter helplessness of the victim and their entire
dependence upon the will of the torturer; the individual is stripped of
integrity. It is the structure of this relationship of torturer to victim that
makes torture, its effects notwithstanding, intrinsically objectionable.[131]
He argues that torture functions not only to undermine the victim's capacity for self-governance, in a broadly Kantian sense, but also to actually force an individual into a position of collusion against oneself; utterly
powerless, the individual becomes complicit in one's own violation.[132] In
this way, the act of torture deliberately perverts human dignity turning
it 'against itself in a way that must be especially offensive to any morality
that fundamentally honours it'.[133] Torture functions to make the body an
enemy of the victim. He notes that 'many of the most common forms of
torture involve somehow pitting the victim against himself, making him

---

[127] Marcy Strauss, 'Torture' (2004) 48 *New York Law School Law Review* 201, 274.
[128] David Sussman, 'What's Wrong with Torture' (2005) 33 *Philosophy and Public Affairs* 1, 3.
[129] *Ibid.*, 13.   [130] *Ibid.*, 4.   [131] *Ibid.*, 13.
[132] *Ibid.*, 4. On this point, see also John Kleinig, 'Ticking Bombs and Torture Warrants'
      (2005) 10 *Deakin Law Review* 614, 619.
[133] Sussman, 'What's Wrong with Torture' 19.

an active participant in his own abuse'.[134] As a consequence, '[t]he victim of torture finds within herself a surrogate of the torturer'.[135]

This analysis recalls Beccaria's point with respect to the unnatural relationship that is established when an accused has to act against himself or herself under torture. Bentham, on the other hand, seemed to consider torture as allowing room for rational and uninhibited choice. According to Bentham, one should succumb or continue to be punished.

Whilst Sussman does stock the deontological armoury against torture, he recognises the difficulty in arriving at an ethical conclusion on the justifiability of torture in the extreme case. He presents deontological arguments against the use of torture; however, he does not purport, through his account of what is wrong with torture, to immediately discount ticking bomb or 'Dirty Harry' dilemmas or to prove that torture is categorically wrong.[136] His analysis is, therefore, essential to an understanding of why it is that torture is categorically banned, but it does not claim to resolve the ticking bomb dilemma.

(3)   Consequentialism for torture

Consequentialism is 'a moral doctrine which says that the right act in any given situation is the one that will produce the best overall outcome, as judged from an impersonal standpoint which gives equal weight to the interests of everyone'.[137] Simply put, consequentialism strives to minimise evil and maximise good for the achievement of the best overall situation.[138] Concentrating on the best overall outcome, it is the ends not that means that determine morality for consequentialists;[139] since the overall outcome is the achievement of the good, then it follows that right action is that action that leads to the fulfilment of the good.[140] Consequentialism has

---

[134] *Ibid.*, 22.   [135]   *Ibid.*, 25.   [136]   *Ibid.*, 13.

[137] Samuel Scheffler (ed.), *Consequentialism and its Critics* (Oxford University Press, 1988), p. 1. G. E. M. Anscombe introduced this term to moral philosophy in 1958. See Alan Donagan, 'Cases of Necessity' in Joram Graf Haber (ed.), *Absolutism and Its Consequentialist Critics* (Boston, MA: Rowman & Littlefield Publishers Inc., 1994), p. 58. See also G. E. M. Anscombe, 'Modern Moral Philosophy' (1958) 33 *Philosophy: The Journal of the Royal Institute of Philosophy* 1, 12.

[138] Scheffler, *Consequentialism and its Critics*, p. 1.

[139] Charles Fried, 'Right and Wrong as Absolute' in Joram Graf Haber (ed.), *Absolutism and its Consequentialist Critics* (Boston, MA: Rowan & Littlefield Publishers Inc., 1994), p. 74.

[140] Michael Plaxton, 'Justifying Absolute Prohibitions on Torture as if Consequences Mattered' in George Kassimeris (ed.), *Warrior's Dishonour: Barbarity, Morality and Torture in Modern Warfare* (Aldershot: Ashgate, 2006), pp. 205, 212.

many forms, utilitarianism, as discussed with respect to Bentham, being the most familiar.[141] Act-consequentialism and rule-consequentialism are distinguished from each other by the latter's employment of 'an ideal set of rules', the purpose of which is to avoid the limitless actions that act-utilitarian calculation authorises.[142] For a rule-consequentialist, therefore, an act is morally wrong if it is a priori forbidden by a rule that is justified by its consequences. Rule-consequentialism thus moves closer to non-absolutist deontology, which, very simply stated, maintains that it is sometimes wrong to do what will produce the best overall outcome.[143] Consequentialism is employed to argue both for and against the use of torture in ticking bomb situations; this demonstrates the conflict over what exactly the best overall situation might constitute.

Consequentialist arguments justifying torture are based on the contention that torture is morally defensible in these limited circumstances because the consequences of not torturing are outweighed by the benefits or outcome that derive from torturing. Although Alan Dershowitz roots his torture warrant proposal in pragmatic rather than moral argumentation, his argument is, nevertheless, underpinned by a rule-utilitarian conception of morality.[144] He criticises quantitative act-utilitarianism, as per Bentham, as 'simpleminded', 'morality by numbers' and without principled safeguards.[145] He defends his own position by arguing that act-utilitarianism ought to be restricted by placing limitations on the kinds of methods that can be used in torturing the suspect and by constraining torture's use with rules stipulating when and on whom it can be used.[146] For example, in the case of a public official confronted with the moral dilemma of the ticking bomb situation, Dershowitz would presumably wish that this public official be bound to ask, first, which rule, if universally obeyed, would bring about the best overall outcome or happiness in this particular situation. One of the rules that the judge or public official

---

[141] Scheffler, *Consequentialism and its Critics*, p. 2.

[142] Michael S. Moore, 'Torture and the Balance of Evils' (1987) 23 *Israel Law Review* 280, 294.

[143] Samuel Scheffler, *The Rejection of Consequentialism: A Philosophical Investigation of the Considerations Underlying Rival Moral Conceptions* (Oxford: Clarendon Press, 1982), p. 2.

[144] For a critique of Dershowitz's moral arguments, see Jonathan Allen, 'Warrant to Torture? A Critique of Dershowitz and Levinson', ACDIS Occasional Paper (University of Illinois: ACDIS Publication Series, 2005); Bob Brecher, *Torture and the Ticking Bomb* (Malden: Blackwell Publishing, 2007).

[145] Alan M. Dershowitz, *Why Terrorism Works: Understanding the Threats, Responding to the Challenge* (New Haven: Yale University Press, 2002), p. 144.

[146] Plaxton, 'Justifying Absolute Prohibitions on Torture', p. 214.

would apply is the prohibition on deliberately punishing the innocent. In applying this rule, the judge would, therefore, have to ask as a second step whether torture of the innocent in this situation is immoral.[147] For Dershowitz, the answer is clear: it is immoral to torture the innocent.

It is unclear, however, how Dershowitz's constraints improve upon the overall cost–benefit analysis. Bentham also attached a number of rules, as part of the calculation, to his cases in order to limit the dangers of torturing the innocent and in order to regulate the torture inflicted. Therefore, Bentham's approach was partially rule-utilitarianism.[148] However, Bentham applied utilitarianism strictly and, therefore, considered the outcome of torture as the priority and not the means involved. Torture of the innocent, however undesirable, is, therefore, never ruled out as a possibility. This is not to say that he sanctions outright the torture of the innocent; rather, in the first case, he accepts the possibility of a wrong determination of guilt and, in the second case, he applies classical act-utilitarianism. For Dershowitz, the prohibition on deliberately punishing the innocent represents the moral rule, the overriding of which is forbidden.[149] In a sense then, Dershowitz's rule-utilitarian assessment is twofold, since the exception to the torture prohibition in ticking bomb circumstances – preventing the death of civilians – already represents a rule to which the public official and judge must adhere. Dershowitz also mentions other rules and principles of morality but does not flesh out what these might constitute. It is, therefore, to be assumed that culpable suspect X will neither meet the requirements for the rule-utilitarian prohibition against torture or the prohibition against deliberately punishing the innocent and would therefore be subjected to (non-lethal) torture.

This limiting principle – the prohibition on punishing the innocent – is particularly vexing. Since the ticking bomb scenario is always construed in such a way that the suspect's guilt is close to certain, why is it necessary to include this limitation? It is included to prevent the torture of, for example, the suspect's mother or children to persuade the unwilling suspect to divulge the information.[150] There is a difficulty, however, in basing

---

[147]   These two stages of rule-utilitarian reasoning are applied with reference to Michael S. Moore's discussion of rule-consequentialism. See Moore, 'Torture and the Balance of Evils' 295.

[148]   Arguably, Bentham's inclusion of this set of rules makes his calculation not act-utilitarian but rule-utilitarian.

[149]   Plaxton notes that the origin of this rule 'has an air of mystery about it'. See Plaxton, 'Justifying Absolute Prohibitions on Torture', p. 214.

[150]   Dershowitz, Why Terrorism Works, p. 146.

the calculation on this principle, for if the perceived consequences of not torturing the suspect's mother or children still exist – that is the death of an unspecified number of civilians – then why does torture not remain, even in rule-utilitarian terms, morally permissible? Is there no exception to this rule, given the extremity of the circumstances? In this regard, Bob Brecher notes:

> [O]n what grounds can one decide which actions are susceptible to utilitarian considerations and which are not? The point is that utilitarianism admits of no exceptions: either right and wrong is a matter of the consequences or it is not. To argue that some thing *justified on utilitarian grounds* can be 'limited by acceptable principles of morality' which are not themselves utilitarian is nonsense.[151]

If torture is no longer an option in this situation, it seems that utilitarianism is no longer being applied, for it is questionable whether, from a utilitarian viewpoint, innocence has a special status.[152] And even if this rule has a special status, it is not self-explanatory from a utilitarian view that it is an exception-less rule. If there is a 'difference in principle ... between torturing the guilty to save the lives of the innocent and torturing innocent people' to save the lives of the innocent, then it is necessary to explain why this prohibition remains infallible on a utilitarian assessment when the prohibition on torture does not, even though the breach of both could according to the assessment bring about the same outcome.

Dershowitz's approach might seem, theoretically, rule-utilitarian; the limiting prohibition on the torture of the innocent might be a utilitarian consideration – in achieving the best overall outcome, the consequences of torturing the innocent do not outweigh the consequences of not torturing – that is, not torturing an innocent individual leads to the most overall happiness. This, however, is unsatisfactory for two connected reasons. First, this balancing of consequences could go either way, and Dershowitz must first explain why it is worse to torture one innocent person than 'to allow' the death of civilians and then hope that this moral intuition against the torture of the innocent is universally shared or at least shared among utilitarians. Second, Dershowitz treats the prohibition on torturing the innocent as a principle, anyhow, and thus as a non-consequentialist moral norm. In considering the foreseeable pitfalls with certain aspects of the ticking bomb dilemma, therefore, he seems to become a non-consequentialist. This lack of commitment to utilitarianism

---

[151] Brecher, *Torture and the Ticking Bomb*, p. 51.   [152] *Ibid.*

proper is indicative of yet another problem in such reasoning. The premise on which the ticking bomb argument is built includes the high probability that torture will work on the suspect in custody. The necessity to include a protection measure to ensure that innocent individuals will not be tortured to achieve the compliance of the suspect unhinges the causal link, which he defends, between torture and preventing the impending act. Furthermore, the inconsistent emphasis on threat and consequences, on the one hand, and the impermissibility of torture, on the other, depending on the innocence of the individual to be tortured points to something logically amiss. By not torturing the suspect's mother because she is innocent, even though, as is inferred, her torture might yield the necessary information, as mentioned above, it is implied that because of the suspect's culpability, torture is somehow deserved or, at least, morally more justifiable, because the suspect has forfeited their own rights in engaging in morally condemnable acts. In his own discussion of torturing the innocent, Dershowitz removes the justificatory logic that might exist for others who defend the use of torture in ticking bomb circumstances – namely, that the culpable may be tortured because of the relevant information that they hold (rather than because they deserve it).

Writing about the moral permissibility of 'other directed torture' – that is the torture of someone other that the suspect in order to induce the suspect's cooperation – Allhoff states that, whilst this kind of torture might be very effective, it is, nevertheless, impermissible because 'the innocent bystander has not done anything to deserve the treatment whereas the terrorist has'.[153] By creating or by being complicit in the situation, the suspect, on the other hand, has forfeited their rights, and, thus, torture no longer constitutes a rights violation.[154] Speculatively, this might also be the underlying rationale in Dershowitz's approach, although he prefers to place the emphasis on why the innocent cannot be tortured, rather than explaining why the allegedly culpable can. Nevertheless, since the culpability of the suspect is so central to the decision to torture, it is clear that there are non-consequentialist factors in play – factors other than the ability to obtain the information needed to prevent the attack and save lives – in the consideration of the justifiability of torturing. This provides further indication that, whilst Dershowitz's argument might look consequentialist, it is overall a non-consequentialist one.

---

[153] Fritz Allhoff, 'Terrorism and Torture' (2003) 17 *International Journal of Applied Philosophy* 105, 114.
[154] *Ibid.*, 108.

Dershowitz does not mull over the moral justifiability question as such, proposing his approach as a normative or harm-minimisation response to a practice that is ongoing.[155] He argues that he is not in favour of torture. The torture warrant proposal offers a pragmatic lesser evil mechanism to better control and limit torture that is already happening.[156] As Brecher points out, this is not an illogical standpoint. It is perfectly reasonable to be morally opposed to a practice and, nevertheless, consider its legalisation as necessary on consequential grounds.[157] It is not clear, however, that this is what Dershowitz is arguing. In Bentham's analysis, utilitarian calculation served as the normative justification for torture as the action that produced the best consequences and overall happiness and, therefore, the appropriate or 'morally right' action.[158] Dershowitz fudges this question. He attempts to conflate legalisation as the lesser evil with utilitarian calculation. In relying on utilitarianism in the first place, however, and in constraining this utilitarianism to the extent that his argument reduces to non-consequentialist justification depending on the suspect's culpability, he cannot escape the reality that through his analysis, even if he does not intend it, he recognises both the moral permissibility of torture in ticking bomb circumstances and the moral justifiability of the legalisation of torture.[159] The limitations that Dershowitz places on the utilitarian argument for the torture warrant system are, as a result, incoherent – 'a moral theory of special pleading'[160] – and, as such, predisposed to the same consequentialist arguments against torture that he attempts to pre-empt. Moreover, because Dershowitz fails to explain the underpinning moral rationale, the attempt to soften the argument by limiting torture only to the culpable appears arbitrary; it is not clear if this intuition derives from the right to self-defence or from the conception that the suspect, through their actions, is responsible for the consequences, that is for the suspect's own torture. Or is it the case, as Allhoff argues, that because of their moral blameworthiness, the suspect has forfeited their rights and is thus deserving of torture? If this is a question of forfeiture of rights and deserved treatment then, first, the moral relevance of such a limitation on claims to rights needs to be elaborated, and, second, the

---

[155] Alan M. Dershowitz, 'The Torture Warrant: A Response to Professor Strauss' (2003) 48 *New York Law School Law Review* 275, 277. Bagaric and Clarke describe Dershowitz's approach as 'harm minimisation rationale'. See Bagaric and Clarke, *Torture*, p. 2.

[156] Brecher, *Torture and the Ticking Bomb*, p. 45.

[157] *Ibid.*, p. 47.   [158] *Ibid.*, p. 48.

[159] Allen, 'Warrant to Torture?', p. 7.

[160] Plaxton, 'Justifying Absolute Prohibitions on Torture', p. 215.

discourse appears altered since torture is no longer construed as just a life-saving technique; it is also a form of punishment.

Mirko Bagaric and Julie Clarke supplement Dershowitz's harm minimisation rationale with an argument defending outright the permissibility of torture in ticking bomb situations. They encourage readers 'to seriously contemplate moving from the question of whether torture is *ever* defensible to the issue of the circumstances in which it is morally permissible'.[161] Bagaric and Clarke condone torture only in 'life-saving circumstances'; the right to life trumps the right to physical integrity.[162] Their condoning of torture is, they contend, based on compassion.[163] Their argument contains both consequentialist and non-consequentialist aspects. Principally, the logic is utilitarian. They maintain that utilitarianism 'provides a sounder foundation for rights than any other competing moral theory'.[164] In that regard, Bagaric and Clarke are critical of the lack of defensible virtues underpinning rights, and they further maintain that absolute rights do not exist. This contention they base on the fact that the right to life is not even sacrosanct.[165]

In their calculation, there are five variables that determine torture's permissibility; the amount of harm to be inflicted is also regulated. Those variables are:

> (1) the number of lives at risk; (2) the immediacy of the harm; (3) the availability of other means to acquire the information; (4) the level of wrongdoing of the agent; and (5) the likelihood that the agent actually does possess the relevant information. Where (1), (2), (4), and (5) rate highly and (3) is low, all forms of harm may be inflicted on the agent – although the aim is to inflict the minimum degree of harm necessary to obtain the relevant information.[166]

The level of wrongdoing of the individual to be tortured is taken into account in deciding whether to torture: 'torture should be confined to people who are responsible in some way for the threatened harm.'[167] On the question of torturing the non-responsible, they state that '[p]eople who are simply aware of the threatened harm, that is, "innocent people", may in some circumstances also be subjected to torture'.[168] They insist, however,

---

[161] Bagaric and Clarke, *Torture*, p. 2.   [162] *Ibid.*, p. 4.

[163] *Ibid.*, p. 48.   [164] *Ibid.*, p. 33.   [165] *Ibid.*, p. 26.

[166] *Ibid.*, pp. 34–5. In an earlier article they stipulated that, '[w]here (1), (2), (4) and (5) rate highly and (3) is low, all forms of harm may be inflicted on the agent – even if this results in death'. See Bagaric and Clarke, 'Not Enough Official Torture in the World?' 611.

[167] Bagaric and Clarke, *Torture*, p. 36.   [168] *Ibid.*, pp. 36–7.

that such individuals must actually possess the relevant information.[169] Bagaric and Clarke do not elaborate on the question of 'other-directed torture', but since the level of wrong-doing is one of the variables in their calculation and since they insist that only those with relevant information may be subjected to torture, it might be assumed that it would be impermissible to torture a suspect's relative in order to compel the suspect's compliance. From their perspective, the level of wrong-doing and the availability of the information conflate, thus maximising the probability of bringing about the best possible outcome through the torture of the subject. On the other hand, however, since their emphasis is on the maximisation of human happiness, and since they are quite aware of the incompatibility of utilitarianism and external constraints, it is conceivable that their calculation would not rule out the torture of an innocent individual if such torture would bring about the best overall outcome:

> The view that punishing the innocent and torturing individuals is the morally correct action in some circumstances is consistent with and accords with the decisions we as individuals and societies as a whole readily have made and continue to make when faced with extreme and desperate circumstances. Once we come to grips with the fact that our decisions in extreme situations will be compartmentalised to desperate predicaments, we do, and should, though perhaps somewhat begrudgingly, take the utilitarian option. In the face of extreme situations, we are quite ready to accept that one should, or even must, sacrifice oneself or others for the good of the whole.[170]

From this account, sacrifice is a utilitarian act; sacrifice of oneself or of others is a utilitarian demand. The individual to be sacrificed, in Bagaric and Clarke's conception, must be one whose sacrifice will bring about human flourishing.[171] In order to demonstrate this readiness to sacrifice, Bagaric and Clarke cite the sacrificial demand of war. The fact that combatants must give their lives in situations of war is, they argue, a representation of classical utilitarianism.[172]

Kahn also makes this connection between the sacrificial demand of both torture and warfare; however, he does not view the existence of this sacrificial violence through the prism of utility. Rather, he recognises in warfare – in killing and being killed – the presence of the sovereign:

> In between the moment when combatants take up the task of self-sacrifice and that in which they effectively surrender, their situation is one of

---

[169] *Ibid.*   [170] *Ibid.*, p. 31.
[171] *Ibid.*, p. 85.   [172] *Ibid.*, p. 31.

'being sacrificed'. In this in-between period, they are very close – politically and phenomenologically – to the classic victim of torture: each is
made to bear the presence of the sovereign in and through the destruction
of his or her body.[173]

Bearing the presence of the sovereign through killing and being killed
is, according to Kahn, political sacrifice, and 'politics … is not a moral
enterprise'.[174] It is not suggested that politics is immoral; rather that it
is not morality that makes the demand for sacrifice – it is the demand
of the sovereign. The sacrificial demand is reciprocally represented by
the hand grenade test[175] and the ticking bomb hypothetical: 'the hand
grenade test measures one's willingness to engage in self-sacrifice, the
ticking bomb one's willingness to sacrifice others'.[176] Bagaric and Clarke
state that, in the extreme circumstance, one must be ready to sacrifice
oneself and others for the good of the whole.[177] In this statement, they
invoke what Kahn describes as the 'intimate connection' between the
two meanings of sacrifice, that is the reciprocal nature of sacrifice. The
torturer must be willing to jump on the hand grenade and this 'willingness to jump on the hand grenade creates the imaginative space for the
torturing search for the ticking time bomb'.[178] To demonstrate what he
means by this reciprocity, Kahn reasons that the sacrifice of the passen-
gers on United Flight 93 in Pennsylvania provided the symbolic, but not
legal, authorisation for the practice of torture in the 'war on terror'.[179] To
Kahn, this space in which the sacrificial operates is a space beyond law,
morality or justice. Rather, it pertains to the existential; the identification with a community or the love of a community motivates sacrifice.
He remarks that in our personal lives we might imagine situations in
which a threat to our families demands a sacrificial response: 'What will
I do when my family is threatened? For love we imagine ourselves doing
the extraordinary: giving ourselves up completely – self-sacrifice –
evokes a reciprocal willingness to take other lives – sacrificing them.'[180]
When Michael Levin conducted an informal poll with four mothers

---

[173] Kahn, *Sacred Violence*, p. 47.
[174] *Ibid.*, p. 79.
[175] The hand grenade scenario tests whether you would be willing to throw yourself on a
hand grenade to prevent death and injury to others.
[176] Kahn, *Sacred Violence*, p. 94.
[177] Bagaric and Clarke, *Torture*, p. 31.
[178] Kahn, *Sacred Violence*, p. 96.
[179] *Ibid.*   [180] *Ibid.*

that asked whether they would approve of torturing a terrorist who had kidnapped their newborn child, perhaps unsurprisingly all answered yes.[181] Yet it is unlikely that those polled responded to this question from a considered moral perspective, having, for example, weighed costs and benefits. Levin, however, makes a leap from this 'empirical' evidence to argue that torture is morally mandatory in ticking bomb situations. According to Levin:

> The most powerful argument against using torture as a punishment or to secure confessions is that such practices disregard the rights of the individual. Well, if the individual is all that important – and he is – it is correspondingly important to protect the rights of individuals threatened by terrorists. If life is so valuable that it must never be taken, the lives of the innocents must be saved *even at the price of hurting* the one who endangers them.[182]

In short, Levin believes that the right to life of the potential victims trumps the right to be free from torture of the alleged suspect because that suspect has relinquished the right not to be tortured through his or her actions.

If we put aside, for the moment, the question of the relationship between ethics and sacrifice, it is worth noting the lack of attention that Bagaric and Clarke afford to the distinction between the sacrifice of oneself and the sacrifice of others. There is an entirely different dialectic between the sacrifice of oneself for the good of the whole and the sacrifice of others for the good of the whole. This difference is even more pronounced when those to be sacrificed are not considered as part of the whole for whose good the sacrifice is being made.

(4)   Consequentialism against torture

One of the most common utilitarian or rule-consequentialist arguments put forward to refute torture's justifiability is the 'slippery slope' argument. This argument essentially holds that once torture is authorised in one set of specific circumstances, it becomes 'routinized and uncontrollable'.[183] Strauss points to integral dangers in the allowance of torture even

---

[181]   Michael Levin, 'The Case for Torture' *Newsweek* (7 June 1982).

[182]   *Ibid.* (emphasis added).

[183]   Sumner B. Twiss, 'Torture, Justification and Human Rights: Toward an Absolute Proscription' (2007) 29 *Human Rights Quarterly* 346, 360.

in limited ticking bomb cases. She questions, for example, how torture can be confined to ticking bomb cases when there may exist 'ordinary' criminal cases where innocent lives may be at risk. She also questions whether the bomb in the ticking bomb case must actually be ticking. This leads her to conclude that 'no matter how one tries to confine the use of torture to extreme, narrow circumstances, the temptation to broaden these circumstances is inevitable'.[184]

Beyond the 'slippery slope' argument, it is argued that the defence of torture damages the society that defends it.[185] Torture, Kremnitzer says, cannot be regarded as compatible with a society based on justice and morality. He views the state's loss of its dignity and moral superiority as a process of self-destruction in which the state surrenders the very values it is founded upon.[186] This goes hand in hand with the argument that by using methods such as torture, the state is adopting the methods of the enemy; not only that, but it is reacting exactly as the enemy wishes:

> The belief that the end justifies the means, the willingness to harm fundamental human values and innocent victims in order to attain a goal, action not in accordance with the law and even contrary to it – these are salient characteristics of terrorism. One of the objectives of terrorist organisations is just that: to cause the state to react in ways that lend it a ruthless tyrannical image. An ever present danger faced by a state confronted with terrorism is that in the course of combating terror and ensuring the state's survival, its character as a law-abiding state will suffer.[187]

Beyond the domestic effect of introducing torture, the torturing state, according to consequentialist reasoning, also suffers in terms of its 'reputation, prestige and international standing'.[188] Strauss observes, in addition, that the practice of torture leads to the loss of the moral high ground in denouncing similar practices worldwide.[189] Strauss defends an absolute torture prohibition having weighed the potential for slippery slopes and the societal costs of torturing against the perceived threat of the ticking bomb scenario. She supplements her position with both a suspicion of the likelihood of the ticking bomb unfolding and a fear of the extent to which the torturer may be tempted to go in extracting information: the torture of a suspect's child, for example.[190]

[184] Strauss, 'Torture' 267
[185] Mordechai Kremnitzer, 'The Landau Commission Report – Was the Security Service Subordinated to the Law, or the Law to the "Needs" of the Security Service?' (1989) 23 Israel Law Review 261.
[186] Ibid., 264.   [187] Ibid., 263.   [188] Ibid., 262.
[189] Strauss, 'Torture' 257.   [190] Ibid., 270, 274.

(5)   Moral intuitionism and considered judgement

In not responding to the ticking bomb dilemma, it could be claimed that Sussman gives teeth to the argument that, from a theoretical perspective, the Kantian position is not the correct moral theory to apply to the ticking bomb situation. Allhoff maintains in that regard that Kantianism, whilst undoubtedly denying the permissibility of torture in such a situation, is, nevertheless, irrelevant.[191] The conflict between absolutism and other moral theories on the question of overriding prima facie moral wrongs is stalled, seemingly irresolvable. Allhoff aims to supersede this stalemate in his argument by relying on the disjuncture that he perceives to exist between a Kantian perspective and ethical intuitionism and/or considered judgement. In this analysis, the permissibility of torture in the ticking bomb case is either self-evident or a considered judgement.[192] Kantianism denies the former and does not cohere with the latter and is, therefore, inapplicable. Allhoff's analysis is wholly theoretical and does not profess to answer the real world applicability of the ticking bomb dilemma as such.[193] There is, however, a difficulty with Allhoff addressing this dilemma purely as a thought experiment. Unlike the trolley problem for example, the ticking bomb hypothetical is given real life credence in policy formation.

Allhoff's refutation of moral theories that adhere to absolutely no torture in ticking bomb situations is significant for a number of reasons. First, his analysis cajoles absolutists to undo their principled objection to torture; in Luban's words 'gotcha!'[194] Second, Allhoff's ultimate conclusion – the irrelevance of a Kantian position as a response to the ticking bomb scenario – forces engagement with the question as to whether strict adherence to the torture prohibition is an ill-considered judgement or counter-intuitive in ticking bomb situations.

(6)   Is there a moral dilemma?

What happens when a moral dilemma arises that appears to create an irresolvable conflict between absolutism and consequentialism? Thomas

---

[191]   Allhoff, 'A Defense of Torture' 257.

[192]   *Ibid.*, 256–60.

[193]   *Ibid.*, 260. Allhoff does, however, conclude that if empirical claims that torture would not maximise happiness in ticking bomb circumstances cannot be empirically proven, then torture must be morally permissible.

[194]   David Luban, 'Liberalism, Torture, and the Ticking Bomb' (2005) 91 *Virginia Law Review* 1425, 1427.

Nagel argues that 'unless the utilitarian considerations favoring violation are overpoweringly weighty and extremely certain', the absolutist position must be adhered to.[195] He opines that moral dilemmas do exist and that these moral dilemmas may never be satisfactorily resolved:

> There may exist principles, not yet codified, which would enable us to resolve such dilemmas. But then again there may not. We must face the pessimistic alternative that these two forms of moral intuition are not capable of being brought together into a single, coherent moral system, and that the world can present us with situations in which there is no honorable or moral course for a man to take, no course free of guilt and responsibility for evil.[196]

Nagel thereby seems to recognise a limit to the applicability of absolutism; a point at which consequentialism might be unavoidable. The exhaustibility of absolutism is not a moral guide, however; rather, at this point a moral dilemma, which it might not be possible to solve with moral justification, governs.[197] In this kind of situation, there is no duty to prioritise the consequences over the breach of an absolute norm, although this might be the intuitive feeling and, thus, the response. Nagel's sense is that these dilemmas constitute a 'moral blind alley' where human action is limited; in other words, these are hopeless dilemmas.[198] For Nagel, however, torture is not to be found in this moral blind alley:

> Even if certain types of dirty tactics become acceptable when the stakes are high enough, the most serious of the prohibited acts, like murder and torture, are not just supposed to require unusually strong justification. They are supposed never to be done, because no quantity of resulting benefit is thought capable of justifying such treatment of a person.[199]

Nagel's assessment does not lead us out of the ethical quandary in the sense that his point will not convince those who insist that a resulting benefit would justify the treatment of the person. The debate revolves incessantly. There is, however, a way out of this ethical impasse. The way out is to recognise that whether or not to torture in ticking bomb situations is not a moral dilemma at all. Several factors contribute to this conclusion.

First, it becomes clear in the analysis of the ethical debate that the ticking bomb scenario bends moral argumentation to its narrative.

---

[195] Nagel, 'War and Massacre' 219.
[196] Ibid., 234.
[197] Larry Alexander, 'Deontology at the Threshold' (2000) 37 San Diego Law Review 893, 896.
[198] Nagel, 'War and Massacre', p. 234.   [199] Ibid.

This is particularly evidenced in the analysis of the consequentialist arguments for the use of torture. In effect, these arguments reduce to a core position that the suspect, because of their alleged culpability, has forfeited their rights and/or 'deserves' to be tortured. By surrounding this core position in doctrines of morality, it is possible to make the argument for torture appear to be ethically motivated in terms of the threat to the potential victims. In reality, however, this is a judgement on the suspect as a rights-holder or on the suspect's blameworthiness and not an ethical judgement on the justifiability of torture. The consequentialist arguments against the use of torture assist in obscuring this core position by seemingly conceding that there is an ethical dilemma involved.

Second, the ticking bomb scenario *is* a fabricated construct for considering the use of torture. This scenario may be described as fabricated not because ticking bomb scenarios could not, or will not, arise, but because there is no causal relation between such a scenario and the practice of torture. Obtaining information is one of the stated prohibited purposes of torture. This prohibited purpose refers to the intention of the state in practising torture; its inclusion does not mean that torture is practised because information is obtainable through the practice of torture. This is not a 'torture does not work' argument. Obtaining information is a justificatory defence used by states for the practice of torture. By listing this as a prohibited purpose, the definition aims to quell this as a defence for the use of torture. But this does not mean that torture is only, or even, practised in order to obtain information. Within the debate on the use of torture in ticking bomb scenarios, it is the identification both with the victims of such ticking bomb scenarios and the public officials charged with preventing such scenarios that allows torture to be constructed in terms of its perpetration for the purpose of obtaining information and of saving lives, that is for 'a good reason'. This construction allows other processes – such as the dehumanisation of the victim – inherent to the practice of torture to fall outside the frame of perceptibility.[200]

The notion that torture might be considered morally permissible in ticking bomb situations on the basis of intuition or a judgement call is, therefore, unsound. It is unsound, on the one hand, because such a basis for thinking about torture is necessarily subjective and, on the other hand, because an intuitive response or a considered judgement is only legitimate

---

[200] Judith Butler, *Frames of War: When is Life Grieveable?* (London: Verso, 2010), p. 64.

once all of the relevant factors have been taken into consideration. Because it equivocates on what is relevant for consideration, the ticking bomb scenario does not provide a legitimate basis for intuitionism or judgement.

Finally, the phenomenon of torture cannot be understood in terms of an ethical dilemma when the juridico-political structure of the exception is grasped. Bagaric and Clarke explain the use of torture as, simultaneously, a utilitarian demand and an act of sacrifice. Kahn's analysis corrects their interpretation of sacrifice by explaining it not as a moral act but as an existential one. He also corrects the idea that the use of torture may be construed on objective moral grounds by showing that the justification of torture is subjectively rooted in the community's identification with the potential victims of torture. However, Kahn's recognition of torture as an aspect of sacrificial politics also misrepresents the juridico-political structure of the act. The person who is subjected to torture is not part of a process of reciprocal sacrifice. Such persons are denied recognition as human and are situated in a zone in which they may be treated as inhuman. Clearly this is not a zone governed by ethics. It is also not a space of sacrifice because the torture victim is not a representative of the community on whose behalf the sacrifice is made; on the contrary, the torture victim is excluded from this community. Whilst excluded from the application of the law and of the norm prohibiting their subjection to torture, they are, at the same time, by being subjected to torture, included within the raw power of the state.

Invariably, the individual at the centre of the torture debate – the individual who might be subjected to torture – is absent from the discussion. This individual is understood as a 'ticking bomb' or a suspected 'terrorist', not as a human. Whilst the human is abstracted from the discussion, when this debate unfurls, it becomes obvious that it is this abstraction of the human victim which makes it possible to debate their possible subjection to torture. This manner in which the human is placed outside the frame of the ticking bomb scenario parallels the real situation in which torture occurs where the human is excluded 'from the frame furnished by the norm'.[201]

C.   Conclusion

'Uninhibited critical analysis' of the philosophical basis for claiming that there is *not* an absolute right not to be subjected to torture leads inescapably

[201]   *Ibid.*, p. 8.

to the question:[202] what does it mean to be, or 'to remain human'?[203] That this question results from such an inquiry explains, in part, why the prohibition of torture *is* an absolute right; to question whether a human is, or should be, human makes no sense on ethical grounds: 'no ethics can claim to exclude a part of humanity, no matter how unpleasant or difficult that humanity is to see.'[204] The absolute prohibition expresses, therefore, an individual human right not to be subjected to torture and, accordingly, to be treated as human. This is one side of the absolute prohibition. The prohibition also endeavours to preclude the exception in order to confirm 'the primacy of [the] norm'[205] and to restrain the power of the state. The prohibition of torture does not simply codify a moral absolute; it codifies the absolute right of the individual not to be reduced, by the state, to a status of rightlessness or bare life, and it codifies the right of the individual not to be purposefully calculated into the mechanisms of state power in order to further the interests of that state, even if that interest is ostensibly 'self-preservation' in a period of crisis.[206]

In the frame of the ticking bomb scenario, however, it is the language by which the human at the core of the ticking bomb scenario is described – 'a terrorist with a ticking bomb' – that makes their dehumanisation, and, hence, their torture, thinkable.

[202] See n. 2 above and accompanying text.
[203] Jean Paul Sartre, 'Preface' in Henri Alleg (tr. John Calder), *The Question* (London: John Calder, 1958), p. 13.
[204] Giorgio Agamben (tr. Daniel Heller-Roazen), *Remnants of Auschwitz: The Witness and the Archive* (New York: Zone Books, 2002), p. 64.
[205] Giorgio Agamben (tr. Kevin Attell), *State of Exception* (University of Chicago Press, 2005), p. 87.
[206] Stanley Cohen, 'Post-Moral Torture: From Guantanamo to Abu Ghraib' (2005) 34 *Index on Censorship* 24, 26.

~

Conclusion

In 1992, in a lecture delivered at the University of Heidelberg, German sociologist Niklas Luhmann presented a ticking bomb scenario as a foil for considering the question: Gibt es in unserer Gesellschaft noch unverzichtbare Normen? – Are there still indispensable norms in our society?[1] Luhmann asks:

> Imagine: You are a high-level law-enforcement officer. In your country – it could be Germany in the not-too-distant future – there are many left- and right-wing terrorists – every day there are murders, fire-bombings, the killing and injury of countless innocent people. You have captured the leader of such a group. Presumably, if you tortured him, you could save many lives – 10, 100, 1,000 – we can vary the situation. Would you do it?[2]

As it turns out, Luhmann is not really interested in whether or not 'you' would do it.[3] He views this case as one of tragic choices and, as such, he deems it to be unanswerable.[4] In essence, Luhmann argues that values are not morally or philosophically indispensable.[5] He indicates that the validity of a value or norm is relative to the practical relevance that it can demonstrate in an individual case.[6] Luhmann's inquiry contradicts Martti Koskenniemi's articulation of the prohibition of torture as an 'unpolitical normative demand'.[7] Koskenniemi describes core rights as having a

[1] Niklas Luhmann, *Gibt es in unserer Gesellschaft noch unverzichtbare Normen?* (Heidelberg: C. F. Müller Juristischer Verlag, 1993), author's translation.
[2] Niklas Luhmann (tr. Todd Cesaratto), 'Are There Still Indispensable Norms in Our Society?' (2008) 14 *Soziale Systeme* 18.
[3] Günter Frankenberg, 'Torture and Taboo: An Essay Concerning Paradigms of Organized Cruelty' (2008) 56 *American Journal of Comparative Law* 402, 405.
[4] Luhmann, 'Are There Still Indispensable Norms in Our Society?' 31.
[5] *Ibid.*, 24. See also Costas Douzinas, 'Torture and Systems Theory' (2008) 14 *Soziale Systeme* 110, 112.
[6] *Ibid.*, 29.
[7] Martti Koskenniemi, 'The Effect of Rights on Political Culture' in Philip Alston (ed.), *The EU and Human Rights* (Oxford University Press, 1999), pp. 99, 114.

'special character' that is dependent upon them 'not being subjected to the kinds of legal-technical arguments and proof that justify – and make vulnerable – "ordinary rights" as policies'.[8] He contends that the right to be free from torture is one such core right, the validity of which 'is not relative to the force of any justification that we can provide for it'.[9]

The debate about torture in ticking bomb situations moves between these two positions. The way in which the ticking bomb scenario informs our perception of the norm prohibiting torture is the first stage in its creation of narratives that argue for the acceptability of torture in the exceptional case. The ticking bomb scenario exploits the notion that torture is inimical to the liberal democracy, and, in so doing, it suggests that the use of torture in this exceptional case is an aberration from the normal state of affairs in which the principle of no-torture governs. In other words, implicit in ticking bomb rationale is the suggestion that the norm prohibiting torture describes reality. By obscuring our view of the reality of torture as practised by liberal democratic states, it also prevents us from thinking about why the torture prohibition is prescribed as an absolute, inalienable right or why it might be considered an 'unpolitical normative demand'.

The clue to understanding the rationale for an absolute prohibition of torture exists in the general formula of torture provisions. There is good reason why the torture prohibition is prohibited in connection with other forms of inhuman and degrading treatment. As the European Commission of Human Rights held in the *Greek Case*, 'all torture must be inhuman and degrading treatment'.[10] Whilst these terms might serve as legal criteria for understanding pain and suffering, they are also descriptive of the status of the subject of such treatment or punishment. From the Latin *degradare* – *de* meaning 'down, away from' and *gradus* meaning 'step or grade' – to degrade means 'to reduce (someone) to a lower rank'.[11] From the Latin *inhumanus* – *in* meaning 'not' and *humanus* meaning 'man, human being' – inhuman means 'not human'.[12] The prohibition of torture thus explicitly includes a prohibition on reducing the human to a status of not-human. Talal Asad remarks: 'The modern history of "torture"

---

[8] *Ibid.*, p. 113.   [9] *Ibid.*
[10] *Denmark et al.* v. *Greece (The Greek Case)* (1969) 12 Yearbook of the European Convention on Human Rights, p. 186.
[11] Catherine Soanes and Angus Stevenson, *Oxford Dictionary of English* revised 2nd edn (Oxford University Press, 2005).
[12] *Ibid.*

is not only a record of the progressive prohibition of cruel, inhuman and degrading practices. It is also part of a more complex story of the modern secular concept of what it means to be truly human.'[13] What it means to be truly human from the perspective of the prohibition on torture is to be recognised as human. Thus, whilst the prohibition of torture embodies the modern sensibility and abhorrence to physical pain,[14] it does not, and should not, only purport to prescribe pain and suffering. It also prescribes the reduction of the human by the state to a status of less than human.

The claim that torture might be justifiable in ticking bomb situations is, fundamentally, a claim that certain individuals do not have the right to have rights and, thus, that the human can be reduced to a status other than human. By positing the individual as 'a terrorist with a ticking bomb', the ticking bomb scenario directs the narrative so that the life or humanness of the subject – the potential victim of torture – is not recognisable.[15]

Practices of torture are regularly described as barbaric or the remnants of barbarism. The word barbaric derives from the Greek *barbarous* meaning foreign.[16] The term barbarian originally described 'a member of a people not belonging to one of the great civilizations'.[17] Michel Foucault describes the barbarian as 'someone who can be understood, characterized, and defined only in relation to a civilization, and by the fact that he exists outside it'.[18] The act of torture marks the threshold between barbarism and civilisation and between inside and outside. It is an act of 'inclusive exclusion'.[19] Through subjection to torture, the barbarian – or the excluded – is included, civilised. The torturer also occupies this position of 'inclusive exclusion' and, as such, the torturer acts at the threshold of barbarism and civilisation.

The act of 'inclusive exclusion' is the subject of J. M. Coetzee's novel *Waiting for the Barbarians*.[20] The novel depicts 'the impact of the torture chamber upon a man of conscience'.[21] The 'man of conscience' is the

---

[13] Talal Asad, 'On Torture or Cruel, Inhuman and Degrading Treatment' (1996) 63 *Social Research* 1081.

[14] *Ibid.*, 1087.

[15] Judith Butler, *Frames of War: When is Life Grieveable?* (London: Verso, 2010), p. 4.

[16] *Oxford English Dictionary.*   [17] *Ibid.*

[18] Michel Foucault (tr. David Macey), *Society Must Be Defended: Lectures at the Collège de France, 1975–76* (London: Penguin Books, 2004), p. 195.

[19] Giorgio Agamben (tr. Daniel Heller-Roazen), *Homo Sacer: Sovereign Power and Bare Life* (Stanford University Press, 1998), p. 21.

[20] J. M. Coetzee, *Waiting for the Barbarians* (London: Vintage Books, 2004).

[21] J. M. Coetzee, 'Into the Dark Chamber: The Novelist and South Africa' *The New York Times* (12 January 1986), p. 13.

magistrate of a tiny frontier settlement. The novel opens with the arrival
of Colonel Joll, an interrogation expert from the Empire's security service, the Third Bureau. Colonel Joll has been sent, under 'the emergency
powers', to investigate the rumoured uprising of the barbarians against
the Empire.[22] He interrogates and tortures captured prisoners, allegedly
involved in this uprising, to 'get the truth'.[23] The Magistrate abhors the use
of torture and is sympathetic to the suffering of the prisoners; however, he
does not intervene to prevent their abuse.[24] With Colonel Joll's arrival, his
authority has been displaced. Having 'completed his inquiries for the time
being', Colonel Joll returns to the capital, and the administration of law
and order passes back to the Magistrate.[25] The Magistrate takes into his
home, and his bed, one of Colonel Joll's torture victims, a young girl who
has been disabled, left partially blind and scarred.[26] Later he travels into
barbarian territory to take the girl back to her people.[27] When he returns,
he finds that the army has arrived to wage its campaign against the barbarians.[28] The Magistrate is imprisoned by the Warrant Officer in the
Third Bureau for 'treasonously consorting with the enemy'.[29] Thereafter,
he is subjected to torture.

The novel traces the Magistrate's search for the meaning and purpose
of torture. He inquires relentlessly into the girl's ordeal, endeavouring to
make sense of her torture at the hands of Colonel Joll: 'It has been growing more and more clear to me that until the marks on this girl's body are
deciphered and understood, I cannot let go of her.'[30] The Magistrate fails,
however, to penetrate the girl's surface and, thus, to reach any general
understanding of her torture.[31] Distressed by the torture of the prisoners, he instead finds himself questioning 'the mysteries of the State' and
his own relationship to Imperial rule.[32] In so doing, he unearths his own
'guilty conscience'.[33] He realises that he is in fact implicated in the torture

---

[22] Coetzee, *Waiting for the Barbarians*, p. 1. For background reading on the novel, see Stef
Craps, 'J. M. Coetzee's *Waiting for the Barbarians* and the Ethics of Testimony' (2007) 88
English Studies 59; Susan Van Santan Gallagher, 'Torture and the Novel: J. M. Coetzee's
"Waiting for the Barbarians"' (1988) 29 *Contemporary Literature* 277.

[23] Coetzee, *Waiting for the Barbarians*, p. 5.

[24] Michael Valdez Moses, 'The Mark of Empire: Writing, History, and Torture in Coetzee's
Waiting for the Barbarians' (1993) 15 *The Kenyon Review* 115, 118.

[25] Coetzee, *Waiting for the Barbarians*, pp. 25–6.

[26] *Ibid.*, pp. 29–31.   [27] *Ibid.*, p. 62.   [28] *Ibid.*, p. 83.

[29] *Ibid.*, p. 85.   [30] *Ibid.*, p. 33.

[31] *Ibid.*, p. 70. See also Craps, 'J. M. Coetzee's *Waiting for the Barbarians*' 62.

[32] Coetzee, *Waiting for the Barbarians*, p. 7.

[33] Jane Poyner, *J. M. Coetzee and the Paradox of Postcolonial Authorship* (Farnham: Ashgate
Publishing, 2009), p. 53.

and, more generally, in the repression of the barbarians. He is implicated, first, because of his 'passive acceptance' of, and his benign involvement in, their torture:[34] 'It has not escaped me that an interrogator can wear two masks, speak with two voices, one harsh, one seductive.'[35] He recognises, second, that by objectifying the girl as a site of torture,[36] and by attempting to read the signs of infamy upon her body,[37] he becomes indistinguishable from her torturers: 'The distance between myself and her torturers, I realise, is negligible; I shudder.'[38] Third, he becomes aware that his actions, whilst well intentioned, nevertheless condone and continue Imperial rule: 'And here I am patching up relations between the men of the future and the men of the past, returning, with apologies, a body we have sucked dry – a go-between, a jackal of Empire in sheep's clothing.'[39]

The Magistrate is 'the figure of the ordinary rule of law'.[40] He represents 'liberal humanist' ideals.[41] Colonel Joll embodies the exceptional. He represents the necessity of safeguarding the Empire.[42] The novel suggests the capacity of state power, operating under necessity, to suppress the principles and protections of the rule of law. It does not, however, simply narrate the supersession of the ordinary by the exceptional. Rather, it depicts their entwinement: 'For I was not, as I liked to think, the indulgent pleasure-loving opposite of the cold rigid Colonel. I was the lie that Empire tells itself when times are easy, he the truth that Empire tells when harsh winds blow. Two sides of Imperial rule, no more, no less.'[43] In the Magistrate's search for the truth about torture, he is led into 'the heart of the labyrinth'.[44] The Magistrate is awakened to the state of exception in which he lives and wherein Imperial rule

---

[34] Sinkwan Cheng, 'Civilization and the Two Faces of Law: J. M. Coetzee's Waiting for the Barbarians' (2003) 24 *Cardozo Law Review* 2349, 2354.

[35] Coetzee, *Waiting for the Barbarians*, p. 8. The Magistrate draws this conclusion after he encourages a barbarian boy to be strong in enduring his torture and to tell the truth.

[36] Cheng, 'Civilization and the Two Faces of Law' 2355, citing Susan Van Santen Gallagher, *A Story of South Africa: J. M. Coetzee's Fiction in Context* (1991), p. 128.

[37] Michel Foucault (tr. Alan Sheridan), *Discipline and Punish: The Birth of the Prison* (London: Penguin Books, 1977), p. 34.

[38] Coetzee, *Waiting for the Barbarians*, p. 61.

[39] *Ibid.*, p. 79.

[40] Thomas P. Crocker, 'Still Waiting for the Barbarians: What is New about Post-September 11 Exceptionalism?' (2007) 19 *Law and Literature* 303, 313.

[41] Cheng, 'Civilization and the Two Faces of Law' 2352.

[42] Coetzee, *Waiting for the Barbarians*, p. 41.

[43] *Ibid.*, p. 148. See also Cheng, 'Civilization and the Two Faces of Law' 2362.

[44] Coetzee, *Waiting for the Barbarians*, p. 149.

pulsates with principles and pain. He faces the dilemma of reconciling his own embroilment in Imperial rule with his principled belief in the inhumanity of torture.

Although the historical and geographical setting is unspecified, the novel is clearly situated in a colonial context. Since Coetzee is both South African and considered a postcolonial writer, the novel has unsurprisingly often been interpreted as a representation of apartheid South Africa.[45] Coetzee, however, denies this interpretation: 'There is nothing about blackness or whiteness in *Waiting for the Barbarians*. The Magistrate and the girl could as well be Russian and Kirghiz, or Han and Mongol, or Turk and Arab, or Arab and Berber.'[46] The novel has also been interpreted, therefore, as translating to the universal,[47] and it has been read allegorically with respect to the use of torture in the aftermath of 11 September within the context of the 'war on terror'.[48]

By situating the actions of the Third Bureau 'in a twilight of legal illegality',[49] the novel suggests the paradigmatic state of exception; the Empire operates outside of the law but, at the same time, its actions have the force of law: '"For the duration of the emergency, as you know", says the Colonel, "the administration of justice is out of the hands of civilians and in the hands of the Bureau."'[50] Furthermore, the novel represents torture as the quintessential act of exception. The barbarian is simultaneously and paradoxically excluded from and included in the legal order by being subjected to the non-application of the law through torture. In Agamben's words, the barbarian is reduced to 'bare life'.[51] The Magistrate searches in vain to discover the meaning of torture and the reasons for the Empire's use of torture against the barbarians. It is not until he is subjected to torture that he realises that it signifies nothing other than the

---

[45] David Atwell, *J. M. Coetzee: South Africa and the Politics of Writing* (Berkeley: University of California Press, 1993), p. 73; Patrick Lenta, '"Legal Illegality": Waiting for the Barbarians after September 11' (2006) 42 *Journal of Postcolonial Writing* 71; See also Van Santan Gallagher, 'Torture and the Novel' 281.

[46] Richard Begam and J. M. Coetzee, 'An Interview with J. M. Coetzee' (1992) 33 *Contemporary Literature* 419, 424.

[47] Anthony Burgess, 'Book Review: The Beast Within' *New York Magazine* (26 April 1982), p. 88.

[48] See Lenta, '"Legal Illegality"' 71; Robert Spencer, 'J. M. Coetzee and Colonial Violence' (2008) 10 *Interventions* 173.

[49] Coetzee, 'Into the Dark Chamber' 13.

[50] Coetzee, *Waiting for the Barbarians*, p. 124

[51] 'Bare life remains included in politics in the form of the exception, that is as something that is included solely through an exclusion.' See Agamben, *Homo Sacer*, p. 11.

Empire's ability to render life bare and to inscribe a meaning of humanity upon the excluded body:

> When Warrant Officer Mandel and his man first brought me back here and lit the lamp and closed the door, I wondered how much pain a plump comfortable old man would be able to endure in the name of his eccentric notions of how the Empire should conduct itself. But my torturers were not interested in degrees of pain. They were interested only in demonstrating to me what it meant to live in a body, as a body, a body which can entertain notions of justice only as long as it is whole and well, which very soon forgets them when its head is gripped and a pipe is pushed down its gullet and pints of salt water are poured into it till it coughs and retches and flails and voids itself. They did not come to force the story out of me of what I had said to the barbarians and what the barbarians had said to me. So I had no chance to throw the high-sounding words I had ready in their faces. They came to my cell to show me the meaning of humanity, and in the space of an hour, they showed me a great deal.[52]

Finally, the novel depicts the delusive power of principles. At first, the Magistrate is reluctant to accept that the Empire he serves employs torture in its administration of justice. In the face of Imperial rule, he is torn. He would prefer to be ignorant of its excesses. Failing that, '[b]ut, alas I did not ride away',[53] he would have the Empire deal conclusively with the problem: 'It would be best if this obscure chapter in the world were terminated at once, if these ugly people were obliterated from the face of the earth and we swore to make a new start, to run an empire in which there would be no more injustice, no more pain.'[54] The Magistrate thus reveals that there are limits to his own conception of justice. He neither wants to concede to a barbarian future nor does he want to face up to the ugliness of the Empire's rule. The Magistrate distances himself from the barbarians and from the unpalatable aspect of Imperial rule. A man of tolerance, he renounces the elimination of the barbarians as his 'way'.[55] However, he cannot avoid excavating the foundations and preconditions on which his principles rest. Following his own subjection to torture, the Magistrate realises that the objective meaning and purpose of torture for which he had been searching cannot be found in an examination of the barbarian 'other'. Moreover, he becomes aware that the principles he represents and the 'notions of justice' he holds are manipulated and, thus, made meaningless by the Empire he serves. As he watches the spectacle of barbarian prisoners being branded as enemies and beaten by soldiers, the Magistrate

---

[52] Coetzee, *Waiting for the Barbarians*, p. 126.
[53] *Ibid.*, p. 9   [54] *Ibid.*, p. 26.   [55] *Ibid.*

protests in the only way he knows how. Rather than 'defending the cause of justice for the barbarians',[56] the Magistrate protests their ill-treatment by shouting 'No!'.[57] This choice of action is deliberate. In his protest the Magistrate does not only renounce the torturous actions of Empire, he also renounces the political and legal usurpation of the idea of justice.

Coetzee's play on the indistinctiveness between civilisation and barbarianism and between inside and outside provides an illuminating counterpart to the fictitious depiction of torture in the ticking bomb scenario. This depiction is fictitious because it omits the reality that torture is an act of 'inclusive exclusion' enabled through a process of dehumanisation and facilitated by a distorted construction of justice and morality. In omitting this reality, the ticking bomb scenario 'exercise[s] the power of a black hole in modern memory'.[58] It asks us to believe that '2 + 2 = 5'.[59]

---

[56] *Ibid.*, p. 118.   [57] *Ibid.*
[58] Darius Rejali, *Torture and Democracy* (Princeton University Press, 2007), p. 547.
[59] George Orwell, *Nineteen Eighty-Four* (London: Penguin Books, 1989), p. 334.

SELECT BIBLIOGRAPHY

Ackerman, Bruce, 'The Emergency Constitution' (2004) 113 *The Yale Law Journal* 1029

Addo, Michael K. and Nicholas Grief, 'Does Article 3 of the European Convention on Human Rights Enshrine Absolute Rights' (1998) 9 *European Journal of International Law* 510

Agamben, Giorgio (tr. Daniel Heller-Roazen), *Homo Sacer: Sovereign Power and Bare Life* (Stanford University Press, 1998)

(trs. Vincenzo Binetti and Cesare Casarino), *Means Without Ends: Notes on Politics* (Minneapolis: University of Minnesota Press, 2000)

(tr. Daniel Heller-Roazen), *Remnants of Auschwitz: The Witness and the Archive* (New York: Zone Books, 2002)

(tr. Kevin Attell), *State of Exception* (University of Chicago Press, 2005)

Aitken, Lord Robert, 'The Aitken Report: An Investigation into Cases of Deliberate Abuse and Unlawful Killing in Iraq in 2003 and 2004' (London: Ministry of Defence, January 2008)

Alexander, Larry, 'Deontology at the Threshold' (2000) 37 *San Diego Law Review* 893

Alleg, Henri (tr. John Calder), *The Question* (London: John Calder Publishers, 1958)

Allen, Jonathan, 'Warrant to Torture? A Critique of Dershowitz and Levinson', ACDIS Occasional Paper (University of Illinois: ACDIS Publication Series 2005)

Allhoff, Fritz, 'A Defense of Torture: Separation of Cases, Ticking Time-Bombs, and Moral Justification' (2005) 19 *International Journal of Applied Philosophy* 243

'Terrorism and Torture' (2003) 17 *International Journal of Applied Philosophy* 105

Alter, Jonathan, 'Time to Think about Torture' *Newsweek* (5 November 2001)

D'Amato, Anthony, 'It's a Bird, It's a Plane, It's *Jus Cogens!*' (1990) *Connecticut Journal of International Law* 1

Ambos, Kai, 'May a State Torture Suspects to Save the Life of Innocents?' (2008) 6 *Journal of International Criminal Justice* 261

Amnesty International, *Report on Torture* 2nd edn (London: Duckworth, 1975)

'USA Human Dignity Denied: Torture and Accountability in the War on Terror', AMR 51/145/2004 (London: Amnesty International, 2004)

'USA: See No Evil: Government Turns the Other Way as Judges Make Findings about Torture and Other Abuse' (London: AMR 51/005/2011, 2011)

Ananiadis, Grigoris, 'Carl Schmitt and Max Adler: The Irreconcilability of Politics and Democracy' in Chantal Mouffe (ed.), *The Challenge of Carl Schmitt* (London: Verso, 1999) 118

Anscombe, G. E. M., 'Modern Moral Philosophy' (1958) 33 *Philosophy: The Journal of the Royal Institute of Philosophy* 1

Arendt, Hannah, *Eichmann in Jerusalem: A Report on the Banality of Evil* (New York: Penguin Books, 1994)

The Origins of Totalitarianism (New York: Harcourt Books, 1968)

Asad, Talal, 'On Torture or Cruel, Inhuman and Degrading Treatment' (1996) 63 *Social Research* 1081

Association for the Prevention of Torture, 'Defusing the Ticking Bomb Scenario: Why We Must Say No To Torture, Always' (Geneva: Association for the Prevention of Torture, 2007)

Association for the Prevention of Torture and Center for Justice and International Law, 'Torture in International Law: A Guide to Jurisprudence' (Geneva: Association for the Prevention of Torture and Center for Justice and International Law, 2008)

Athey, Stephanie, 'The Terrorist we Torture: The Tale of Abdul Hakim Murad' (2007) 24 *South Central Review* 73

Atwell, David, *J. M. Coetzee: South Africa and the Politics of Writing* (Berkeley: University of California Press, 1993)

Aussaresses, Paul, *Services Spéciaux: Algérie 1955–1957* (Paris: Perrin, 2001)

Bagaric, Mirko and Julie Clarke, 'Not Enough (Official) Torture in the World? The Circumstances in Which Torture is Morally Justifiable' (2005) 39 *University of San Francisco Law Review* 581

Torture: When the Unthinkable is Morally Permissible (Albany: State University of New York Press, 2007)

'Tortured Responses (A Reply to Our Critics): Physically Persuading Suspects Is Morally Preferable to Allowing the Innocent to Be Murdered' (2006) 40 *University of San Francisco Law Review* 1

Bassiouni, M. Cherif, *The Institutionalisation of Torture by the Bush Administration: Is Anyone Responsible?* (Antwerp: Intersentia, 2010)

'The Institutionalisation of Torture under the Bush Administration' (2006) 37 *Case Western Reserve Journal of International Law* 389

Beccaria, Cesare (tr. David Young), *On Crimes and Punishments* (Indianapolis: Hackett Publishing Company, 1986)

Begam, Richard and Coetzee, J. M., 'An Interview with J. M. Coetzee' (1992) 33 *Contemporary Literature* 419

Beigbeder, Yves, *Judging War Crimes and Torture: French Justice and International Tribunals and Commissions (1940-2005)* (Leiden: Martinus Nijhoff Publishers, 2006)

Benjamin, Walter (tr. Edmund Jephcott), 'Critique of Violence' in Marcus Bullock and Michael W. Jennings (eds.), *Walter Benjamin: Selected Writings, Vol. I, 1913-1926* (Cambridge, MA: The Belknap Press, 1996) 236

  (tr. Harry Zohn), 'On the Concept of History' in Howard Eiland and Michael W. Jennings (eds.), *Walter Benjamin: Selected Writings, Vol. IV, 1938-1940* (Cambridge, MA: The Belknap Press, 2003) 389

Bentham, Jeremy, 'Anarchial Fallacies' in John Bowring (ed.), *The Works of Jeremy Bentham: Vol. II* (Edinburgh: William Tait, 1859) 498

  An Introduction to the Principles of Morals and Legislation (New York: Dover Philosophical Classics, 2007)

Benvenisti, Eyal, 'The Role of National Courts in Preventing Torture of Suspected Terrorists' (1997) 8 *European Journal of International Law* 596

Bernstein, Richard, 'Kidnapping has the Germans Debating Police Torture' *New York Times* (10 April 2003)

Bianchi, Andrea, 'Human Rights and the Magic of *Jus Cogens*' (2008) 19 *European Journal of International Law* 491

Bossuyt, M. J., *Guide to the 'Travaux Préparatoires' of the International Covenant on Civil and Political Rights* (Dordrecht: Martinus Nijhoff Publishers, 1987)

Boulesbaa, Ahcene, 'An Analysis of the 1984 Draft Convention Against Torture and Other Cruel, Inhuman or Degrading Treatment or Punishment' (1986) 4 *Dickinson Journal of International Law* 185

  The UN Convention on Torture and the Prospects of Enforcement (The Hague: Martinus Nijhoff Publishers, 1999)

Branche, Raphaëlle, 'Torture of Terrorists? Use of Torture in a "War Against Terrorism": Justifications, Methods and Effects: the Case of France in Algeria, 1954-1962' (2007) 89 *International Review of the Red Cross* 543

Brecher, Bob, *Torture and the Ticking Bomb* (Malden: Blackwell Publishing, 2007)

Brzenziki, Matthew, 'Bust and Boom' *The Washington Post* (30 December 2001) W09

Burgers, J. Herman and Hans Danelius (eds.), *The United Nations Convention against Torture: A Handbook on the Convention against Torture and Other Cruel, Inhuman and Degrading Treatment or Punishment* (Dordrecht: Martinus Nijhoff Publishers, 1988)

Burgess, Anthony, 'Book Review: The Beast Within' *New York Magazine* (26 April 1982) 88

Butler, Judith, *Frames of War: When is Life Grieveable?* (London: Verso, 2010)

  'I Merely Belong to Them' (2007) 29 *London Review of Books* 26

  Precarious Life: The Powers of Mourning and Violence (London: Verso, 2004).

Camus, Albert, *Caligula and Other Plays* (London: Penguin Books, 1984)

Chadwick, Elizabeth, *Self Determination, Terrorism and the International Humanitarian Law of Armed Conflict* (The Hague: Martinus Nijhoff Publishers, 1996)

Cheng, Sinkwan, 'Civilization and the Two Faces of Law: J. M. Coetzee's Waiting for the Barbarians' (2003) 24 *Cardozo Law Review* 2349

Clark, Ann Marie, *Diplomacy of Conscience: Amnesty International and Changing Human Rights Norms* (Princeton University Press, 2001)

Coetzee, J. M., 'Into the Dark Chamber: The Novelist and South Africa' *The New York Times* (12 January 1986) 13

Waiting for the Barbarians (London: Vintage Books, 2004)

Cohen, Stanley, 'Post-Moral Torture: From Guantanamo to Abu Ghraib' (2005) 34 *Index on Censorship* 24

Cohen, Stanley and Daphna Golan, 'The Interrogation of Palestinians During the Intifada: Follow Up to March 1991 B'Tselem Report' (Jerusalem: B'Tselem, 1992)

'The Interrogation of Palestinians During the Intifada: Ill-Treatment, "Moderate Physical Pressure" or Torture?' (Jerusalem: B'Tselem, 1991)

Craps, Stef, 'J. M. Coetzee's *Waiting for the Barbarians* and the Ethics of Testimony' (2007) 88 *English Studies* 59

Crelinsten, Ronald, 'How to Make a Torturer' in William F. Schulz (ed.), *The Phenomenon of Torture: Readings and Commentary* (Philadelphia: University of Pennsylvania Press, 2007) 210

Crocker, Thomas P., 'Still Waiting for the Barbarians: What is New about Post-September 11 Exceptionalism?' (2007) 19 *Law and Literature* 303

Crook, John R., (ed.), 'Contemporary Practice of the United States Relating to International Law' (2005) 99 *American Journal of International Law* 479

Cullen, Anthony, *The Concept of Non-International Armed Conflict in International Humanitarian Law* (Cambridge University Press, 2010)

'Defining Torture in International Law: A Critique of the Concept Employed by the European Court of Human Rights' (2003) 34 *California Western International Law Journal* 29

Davidson, Scott, 'The Civil and Political Rights Protected in the Inter-American Human Rights System' in David J. Harris and Stephen Livingstone (eds.), *The Inter-American System of Human Rights* (Oxford University Press, 2004) 213

de Londras, Fiona, 'Book Review: Paul W. Kahn, Sacred Violence' (2009) 19 *Law and Politics Book Review* 371

'International Decision: *Saadi* v. *Italy*' (2008) 102 *American Journal of International Law* 616

de Wet, Erika, 'The Prohibition of Torture as an International Norm of *Jus Cogens* and its Implications for National and Customary Law' (2004) 15 *European Journal of International Law* 97

Dershowitz, Alan M., 'Is it Necessary to Apply Physical Pressure to Terrorists and to Lie about it?' (1989) 23 *Israel Law Review* 192

'Is there a Torturous Road to Justice', *Los Angeles Times* (8 November 2001)

'Should we Fight Terror with Torture' *The Independent* (3 July 2006) 1

'Terrorism and Torture', *The Irish Times* (10 January 2003), 15

'The Torture Warrant: A Response to Professor Strauss' (2003) 48 *New York Law School Law Review* 275

'Tortured Reasoning' in Sanford Levinson (ed.), *Torture: A Collection* (Oxford University Press, 2004) 257

Why Terrorism Works: Understanding the Threats, Responding to the Challenge (New Haven: Yale University Press, 2002)

Dewulf, Steven, *The Signature of Evil: (Re)Defining Torture in International Law* (Antwerp: Intersentia, 2011)

Dine, Philip, 'Anglo-Saxon Literary and Filmic Representations of the French Army in Algeria' in Martin S. Alexander, Martin Evans and J. F. V. Keiger (eds.), *The Algerian War and the French Army, 1954–62: Experiences, Images, Testimonies* (New York: Palgrave Macmillan, 2002) 137

Images of the Algerian War: French Fiction and Film, 1954–1992 (Oxford: Clarendon Press, 1994)

Donagan, Alan, 'Cases of Necessity' in Joram Graf Haber (ed.), *Absolutism and Its Consequentialist Critics* (Boston, MA: Rowman & Littlefield Publishers Inc., 1994) 41

Dörmann, Knut, *Elements of War Crimes under the Rome Statute of the International Criminal Court: Sources and Commentary* (Cambridge University Press, 2003)

Douzinas, Costas, *Human Rights and the End of Empire: The Political Philosophy of Cosmopolitanism* (Abingdon: Routledge-Cavendish, 2007)

The End of Human Rights (Oxford: Hart Publishing, 2000)

'Torture and Systems Theory' (2008) 14 *Soziale Systeme* 110

Droege, Cordula, '"In Truth the Leitmotiv": the Prohibition of Torture and Other Forms of Ill-Treatment in International Humanitarian Law' (2007) 89 *International Review of the Red Cross* 515

Dworkin, Ronald, *Taking Rights Seriously* (London: Duckworth, 1977)

Dyzenhaus, David, 'The Compulsion of Legality' in Victor V. Ramraj (ed.), *Emergencies and the Limits of Legality* (Cambridge University Press, 2008) 33

The Constitution of Law: Legality in a Time of Emergency (Cambridge University Press, 2006)

Eftekhari, Shiva, 'France and the Algerian War: From a Policy of "Forgetting" to a Framework for Accountability' (2003) 34 *Columbia Human Rights Law Review* 413

Ehlstain, Jean Bethke, 'Reflection on the Problem of Dirty Hands' in Sanford Levinson (ed.), *Torture: A Collection* (Oxford University Press, 2004) 77

Evans, Malcolm D. and Rodney Morgan, *Preventing Torture: A Study of the European Convention for the Prevention of Torture and Inhuman or Degrading Treatment or Punishment* (Oxford University Press, 1998)

'Excerpts of the Report of the Commission of Inquiry into the Methods of Investigation of the General Security Service Regarding Hostile Terrorist Activity' (1989) 23 *Israel Law Review* 146

Feldman, Leonard C., 'Terminal Exceptions: Law and Sovereignty at the Airport Threshold' (2007) 3 *Law, Culture and Humanities* 320

Feller, S. Z., 'Not Actual "Necessity" but Possible "Justification"; Not "Moderate" Pressure but Either "Unlimited" or "None at All"' (1989) 23 *Israel Law Review* 201

Fitzpatrick, Joan, *Human Rights in Crisis: The International System for Protecting Rights During States of Emergency* (Philadelphia: University of Pennsylvania Press, 1994)

'Speaking Law to Power: The War against Terrorism and Human Rights' (2003) 14 *European Journal of International Law* 241

Foucault, Michel (tr. Alan Sheridan), *Discipline and Punish: The Birth of the Prison* (London: Penguin Books, 1977)

(tr. David Macey), *Society Must Be Defended: Lectures at the Collège de France, 1975–76* (London: Penguin Books, 2004)

Frankenberg, Günter, 'Torture and Taboo: An Essay Concerning Paradigms of Organized Cruelty' (2008) 56 *American Journal of Comparative Law* 402

Fried, Charles, 'Right and Wrong as Absolute' in Joram Graf Haber (ed.), *Absolutism and its Consequentialist Critics* (Boston, MA: Rowan & Littlefield Publishers Inc., 1994) 73

Gage, Sir William, 'The Report of the Baha Mousa Inquiry' (2011 HC 1452)

Galli, Carlo, 'Carl Schmitt's Antiliberalism: its Theoretical and Historical Sources and its Philosophical and Political Meaning' (2000) 21 *Cardozo Law Review* 1597

Ginbar, Yuval, 'Legitimizing Torture: The Israeli High Court of Justice Rulings in the Bilbeisi, Hamdan and Mubarak Cases: An Annotated Sourcebook' (Jerusalem: B'Tselem, 1997)

Why Not Torture Terrorists? Moral, Practical, and Legal Aspects of the 'Ticking Bomb' Justification for Torture (Oxford University Press, 2008)

Green, Adam, 'Normalizing Torture: One Rollicking Hour At a Time', *The New York Times* (22 May 2005) 34

Greenberg, Karen J. and Joshua L. Dratel (eds.), *The Torture Papers: The Road to Abu Ghraib* (Cambridge University Press, 2005)

Greer, Steven C., *The Margin of Appreciation: Interpretation and Discretion under the European Convention on Human Rights* (Strasbourg: Council of Europe Publishing, 2000)

'Should Police Threats to Torture Suspects Always be Severely Punished? Reflections on the Gäfgen Case' (2011) 11 *Human Rights Law Review* 67

Gross, Oren, 'Are Torture Warrants Warranted? Pragmatic Absolutism and Official Disobedience' (2004) 88 *Minnesota Law Review* 1481

'Chaos and Rules: Should Reponses to Violent Crises Always Be Constitutional?' (2003) 112 *Yale Law Journal* 1011

'Extra-Legality and the Ethic of Political Responsibility' in Victor V. Ramraj (ed.), *Emergencies and the Limits of Legality* (Cambridge University Press, 2008) 60

'The Normless and Exceptionless Exception: Carl Schmitt's Theory of Emergency Powers and the "Norm/Exception" Dichotomy' (2000) 21 *Cardozo Law Review* 1825

'The Prohibition on Torture and the Limits of the Law' in Sanford Levinson (ed.), *Torture: A Collection* (Oxford University Press, 2004) 229

'What "Emergency" Regime?' (2006) 13 *Constellations* 74

Gross, Oren and Fionnuala Ní Aoláin, *Law in Times of Crisis: Emergency Powers in Theory and Practice* (Cambridge University Press, 2006)

Gullì, Bruno, 'The Ontology and Politics of Exception: Reflections on the Work of Giorgio Agamben' in Matthew Calarco and Stephen DeCaroli (eds.), *Giorgio Agamben: Sovereignty and Life* (Stanford University Press, 2007) 219

Hannah, Matthew, 'Torture and the Ticking Bomb: The War on Terrorism as a Geographical Imagination of Power/Knowledge' (2006) 96 *Annals of the Association of American Geographers* 622

Hannaiken, Lauri, *Peremptory Norms (Jus Cogens) in International Law: Historical Development, Criteria, Present Status* (Helsinki: Lakimiesliiton Kustannus Finnish Lawyer's Publishing Company, 1988)

Hathaway, Oona A., 'Do Human Rights Treaties Make a Difference?' (2002) 111 *Yale Law Journal* 1870

'The Promise and Limits of the International Law of Torture' in Sanford Levinson (ed.), *Torture: A Collection* (Oxford University Press, 2004) 199

Heyns, Christof (ed.), *Human Rights Law in Africa* (The Hague: Kluwer Law International, 2002)

Higgins, Rosalyn, 'Derogations under Human Rights Treaties' (1976) 48 *British Yearbook of International Law* 281

Hoh, Harold Hongju, 'Can the President Be Torturer in Chief?' (2005) 81 *Indiana Law Journal* 1145

Hope, David, 'Torture' (2004) 53 *International Comparative Law Quarterly* 807

Horne, Alistair, *A Savage War of Peace: Algeria 1954–1962* (New York Review of Books, 2006)

'Shades of Abu Ghraib' (2009) Nov/Dec *The National Interest* 23

Human Rights Watch, 'Cruel Britannia: British Complicity in the Torture and Ill-Treatment of Terror Suspects in Pakistan' (New York: Human Rights Watch, 2009)

Humphreys, Stephen, 'Legalising Lawlessness: On Giorgio Agamben's State of Exception' (2006) 17 *European Journal of International Law* 677

Hussain, Nasser, 'Beyond Norm and Exception: Guantánamo' (2007) 33 *Critical Inquiry* 734

The Jurisprudence of Emergency: Colonialism and the Rule of Law (Ann Arbor: University of Michigan, 2003)

Ignatieff, Michael, *The Lesser Evil: Political Ethics in an Age of Terror* (Princeton University Press, 2004)

Ingelse, Chris, *The UN Committee Against Torture: An Assessment* (The Hague: Kluwer Law International, 2001)

Jessberger, Florian, 'Bad Torture – Good Torture? What International Criminal Lawyers May Learn from the Recent Trial of Police Officers in Germany' (2005) 3 *Journal of International Criminal Justice* 1059

Johns, Fleur, 'Guantánamo Bay and the Annihilation of the Exception' (2005) 16 *European Journal of International Law* 613

Joint Committee on Human Rights, 'Allegations of UK complicity in Torture' (2008–09, HL 152, HC 230)

Joll, James, *Europe since 1870: An International History* 4th edn (London: Penguin Books, 1990)

Kahn, Paul W., *Sacred Violence: Torture, Terror, and Sovereignty* (Ann Arbor: University of Michigan Press, 2008)

Kaltenbeck, Franz, 'On Torture and State Crime' (2003) 24 *Cardozo Law Review* 2381

Kaplan, Fredy H., 'Combating Political Torture in Latin America: An Analysis of the Organization of American States Inter-American Convention to Prevent and Punish Torture' (1989) 15 *Brooklyn Journal of International Law* 399

Kant, Immanuel (tr. James W. Ellington), *Grounding for the Metaphyics of Morals: On a Supposed Right to Lie Because of Philanthropic Concerns* (Indianapolis: Hackett Publishing Company, 1993)

Kanwar, Vik, 'Book Review: Giorgio Agamben, State of Exception' (2006) 4 *International Journal of Constitutional Law* 567

Klabbers, Jan, 'Rebel with a Cause? Terrorists and Humanitarian Law' (2003) 14 *European Journal of International Law* 299

Klayman, Barry M., 'The Definition of Torture in International Law' (1978) 51 *Temple Law Quarterly* 449

Kleinig, John, 'Ticking Bombs and Torture Warrants' (2005) 10 *Deakin Law Review* 614

Koepnick, Lutz, *Walter Benjamin and the Aesthetics of Power* (University of Nebraska Press, 1999)

Koskenniemi, Martti, 'The Effect of Rights on Political Culture' in Philip Alston (ed.), *The EU and Human Rights* (Oxford University Press 1999) 99

Kreimer, Seth F., '"Torture Lite", "Full Bodied" Torture, and the Insulation of Legal Conscience' (2005) 1 *Journal of National Security Law and Policy* 187

Kremnitzer, Mordechai, 'The Landau Commission Report – Was the Security Service Subordinated to the Law, or the Law to the "Needs" of the Security Service?' (1989) 23 *Israel Law Review* 216

Kremnitzer, Mordechai and Re'em Segev, 'The Legality of Interrogational Torture: A Question of Proper Authorization or a Substantive Moral Issue?' (2000) 34 *Israel Law Review* 509

Kretzmer, David, *The Occupation of Justice: The Supreme Court of Israel and the Occupied Territories* (Albany: State University of New York Press, 2002)

Kutz, Christopher, 'Torture, Necessity and Existential Politics' (2007) 95 *California Law Review* 235

Lacquer, Walter, *Terrorism: A Study of National and International Political Violence* (Boston, MA: Little, Brown and Company, 1977)

Langbein, John H., 'The Legal History of Torture' in Sanford Levinson, *Torture: A Collection* (Oxford University Press, 2004) 93

    Torture and the Law of Proof: Europe and England in the Ancien Régime (University of Chicago Press, 2006)

    'Torture and Plea Bargaining' (1978) 46 *University of Chicago Law Review* 3

Lartéguy, Jean, *Les Centurions* (Paris: Presses de la Cité, 1960)

Lazreg, Marnia, *Torture and the Twilight of Empire: From Algiers to Baghdad* (Princeton University Press, 2008)

Le Sueur, James D., 'Torture and the Decolonisation of French Algeria: Nationalism, "Race" and Violence during Colonial Incarceration' in Graeme Harper (ed.), *Colonial and Postcolonial Incarceration* (London: Continuum, 2001) 161

Ledwidge, Frank and Lucas Oppenheim, 'Preventing Torture: Realities and Perceptions' (2006) 30 *The Fletcher Forum for World Affairs* 165

Lenta, Patrick, '"Legal Illegality": Waiting for the Barbarians after September 11' (2006) 42 *Journal of Postcolonial Writing* 71

Levin, Michael, 'The Case for Torture' *Newsweek* (7 June 1982)

Levinson, Sanford, 'Contemplating Torture: An Introduction' in Sanford Levinson (ed.), *Torture: A Collection* (Oxford University Press, 2004) 23

    'In Quest of a "Common Conscience": Reflections on the Current Debate About Torture' (2005) 1 *Journal of National Security Law and Policy* 231

    '"Precommitment" and Postcommitment": The Ban on Torture in the Wake of September 11' (2003) 81 *Texas Law Review* 2013

    'Preserving Constitutional Norms in Times of Permanent Emergencies' (2006) 13 *Constellations* 59

    'Slavery and the Phenomenology of Torture' (2007) 74 *Social Research* 149

Leyland, Peter, *The Constitution of the United Kingdom: A Contextual Analysis* 2nd edn (Oxford: Hart Publishing, 2012)

Lippman, Matthew, 'The Development and Drafting of the United Nations Convention Against Torture and Other Cruel, Inhuman or Degrading Treatment or Punishment' (1994) 17 *Boston College International and Comparative Law Review* 275

Luban, David, 'Liberalism, Torture, and the Ticking Bomb' (2005) 91 *Virginia Law Review* 1425

Luhmann, Niklas (tr. Todd Cesaratto), 'Are There Still Indispensable Norms in Our Society?' (2008) 14 *Soziale Systeme* 18

    Gibt es in unserer Gesellschaft noch unverzichtbare Normen? (Heidelberg: C. F. Müller Juristischer Verlag, 1993)

Lukes, Stephen, 'Liberal Democratic Torture' (2006) 36 *British Journal of Political Science* 1

Machiavelli (tr. C. E. Donald), *The Prince* (Ware: Wordsworth Editions, 1997)

MacIntyre, Alasdair, *A Short History of Ethics* (London: Routledge, 1967)

MacMaster, Neil, 'The Torture Controversy (1998–2002): Towards a "New History" of the Algerian War? (2002) 10 *Modern and Contemporary France* 449

'Torture: from Algiers to Abu Ghraib' (2004) 46 *Race & Class* 1

Macpherson, C. B., *The Real World of Democracy* (Oxford University Press, 1966)

Mann, Itamar and Omer Shatz, 'The Necessity Procedure: Laws of Torture in Israel and Beyond, 1987–2009' (2010) 6 *Unbound: Harvard Journal of the Legal Left* 59

Maran, Rita, *Torture: The Role of Ideology in the French–Algerian War* (New York: Praeger Publishers, 1989)

Marty, Dick, 'Alleged Secret Detentions and Unlawful Inter-State Transfers of Detainees Involving Council of Europe Member States', Council of Europe doc. 10957 (12 June 2006)

'Secret Detentions and Illegal Transfers of Detainees involving Council of Europe Member States: Second Report', Council of Europe doc. 11302 (7 June 2007)

Mayer, Jane, 'Whatever It Takes: The Politics of the Man Behind 24' *The New Yorker* (19 February 2007) 66

McCoy, Alfred W., *A Question of Torture: CIA Interrogation: From the Cold War to the War on Terror* (New York: Metropolitan Books, 2006)

McLoughlin, Daniel, 'In Force without Significance: Kantian Nihilism and Agamben's Critique of Law' (2009) 20 *Law and Critique* 245

Meron, Theodor, *Human Rights and Humanitarian Norms as Customary Law* (Oxford: Clarendon Press, 1989)

'The Humanization of Humanitarian Law' (2000) 94 *American Journal of International Law* 239

The Humanization of International Law (Leiden: Martinus Nijhoff Publishers, 2006)

Michaelson, Christopher, 'The Renaissance of Non-Refoulement? The Othman (Abu Qatada) Decision of the European Court of Human Rights (2012) 61 *International and Comparative Law Quarterly* 750

Moeckli, Daniel, '*Saadi* v. *Italy*: The Rules of the Game Have *Not* Changed' (2008) 3 *Human Rights Law Review* 534

Moir, Lindsay, *The Law of Internal Armed Conflict* (Cambridge University Press, 2002)

Montesquieu, Charles De Secondat (Baron de), *The Spirit of the Laws: Vol. I* (New York: Hafner Publishing Company, 1949)

Moore, Michael S., 'Torture and the Balance of Evils' (1987) 23 *Israel Law Review* 280

Morgan, Rod, 'The Utilitarian Justification of Torture: Denial, Desert and Disinformation' (2000) 2 *Punishment & Society* 181

Morsink, Johannes, *The Universal Declaration of Human Rights: Origins, Drafting and Intent* (Philadelphia: University of Pennsylvania Press, 1999)

Murphy, Ray, 'Prisoner of War Status and the Question of the Guantánamo Bay Detainees' (2003) 3 *Human Rights Law Review* 257

Nagan, Winston P. and Lucie Atkins, 'The International Law of Torture: From Universal Proscription to Effective Application and Enforcement' (2001) 14 *Harvard Human Rights Law Journal* 87

Nagel, Thomas, 'War and Massacre' in Joram Graf Haber (ed.), *Absolutism and Its Consequentialist Critics* (Boston, MA: Rowman & Littlefield Publishers Inc., 1994)

Ní Aoláin, Fionnuala, 'The European Convention on Human Rights and Its Prohibition on Torture' in Sanford Levinson (ed.), *Torture: A Collection* (Oxford University Press, 2004) 213

   The Politics of Force: Conflict Management and State Violence in Northern Ireland (Belfast: Blackstaff Press, 2000)

Norris, Andrew, 'Sovereignty, Exception, and Norm' (2007) 34 *Journal of Law and Society* 31

Nowak, Manfred, *UN Covenant on Civil and Political Rights: CCPR Commentary* 2nd edn (Kehl: N. P. Engel Verlag, 2005)

   'What Practices Constitute Torture? US and UN Standards' (2006) 28 *Human Rights Quarterly* 809

Nowak, Manfred and Elizabeth McArthur, 'The Distinction between Torture and Other Cruel, Inhuman or Degrading Treatment or Punishment' (2006) 16 *Torture* 147

   The United Nations Convention against Torture: A Commentary (Oxford University Press, 2008)

Nussbaum, Martha, 'The Costs of Tragedy: Some Moral Limits of Cost–Benefit Analysis', (2000) 29 *Journal of Legal Studies* 1005

O'Connell, David, 'Jean Lartéguy: A Popular Phenomenon' (1972) 45 *The French Review* 1087

Orakhelashvili, Alexander, *Peremptory Norms in International Law* (Oxford University Press, 2006)

Orwell, George, *Nineteen Eighty-Four* (London: Penguin Books, 1989)

Ouguergouz, Fatsah, *The African Charter on Human and Peoples' Rights: A Comprehensive Agenda for Human Dignity and Sustainable Democracy in Africa* (The Hague: Kluwer Law International, 2003)

Parry, John T., 'Escalation and Necessity: Defining Torture at Home and Abroad' in Sanford Levinson (ed.), *Torture: A Collection* (Oxford University Press, 2004) 145

   'The Shape of Modern Torture: Extraordinary Rendition and Ghost Detainees' (2005) 6 *Melbourne Journal of International Law* 516

   'Torture Warrants the Rule of Law' (2008) 71 *Albany Law Review* 885

Understanding Torture: Law, Violence and Political Identity (Ann Arbor: University of Michigan Press, 2010)

Paust, Jordan J., 'Above the Law: Unlawful Executive Authorizations Regarding Detainee Treatment, Secret Renditions, Domestic Spying, and Claims to Unchecked Executive Power' (2007) 2 *Utah Law Review* 345

'The Reality of *Jus Cogens*' (1991) 7 *Connecticut Journal of International Law* 81

Pennegård, Ann-Marie Bolin, 'Article 5' in Gudmundur Alfredsson and Asbjørn Eide (eds.), *The Universal Declaration of Human Rights: A Common Standard of Achievement* (The Hague: Martinus Nijhoff Publishers, 1999) 121

Peters, Edward, *Torture* (Philadelphia: University of Pennsylvania Press, 1996)

Pictet, Jean S. (ed.), *Commentary I Geneva Convention for the Amelioration of the Condition of the Wounded and Sick in Armed Forces in the Field* (Geneva: ICRC, 1952)

(ed.), *Commentary II Convention for the Amelioration of the Condition of Wounded, Sick and Shipwrecked Members of Armed Forces at Sea* (Geneva: ICRC, 1960)

(ed.), *Commentary III Convention Relative to the Treatment of Prisoners of War* (Geneva: ICRC, 1960)

(ed.), *Commentary IV Convention Relative to the Protection of Civilian Persons in Time of War* (Geneva: ICRC, 1958)

Plaxton, Michael, 'Justifying Absolute Prohibitions on Torture as if Consequences Mattered' in George Kassimeris (ed.), *Warrior's Dishonour: Barbarity, Morality and Torture in Modern Warfare* (Aldershot: Ashgate, 2006) 205

Posner, Richard A., *Not a Suicide Pact: The Constitution in a Time of National Emergency* (New York: Oxford University Press, 2007)

'Torture, Terrorism, and Interrogation' in Sanford Levinson (ed.), *Torture: A Collection* (Oxford University Press, 2004) 291

Posner, Eric A. and Adrian Vermeule, 'Should Coercive Interrogation be Legal?' (2005) 84 *Chicago Public Law and Legal Theory Working Paper* 1

Terror in the Balance: Security, Liberty and the Courts (New York: Oxford University Press, 2007)

Poyner, Jane, *J. M. Coetzee and the Paradox of Postcolonial Authorship* (Farnham: Ashgate, 2009)

Ralph, Jason, 'The Laws of War and the State of the American Exception' (2009) 35 *Review of International Studies* 631

Ramraj, Victor V., 'No Doctrine More Pernicious? Emergencies and the Limits of Legality' in Victor V. Ramraj (ed.), *Emergencies and the Limits of Legality* (Cambridge University Press, 2008) 3

Rasch, William, 'From Sovereign Ban to Banning Sovereignty' in Matthew Calarco and Steven DeCaroli (eds.), *Sovereignty and Life* (Stanford University Press, 2007) 92

Rawls, John, *A Theory of Justice* (Cambridge, MA: The Belknap Press, 1971)

Reichman, Amnon and Tsvi Kahana, 'Israel and the Recognition of Torture: Domestic and International Aspects' in Craig Scott (ed.), *Torture as Tort: Comparative Perspectives on the Development of Transnational Human Rights Litigation* (Oxford: Hart Publishing, 2001) 631

Rejali, Darius, *Torture and Democracy* (Princeton University Press, 2007)
    Torture and Modernity: Self, Society and State in Modern Iran (Boulder: Westview Press, 1994)

Rodley, Nigel S., 'The Definition(s) of Torture in International Law' (2002) 55 *Current Legal Problems* 467
    The Treatment of Prisoners Under International Law 2nd edn (Oxford University Press, 1999)

Rodley, Nigel S. and Matt Pollard, *The Treatment of Prisoners Under International Law* 3rd edn (Oxford University Press, 2010)

Ross, James, 'A History of Torture' in Kenneth Roth and Minky Worden (eds.), *Torture: A Human Rights Perspective?* (New York: Human Rights Watch, 2005) 3

Rossiter, Clinton, *Crisis Government in the Modern Democracies* (Princeton University Press, 1948)

Rumney, Philip N. S., 'Is Coercive Interrogation of Terrorist Suspects Effective? A Response to Bagaric and Clarke' (2006) 40 *University of San Francisco Law Review* 479

Sarat, Austin, 'Introduction: Toward New Conceptions of the Relationship of Law and Sovereignty under Conditions of Emergency' in Austin Sarat (ed.), *Sovereignty, Emergency, Legality* (Cambridge University Press, 2010) 1

Scarry, Elaine, 'Five Errors in the Reasoning of Alan Dershowitz' in Sanford Levinson (ed.), *Torture: A Collection* (Oxford University Press, 2004) 281

Schabas, William A., 'The Crime of Torture and the International Criminal Tribunals' (2006) 37 *Case Western Reserve Journal of International Law* 349
    The Death Penalty as Cruel Treatment and Torture: Capital Punishment Challenged in the World's Courts (Boston, MA: Northeastern University Press, 1996)
    The International Criminal Court: A Commentary on the Rome Statute (Oxford University Press, 2010)
    The UN International Tribunals: The Former Yugoslavia, Rwanda and Sierra Leone (Cambridge University Press, 2006)

Schabas, William A. and Aisling O'Sullivan, 'Of Politics and Poor Weather: How Ireland Decided to Sue the United Kingdom under the European Convention on Human Rights' (2007) 2 *Irish Yearbook of International Law* 3

Schachter, Oscar, 'Editorial Comment: Human Dignity as a Normative Concept' (1983) 77 *American Journal of International Law* 848

Schapiro, Tamar, 'Kantian Rigorism and Mitigating Circumstances' (2006) 117 *Ethics* 32

Scheffler, Samuel, *The Rejection of Consequentialism: A Philosophical Investigation of the Considerations Underlying Rival Moral Conceptions* (Oxford: Clarendon Press, 1982)

(ed.), *Consequentialism and its Critics* (Oxford University Press, 1988)

Scheuerman, William E., 'Carl Schmitt and the Road to Abu Ghraib' (2006) 13 *Constellations* 108

Carl Schmitt: The End of Law (Boston, MA: Rowman & Littlefield Publishers, 1999)

'International Law as Historical Myth' (2004) 11 *Constellations* 537

Schmitt, Carl (tr. George Schwab), *The Concept of the Political* (University of Chicago Press, 2007)

Die Diktatur: Von den Anfängen des modernen Souveränitätsgedankens bis zum proletarischen Klassenkampf (Berlin: Duncker & Humblot, 2006)

(tr. George Schwab), *Political Theology: Four Chapters on the Concept of Sovereignty* (University of Chicago Press, 2005)

Scholten, Bas, 'Defending Our Legal Practices: A Legal Critique of Giorgio Agamben's State of Exception' (2009) 1 *Amsterdam Law Forum* 113

Schulz, William F. (ed.), *The Phenomenon of Torture: Readings and Commentary* (Philadelphia: University of Pennsylvania Press, 2007)

Seidman, Louis Michael, 'Torture's Truth' (2005) 72 *University of Chicago Law Review* 881

Shatz, Adam, 'The Torture of Algiers' *The New York Review of Books* (21 November 2002)

Shue, Henry, 'Torture' (1978) 7 *Philosophy and Public Affairs* 124

'Torture in Dreamland: Disposing of the Ticking Bomb' (2006) 37 *Case Western Reserve Journal of International Law* 231

Simpson, Alfred William Brian, *Human Rights and the End of Empire: Britain and the Genesis of the European Convention* (Oxford University Press, 2001)

Soanes, Catherine and Angus Stevenson, *Oxford Dictionary of English* (revised 2nd edn, Oxford University Press, 2005)

Spencer, Robert, 'J. M. Coetzee and Colonial Violence' (2008) 10 *Interventions* 173

Spjut, Raj, 'Notes and Comments: Torture under the European Convention on Human Rights' (1979) 73 *American Journal of International Law* 267

Staub, Eric, 'Psychology and Torture' in William F. Schulz (ed.), *The Phenomenon of Torture: Readings and Commentary* (Philadelphia: University of Pennsylvania Press, 2007) 204

Strauss, Marcy, 'Torture' (2004) 48 *New York Law School Law Review* 201

Struck, Doug, 'Borderless Network of Terror: Bin Laden Followers Reach Across the Globe' *The Washington Post* (23 September 2001) A01

Sussman, David, 'Defining Torture' (2006) 37 *Case Western Reserve Journal of International Law* 225

'What's Wrong with Torture' (2005) 33 *Philosophy and Public Affairs* 1

Tindale, Christopher, 'Tragic Choices: Reaffirming Absolutes in the Torture Debate' (2005) 19 *International Journal of Applied Philosophy* 209

Twining, W. L. and P. E. Twining, 'Bentham on Torture' (1973) 24 *Northern Ireland Legal Quarterly* 305

Twiss, Sumner B., 'Torture, Justification and Human Rights: Toward an Absolute Proscription' (2007) 29 *Human Rights Quarterly* 346

UNCAT 'Consideration of Reports Submitted by States Parties under Article 19 of the Convention: Israel' UN Doc. CAT/C/ISR/CO/4 (23 June 2009)

UNCHR 'Report of the Special Rapporteur on the Question of Torture, Manfred Nowak' (2005) UN Doc. E/CN.4/2006/6

UNGA, 'Report of the Committee against Torture' UN Doc. A/49/44 (1993)
  'Report of the Committee against Torture' UN Doc. A/52/44 (1997)
  'Report of the Committee against Torture' UN Doc. A/53/44 (1998)
  'Report of the Committee against Torture' UN Doc. A/57/44 (2002)

UNHRC, Joint Study on Global Practices in Relation to Secret Detention in the Context of Countering Terrorism of the Special Rapporteur on the Promotion and Protection of Human Rights and Fundamental Freedoms while Countering Terrorism, Martin Scheinin; the Special Rapporteur on Torture and Other Cruel, Inhuman and Degrading Treatment or Punishment, Manfred Nowak; the Working Group on Arbitrary Detention represented by its Vice Chair, Shadeen Sardar Ali; and the Working Group on Enforced or Involuntary Disappearances represented by its Chair, Jeremy Sarkin (2010) UN Doc. A/HRC/14/42

'Report of the Special Rapporteur on Torture and Other Cruel, Inhuman and Degrading Treatment or Punishment, Manfred Nowak' (2010) UN Doc. A/HRC/13/39

'Report of the Special Rapporteur on Torture and Other Cruel, Inhuman and Degrading Treatment or Punishment, Manfred Nowak: Study on the Phenomena of Torture, Cruel, Inhuman and Degrading Treatment or Punishment in the World, Including an Assessment of Conditions of Detention' (2010) UN Doc. A/HRC/13/39/Add. 5

Valdez Moses, Michael, 'The Mark of Empire: Writing, History, and Torture in Coetzee's *Waiting for the Barbarians*' (1993) 15 *The Kenyon Review* 115

van Cleef Greenberg, Eldon, 'Law and the Conduct of the Algerian Revolution' (1970) 11 *Harvard International Law Journal* 37

Van Santan Gallagher, Susan, 'Torture and the Novel: J. M. Coetzee's "Waiting for the Barbarians"' (1988) 29 *Contemporary Literature* 277

Venator Santiago, Charles R., 'From the Insular Cases to Camp X-Ray: Agamben's State of Exception and United States Territorial Law' (2006) 39 *Studies in Law, Politics and Society* 15

Vermeule, Adrian, 'Our Schmittian Administrative Law' (2009) 122 *Harvard Law Review* 1095

Viljoen, Frans and Chidi Odinkalu, *The Prohibition of Torture and Ill-Treatment in the African Human Rights System: A Handbook for Victims and their*

Advocates (OMCT Handbook Series Vol. 3, World Organisation against Torture 2006)

Voltaire, 'Torture and Capital Punishment' in William F. Schulz (ed.), *The Phenomenon of Torture: Readings and Commentary* (Philadelphia: University of Pennsylvania Press, 2007) 36

Waldron, Jeremy, 'Torture and Positive Law: Jurisprudence for the White House' (2005) 105 *Columbia Law Review* 1681

Walzer, Michael, 'The Problem of Dirty Hands' (1973) 2 *Philosophy and Public Affairs* 160

Walzer, Michael, *Just and Unjust Wars* (New York: Basic Books, 1977)

Weber, Max, 'Politics as a Vocation' in Hans Heinrich Gerth and Charles Wright Mills (eds.), *From Max Weber: Essays in Sociology* (London: Routledge, 1948) 77

Weber, Samuel, 'Taking Exception to Decision: Walter Benjamin and Carl Schmitt' (1992) 22 *Diacritics* 5

Weisberg, Richard H., 'Loose Professionalism, or Why Lawyers Take the Lead on Torture' in Sanford Levinson (ed.), *Torture: A Collection* (Oxford University Press, 2004) 299

Weissbrodt, David and Amy Bergquist, 'Extraordinary Rendition and the Torture Convention' (2006) 46 *Virginia Journal of International Law* 585

Wilson, Heather A., *International Law and the Use of Force by National Liberation Movements* (Oxford University Press, 1988)

Wisnewski, J. Jeremy and R. D. Emerick, *The Ethics of Torture* (London: Continuum, 2009)

Wolcher, Louis, *Law's Task: The Tragic Circle of Law, Justice and Human Suffering* (Aldershot: Ashgate, 2008)

Žižek, Slavoj, *Welcome to the Desert of the Real* (London: Verso, 2002)

INDEX

Lightning Source UK Ltd.
Milton Keynes UK
UKOW01f0030080717
304866UK00021B/594/P